# CROSSCULTURAL COMMUNICATION

### *By The Same Author*

- Phonology of Banda Dialect, Chetna Prakashan, Nagpur, 1996.
- Equality of Religions, Mohit Publications, New Delhi, 1995.
- Creativity and Values, Arya Book Depot, New Delhi, 1992.
- A Search for Human Values, Arya Book Depot, New Delhi, 1992
- New Education Policy, Krishna Bros., Ajmer, 1987.
- Value Education : Theory and Practice, Krishna Bros., Ajmer, 1986.
- Current Trends and Problems of Progressive Education, Krishna Bros., Ajmer, 1985.
- Anglo-Hindi-Sanskrit Practical Grammar, Nagpur, 1967.

**About the Author**

**Dr N.L. Gupta** (*b.* 1940) is the first scholar to obtain a Ph.D. from two different faculties of Nagpur University. He has a series of Post-Graduate degrees and many firsts at his credit. He is the first candidate to submit a thesis for D. Litt. in R.S. University Raipur. He is the first writer to get subsidy for a Hindi book *Berar Ke Sufi Shayar* from Governor of Maharashtra, which is oftly quoted by Urdu Scholars. Recently he has been awarded by Maharashtra Hindi Granth Academy for the best work on Literary criticism styled as "Nav-Manavatavadi Chintan" (Neo-humanistic Thought).

Dr. Gupta is a prolific writer. Besides many research papers, he has 35 books in both Hindi and English at his credit. Dr Gupta's writings have a very broad spectrum of themes which include Literature, History, Culture, Education, Sociology, Philosophy, Theology and so on. He is considered to be the authority on 'Value Education' on which he has contributed as many as six books with different angles. Latest in the series was *Education and Values in the Mahabharata, Mulya Parak Shiksha* of about 400 pages published from Ajmer, has been profusely quoted by the scholars.

Presently Dr Gupta is working as Assistant Commissioner, Kendriya Vidyalaya Sangathan, Bhubaneshwar, Orissa.

# CROSSCULTURAL COMMUNICATION

## Global Perspective

N.L. GUPTA, D. Litt.
Assistant Commissioner
Kendriya Vidyalaya Sangathan
Bhubaneswar Region, Bhubaneswar

CONCEPT PUBLISHING COMPANY, NEW DELHI-110059

ISBN 81-7022-621-X (PB)

First Published 1998



*Published and Printed by*
Ashok Kumar Mittal
**Concept Publishing Company**
A/15-16, Commercial Block, Mohan Garden,
New Delhi-110059. (INDIA)

Phones : 5554042, 5504042
Fax : 091-11-5598898

# Preface

Universally speaking we are living in the world of sharing and interdependence in the family, society or nation at large. But with the violent strides of modern science and technology, particularly info-technology where Cyberspace has made a mark and influenced our materialistic world considerably, this sharing has crossed the boundaries of individual nation, may it be a developed country like France, developing like India or an underdeveloped country like Ghana in Africa. The value of nationalism is an important value, no doubt; but now the more important is internationalism which comes through international understanding that begets universal Brotherhood ('Vasudhaiv Kutumbakam'). With this mental disposition the entire world becomes like a nest ('Yatra Vishawam Bhavatyekneedam') and the Western call it a 'global village'.

Crosscultural Communication, hereafter called CC, though a subject of academic novelty, is a crosscultural training which is termed as cultural assimilator by the virtue of its function and character. It is an approach for increasing understanding between individual or societal members of two cultures. It is the need of the hour, if we want to establish peace and harmony in the society, we cannot afford to ignore it. If we want to dispense with the tribal character of religion or culture we have to develop crosscultural awareness, as Dr S. Radhakrishnan has put it– "The tribal character of religion can be traced to early times when the function of religion was said to be the training of its adherents to a patriotic docility".

The address of Swami Vivekanand in the last session of Religious Parliament (27 Sep. 1893) at Chicago is noteworthy in which he apparently said– "The Christian is not to become a Hindu or Buddhist, nor Hindu or a Buddhist to become a Christian. But each must assimilate the spirit of the others and yet preserve his individuality and grow according to his own law of growth". This statement is clear indicative of the fact that he believed in "equality of religions" instead of "unity of religions" and thus advocated for religious pluralism. His ideas can be translated into action by healthy crosscultural communication effectively.

For healthy and productive crosscultural communication combating or racism, prejudices and discriminatory attitudes is necessary. To accomplish this objective we have to minimize negative attitude and behaviour and instil positive view toward the people, society and nation at large. Negative attitudes are originated by negative values. What are negative values? Fear, hatred, jealousy, doubt, greed, deceit, inferiority, fault-finding, egoism, insistance, aversion etc., may be termed as negative values, which influence individual's conduct and behaviour negatively. These negative values are derived from various mis-conception and lack of self-actualization. No doubt, heridity and harmones do play their role in the gamut of entire phenomena.

Crosscultural communication is necessary for our socio-economic growth also because in our modern world no nation is self-supporting fully. For one thing or the other one nation has to depend on other(s). Economic progress depends on industrial growth and industrial growth requires some technology. International flow of scientific and technological knowledge called 'Technology Transfer' is a very vital instrument for crosscultural communication. The transnational corporation plays an important role in this process. Such corporation stands for international spreading of research and development and deploy the technology systemetically through their networks all over the world. Their main clients are the developing countries.

For free frank and harmonious new world order the following democratic values incorporated in the Universal Declaration of Human Rights and adopted in the United Nations General Assembly in 1948, are of vital significance :

1. acceptance and appreciation of cultural diversity
2. respect for human dignity and universal human rights.
3. responsibility to the world community, and
4. reverence for the earth.

The declaration has been designed to serve "as a common standard of achievement for all peoples and all nations". The declaration states that all persons are born free and equal in dignity and expresses basic civil, economic, political and social rights of all humans. It is a statement of moral standards to be followed by all nations. It stresses the fact that every one has the right to life, liberty and security of person, equality before law, freedom of movement etc. irrespective of caste, creed, colour, sex or language.

Besides introductory chapter and two appendices there are following eight chapters in this book through which a survey of various global currents and cross-currents, communication and cross-communication in the pertinent and prominent areas like religion, culture, politics, economic, art, philosophy, literature, trade and commerce etc., has been made :

1. Conceptual Analysis
2. Cultural Pluralism : Global Phenomena
3. Crosscultural Communication : Multi-religious Perspective
4. Religion and Politics
5. Inter-dependence : Socio-economic Perspectives
6. Cross-currents in Philosophy, Art and Literature
7. Human Values and Crosscultural Understanding
8. Towards New World-Order

In order to make the work comprehensive and more useful the following two appendinces have been appended at the end of the book :

1. Biographical notes
2. World's Main Events : at a Glance

To make the references comprehensive about 150 biographical notes and other references have been given in a synoptical and lucid manner. Under the heading bibliography, there are particulars of about 200 books have been given. This will not only help the readers to comprehend the subject but also inspire those scholars for furtherance of such studies, who are interested in the subject of C.C.

The author take this opportunity to acknowledge his debt with all sincerity to a host of scholars, oriental as well as oxidental, without whose indepth studies and monumental works no work of this unique type could have been possible. The thrust has been given to present inter-mingling of various micro and macro-cultures of the world i.e., the impact of one culture on the other, meeting points of the East and the West, convergent and divergent varieties of the Eastern responses etc. in a precise and lucid manner. While writing this volume covering a vast and the most complex area of CC the author, at places, had to be selective and precise. Thus it is just possible that at a few places the readers may feel something lacking, which is but natural in such type of works.

In fact, the MSS of the book was given to the publisher in 1995, 'International year of tolerance', as declared by UNO. But due to certain pre-occupations, he could not take it up for publication earlier. However, it is good that it is being published at the threshold of 50th anniversary of Indian independence. For this I extend my hearty thanks to Shri Ashok

Kumar Mittal of Concept Publishing Company, New Delhi, who has shown appreciable zeal and enthusiasm in bringing out this volume in an excellent get-up, befitting to the reputation of his Company.

HP-7 Laxmisagar **N.L. Gupta**
BHUBANESWAR

# CONTENTS

# INTRODUCTION

The first thing that is absolutely necessary for the smooth and peaceful existence of the human race is the building up of a good society. In the simplest term a good society means a group of good people. For establishing the peace in the society, nation and the world at large the value of tolerance is very essential. The two values-peace and tolerance are not only supplementary but also complimentary to each other. This is why UNO has declared 1995 as the International year of Tolerance. The theme of 1994 was also an extremely important one and as such international community responded to it positively, the Cairo conference on population being one of its major highlights. It was a year when after centuries of aparthied the African National Congress won first ever democratic elections and Nelson Mandela became the first Black President of South Africa.

**Theme**

It is needless to mention that tolerance is a value of tremendous importance, since it is fountain head of the values like compassion, common good, self-support, self-control, gentlemanliness, national unity, kindness, secularism and so on. With the collapse of communism and the decline and fall of USSR the world has no power blocks, no parasitization between East and West. It remains, however, a multipolar or pluralistic world of diverse nationalities, creeds, colours and races. At times we observe conflicts in ideologies among developed, developing and under-developed countries. The world is shrinking very fast and with the violent strides of info-technology and the proliferation of television channels that cross all barriers of race and language, tolerance, recognition and acceptance of other communities, as they are, mutual respect and dignity of human beings have emerged as the basic values implicit in the pluralistic society.

This book is just an humble effort in tune with the noble and humanistic mission of UNO–producing a survey of various currents and cross-currents, communication and cross-cummunication in the vital areas like religion, culture, politics, economics, art, literature and so on among various developed, developing and underdeveloped countries of the world.

The subject of *Crosscultural Communication* is a subject of academic novelty, atleast in India. Of course, in many of the universities of United States of America it has already found a place even at Post-graduate level. One of the reasons behind this might have been that evils of racism prevailed in America due to black and white problems, as Dr. King, receipient of Nobel Prize for peace, pointed out in 1967: "America had failed to tackle positively and forthrightly the triple evils of racism, extreme materialism and militarism." In 1973 George Washington proclaimed that the "Bosom of America is open to receive not only the opulent and respectable stranger, but the oppressed and persecuted of all Nations and Religions whom we shall welcome to a participation of all our rights and privileges". In this policy statement, obviously, slaves and free blacks were not included, nor the native peoples or Maxicans of South-west. With the passage of time the folly came to be realised gradually as late as in 1965, i.e., after 172 years. Referring to the immigration Law, President Lydon Johnson announced : "It does repair a very deep and painful flaw in the fabric of the American nation."

Under such racist circumstances an emphasis on combating racism has become imperative in USA. Crosscultural communication has lot of potential in it for the purpose. As a sequel the discipline like multicultural education has become a fashion of the day in USA.

## Melting-pot Theory

The concept of the melting-pot was proposed by the playwright Israel Zangwill in his 1909 play 'The Melting-pot'. In that work a Russina-Jewish immigrant described the United States in this speech:

"America is God's Crucible, the great Melting Pot where all races of Europe are melting and reforming ! Here you stand, good folk, think I, when I see them at Ellis Island, here you stand in your fifty groups with your fifty hatreds and rivalries, but you won't be long like that, brother, for this are the fires of God. A fig for your feuds and vendettas ! Germans and Frenchmen, Ireshmen and Englishmen, Jews and Russians-Into the Crucible with you all. God is making the American. . . . The real American has not yet arrived. He is only in the crucible, I tell you – he will be the fusion of all races, the coming superman" (Zangwill, 1909, p. 37).

The melting pot ideal was considered as promising one for fusing persons from old and new immigrant groups into a new common American society. This happened in India centuries ago when various non-Aryan tribes poured into it. There were mainly two inherent defects in the ideology. Firstly, it never proposed to melt all ethnic and cultural groups, as it happened in America many immigrants of Afro-Asian origin could not or did not adopt American ways of life for various socio-economic reasons. Even in Zangwill's speech there is no mention of adding American Indian, Blacks, Hispanics, other than immigrants from Spain, or Asians to this crucible. Secondly, it was rather over-expectation to think that various ethnic groups having divergent ethno-cultural background and varied interest will be melt into one cultural pot in total.

In response to Pandit Jawaharlal Nehru's three articles (appeared in Modern Review of Calcutta) regarding spiritual unrest in the Islamic world whatever Dr. Muhammad exaspired indirectly indicate the failings of the Theory of 'Melting Pot'. Dr. Iqbal responded:

> "He (Pt. Nehru) thinks, wrongly in my opinion, that the only way to Indian nationalism lies in a total suppression of the cultural entities of the country through the interaction of which alone India can evolve a rich and endruing culture. A nationalism achieved by such methods can mean nothing but mutual bitterness and even oppression. It is equally obvious that the Qadian, too, feel nervous by the political awakening of the Indian Muslims, because they feel that the rise in political prestige of the Indian Muslims is sure to defeat their designs to carve out from the Ummat of the Arbaian Prophet a new Ummat for the Indian Prophet. It is no small surprise to me that my effort to impress upon the Indian Muslims the extreme necessity of internal cohesion in the present critical moment of their history in India; and my warning them against the forces of disintegration, maquerading as Reformist movements, should have given the Pandit occasion to sympathise with such forces."[1]

But here Iqbal's view-point is on extreme side. Just for internal cohesion of the group or section of the society peace and harmony of the larger group or macro-culture cannot be overlooked. Moreover, the identity of the individual or a small group with certain ethnic traits may not lead to security or may not fulfil his requirement or may not resolve the problems, which individual life poses, particularly when we are living in the era of inter-dependence. Thus one has to maintain the identity in such a fashion that the window of his mind is not closed and airs of other faiths and culture are also allowed to provide a sort of soothing and consoling affect to one's own conscience. On this point the observation of George DE Voc is noteworthy. He maintains :

"Man's capacity to identify brings human conflicts within him. Man experiences conflict intra-physically. Potentially permeable to the feelings and experiences of others, given also to the project of his feelings into objects and beings about him, he finds that his culture only imperfectly helps him attain, with relative degrees of a suredness, a secure social self-identity. This social self-identity tends to be somewhat less secure in situations in which a pronounced continuous dependence upon an exploited group cannot be resolved."[2]

*Culture assimilators* have been developed for a number of nations such as Israel and Iran, and for black and white cultures within the United States. In fact, crosscultural training is called culture assimilator, an approach for increasing understanding between members of two cultures.

## Cultural Assimilation and Other Theories

Culturally speaking an assimilation is the process by which microcultures become a synonymous with macroculture. Either cultural patterns that distinguished them from macroculture have disappeared, or their distinctive cultural patterns have been adopted by macroculture so that there is no longer a distinct or separate culture, or the combination of the two has occurred. Macroculture is a culture which represent the entire country. Therefore, it is also at times, used as synonymous of the national culture, though the scholars are not unanimous on the point of the national culture. The theory of 'melting pot' stands no good in the modern complex society. Therefore, cultural pluralism is emerging as order of the day–with the end of 342 years of the White domination in South Africa.

Cultural pluralism theory has got a new impetus, that warrants greater inclination towards democratization. Moreover, recent failure of Communism and distortion of dictatorial societies stand as vital testimony. End of aparthied is another good and healthy sign paving the path for the unity of mankind. When Mandela assumed charge as president of South Africa he expelled the demon of racism and hatred from Africa, if not from the whole world.

## Why Crosscultural Communication

The art of communication is to be learned by one and all in a democratic society. In a culturally and linguistically pluralistic society clear and transparent communication is very essential, if we are to understand each other and if we are to be understood by others. There is no gain- saying the fact that the mass media are primary communcators of information about the wider world. But there are obviously certain limitations with the mass media. The media cannot take the place of the thoughtful books.

Gap in communication leads to prejudice and distortion that most often bring about greater mischief in the world. Once Confucious was asked by the king:

"If he is conferred with kingship what is that area he would like to give top priority." Very rightly he responded,"Language" i.e., communication-skill. In case, Language is not clear, communication will not be complete and incomplete communication will obviously lead to misunderstanding and prejudice that will widen the gap among the people, that in turn will beget hatred and enmity, instead of cooperation and friendship, and thus there will be no peace in society and nation at large.

Similarly, among various countries crosscultural communication is very necessary so that they can understand each other through religion, culture, art, literature, foreign policies, fiscal policies, etc. Such type of bridges of understanding will help to lessen and minimize the gap between two cultures. Thirukkural, a noted Tamil poet, who has been translated in more than twenty-five languages and who had been famous for his ethical themes and bravity, has very aptly remarked on power of speech:

> The goodness called goodness of speech
> Is goodness which nothing can reach
> Since gain or ruin speeches bring
> Guard against the slips of tongue.
> Weight the words and speak, because
> No wealth or virtue words surpass.
> They overspeak who do not seek
> A few and flawless words to speak.

In Chhandogya Upnishad (Narad and Sanatkumar–Dialogue) it is said that speech is greater than words, mind is greater than speech, will is greater than mind, consciousness is greater than will, meditation is greater than will and power of understanding is greater than meditation. Sanatkumar, Surmonizing Narad Atma-Vidya or Brahmavidya (Knowledge of the Supreme) says: "Power of understanding being *sine quo non* for proper meditation, that is greater than meditation. If we cannot correctly understand and discriminate between good and bad, truth and untruth, and discriminate between good and bad, truth and untruth, and the like pairs of opposites, how can we meditate?" Thus there is no doubt that the power of understanding is linked with the speech, one of the tools of communication.

## Freedom and Crosscultural Communication

Many political thinkers like Churchill hold that democracy is cumbersome, slow, uncertain and inefficient, but there is no other way out since all other systems tried in course of human history have proved worse and democracy, by and large, had proved to be not only a political system but a way of life. J. Krishnamurty has rightly said: "Freedom is very necessary in our life. Freedom is obviously not to do whatever you like, though this has been considered freedom and has been the way of our life." Crosscultural communication, no doubt, prevails when freedom of expression is there, which is feasible in democratic society only. Recently freedom House, in its annual survey titled "freedom in the world", claimed "inter-ethnic and intersectarian strife are substantial factors in the erosion of liberties in the partly-free countries of India, Turkey, Mali and Niger".

## Cultural Consciousness Essential

For combating prejudices and racism and develop transcultural understaning crosscultural awareness is essential. For this purpose an individual must have an understanding of his or her own worldview. It is universally acknowledged truth that humans have the capacity to reduce their ethnocentrism. The only need is to awaken their cultural consciousness. Hanvey has mentioned two dimensions of cultural consciousness–

(1) *Perspective Consciousness*: It is defined as recognition or awareness on the part of the individual that he or she has a view of the world that is not universally shared, that this view of the world has been and continuous to be shaped influences that often escape conscious detection, and that others have view of the world that are profoundly different from one's own.

(2) *Crosscultural Awareness*: This refers to an awareness of the diversity of ideas and practices to be found in human societies around the world, of how such ideas and practices compare, and including some recognition of how the ideas and ways of one's own society might be viewed from other vantage points".[3]

The distinct aim of these two dimensions is to form a harmonious and complex-free society in which values like truth, non-violence, peace, love and freedom etc. may flourish making way to international understanding and ultimately world peace. Lastly with Daiṣakuikeda and Wilson we must realise that "Throughout the world, and at ever widening levels of society, people now encounter new knowledge, meet new types of demands, become involved in patterns of social orgainization have to learn, for their work, in their househods, and new procedures.

Today's man discovers that he is recurrently in need of re-education. Whereas in the past, the individual learned in childhood the rudiments necessary for the type of life he was likely to lead and found subseqent learning to be a cumulative process, building up into a fund much diminished. Experience is often a hindrance, attaching one to out-of-date measures, and unlearning and relearning become everyday necessities".[4]

**Interdependence**

Today we are living in the era of interdependence. No nation can afford to be secluded and isolated, howsoever rich or affluent it may claim to be. It has to depend on some country for one thing or another either it is raw material or finished goods, technical know-how or info-technology and so on. Interdependence is not only among the countries but also among the various aspects of our contemporary life. Therefore, interdependence is to be found in several spheres i.e., military, political, economic, technology transfer etc. That is why the promoters of new thinking hold: "understandably, our programme begins with military issues and then goes on to political ones. The military-political sphere, primarily the reduction and elimination of nuclear armaments, forms the basis for ensuring security. But can the world be safe, if whole continents can find themselves on the brink of starvation? Can the world be safe when scores of countries are being overwhelmed by a burden of debts? Can the world be safe while on the verge of an ecological catastrophe? This is why our programme takes into account all these components of the problem of ensuring security."[5]

Moreover, the world peace may stand threatened unless the human dignity is not looked after. The world cannot be safe when human rights are being trapled upon, when the right to life is threatened. Human life is endangered not only by nuclear destruction but also by the lack of the basic conditions for existence. Even in this nuclear age hundreds of thousands of people are suffering from starvation and various diseases. Due to fast erosion of human values the rate of offences and crimes has gone on quite higher side. In one of the recent surveys in a affluent country like United States the frequency of criminal offences, violent crimes and property crimes are constantly increasing.

Increase in offences and crimes is a gobal phenomena. Hunger and unemployment–these two are prominent reasons for such offences particularly in the lower strata of the societies and as such these require immediate attention of the world community.

## Integrated Philosophy

Today we are confronted mainly with three problems, all over the world– poverty, unemployment and social disharmony. The last one is mainly due to lack of proper cultural communication. We are living in the era of communication. Of all sorts of communication cultural communication is the most subtle and significant as it establishes linkage between two or more persons or ethnic groups. Crosscultural communication has still wider scope because it links one culture to another, one society and nation at large to another. It has the components to establish social harmony and cordinality in society provided it is unbiased and unprejudiced. Let's vitalise and revitalise it.

For this Dr. Karan Singh has rightly said, "We need the mind to be illuminated by *Jnana* (Wisdom), the heart to be flooded by *bhakti* (Devotion), the will to be disciplined by *karma* (Action), and the psyche to be spiritiualized by *raja* (*yoga* practice). It is only if we are able to develop all these four elements of our personality that we will achieve the spacity to function as integrated and harmonious human beings, capable of building a new, global civilization on planet earth. And, surely, we can today accept no lesser goal than to be pioneers of global consciousness that is painfully struggling to be born on our beautiful planet, on Mother Earth that has nurtured the human race up from the slime of the primeval ocean to where we stand today, poised on the threshold of a new leap forward."[6]

### REFERENCES

1. Dr. Muhammad Iqbal, *Islam and Ahmadism*, p. 2
2. *Conflict in Society*, p.80, a paper titled as "Conflict exploitation in human system; Some Theoretical Perspectives from the Study of Personality in Culture by George DE Voc.
3. *Multicultural Education*, p. 64.
4. Daisakuikeda and Bryan Wilson, Human Values in a Changing World, p. 105.
5. Vadim Zagladin, To Restructure and Humanise International Relations, p. 118.
6. Dr. Karan Singh, *Essays on Hinduism*, p. 92.

# 1

# CONCEPTUAL ANALYSIS

## Introduction

Essentiality of interaction, Evolutionary process, conflict problems and crosscultural communication, Need and objectives; Theories of Assimilation of Cultures, Melting-pot theory, Anglo-confirmity Theory, Cultural Pluralism Theory; Stereotypes and crosscultural communication, Indoctrination and Ideological conflicts Indoctrination defined, role of politics, indoctrination and education, Epistemological Influences; Environmentalism, Enculturation and socialization, Cultural Relativism and Myths, Prejudices and Personality, Indicatores of Crosscultural Communication, Crosscultural Communication and Body Language, non-verbal communication, para-language, syberspace; Highway of communication.

We start with the idea of being and the idea of *not-being* follows naturally. These two ideas opposing each other, a new higher thought in which the opposition arises. The opposition of being and not being is overcome in the idea of *becoming*. The new thought leads to a new contradiction which in turn takes us to a higher thought reconcilling both, and the process goes on until we reach the *Absolute Idea*.– ***Hegel***

## Essentiality of Interaction

According to Hegel, the logic is an analysis not of methods of reasoning, but of the concepts used in reasoning. Emanual Kant call them as being, quality, quantity, relations etc. Hegel says: "The most pervasive of them all is Relation, every idea is a group of relation, we can think of some thing only by relating it to some thing else, and perceiving its similiarities and differences. An idea without relations of any kind is empty. That is why he concludes–

"Pure Being and Nothing are the same". On this analogy we can say that pure culture is no culture, we can understand our own culture by relating it to other cultures and perceiving its similarities and its difference. Without having this exercise the total perception or perception of the whole will not be feasible, it will be just a partial perception. Until and unless the total perception will not be there our understanding will not be clear and unless understanding is clear, we may be victim of prejudices, biased, in turn, which may lead to discrimination. Discrimination among the group leads to mutual scapegoating and scapegoating ultimately leads to hostility among the groups. This type of hostility has no bounds, no limits, it may go to any extent, members of the hostile groups may kill each other.

Knowledge of other cultures is an instrument of better understanding–of our own culture. Therefore, crosscultural or intercultual communication is the need of the day, a universal requirement. If we want peace and harmony in society, in state, in nation and the world at large, unity of mankind is not only desirable but necessary also. For the enrichment of one's own culture also the knowledge and understanding of other culture is essential. George Santayana has rightly said, "The Jews, the Greeks, the Romans, the English were never so great as when they confronted other nations, reacting against them and at the same time, perhaps, adopting their culture.....".

## Evolutionary Process

Crosscultural communication is a long evolutionary process, since the modes of intentional communication (Language, signs, gestures etc.) are themselves evolutionary. Due to rapid explosion of knowledge and violent strides of science and technology intercultural competence of the individuals will be ever subject to change alongwith the value system of different countries in the new world-order. Gignatic projects for various establishments in the space are taking shape and as such the possibility of transplanetary communication cannot be ruled out. Synthesis of various ideas, cultures, religions etc. is already on the wheel. Twenty-first century will definitely be different from the present one. We shall reap as we are sowing. This is the nature of law. The cake will be so, as its ingredients are. In American context E. Trueblood has rightly observed in his famous book *The life we Prize*, which is very true for other cultures also:

> "In our present predicament we seem like chessplayers who have been maneuvered into positions in which all of the available moves

are really damaging ones. We begin to see deemly, that what is occurring, in part, is a terrible working of moral law, but this is hard for us to believe or to understand. The resentment of Asians seems unreasonable and unjustified, and it is unjustified, if we are concerned only with contemporary events, but what we are reaping is a delayed harvest. Every white man who violated, in years past, the Principle of the innate dignity of every human being by saying "boy" to a Chinese man, was helping to build-up the fiery hatred which finally has burst upon us with such apparent unreason, at the very time that we are trying to maintain a lofty principle of at great sacrifice ourselves."

To sacrifice man at the altar of principles, may it be Indian, American, Chinese or Japanese, is rather inhuman and so immoral. Here we are reminded of Marxian Dictum: "Man is the root of Mankind" and that of Protgores: "Man is measure for all things". Alike M.N. Roy we may hope that "A brotherhood of men attracted by the adventure of ideas, keenly conscious of the urge for freedom, fired with the vision of a free society of free men, and motivated by the will to remake the world, so as to restore the individual in his position of primacy and dignity, will show the way out of the contemporary crisis of modern civilization."[1]

Crosscultural communication can go a long way in the quest of new world-order as its focus is on cultural self-awareness. Persons will achieve a psychological balance between cultural pride and identity on the one hand and appreciation of other cultures on the other hand. But the quest is unending and may continue till the man exists on this planet. This quest is going on, and let's hope with Arun Mitra, that it will go on. It is not a matter of being victor or vanquished, achieving success or unsuccess, loss or gain; but of working for it with full zeal and confidence and waiting with tolerance and patience, as he says:

Torrents of rain and gusty wind
I can't make out your words in their midst
Wet with tears and besides, the whirlwinds within
Let the earth be warm, let the water drip away
Their angles will be clear
As the points of steel
Then shall I be able to feel anguish
And you'll left your face and flash
Like a burnt god

Then all will come within the fold of my senses
Every blazing step and the ferry-port
Will assume the true image of
Your words
Now let me wait.[2]

**Conflict Problems and Crosscultural Communication**

In Great Britain in sixties a new discipline emerged to inquire into conflict-problems of the mankind. It was a multi-disciplinary field of enquiry into causes and control of conflict in human society. The subject had already been recognized in the United States where a centre for Research on Conflict Resolution had been created at the university of Michigan in 1959. Due to rapid strides of science and technology the problem of cultural conflict increased considerably. It was realized by the continental Europe also, where a Peace Research Institute exist within the Institute for Social Research in Oslo. The Centre in Michigan publishes the *Journal of Conflict Resolution* and the institute in Oslo brings out the Journal of *Peace Research* incorporating research papers in the field. Formal recognition of this new area of discourse in Britain occurred in June 1963 when a meeting was convened at Windsor which resulted in the formation of "Conflict Research Society".

On this very theme the CIBA foundation, a unique international institution in portland place, offers accommodation to scientists from all over the world. Foremost in its activities is the organization of small conferences, the proceedings of which are published in book form.

The concept of cross cultural communication may be searched in such attempts made at international level. Highlighting the nature and character of the symposium, in one of the volumes published by CIBA foundation, it is said :

> "The symposium is essentially inter-disciplinary, involving sociology, anthropology, social psychology, system analysis, political science, history and international law. Possibly the meeting may itself contribute to the exploration of the mutual relevance of these various points of view. By discussing the actiology of group conflicts at a number of levels and trying to identify new complexities of structure and function at each succeeding level, it is hoped that it may eventually be possible to elucidate some of the sociological processes leading to war".

Cultural institutions in general are not necessarily adaptive in the Darwinian sense. It does not appear possible to explain cultural evolution by a process of natural selection that encourages the persistence of useful social customs and eliminates maladaptive ones : the pace of social change is too fast for any such equilibrium to be achieved. Now Science and technology have enabled man to reverse to some extent the age-old process of adaptation to environment by assisting him to adapt his physical environment to himself. Scientific consideration of man's social environment and its manipulation has only just begun."[3]

In modern times the crux of the human problem is how to imbibe the capacity to combine material progress with survival. It will be possible only when intellectual focus of a man will be on the problems of conflict in society. How to overcome it, of course, developed cultural traditions can help him to govern and regulate his role behaviour and remove or at least eliminate those factors leading to microcultural conflicts. The sources of conflict in any society may be in multitude; but they are mostly psycho-sociological in character. In a large number of group a man considerably developed capacity to internalize constraint as part of his learning of culture. This type of learning starts from the very childhood and the family has a great role to play therein. The phenomenon of socialization is directly related to the socio-cultural values prevailing in a group. Emile Durkheim, a noted social scientist, in his classical work. *The Elementary Forms of Religious Life*, has given an elaborate analysis of socialization within society. It has heitalped to solve the dilemma faced by previous social theoreticians, such as Hobbes, Rousseau and Locke, in explaining integrated processes that keep society together by discussing how it is the very essence of man's social nature itself for him to experience a strong sense of inner constraints. By instinct a man aspire for assertion and recognition regardless of his age, caste, creed, colour or the social status. We should not forget this basic fact. This constraint keeps societies integrated without the need to resort to the fiction of social contract or to rely on the use of instrumental power or coercion.

Historically speaking no great culture of the ancient world could become great, magnanious and appealing without assimilation of certain elements of other cultures. No human being, a group or a culture can be adjudged superior or inferior in isolation. It can be evaluated, adjudged and better understood in relation to other cultures only.

## Need

We are passing through a very unique crisis, which can be termed as cultural crisis, not economic crisis. It is transitional period when our traditional values are at stake and new value-system is yet in making. It is not only moral but a human-crisis. Human beings are facing a number of critical concerns, which warrant our immediate attention, which include destruction of ozone layer, ecological imbalance, pollution, poverty, over-population, threat of nuclear armament, world-hunger, spread of AIDS etc. Any sort of negligence to these problems may lead us towards destruction. In order to resolve these problems besides global co-operation, this type of mutual co-operation will be feasible where there will be mutual understanding between various cultural groups, societies and various nations of the world. For this purpose, crosscultural understanding is necessary and for such type of understanding proper crosscultural communication in various groups of macro-culture as well as among various micro-cultures is essential.

**Objectives**

Objectives of Crosscultural Communication may be enumerated as under :
To Develop:

1. A good self-concept and self-understanding.
2. Sensitivity to and understanding of others, including cultural groups in India and abroad.
3. The ability to perceive and understand multiple cultural and national interpretations of events, values and individual or group behaviour.
4. The ability to make decisions on multicultural analysis and synthesis.
5. Openmindedness toward customs and rituals prevailing in other cultures.
6. International understanding.
7. Pride in self.
8. Respect for other religions, in a multi-racial, multi-cultural and multi-linguistic society.

**Theories of Assimilation of Cultures**

Gorden (1964) has developed three theories to describe the role of distinct cultures in the assimilation strategies predominant in the twentieth century– the melting pot, Anglo conformity and cultural pluralism in the American perspective. These theories were used to describe the process of assimilation that was popularly supported by the dominant culture of the period and by government policies particularly related to immigration and civil rights.

Due to system of slavery America has been facing racial problems. The presence or the blacks-Negroes doesn't confirm the concept of equality as enshrined in the American constitution, in the field of socio-economic or legal they are still treated as second rate citizens in some particularly southern, parts of United States. According to Commager "Partly because he was a black, partly because he has less training, and less education than his white competitor, the Negro was generally last to be hired and first to be fired." In the northern states of America, because of their prosperity, they have been able to get equal status with the white counterparts; but in the southern states inequality hatred and depression still prevail.

In 1860 Abraham Lincon, the 16th President of America, has tried his best to abolish slavery. Consequently in 1865 by the 13th amendment the slavery was abolished and about 40 lacs Negroes were able to breathe in the atmosphere of equality. By the 14th and 15th amendment the class distinction was removed and the Negroes got the right to vote. These amendments, of course, got a practical shape in the Northern region; but in the Sourthern region nothing constructive could be done. Their status was that of second grade citizens. It was only after 1963 when Martin King Luther led a procession of Negroes and Whites that some reformative steps have been taken in this direction. In 1970 the Supreme Court, in one of its historical decisions, has given the equal rights of admission to the children of blacks and whites, that is why United States is facing the problems of "Multicultural Education". "Multiethnic Education" and so on.

## Melting Pot Theory

The concept of the melting pot was proposed by the playwright Israel Zangwill in his 1909 play. The Melting Pot, where a Russian-Jewish grant described the United States in this speech:

> America is God's crucible, the great Melting Pot where all recess of Europe are melting and reforming. Here you stand, good folk, think I, when I see them at Ellis Island, here you stand in your fifty groups with your fifty hatreds and rivalries, but you won't be long like that, brothers, for there are the fires of God. A fig for your feuds and

> vendeltas: Germans and Frenchmen, Irishmen and Englishmen, Jews and Russians into the crucible with you all: God is making the Americans. . . . The real American has not yet arrived. He is only in the crucible, I tell you–he will be the fusion of all races, the coming superman (Zangwill, 1909, p. 37).[4]

It is just historical coincident that when Zangwill profounded his theory (melting pot) through one of his play, in India noted Bengali Poet and Nobel laureate, Ravindra Nath Tagore, indicated the same theme through one of his poems, entitled "Aee Mahamanaver Sangar Teere" (Come to the sea-shore of superman) wherein he says:

> Hethai Arya, Hetha Anarya, Hethai Dravid-Cheen, Shak-Hun-Dal, Pathan-Mogul Ek Dehe Holo leen. (Here came Aryans, Non-aryans. Here came Dravidians and Chinese. Band of Shakas, Hunas, Pathans and Moghuls also made an advent and got assimilated in the body of India).

With the various invaders several cultures poured down in India; but ultimately were assimilated in the melting pot (india) and formed one composite culture of India. Similarly, "The melting pot ideal was quickly adopted as a promising ideal for fusing various new and old immigrant groups into a new American society. One of the ideological fallings of the melting pot was that it never proposed to melt all ethnic and cultural groups. Even in Zangwill's speech there is no mention of adding American Indians, Blacks, Hispanics other than immigrants from spain, or Asians to this crucible. Although the prospect of being a part of the pot that would create the real Americans seemed an attractive idea to many immigrants, other groups, particularly American Indians, fought against becoming the one model American. To melt into the American society required abandoning customs, dress, and language so that one would think, feel, and act like an American."[5]

Melting pot theory is an ideal and there had always been some difference between the ideal and actual practice. So, the case is with this theory. Some groups or micro-cultures or even persons do not like to part with their customs or age-old tradition and feel reluctance to adopt macroculture or national culture. This generally happens to the minority group for various socio-religious reasons and prove to be hard nut to bring them into the mainstream of the society or the nation at large.

**Anglo-confirmity Theory**

This theory is applicable to the macroculture of United States of America, where the microcultures of Immigrants and minority group was not expected to contribute equally as visualised in melting pot theory. The very expectation from the microcultural groups were far less than expected in the melting pot theory. "They were required to attend schools to learn the language, values, traits, dress and customs of the dominant culture. To be accepted as Americans, members of these immigrant groups had to confirm to the patterns of thinking, feeling and behaving of the WASP culture." But eventually the requirement was not fulfilled and the expectations were not translated into action fully.

Here we would like to make it clear that inter-cultural contact does not necessarily lead to cultural assimilation. For this purpose proper psychological balance between pride in one's own culture and the appreciation of cultures very different from our own. "The Anglo-conformity theory described what was expected of migrant and minority groups, but it did not describe how these groups chose to adopt the WASP culture as their own, many refused to assimilate into dominant culture and maintained separate ethnic communities and enclaves within the society. They developed within groups institutions, agencies, and power structures for services within their ethnic communities (Hunter, 1974). Little Italy, China town, and Harlem are examples of communities that still exist and reflect the ethnic identity of their inhabitants, some religious groups, pertinently the Hutterities and the Amish, also continue to maintain their own communities. The reality of the preservation of communal life and significant portions of the culture of these groups within the context of American citizenship was termed cultural pluralism by sociologists and educators."[6]

In fact, earlier defences of the ideal of 'the melting pot' 'Assimilation', and acculturation are being challenged because their assumptions were that ethnics would surrender their various heritages to join the dominant culture. Here, in this case man's natural instincts of self-assertion and self-identification were not taken into account. Moreover, the degree of difference among microcultures is also significant. For example, Europeans and Americans, Hindus and Jains — there is a certain affinity of culture and as such for Europeans and Jains it is easier to adopt the dominant cultures, namely, American and Indian respectively. But for the American Indians and blacks, due to lack of cultural affinity, adoption of dominant culture carries various threads of doubt, it may be feasible and otherwise also. These days with a new emphasis on the conservation of ethnic heritages, the American Indians and blacks do not like to loose their ethnic distinctiveness.

**Cultural Pluralism Theory**

Like India, the United States of America (U.S.A.) consists of people of different Languages, races, sects and religions. According to census of 1980 its population is about·twenty-three crores, whereas India's population in 1981 was more than eighty-four crores. The people of united states mainly speak English and Christianity is the faith of bulk of people. There are 5.5 million jews. Important religious organizations are – Protestant bodies, Roman Catholic Church, Old Catholic, Polish National Catholic, Armeman and Buddhists. The constitution of United States, like Indian constitution, protects the freedom of each citizen to choose his or her faith and worship according to one's conscience.

India is a secular state, which means that the decisions of the state should not be taken on religious grounds. Religion and Politics should be separated. This also sounds that all religions would be equal before the state. A secular state does not mean that citizens cannot practice their religion; but no religion is given preference over other. Article 25 provides freedom of religion to all Indian citizens. As per article 26 Religious communities can also set-up charitable institutions of their own. In fact, many educational institution are run by such charities. Similarly, the first amendment of the American constitution provides that the "Congress shall make no law respecting and establishment of religion, or prohibiting the free exercise thereof.

'Cultural Pluralism' is an ideal according to which all groups should live and work together while maintaining and preserving their cultural identity. In such a phenomenon problem of possible contradiction arises. According to the views of some social scientists, emphasis on cultural distrinctiveness works against allegiance to a common American culture and has the possibility of promoting divisiveness and enhancing social segregation, whereas others see "cultural pluralism as the only tenable basis for equality and human rights for all. Historically speaking after Second World War, minority ethnic groups including the blacks became increasingly powerful both politically and socially, and refuse to tolerate discrimination by the dominant WASP cultural group and its political and social institutions. In the 60s with the sustained efforts of a Negro Leader, Martin King Luther, the black power movement stressed the social and political advantages for blacks to identify strongly with their ethnic groups. There is no gainsaying the fact that some members of cultural groups strongly support the development of identity and commitment with their cultural group to the extent of exclusion of influence from the dominant culture or other cultural groups.

## Stereotypes and Crosscultural Communication

For effective crosscultural communication elimination of stereotypes is necessary. Stereotype is, in fact, a hypothesis based on exaggerated and inaccurate generalization used to describe all members of a group. "Stereotypes are erroneous beliefs, either–favourable or unfavourable, which are applied universally and without exception. Some common stereotypes are : athletes are dumb; Jews are stingy; Japanese Americans are highly intelligent; Blacks are violent, fat people are lazy and lack self-discipline, sorority girls are superficial; whites are racially prejudiced; Blacks are sexually promiscious; and Hispanics speak Spanish. Often there is just enough fact to make a stereotype true. For example, there are some dumb blondes, interfering mother-in-law, cruel stepmothers, and Asian whiz kids, and those Kernels of truth work to keep the stereotypes alive."[7]

Many a time there is over-generalisation. For example it is said that all Jews are highly intelligent. In history three Jews had been very famous as far as calibre and creative talent are concerned, i.e., famous scientist and propounder of the theory of relatively, Albert Einstein; founder of the school of Psycho-analysis in psychology, Sigmund Friud; and the great champion of communism, Karl Marx. But, by using stereotype that all the Jews are highly intelligent is just overgeneralization of the historical illustrations made above. In 'Merchant of Venice', a Shakespearian play, one Jew merchant named Shellock has been depicted as the most miser and cunning. There may be other few examples also. But, on the basis of a few facts we cannot believe in generalized stereotype – ''Jews are stingy.''

Such categorization, of course, help our perception to some extent by giving some information about a group or particular caste, sect or race. But, such generalizations, at times, are felt very deceptive. It is just to simplify our problems, and make our understanding easier as it is not possible or rather practical to employ all the information about surrounding or environment of the individuals we come into contact. From the Indian scenario a few stereotypes may be numerated: All drivers (professional) are drunken, Marwaris are miser, Jains are vegetarians. Baniyas are good businessmen, Punjabees are adventurous, Bengalis are fish-eaters, etc. As we have already mentioned that such generalization are deceptive. It is true in Indian context also. Actually the virtues or vices of an individual are manifested in his relationship with others, not in isolation. Some peole argue that stereotypes and prejudice help develop strong in-group feelings and safeguard the nurturing of ethnic traditions and beliefs. This argument is against the basic assumption and aspiration of healthy crosscultural communication and also against the unity of mankind. Crosscultural Communication is based on the assumption of cultural pluralism. A basic assumption of crosscultural communication is that a group can have a good crosscultural communication even with the retention its original culture. Thus, a group can be called multicultural without damaging its own beliefs and traditions if there is a spirit of tolerance and proper understanding. Crosscultural communication does not aim at harming anybody's feeling or erosion of any belief or tradition; but it stands for concern and respect for other cultures.

## Indoctrination and Ideological Conflict

> "A religious belief could only be something like a passionate commitment to a system of reference. Hence, although its belief, it's really a way of living, or a way of assessing life. Confusing religious doctrines with empirical ones is a blunder that reduces all such beliefs to superstition. Religious belief is not reasonable nor it pretend to be, and it is ludicrous to make it appear to be reasonable. Those who try to make religious belief appear to be reasonable by appealing to facts and evidence, are unreasonable and that if this is religious belief, it's all superstition."[8]
>
> – *Wittgenstein*

## Indoctrination Defined

Indoctrination is interpreted as 'the deliberate action of changing and increasing the number of unquestioned things in a culture' because indoctrinated individual is not supposed to question 'why'. Belief is after all belief as it is followed and belief has not rationales as Wittgenstein has observed above. According to John Wilson: The central religious questions are about the appropriateness of certain attitudes and emotion, particularly the attitude of worship towards certain objects. Philosophical problems about freedom and indoctrination will not worry us any longer when we understand that in religion, just as in morality, politics, aesthetics and other forms of thought and practice, two forms of commitment are required–In tradition ('content') and to the impartial questioning and analysing of religious beliefs ('form'). This means that the process of indoctrination is not assumed to be accomplished unless it is exercised at intellectual as well as emotional level when the individual is upset equally at emotional level also the process is very much facilitated. This happened so with Dr. B.R. Ambedkar. Being very much perturbed and harassed by the atrocities of Hinduism, particularly with the problem of untouchability he resolved "I am born as Hindu but I will not die as Hindu" and before one year of his death he took *deeksha* of Buddhism alongwith his thousands of followers at Nagpur. Prior to taking *deeksha* he studied the Buddhist scriptures thoroughly and contributed a lot towards Buddhist studies.

Dr. B.R. Ambedkar was well-known leader of scheduled castes and down-trodden masses attending their economic, social and political problems. In 1950 he made known publicly his determination to revive Buddhism in India. In the same year concluding one of his articles named. *"The Buddha and future of His Religion"* he proclaimed that Buddhism was the only religion which the world could have because of its emphasis on reason, morality, liberty, equality and fraternity. This very example reveals that the vitality of propaganda of any faith or religion depends upon its ingredients, the content as well as its form. D.C. Ahir observes that, "The most outstanding event of the 2500th Buddha Jayanti Celebrations took place on October 14 of that year (1956). On that day Dr. Ambedkar took formal refuge to in Buddha-Dhamma, alongwith half a million followers at an impressive and historic ceremony held at Nagpur and gave a clarion call to his followers to take refuge in the Buddha, the Dhamma and the Sangha. With the turning of the wheel of law by Dr. Ambedkar at Nagpur on 14th October 1956, the revival movement entered into an era of intense activity which can be rightly called the 'Ambedkar Era' of Indian Buddhism. It is worth-noting that within a period of five years (1956–1961) the population of Buddhists registered a spectacular increase of 1670. 71per cent i.e., form 1,80,823 to 32,50,227. This figure might have further gone up by now as the mass conversions initiated by Dr. Ambedkar have been continuing unabated."[9]

The word 'doctrine' is sometime, by some people, politicians in particular, defined very vaguely. They refuse to accept that the primary locus of indoctrination is religion. In a secular state like India indoctrination in a particular creed, sect or religion in any government institution is not desirable, it is rather objectionable. India is a secular state. This means, that decisions of the state should not be taken on religious grounds. This also means that all religions would be equal before the state. A secular state does not mean that citizens cannot practice their religion. But no religion is given preference over other. According to this, Indian Constitution gives a right to freedom of religion to all Indian citizens. All citizens can practice their religion (Article 25). However, these activities of the religious communities which are not religious, which are known as secular are governed by law. For example, religious communities can govern financial activities of religious bodies. Establishing of charitable institutions also can be restricted in the interest of public order, morality and health but religious education cannot be given in institutions that are run by the State (Aıticle 28). If this is allowed, the principal of secularism will be at stake.

**Intellectual vs Emotional Indoctrination**

Moverover, psychologically without emotional excitement merely intellectual indoctrination is not found to be effective. William Sargant observes : "Intellectual indoctrination without emotional excitment is remarkably ineffective, as the empty pews of most English churches prove; the social pressure which once sent even the agnostic or lukwarm to Sunday matins having long been relaxed. and recently we found ourselves welcoming a high-powered American Fundamentalist who had come to in back for the churches the congregations that they had lost."[10]

If the inculcation of any principle or doctrine is to be made enduring and lasting 'free choice' must be opened to an individual or institution by providing complete freedom. Without such freedom free choice will not be feasible. "Freedom of religious faith, together with freedom of thought and conscience among the most important human rights has been won in the West with great sacrifices; and it is our duty to guard it jealously. Yet I believe that freedom of faith should include both the rights to embrace any religion one chooses and right to conduct missionary activities to carry that faith to other people."[11] Some nations permit only the former and prohibit the latter. The worse situation, which hampers the crosscultural communication, is to allow missionary work against religion and forbid it in its name. This very trend is noticeable in the specialist nation. Unless both of these two rights are granted simultaneously maintenance and nurture of religion are difficult, if not quite impossible. If the religion and its main tenets are not publicized, the religion may die out. We may say that human religious conscience is difficult to maintain if both the rights are not granted.

**Role of Politics**

It may appear astonishing, but a historical fact that in cultures perceiving themselves to be champions of liberty call for the suppression of unpalatable truths. "Event in Tiananmen Square in 1989 and the case of Salman Sushdie's novel 'the Satanic Verses' bring it home to us, if we needed reminding, that the issues of censorship and freedom of expression are very live ones. But at the same time, these dramatic events are taking place more familiar, but no less working, examples can be found in the schooling system. The West Vancouver Branch of British Columbia Federation of English Teachers have recently resolved not to teach Shakespeare's "Merchant of Venic" on the grounds that it is racialist; elsewhere in Canada Jim Keegstra has been found guilty of wilfully promoting hatred against Jews, for arguing that the familiar story of the Nazi treatment of Jews is substantially incorrect, is in fact a Jewish plot (Bercuson and Wertheimer, 1985). In the United States creationists still seek to prevent the teaching of the theory of evolution, often with success. In certain school districts in Britian, books are unashamedly vetted and censored by political criteria. Censorship, which we perhaps tend to think of as a feature of other more repressive societies, is part of our everyday life."[12] In India also for fear of hurting the secular status we do not teach 'g' for Ganesh ('God of wisdom') but for 'Gadha' (donkey). In many cases we can observe that with the change of the Government in a state the very base of the curriculum is also changed. The opposite party levelled allegations also against the ruling party (Bhartiya Janata Party in M.P. 1991–93) for indoctrination damaging the secular character of the syllabus. Ultimately, the entire endeavour of the ruling party was quashed soon after the change of the party. It is just an example. As a whole indoctrination is a very serious political problem in the world.

**Indoctrination and Education**

In very religious communities and institutions also the paradigm cases are found. "The ordinary uses of 'indoctrination' suggest that it has to do with the transmission or inculcation of doctrinal beliefs. Indoctrination does not imply a specific activity or activities but confirmity to some specific beliefs and rules that are at the foundation of particular ideology. Just as we educate people by teaching them the huminities, the sciences and the arts, we doctrinate people by teaching them particular doctrines. The difference between education and indoctrination lies in the nature of critieria employed . . . . . Successful indocrination results in the acceptance of doctrinal beliefs and commitment to them. Whereas successful educational engagement aim at some worthwhile understanding."[13]

If a student, after careful consideration, rejects the doctrines he has been taught, the indoctrinator has failed in his or her task. It so happened with Dr. S. Radhakrishnan, as he himself has written in his autobiography:

> "My Search for Truth" that he was so much perplexed and innerly hurt with the sense of hatred towards his own faith (Hinduism) by the indoctrinators (missionaries) that he was compelled to know the truth by studying deeply the sacred literature of his own faith (Hinduism). After having studied deeply all the aspects of Religion he concluded that Religion is not a principal or doctrine but an experience of life, a way of life, without which a man is incomplete. The essence of religion is not in dogmas and creed, nor in rites and ceremonies as these modes, at times, prove to be repulsive for a man. According to him" India is not a racial identity, for a racialist destiny is spurious. Pure racial types are an ideal figment of anthropology. In real life it is not easy to find individuals who combine all the characters of the same type. Men everywhere exhibit features belonging to different racial types, and even members of the same family hardly ever possesses the same racial characters. Indian culture is not racially exclusive, but has affected men of all races. It is international in feeling and action. As the typical religion of India, Hinduism represents this spirit. The spirit that has such extraordinary vitality as to servive political and social changes. From the beginning of recorded history. Hinduism has borne witness to the sacred flame of spirit which must remain for ever, even while dynasties crash and empires tumble into ruins. It alone can give our civilization a soul, and men and women a principle to live by."[14]

**Epistemological Influences**

Lastly, we should not forget that freedom is not a licence. It is for creation and not for destruction to say with will Durant that "Will is free in so far as life is creative, in so far as it enters, with its remolding energy, as one of the determining conditions of choice and action."[15] Since the main storehouse of doctrines is said to be religion, if this precaution is not taken it may lead to disharmony of the group or society. There are some other types of doctrines, such as-political, psychological etc. These are not so harmful, in the words of Ben Spiecker and Roger Straughan, these doctrines are "Like dead rats in epistemological sanctuaries–when they are pointed out by critics they cause great embarrassment to their originators or perpetrators." Few examples are as under :

| | | |
|---|---|---|
| (1) Carl Marx | – | "Every historical event is the product of economic forces." |
| (2) Skinner | – | "Operant response increases its probability when followed by a reinforcing situation." |
| (3) Sigmund Freud | – | "All human actions are determined by unconscious forces." |
| (4) J. Load | – | "All life-phenomena are determined by Chemical process." |
| 5) E.A. Schafer | – | "Living beings are governed by Laws identical with those which govern inanimate matter. |
| (6) Sir Ray Lankester | – | "The materialist and mechanical scheme of nature (including man's nature) elaborated by physical science, is true and trustworthy. |
| (7) Bertrand Russel | – | "It is a working hypothesis that the human body acts according to the same laws of physics and chemistry as those which govern the dead matter, and that it differs from the dead matter, but by the extraordinary complexity of its structure." |

Of these seven, the first–three received world-wide acclaim and there are host of books by eminent authors and there had been a certain span of period in the 20th century when these doctrines gained lot of popularity. It is also true that political philosophers like Carl Marx and lenin brought about lot of changes in the socio-politico-cultural spheres of the world. But now as USSR stands withered, the Marxist philosophy has also withered, except its humanistic view where he says that "Man is the measure for everything. Prof. Carow Hund says,"Finally, Marx's Thesis that all conflict among men arises from class struggle, albeit of undoubted tactical values as calculated to convince the masses that their misfortunes are attributed to the capitalist system and will disappear with the victory of the proletariat, is nonetheless fallacious. For the supreme source of conflict in life is the inevitable opposition between the claims of the individual and those of society, a conflict which is not reducible to class-struggle and cannot be dialectically resolved because it is a part of unchanging human situation." Recent events in Russia falsified the Marx prophecy that capitalism will slowly weaken itself. On the contrary, we find that capitalism has considerably strengthened itself.

On Skinner's as well as Freud's theories there had been many improvisations by their followers. The rest of the four are just scientific generalization which did not or rather could not hold good after detailed examination by the experts. Herber Spencer applied the physical concepts of "organism" and "embryonic evolution" to the human phenomena of history and sociology, and the result was disastrous. Har Dayal holds that "Such method leads only to confusion and error. Sound philosophy demands that the special laws governing each of the five orders of phenomena should be formulated on the basis of observed and ascertained facts. The attempt of foist all the physical and chemical laws upon Zoology or Zoological laws upon psychology and sociology must be abandoned. Each branch of science deals with its own phenomena and discovers its special laws, besides those universal laws that apply to all phenomena."[16] He further adds that "Henry Bergson's Elan Vital, H.A.E. Driesch's entelechy, William Mcdougall's soul and other such terms are really meaningless and superfluous. They are merely metaphysical abstractions. Science deals with phenomena and their laws; it shuns vague and mystical abstractions that only confuse the mind."[17]

Above all enquiry we must bear in mind that an animal is not a mere mechanical apparatus, it is something more than that as it has a nervous system and has a thinking power. It is important to note that modern philosophers like schopenhauer and nietzsche, with all their hostility to traditional theology, rejected mechanism clearly; because machine can do only numbering calculating, weighing, seeing, handling etc, nothing more. It cannot differentiate between the good and bad.

## Environmentalism

Environment has a very wide and varied effect on the working habits, food-habits, conduct and character of human beings. The country like India where the tropical climate and human fertility have contributed towards the growth of a dense population, low wages have been the result leading to a great inequality in the distribution of wealth which ultimately leads to an inequality in the social status. Montesqeue, like many other environmentalists, has been influenced by the environmental factors as the moulder of human character. He holds that "people in cold countries are stronger physically, more courageous, franker, less cunning than those of the South who are like old men, timorous, weak in body, indolent and passive". According to Montesque,

> "Islands peoples are more jealous of their liberties than those of continents. Islands are commonly of small extent; one part of the people cannot be so easily employed to oppress the other; the sea separates them from great empires; tyranny cannot so well support itself within a small compass; conquerors are stopped by the sea, and the islanders being without the reach of their arms more easily preserve their own laws."[18]

In fact the nature of thought and deeds, bearings and behaviour, mind and manners etc. have considerable impact of the environment. Inter-action between a man and environment is a constant process continuing from the time immemorable. Gottingen made a judicious attempt in this regard in his *Kosmos* upon the "evolution of Mediterranean civilization, "The influence of the sea was speedily manifested in the growing power of the Phoenicians and subsequently in that of the Hellenic nations and in the rapid extension of the sphere of general ideas ...... The active life of the Greeks, especially of the Ionians; and their early predilection for maritime expeditions found a rich field for its development in the remarkable configuration of the Mediterranean, and in its relative position to the oceans situated to the South and West."[19]

Environmentalism is well illustrated by Buckle, in *History of Civilization in England.* Buckle attempted to elevate history to other branches of speculation. Other scientists conducted an enquiry with a lot of data at their disposal. They aimed at discovering in it a pattern of regularity which led them to recognise and formulate the fundamental laws "We are driven to the conclusion that the actions of men, being determined solely by their antecedents must have a character of uniformity, that is to say must, under precisely the same circumstances, always issue in precisely the same results. And as well antecedents are either in the mind or out of it, we clearly see that all the variations in the results, in other words, all the changes of which history is full, all the vicissitudes of the human race, their progress or their decay, their happiness or their misery, must be the fruit of a double action, an action of external phenomena upon the mind and another action of mind upon the phenomena . . . . thus we have man modifying nature and nature modifying man, while out of this reciprocal modification all events must necessarily spring."[20]

## Enculturation and Socialization

Enculturation and socialization are the processes taking place in one's life right from the early childhood. Various formal and informal agencies knowingly or unknowingly, directly or indirectly get involved in these processes, which include parents, nurses, physicians, teachers etc. As a matter of social obligations these agencies import various types of instructions formally or informally in order to socialize the child, though they may not take it as a process. It is done so naturally and unconsciously that no need is felt to give the process any particular and formal nomenclature; but they go on modifying the attitude, behaviour and so of the child through the technique of reward and punishment, appreciation and displeasure or through direct demonstration of certain behavioural patterns within acceptable norms of the society. Thus, individuals get socialized and encluturated in confirmity with the patterns of culture and value-system of the society they live in. The culture in which one is born becomes insignificant unless one is also socialized in the same culture as Kluckhohn has illustrated.

> "I met in New York city a young man who did not speak a word of English and was obviously bewildered by American ways. By 'blood' he was as American as you or I for his parents had gone from Indiana to China as missionaries. Orphaned in infancy, he was reared by a Chinese family in a remote village. All who met him found him more Chinese than American. The facts of his blue eyes and light hairs were less impressive than a Chinese style of gait. Chinese arm and hand movements, Chinese facial expressions, and Chinese modes of thought. The biologican heritage was American, but the cultural training had been Chinese. He returned to China."[21]

Many such examples can be cited from our society also. Various tribes living in remote islands leading backward life are still repulsive of the process of urbanisation. In spite of a few changes in certain facts of life their modes of thoughts are still coloured with tribal culture. With the rapid strides of advancement they are gradually adopting urban life-style. Similarly, the Eskimo who lives with extreme cold, snow ice and sea have developed culture different from the pacific. Islanders shom-pen tribes of Nicobar Islands are on violent strides towards the process of modernization. Majority of the group has adopted christianity and they are moving very fast to adopt developed and modern life-styles. Thus, we can say that culture is learnt and it is subject to adaptation since cultures have developed to accommodate certain environmental and available natural and technological resources.

Let us take one example from Indian perspective. Amir Khusrau, the poet and musician was a Turk by birth. But, he lived in India for most of the span of his life. He served as poet laureate to at least six Sultans, the last being Ghiyasuddin Tughlaq. For many years he had to stay in other provinces with his masters to accompany them in their marches. In 1284 he became the disciple of the famous Chishtiya Sufi Saint Nizamuddin Auliya and became a full-fledged sufi. His statements and writings show that he knew Hindi better than Arabic and he was also proud of it. At one place he says: "I am an Indian Turk and I can reply to you in Hindi. I have no Egyptian sugar to talk of Arabia and Arabic. As I am in fact the parrot of India, question me in Hindui, that I may talk sweetly."[22]

**Cultural Relativism and Myths**

As far as democratic values like liberty and equality are concerned and peace and harmony in a special group is desired cultural myths stand as dysfunctional to our efforts. In the name of culture atrocities and injustice on human beings violating all norms of decency and human dignity cannot be ignored. All those beliefs and practices which discriminate between humans on the basis of gender, race, religion, language, or any socio-political affinity are also dysfunctional to smooth crosscultural communication.

In fact the word 'myth' is used in the classical sense. A myth is an answer to an unanswerable question which has been socialized, politicized, and traditionalized by a society. 'Mythology' is the study of myths, both classical and current. Classical myths have their own significance particularly to examine the origin of a particular religion, as Max Muller Says :

> "The more we go back, the more we examine the earliest germs of any religion, the purer I believe we shall find the conceptions of the Deity". But to instil the value of scientific temper and develop awareness among future citizens and leaders myths must be properly explained. W.J. Wilkins, in the preface to second edition of 'Hindu Mythology' writes : "It is most instructive to notice the marked deterioration in the quality of the teaching, deities as described by

the earlier sages being vastly better than their successors declare them to be. Non-Christian Bibles are all development in the wrong direction. They begin with some flashes of true light, and end in darkness".[23]

Pedagogically speaking "Education" is the invention contrived and used by humans to move from where we are to where we want to go. The pertinent question is which way we should go? It has been answered in "Alice in Wonderland" very simply but subtly :

> "Could you tell me, please, which way I
> ought to go from here? Said Alice,
> 'That depends a good deal on where you
> want to get to' said Cheshire Cat".

If we wish to establish peace and harmony in the society combating prejudices, tension, conflicts, crime and terrorism we have to demythologize the society and establish it on rational and scientific ground so that the people may not be victimized on the count of religion or socalled cultural conventions, which neither suit to the fast-changing society nor conducive to the human dignity.

Elaborating the urgent need for education in Human Rights Nelsion Haggerson writes :

"Demythologizing is a special form of education which aims at bringing myths to the awareness of educands, determining whether they are currently viable, . . . . and replacing them with new myths by which to live and rear new generations of children. Demythologizing includes inquiring into the existence and nature of the educands, and implementing curricular and instructional endeavours which assist them in replacing faculty myths with viable ones."[24] In order to prepare future leaders the teaching of Economic, History, Sociology and transcultural communication in the right perspectives is very essential. For want of proper education and awareness the common people are easily misled by charlatans, socalled patriots and priests. In this regard, Hood has satirically but rightly observed :

> *"The history of mankind to trace*
> *Since Eve, the first of dupes or doom unriddled.*
> *A certain portion of the human race*

*Has certainly a taste for being diddled*
*No matter what, to pasture cows on stubble*
*To twist sea-sand into a solid rope.*
*To make french bricks and fancy-bread of rubble,*
*Or light with gas the whole celestial cope -*
*Only propose to blow a bubble,*
*And Lord ! what hundreds will subscribe for soap"*[25]

Each culture has its own mores and morals, traditions and conventions, ethos and ethics, good and bad life-styles. Whatever bad elements we observe in other cultures, they are not said to be bad provided the human rights and dignity or social cohesiveness are not at stake. Thus one has no right to either criticize or change those traditions or myths of other cultures. Nelson Haggerson has aptly pointed out :

"When you think of the "Ugly American" or the "Arrogant Englishman" images, it is easy to understand why cultural relativists have strong argument. On the other hand, when you think of the world as a "global village" and you think that in one part of that global village women are subject to atrocities as part of their "Culture", whereas women another part of the world are "equals" you begin to wonder why some women have rights of safety, dignity and freedom and others seem to have few, if any such rights. You begin to question the efficacy of the cultural relativity myth".[26]

Thus we see that the theory concept of relativism in cultures may not be efficacious as far as the cause of human rights and dignity of mankind are concerned. Of course, for healthy and efficacious crosscultural communication it is essential to know how different cultures view man, women, children, microcultures, races, ethnic groups, religious groups and so on.

## Prejudices and Personality

Personality is a psycho–physical mechanism, psychic complex often stand as odds and obstacles in the way of balanced development of one's personality, Gordon Allport, the greatest authority on prejudice and personality, agrees that humans prefers the familiar, but he explains that this is because of "the principles of ease, least effort, congeniality, and pride in one's own culture", not prejudice. Thus liking or disliking of other culture or way of thinking, believing, judging, acting etc. can not always be attributed to one's prejudices. It is just possible that one may dislike other's company for want of congeniality or for the fear of some sort of uneasiness. Allport visualizes social relationships among groups along a continuum from friendly to hostile and in the descending order he indicates eight phases in this manner :

Friendly - cooperation - respect -
tolerance - predilection - prejudice -
discrimination - scapegoating - hostile.[27]

As far as loyality of the individual is concerned, it is found to be towards one's family but it goes on decreasing as he moves towards the out circles i.e. *neighbourhood, city, state, nation, racial stock and lastly, the mankind.* On the part of individual lot of efforts are required conscious or unconscious to move oneself from one to another outer circles, i.e., from family to neighbourhood, from neighbourhood to city, city to state, state to nation, nations to race and from race to mankind, while bridging the gap between the two, an individual has to cherisn and embibe higher and sublime human values.

**Confucian Formula Eliminating Prejudices**

Confucianism was not a welcome doctrine during the regime of Mao Tze-Tung. During early years of Communists, Confucianism received very rough treatment. In his early writing Mao blasted Confucianism as semi-feudal; but after some years he advised his countrymen to study confucius as well as Marx. Now even the Communist are pondering over the following basic formula of Confucius, wherein righteousness (Dharma – according to Hindu terminology) has been treated as the basic element; and family as the basic unit for peace in nation and the world at large.

If there be righteousness in the heart
there will be beauty in the character.
If there be beauty in the character
there will be harmony in the home.
If there be harmony in the home
there will be order in the nation
If there be harmony in the nation
there will be peace in the world.[28]

By the virtue of its merit and magnanimity Confucianism became China's state religion during Han Dynasty (206 BC — 220). In 130 B.C. it was made the basic discipline for the training of Government officials and it continued till the establishment of the Republic in 1912.

**Indicators of Crosscultural Communication**

To understand the concept of crosscultural communication the knowledge of the following periods, movements and various personalities in proper perspective of universal history may be of immense help. In this treatise an attempt will be made to present the view-panels in respect of most of the aspects if not all, in a very precise and pertinent manner making the way for streamlining crosscultural communication :

— Early Egypt, Sculpture and Architecture.
— Akhanation : his Life and Work.
— War between Persia and Hellas.
— Greek Democracy and Socialism.
— Greek Philosophy from Thales to Plotinus.
— Greek Art (Sculpture and Architecture).
— Homer's "Odyssey".
— Greek Tragedy (Eschylus, Sophocles, Euripides).
— The Scientists and Scholars of Alexandria in the forty-eighth century A.H. (third century B.C).
— The Hebrew Prophets.
— Origin and Growth of the Christian Church : its Martyrs and Apostles.
— Zoroaster and the Rise of Zoroastrianism.
— Budha and Buddhism in India. Asoka, Jainism.
— Nagarjuna and the Mahayana, Gandhara Sculpture.
— Kung-fu-tzu (Confucius), Mencius, and their movements.
— Early History of Rome, Democracy and Republicanism
— Class struggles in Rome.
— The Reign of Justinian. Roman Law. Byzantine Art.
— The Rise of Monasticism in Egypt. The Orders of St. Basil and St. Benedict.
— Spread of Christianity in Europe. Irish Saints and Scholars.
— St. Francis and his Order. The Spiritual Friars.
— Muhammad and early Islam.
— The Islamia Renaissance; Moslem Philosophy and Science (fifty-

ninth to sixty-second centuries).

- Sufism and its Saints.
- The Dervish Orders.
- Persian Didactic Poetry.
- The Tang Dynasty in China. Progress of Buddhism. Chinese Painting.
- The Gupta Empire in India. Indian Literature and art. The Ramayana.
- The Sassanian Period in Persia.
- The Renaissance in the Byzantine Empire (fifty-ninth century A.H.) (ninth A.D.) Photius and Arethas.
- Early Renaissance in Europe (fifty-second and fifty-third centuries).
- The war between the Communes of Lombardy and the Emperor.
- The Great Renaissance in Italy and Europe (sixty-fourth, sixty-fifth and sixty-sixth centuries). The New Schools and Colleges. Democracy at Florence. Italian Painting, Sculpture, and Architecture.
- The Vaishnava Saints of N. India. Reformers, Modern Hindu Sects. Tamil Saints.
- The Buddhist Religious Leaders of China and Japan : their Sects and Schools, Japanese Sculpture.
- The Sung Philosophers in China.
- Discovery of the Cape route and of America, Columbia.
- The Protestant Reformation, Luther, Calvin, Zwingli, Anabaptists, Puritans, Socinians, Non-conformists in England and America, Gustavus Adolphus. The Dutch War of Independence.
- India's War of Independence against the Moguls. Mogul and Rajput Painting. Mogul Architecture in N. India, Hindu Architecture in S. India.
- Progress of Science since 6400 in Europe and America.
- German music from Bach to Wagner.
- Modern English Poetry. French Tragedy and Comedy. German Drama, Lyrics, and Short Stories. Russian Novels and Ballet, French and English Landscape-Painters.
- Modern Democracy. English, American and French Revolutions. European and South American National Movements. Parliaments. Abolition of Slavery.
- Socialism in Europe. The Russian Revolution. The Jesuits in

Paraguay. The Communist Colonies of N. America.
— Modern Philosophy and Religion. Positivism. Spinoza. Spencer Free thought and Ethical Movements in Europe and America. Theosophy. The Brahmo Samaj, Bahaism, Oomoto in Japan.
— The Peace Movement. Esperanto. The UNO.

**Crosscultural Communication and Body Language**

There are mainly three constituents of our speech, which include :

1. Words, sentences etc.
2. Modulation, pitch etc. of the voice of the speaker
3. Movements and postures of various parts of the body.

The former two fall under the category of verbal communication; whereas the third one comes under non-verbal communication, which is popularly known as a 'body language'. It is said that the contribution of words in conveying the purport is only 25 per cent, of modulation etc. 15 per cent and 60 per cent of various movements and postures of the body. Therefore, to observe and understand the language of the body is very important. That is why we enjoy listening to the speakers, more than going through his or her script. Similarly, conversation is found to be more enjoyable in light than in darkness. Clinical studies have revealed that the extent to which body language can actually contradict verbal communications. A classic example is the young woman who told her psychiatrist that she loved her boy friend very much while nodding her head from left to right and vice-versa in subconscious denial.

The importance of non-verbal communication is illustrated by the amount of meaning it carries in a normal conversation. Knapp (1972) suggests that in a typical conversation between two people, less than 35 per cent of the social meaning is actually transmitted by words, whereas more than 65 per cent of the social meaning is, conveyed, through non-verbal channels. The meaning conveyed by these channels includes not only surface message but the undercurrent of emotions or feelings also. The listerner not only hears words; but he also watches gestures and postures (body language) of the speaker.

Body language is also called Kinesics. Dr. Ray Birdwhistell, who has attempted to outline and tried to make it a science, contributed a manual called "An introduction to Kinesics". He has also attempted to put together a notational system for kinesics or body language. "Kine" means a smallest recordable movement of the body. He holds that all movements of the body have meaning. None are accidental. Once this is accepted we can proceed to a study of every movement. He finds that this basic assumption is the most difficult one to accept. Perhaps scratching the nose is an indication of disagreement, but it may also be an indication of an itchy nose. This is where the real trouble in Kinesics lies, in separating the significant from the insignificant gestures, the meaningfully from the purely random, or from the carefully learned.

Culture is said to be a guiding factor in all body language, and this is particularly true of body-zones. Dr. Hall holds that "basic differences between cultures lies in the way they handle space . . . . . . Latin Americans stand closer when they talk than Chinese or Negros, and Arabs stand even closer than Latins do. "Along with this closeness, there is a pushing and a sharing in the Arab world that Americans there are boundaries in a public place when he is waiting in line he believes that his place there is inviolate. The Arab has no concept of privacy in a public place, and if he can push his way into a line, he feels perfectly within his rights to do so.

As the Japanese lack of a word for privacy indicates a certain attitude towards other people, so the Arab lack of a word for rape indicates a certain attitude towards the body. To an American the body is sacred. To the Arab, who thinks nothing of showing and pushing and even pinching women in public, violation of the body is a minor thing. However, violation of the ego by insult is a major problem."[29] Thus Dr. Hall, discussing various aspects of Body Language peeps into crosscultural implication of his 'proxemics'. According to Christine I. Binnett" Variations in proxemics within a high-or low-context culture do exist, however In China, for example, gender makes a difference. It is common to see males walking hand in hand (or even intertwined) with males, and females with females. This does not signify being gay or lesbian, as it would in some cultures. Traditionally, heterosexual touching was strictly private in China, though today this is changing in most urban areas. Despite these changes, deeply rooted cultural expectations related to dating and courtship are likely to cause misunderstandings between Chinese and Americans."[30] In his research Hall has tried to prove that handling space by different culture is one of the prominent indicators of cultural characteristic of the people as far as communication is concerned. The focal point of his crosscultural research is the way humans use and organise space, as he himself elaborates:

"My own interest in space as a cultural phenomenon stemmed from the observation that Amercians overseas were confronted with a variety of difficulties because of cultural differences in the handling of space. People stood "too close" during conversations, and when the Americans backed away to a comfortable conversational distance, this was taken to mean that Americans were cold, all of, withdrawn, and disinterested in the people of the country. U.S. housewives muttered about "waste-space" in houses in the Middle East. In England, Americans, who were used to neighbourliness, were hurt when they discovered that their neighbours were no more accessible or friendly than other people, and in Latin America, ex-suburbanites, accused to unfenced yards, found that the high walls were made them feel "shut out". Even in Germany, where so many of our countrymen felt at home radically different patterns in the use of space led to unexpected tensions."[31]

## Non-verbal Communication

Acknowledging differences within foreign cultures can alert us to more subtle differences at home. Greetings are one example and illustrate how the accepted behaviours of one culture may be seriously misunderstood in another.

The Copper Eskimo welcome strangers with a buffet on the head or shoulders with the first, while the north-west Amazonians slap one another on the back in greeting, Polynesian men greet one another by embracing and rubbing each other's back; Spanish-American males greet one another by a stereotyped embrace, head over the right shoulder of the partner, three pats on the back, head over reciprocal left shoulder, three more pats. In the Torres Straits, the old form of greeting was to bend the right hand into a hook, then mutually scratching palms by drawing away the right hand, repeating this several times. An Ainu, meeting his sister, grasped her hands in his for a few seconds, suddenly released is hold, grasped her by both ears and gave the peculiar Ainu greeting cry; then they stroked one another down the face and shoulders. Kayan males in Borneo grasp each other by the forearm, while a host throws his arm over the shoulder of a guest and strokes him endearingly with the palm of his hand. When two Kurd males meet, they graps one another's right hand, raise them both, and alternately kiss the other's hand. Andamanese greet one another by one sitting down in the lap of the other, arms around each other's necks and weeping for a while; two brothers, father and son, mother and daughter, and husband and wife, or even two friends may do this; the husband sits in the lap of the wife. Friends "goodbye" consists in raising the hand of the other to the mouth and gently blowing on it, reciprocally. At Matavi a full-dress greeting after long absence requires scratching the head and temples with a shark's tooth, violently and with much bleeding. This brief list could be easily enlarged by other anthropologists.[32] Leubitz[33] identifies four functions of non-verbal communication :

1. Non-verbal communication relays messages. A person's attitude, personality, or manner of dress may communicate.
2. Non-verbal communication can augment verbal communication. When upset, an individual may say. "I feel terrible about the way things have turned out." At the same time the individual may be crying. The spoken words are reinforced by the non-verbal act of crying.
3. Non-verbal communication may contradict verbal communication. A wife finds her husband nervously pacing the floor and puffing on his cigarette when he returns home from the office. When asked if he had a bad day, he snaps back, "No everything is just fine."
4. Non-verbal communication can replace verbal communication. When verbal communication is not possible for some reason.

## Paralanguage

Non-verbal communication is not necessarily non-vocal often what is being said depends on the manner in which it is said. For example the single word 'yes' can carry a message of finance, resignation, acknowledgment, interest, agreement and enthusiasm (Barnlund 1968).

According to Swensen (1973) Paralanguage includes all production of sounds that is vocal but non-verbal. It includes voice quality, ways of verbal expression, and sounds that are not verbal, such as laughing and crying. It is what is communicated through sounds that are not contained in words themselves. Trager (1958) identified two categories of pra-language – vocalization and vocal qualities. Vocalizations are sounds and noises that are not words. Vocalizations are further divided into three types :

1. Vocal characterisers, which include sounds, such as laughing, crying, sighing and coughing.

2. Vocal qualifiers, which include characteristics of sounds, such as intensity (lud or soft) and pitch (high and low) ; and
3. Vocal segregates, which are sounds other than words, such as uhhuh, mmmm, shhh etc.

**Cyberspace : Information Highway**

Cyberspace is a language of technologically enhanced culture that has invaded the west especially after the advent of computers. The term 'Cyberspace' was first used by *William Gibson*. In his story "Burning Chrome" he described those who use devices known as *Cyberdecks* to transcend their normal sensuous organs, assimilating themselves to interface with the world, through their computers, a state that is more close to semi-transcendental level of mind. Cyberspace is, actually a place where several people from different continents met, not physically but through multimedia, to exchange their ideas or seeking solutions to their problems or providing the required data from their side of world to the needy from another side through various bulletin board services (BBs). To be precise it is a network of computer systems. Three such networks operating world over are – Compuserve, America Orline and Internet. Of these the last one is the biggest one, which is also known as *Information Highway*.

It is an example of science realising the dream of science fiction writers. Of scientists picking-up where the fiction-writers left. File transfer modems attached to computer were referred to as *cyberdeeks* in the yester-year fiction. In fact the science fiction writers visualised and provided a necessary vision into the future thus making it easier for scientists to pursue an ideal target through their logical experiments to create a new invention or improve on the earlier version.

The idea of *talking and listening computers* was reflected in the wonderful science-fiction film '2001'. Charles Babbage writers'. "In fact, such a type of computer has been a dream of computer scientists for a long time. It now seems fulfilments. Although listening and speaking computers have already been installed at various airports in the United States, they have some serious drawbacks. They have a highly limited vocabulary and can misunderstand words if they are mispronounced or are spoken with a different accent. For instance, if the human being has a cold or cough, the computer would not be able to respond to the person's instructions, which it does ordinarily. Or instead of an American, if an Indian addresses some instructions, the computers would not be able to understand him. Experts, however, think that all this is likely to change soon. Computers would be able to respond to any voice spoken with any accent, whether the person has a cold or no cold."[34] By now such shortcomings have been removed and talking directly to the computers has become easy and fun. Such a computers would particularly be of great help to handicapped persons, who are not able to make use of their hands and perform any task.

*Internet*—As we have mentioned 'Internet' is the biggest network operating all over the world. It is a loose connection of millions of computers at verious countries and the users of these computers, or nodes, as they are usually called, exchange information. There is no central administration of the internet system. That is why it is referred to as a loose connection of computers. Vishal Malhotra and Guriqbal Singh inform : "Originally christened as Arpanet in 1969, it was launched on an experimental basis as a network of the advanced research projects agency of the US, Department of Defence with the prime objective of facilitating direct communication among the research project grant scientists. From an humble beginning of a mere four computers, the Arpanet has come a long way. According to the latest figures available, the Internet is estimated to expanding by 1.08 million members a month. The members can share information, download the complete text of important government documents and treatise for example, the North American Free Trade Agreement or the Maastricht Treaty, consumer interest news, NASA space flight information, Japanese economic newswire copies and what not."[35]

## REFERENCES

1. M.N. Roy, *Reason, Romanticism and Revolution*, p. 498.
2. Arun Mitra, *The Quest Goes on & other Poems* (Sahitya Academy)
3. Anthony de Reuck and Julie Knight (Ed), *Conflict in Society*. Preface, p. VIII-IX.
4. Quoted from *Multicultural Education in a Pluralistic Society*. p.23 24.
5. Ibid, p. 24.
6. *Multicultural Education in a Pluralistic Society*, p. 25.
7. *Comprehensive Multicultural Education*, p.17.
8. Wittgenstein, L., *Culture and Values*, p. 64.
9. D.C. Ahir: *Buddhism in Modern India*, pp. 36-37.
10. William Sargant : *Battle for the Mind*, p.100.
11. *Human Values in the Changing World*, p. 309.
12. Ben Spiecker and Roger Straughan, *Freedom and Indoctrination in Education*, p. 94.
13. *Ibid.*, pp.6–7.
14. Dr. S. Radhakrishnan, *Religion and Society*, p. 43.
15. Will Durant, *Pleasures of Philosophy*, p. 66–5.
16. Har Dayal : *Hints for Self-culture*, p. 27–28.
17. *Ibid.*, p. 28.

18. Quoted from *Anthoropography*, Balbir Singh Negi, p. 2.
19. *Ibid*, p. 3.
20. *History of Civilization in England*, p. 15.
21. Kluckholm C, Mirrir for man : The Relation of Anthropology to Modern life, p. 19.
22. Dr. M.W. Mirza : *The life and Works of Amir Khusrau*, p. 20.
23. W.J. Wilkins, *Hindu Mythology*, Second Edition, preface.
24. From Key-note address delivered in WCCI – India Fourth Regional Conf. at Faridabad 10–12 December 1991.
25. Quoted in *Hints for Self-culture*, p. 292.
26. *Ibid*.
27. Quoted by, Christine I Bennet in his book *Comprehensive Multicultural Education*, p. 19.
28. *The Religions of Man*, p. 182.
29. Julius Fast : *Body Language*, p. 29.
30. *Comprehensive Multicultural Education*, p. 63.
31. Hall : *Beyond Culture*, p. 58.
32. W. Labarre, "Paralinguistics, Kinesics and cultural Anthropology" in "Intercultural Communication : A Reader" quoted by Christine I Bennett in *Comprehensive Multicultural Education*, p. 61.
33. Leubitz L. *Non-verbal Communication : A guide for teachers.*
34. "Charles Babbage and Computers" in *Inventions That Made History*, p. 75.
35. *Hindustan Times*, 7th December 1994.

# 2

# CULTURAL PLURALISM
## Global Pheomena

What is culture ? Multiethnic society, Hooton's Classification, Communal conflicrts *Vs* Racial conflict, Culture and human values-value tenets, values and Human rights, Cultural consciousness ; Monochronic and Polychronic cultures, culture and faith, Assimilative process in America – the process, Cultural diversity, Culture within Culture, Asian Americans, Indian Americans, the Navajo way; Multiculturism, cultural change and biological considerations; Science and Culture : A pragmatic View, Aryan' Love for Learning. Sumerians and their contribution, Malaysia and India : Cultural Bonds.

**What is Culture ?**

Anthropologists have defined culture in a variety of ways. Prior to the late 1950s, it was typically defined in terms of patterns of behaviour and customs. As early as 1871, for example, Tylor defined culture as "that complex whole which includes knowledge, belief, art, morals, law, custom and any other capabilities and habits acquired by man as a member of society".

This definition contrasts with more recent definitions of culture that focus on shared knowledge and belief systems, rather than on habits and behavior. Spradley and McCurdy define culture as "the acquired knowledge that people use to interpret experience generate social behaviour". They also assert that cultural knowledge "is like a recipe for producing behavior and artifacts." Good-enough explains further :

> A society's culture consists of whatever it is one has to know or believe in order to operate in a manner acceptable to its members, and do so in any role that they accept for any one of themselves. Culture, being what people have to learn as distinct from their biological heritage, must consist of the end product of learning :

knowledge, in most general, if relative, sense of the term. By this definition, we should note that culture is not a material phenomenon; it does not consists of things, people, behaviour, or emotions. It is rather an organization of these things. It is the forms of things that people have in mind, their models for perceiving, relating and otherwise interpreting them. As such, the things people say and do, their social arrangements and events, are products or by-products of their culture as they apply it to the task of perceiving and dealing with their circumstances.

According to LeVine, Culture is "a shared organization of ideas that includes the intellectual, moral and aesthetic standards prevalent in a community and the meanings of communicative actions". Triandis makes a distinction between subjective culture, the "world view or the way a cultural group perceives its environment, including stereotypes, role perceptions, norms, attitudes, values, ideals and perceived relationships between events and behaviors, and ——. material or concrete culture which includes the objects and artifacts of a culture".

Wissler[1] has classified the common features of human civilization under the following heads : Speech, Material Traits, Arts, Mythology, Knowledge, Religion, Family and Social Systems, Property, Government, War. These are common to all known forms of human civilization, so the question arises, is there anything which lies at the uniformity of pattern ? There are various types of speculations towards this question. Wissler[2] has suggested the hypothesis that there might be culture-building instinct in man, which compels him to build civilization after a definite pattern, wherever he might be born. That instinct is like the instinct of the bee which compels it to build its hive after a definite general pattern all over the world. In other words, the character is transmissible by heredity and not subject to environmental influences.

In fact, culture is an adaptive behaviour. In the process of adaptation to the environment man forms his life-styles, which uncludes food habits, shelter, passtimes, dresses etc. Thus culture can be learnt, cultural traits, except very few, can be transmitted. Preservation, maintenance and transmission-these are the natural phases of culture. Functional uniformity of nature is the basis of science as well as life. The natural aspects of human life are common and uniform. But the language, art, literature, religion and philosophy differ from country to country, from continent to continent, from race to race and so on.

## Multiethnic Society

In a country like India where variety of races, sects, religions, and languages and dilects have been flourishing it is but natural that various microcultures may exist still India has been striving for unity in diversity and to considerable extent she has been successful too in this venture through multidimensional efforts. We take pride in this cultural pluralism but for certain group of people this very feature is not so appreciable. In fact "cultural pluralism is considered dangerous to society by those who believe it heightens ethnic group identity and leads to separatism, intergroup antagonism, and fragmentation. This misconception overlooks a crucial ingredient of pluralism. All ethnic groups are expected to conform to those elements of the macroculture that are necessary for society."[3]

While promoting the noble cause of crosscultural communication India is at an advantageous position as there is no problem of racist supremacy as it is confronted by the United States and U.K. and other countries suffering from white supremacy. In order to bring about excellence in education they have introduced multicultural education because in a racist society due to white supremacy equity, a prime democratic value, lacks very much. The problem of racist superiority is an inherent element in the history of these nations. In India it is not so. Showing concern to this problem prevailing particularly in States Christine L. Benett observes : "Equity is not only a matter of bettering our country's educational system. It is required if we value this nation's democratic ideals : basic human rights, social justice, respect for alternative life-choices, and equal opportunity for all. Making reality fit these ideals, however, is not always easy. It is ideally un-American to be racist or sexist, for example, but because many teachers are fearful about teaching attitudes and values, they ignore the issues of prejudice and discrimination. Multicultural education, on the other hand, confronts the fact that this is a racist society with a history of white supremacy."[4]

According to Dr. B.S. Guha, no less than six racial elements have contributed to build up the population of India.

1. The Negrito, immigrant from Africa, is now all but extinct in India. A small group still survives in the Andamans, while traces of this race are found among the Kadars and Palayans of Cochin and Travancore, the Nagas of Assam, and a few other tribes in India.
2. The Proto-Australoids, who came from the west, form one of the basic elements of Indian population. By admixture with other

elements, specially with the Negritos who came before, and the Mongoloids who came after them, they gave rise to Kol or Munda type, the Mon-Khmer type in Assam, Burma, and Indo-China, and various other primitive types now found in the islands of the Indian Archipelago and those of Melanesia and Polynesia. The speeches of these peoples, scattered in wide areas extending from Kashmir to Easter Island, belong to the same Family of Languages known as Austric.

3. The Mongoloids are divided into two sub-groups. The Paleo-Mongoloids are represented by tribes living in Assam, Chittagong Hills, and the Indo-Burmese frontiers. The Tibeto-Mongoloids, a more pronounced and advanced Mongoloid type must have immigrated from Tibet in comparatively later times into Sikkim and Bhutan.
4. The Mediterranean peoples, with different sub-types, all came from the west and spoke the Dravidian language, now represented by Tamil, Telugu, Kannada, and Malayalam.
5. The Alpine, Dinaric, and Armenoid, forming sub-groups of one physical type, probably came from Central Asia. They form main elements in the population of Bengal, Orissa and Gujarat and are also found scattered in other parts of India, including South Indian Peninsula.
6. The Nordic Group who spoke the Aryan language, of which the earliest specimen is preserved in the Vedas.

Those who would equate a stand against racism with preaching values can be told that it is undemocratic, and antihuman to be racist. We can then proceed as follows :

- Recognize racist history and its impact on oppressors and victims.
- Examine our own attitudes, experiences, and behaviours concerning racism.
- Understand the origins of racism and why people hold racial prejudices and stereotypes.
- Understand the differences among individual, institutional, and cultural racism.
- Be able to identify racist images in the language and illustration of books, films, television, news media, and advertising.
- Be able to identify current examples of racism in our immediate community and society as a whole.
- Identify specific ways of combatting racism.
- Become antiracist in our own behaviour.

**Hooton's Classification**

| Primary Stocks and Races | Skin Colour | Hair Colour | Eye Colour | Hair Form | Head Form |
|---|---|---|---|---|---|
| White or Caucasoid | Light brown | Black | Never black | Wavy or straight | — |
| 1. Mediterranean | — | dark brown to black | dark brown to brown | — | cephalic Index less than 80 |
| A. Upper Palaeolithic or Atlanto-Mediterranean | generally dark | — | — | very wavy or curly | dolichocephalic |
| B. Iranian Plateau or Indo-Afghan | — | — | — | — | — |
| C. Classic Mediteranean | — | — | — | — | — |
| 2. Ainu | light brown or greyish | dark brown to black | dark to brown | — | cephalic Index less than 80 |
| 3. Keltic | Pale-white often freckled | dark brown | blue grey or pale mixed | wavy or curly | C.I. less than 80 |
| 4. Nordic | usually pink or ruddy | golden | blue or grey | wavy or straight | C.I. less than 80 |
| 5. Alpine | olive or brunet white | dark brown | dark brown | — | globular head or (over 80) |
| 6. East Baltic | creamy or ivory white | golden | grey, light-blue | straight | C.I. over 63 |
| 7. Armenoid | olive | dark brown to black | dark brown to brown | wavy or curly | C.I. over 80 |

**of World Races** —(*Contd.*)

| Nose Form | Face Form | Stature | Distribution | Remarks |
|---|---|---|---|---|
| usually higher | — | — | — | Buttocks usually prominent amongst females & Breastis hemispherical amongst women. |
| — | — | — | — | — |
| usually straight | often very long | usually tall | Sporadic in refuge areas of Europe and the Middle East, common in Ireland, Scotland, Wales. | — |
| High, broad or medium | — | usually medium | Mostly in Iran and Iraq. | — |
| — | Face narrow and oval | usually under 166 cm. | Arabia, Near East, whole Mediterranean basin, sporadically in Eastern, central & northwestern Europe. | — |
| root depressed and concalle profile | short to medium | short or average 158 cm. | North Japan, Sakhaline and Yezo | Mongolold admixture may be detected in females |
| very long | long narrow | Tall | Ireland, Scottish highlands, Wales, western Europe | long arms and legs, short trunk. |
| High and narrow | — | Tall | Scandinavia, Sweden, Baltic and Britain | — |
| Nasal Index 63 | broad and short | medium to short | Central Zone of Europe and France, Urals, Norway, Near East, North-west Africa. | |
| N.I. over 65 | — | — | Finland, Russia, Poland and Baltic countries | wavy head hair, sparse body hair. |
| under 63 | Narrow and elongated | medium | Turkey, Syria, Palestine, Iraq and Balkan Countries | — |

**Hooton's Classification**

| Primary Stocks and Races | Skin Colour | Hair Colour | Eye Colour | Hair Form | Head Form |
|---|---|---|---|---|---|
| 8. Dinaric | variable | medium to dark brown | brown to light | usually wavy | C.I. 80 and over |
| 9. Nordic Alpine | — | dark | dark | red hair | C.I. over 80 |
| 10. Nordic Mediterranean | — | dark | light | — | C.I. under 80 |
| 11. Australian | chocolate | dark brown | dark brown | curly | usually 80 |
| (a) Murrian | light red brown | — | dark brown | wavy | over 80 |
| (b) Carpentarian | dark | — | dark brown | — | — |
| (c) Tasmanoid | darker | dark brown | — | smaller | — |
| 12. Indo-Dravi-dian | dark brown | black | dark brown | Frizzly | C.I. under 80 |
| (a) Classi Indo-dravidian | — | — | — | Straight | C.I. 74.3 |
| (b) Armenoid (Iranian) | Pale-white | — | — | Straight | overage 81.8 |
| (c) Indo-Nordic | rosy white | dark brown | grey or blue | Straight | C.I. 73.1 |
| (d) Australoid | chocolate brown | — | — | wavy to curly | dolichoce-phalic |
| (c) Negritoid | black | dark brown | — | Frizzly | long |
| 13. Polinesian | yellow brown | dark | — | wavy | C.I. 80 |
| Negroid | black | dark brown | dark brown | Frizzly | dolichoce phalic |

**of World Races —**(*Contd.*)

| Nose Form | Face Form | Stature | Distribution | Remarks |
|---|---|---|---|---|
| N.I. under 63 | much longer | very Tall (over 170 cm. | British Isles, Yugo-slavia, Central European Countries | Lips thinner than the Armenoids. |
| N.I. 63 | — | — | U.S.A. and Irish states | — |
| — | — | under 170 cm. | Ireland and U.S.A. | — |
| under 85 | Facial Index under 90 | average 160 cm. | — | — |
| longer | — | — | South Australia and Queensland. Forest of Tasmania | — |
| — | — | Tall | N. Australia, and Gulf of Carpentaria | — |
| — | — | Short | Queensland and Tropical Forest of Tasmania | Small Ears. |
| — | leptoprosopic | variable | India and Ceylon. | — |
| N.I. 73 | — | Short | Punjab. | — |
| long (69.8) | — | medium | western Littoral and Bengal | — |
| N.I. 67.1 | — | medium | N.W. Himalayas, Pakistan and Afghanistan. | — |
| chomalr rhine | — | short | Central and Southern India | Represented by Bhils and Chenchus. |
| — | — | short | Southern India (Kadar and Pulayans). | Thickcorted lips |
| — | — | over 167 | Newzealand, Hawaii, Thailand, Indochina and Philippines Islands. | — |
| Nasal Index 85 | | Short | — | Breast form Conical and buttocks usually less projecting among female |

## Hooton's Classification-

| Primary Stocks and Races | Skin Colour | Hair Colour | Eye Colour | Hair Form | Head Form |
|---|---|---|---|---|---|
| 14. African Negro | — | — | — | — | — |
| 15. Nilolic Negro | black or bluish black | — | — | — | cephalic Index under 76 |
| 16. Negrito | yellowish or brown | black | — | woolly | — |
| (a) Infantile | dark brown | — | — | — | over 80 |
| (b) Adulti form | greyish yellow | — | light brown | — | mesocephalic |
| 17. Tasmanian | Black or dark brown | black | — | Frizzliy | cephalic Index under 76 |
| 18. Melanesian | dark brown or black | black or 'foxy' | dark brown to black | Frizzly | — |
| a) Papuan | nearly black | dark brown | — | Frizzly | — |
| b) Melanesian | — | — | — | Frizzly | mesocephalic |
| 19. Bushmen-Hottentot | yellow to yellow brown | Black | Dark brown to black | Tiny or peppercorn | dolichoce-phalic or under 78 |
| (a) Bushmen | yellow to brown | — | — | — | C.I. over 75 |
| (b) Hottentot | yellowish to brown | — | — | — | cephalic under 75 |

**of World Races —(*Contd.*)**

| Nose Form | Face Form | Stature | Distribution | Remarks |
|---|---|---|---|---|
| — | — | variable 165 to 170 cm. | Sudanese, Buntu in west and central Africa and South Africa except Shari | — |
| Platyrrhine | — | over 170 cm. | Upper waters of white Nile | |
| — | — | less than 150 cm. | — | — |
| narrow at root | Short to broad | somewhat Tall | Congo Forests, Andaman Islands, Malay Peninsula, Philippines and New Guinea. | — |
| — | long and narrow | — | Congo Forest area, New Guinea, and Malaya Peninsula. | Broad sholdered, broad and high pelvis, short legs & long arms. |
| — | Euryprosopic | — | Tasmania and Australia | well developed muscular & prominent buttocks and abdomen slender limps. |
| Hyperchamaerrhine | — | Low less than 165 cm. | — | Elongation of forearms & long legs. |
| chamaerrhine | — | — | New Guinea and Islands of Melanesia. | — |
| — | — | — | Melanesian Islands, New Guinea and other Coastal regions | — |
| Nasal Index 85 | — | under 160 cm. | — | Buttocks-marked steatopygia in females. |
| — | — | average 144 cm. | Kalahari Desert, South Africa | — |
| — | Elongated | receding 150 cm. | South west Africa and formerly in Cape Colony | Steaopygia more pronounced in female. |

**Hooton's Classification-**

| Primary Stocks and Races | Skin Colour | Hair Colour | Eye Colour | Hair Form | Head Form |
|---|---|---|---|---|---|
| 20. Classi Mongoloid | yellow to brown | black | dark brown | Straight | — |
| 21. Arctic Mongoloid | — | — | — | — | C.I. less than 80 |
| 22. Indonesian | dark to yellow brown | black | dark brown | Straight | — |
| (a) Malay-Mongoloid | light yellow brown | — | — | Straight | cephalic Index over 80 |
| (b) Indonesian | light red brown | — | — | wavy | C.I. under 80 |
| 23. American Indian | yellow to brown or red brown | black srarely dark | dark brown to blue | Straight coarse and wavy | — |
| (a) Brachy cephalic | — | — | — | — | Cephalic Index 80 or over |
| (b) Dolicho-cephalic | — | — | — | — | Cephalic Index under 80 |

**of World Races** —(*Contd.*)

| Nose Form | Face Form | Stature | Distribution | Remarks |
|---|---|---|---|---|
| — | — | — | — | Epicanthic fold. |
| Nasal Index 70 | very broad | under 160 cm. | North East Asia, Arctic regions of North America | Epicanthic fold not found in adult males. |
| Nasal Index 80 | — | under 165 cm. | — | — |
| — | Narrow | — | Indochina, Burma, Indonesia, Philippines, Thailand, Malaya Archipelago. | — |
|  |  |  |  | — |
| — | — | — | Indonesia, Burma, Thailand, Malay peninsula. |  |
| Nasal Index over 80 | — | — | — | External eye-fold common. |
| — | — | — | Sporadic in the N. American area, central and Southern America. | — |
| — | — | — | Canada, U.S.A. and New world. | — |

## Communal Conflict vs Racial Conflict

The terms 'community' and 'Race' are distinctively of different semantic shades; but at times for some specific reasons they are used for identical purport. As far as the background or the cause of 'communal conflict' and 'racial conflict' is concerned, it is predominantly political one. In other words we can say that both of these are the result of a political process, may it be a developing country like India or a developed country like United States of America. Ratna Naidu confirming their identical background says that "politicization has taken place not on single polarized issues, such as conflict or interests between classes, but multiple community centered issues (health, housing, education, transportation, location of industry, land-use and so on). The consequence of this is the advance countries has been the creation of "communal" societies, "where more and more groups act as Veto powers and check each other's purposes". She further adds that "in societies where minorities refuse to assimilate either at will or under pressure and are not placed in an autonomously governable region, communal conflict is endemic. Communalism is a term peculiar to former British colonies and therefore, the nature of the communal conflict between Tamils and Sinhalese, the Hindus and the Muslims or the Malay and the Chinese is of the same psycho-social genre and similar is its paralyzing impact upon the body politic."[5]

India, being multi-cultural, multilingual and multiracial country it communal problems are very complex. "Neither a mere acceptance of theory of plurality nor its ramifications alone can explain the nature, structure and inevitable consequences of existing empirical inter-community relations in various regions, zones, lanes and by-lanes. At some place it is the economic factors that pre-dominate the pattern of relations, at others it is historicity that governs human inter-actions. Still at others socio-cultural parameters determine the importance to be attached to religion or community. Thus no linear theories can either express nor explain the empirical nexus that operates in India approaching 20th century".6

## Culture and Human Values

One may ask what is the relationship between Culture and Values ? There are multiple origins of values but the values of the Eastern World owe a great deal to culture specially philosophy and religion. Philosophical and religious tenets are significant originators of our values. Culture is one of the significant sources of values. Since culture differs from nation to nation, cultural tenets also differ. Consequently values and morals also differ from nation to nation, age to age and place to place. Analysis of various human values can be done on the basis of cultural tenets of a particular culture as the culture and conventions. These two are the main sources of values. When various values inter-act with the actual human behaviour and individual traits our traditional values are affected in positive or negative way. The process of inter-action leads to commission or commission of certain human values, which in turn affects entire gamut of cultural phenomena. This process goes on repeating itself. This can be explained through the following diagram :

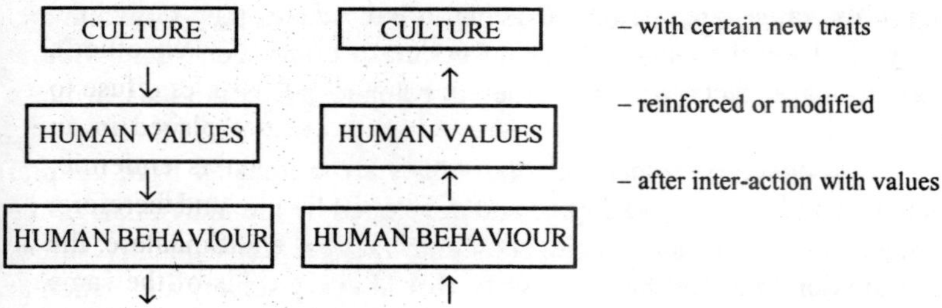


**Value-tenets**

American value-tenets are admixture of religious and secular tenets and based on materialism. Indian value tenets are based on spiritualism. Therefore, American and Indian values also differ to great extent. This hypothesis will be clear if we compare the value tenets of these two countries, which are as under :

| Indian Value-Tenets | American Value-Tenets |
|---|---|
| 1. Spiritualism is superior to materialism. | |
| 2. Human body does not consist of physical body only. | Material progress is important. |
| 3. The principle of universal soul. | |
| 4. The principle of transmigration of soul. | |
| 5. Moksha is ultimate aim. | Individual is of Supreme importance. |

| | | |
|---|---|---|
| 6. | Law of Karma | |
| 7. | Importance of knowledge | Life has purpose. |
| 8. | Contact is vital factor for formation of character. | |
| 9. | Will of God is supreme. | Certain basic social institutions are important. |
| 10. | The principle of other-worldliness. | Selected other miscell-aneous beliefs and attitudes are important. |

There is a very close link between values and culture. Values originate from cultural tenets and help to shape and maintain the cultural structure of the society. On the other hand culture conditions the various values developed by the individuals. "In respect to individuals and cultures, values are circular. Existing in individuals, they flow into and help to shape the culture. Existing in cultures, they condition, without categorically dictating, the values developed by individuals in these culture."[7]

It is observed sometimes that values are originated from cultural tenets, but they are not adopted and developed by the individuals of the society for good many socio–economic factors. Consequently values remain dormant. But history reveals that in every society and nation at large there had been certain great personalities to counter several evils of the society and strengthen the various cultural values for the wider interest of the mankind.

According to a section of educationist search for new human values, which would be more consonant with the global consciousness of our times and responsive to the change brought about by science and technology and to the urgency of wide-scale problems being faced by man-kind, are suggested.

## Values and Human Rights

Dr. Prem Kirpal, Former Secretary of Education, Government of India has rightly pointed out that "the charter of the United Nations, the constitution of UNESCO and the Declaration of Human Rights Embodies Statements, principles and norms for the observance by the member-states are very conducive to the evolution of proper human values that can be practiced and shared by all in the making of a new humanism for the emerging global community". In this context he has mentioned the following value concepts :

1. Man and his own self : The human person, The Inner Man.
2. Man and his fellowmen : Society : Human Relations.
3. Man and his habital : Natural : Space
4. Man and his work.
5. Man and his Art.
6. Man and Technology.
7. Man and his Technology.
8. Man and Time : The stream of past, present and future.
9. Man and his cosmos (Man and his universe; the meaning and purpose of existence).

Besides these traditional and modern value concepts mostly applicable to the individual there are a few values to be observed by societies and nations for the harmonious growth of human being and global peace. Some of such value–concepts have been enumerated in the declaration of congress for Human Unity held at Philadelphia in May, 1976. They are as following :

A. Compassionate Love.
B. Intrinsic Worth of each human being.
C. Right for all people to develop their creativity.
D. The inter-dependence of all nations.
E. Solidarity.
F. Freedom and justice for all people.
G. Complete disarmament.
H. Decentralization of power.
I. Freedom of expression of thought.
J. The right to work for just rewards.
K. Preservation of natural and cultural environments.
L. The adjustment of economic structures for greater equality and justice for people.
M. Abolition of all forms of slavery torture and capital punishment.

**Monochronic and Polychronic Cultures**

The concept of monochronic and polychronic cultures is based on the use of time the culture exercises. In European society they are known as White time and Black time respectively. The concept represents a life-style prevailing in a culture particularly in term of usage of time. White time is monochronic time where things are accomplished one-at-a-time in a linear fashion familiar with low-context Anglo-Western Europeans. Events occur strictly according to time-schedule. Black time, Polychronic time, is the opposite, where time management is not so systematic. The notion of black time may be expanded to include people from polychronic cultures, for example, southern European. In high-context cultures, time is polychronic.

In polychronic cultures many activities take place simultaneously– and schedules are invisible. Logically speaking there cannot be a time of demarcation to separate polychronic and monochronic cultures. An individual cannot be exclusively polychronic or monochronic at all the places, and at all the times. There are many examples of a few scholars, who had been monochronic at times, otherwise, usually polychronic. In Jain literature we find the terms like 'Shatavdhani', 'Dashavdhani' etc. which mean attending to hundred person, ten persons respectively. Thus, no rigidity can be predicted in respect of these two terms. Hall holds that "polychronic cultures are by their very nature oriented to people. Any human being who is naturally drawn to other human beings and who live in a world dominated by human relationships will be either pushed or pulled toward the polychronic end of the time spectrum. If you value people, you must hear them out and cannot cut them off simply because of a schedule".[8]

## Culture and Faith

As compared to the faith, culture is a very broad-based concept. A faith is a part of culture. Besides faith, in any culture there are host of other credentials of social and religious life which include art, literature, philosophy, various social institutions and so on. Religion is an important aspect of culture, but they are not identical. Religion's development incorporates two components-faith and culture, faith is religious, but culture is not so. It may be secular and in many cases it stands a secular as we may visualize various secular elements in the Indian Macroculture. The fight against communalism may be effective and successful if the cultural tradition is appropriated and harnessed with secular forces available in surroundings. Today culture stands at the centre of communal mobilization. Therefore, all the forces must be mobilized to wage the struggle in the domain of culture removing all confusions. Here the caution given by Dr. Radhakrishnan is noteworthy. He observes that –

> "It is one of the tragic confusions of religious history that as a faith becomes credal, the creed by which man communes with the Divine supplants the Divine. The prophet who announces the message becomes himself an object of worship supplanting the higher truth in which he believes. We become ambitious for our formulas, for our prophets, for our organizations."[9]

When religion is secularized it comes very close to Humanism. Therefore, human values is the central faith of humanist. Any religion sans higher human values like love, peace, non-violence, truth, justice etc. cannot be appealing nor it can survive. Kant's attitude to moral law is deeply religious. He desired that religion must be based not on the logic of theoretical reasons but on the practical reason of the moral sense, it follows that any Bible or revelation must be judged by its value for morality and cannot itself be the judge of moral code. According to Immanuel Kant, Churches and Dogmas have value only in so far as they assist the moral development of race. When mere creeds or ceremonies usurp priority over moral excellence as a test of religion, religion disappears. In his own words –

> "Christ has brought the Kingdom of God nearer to earth; but he has been misunderstood and in place of God's Kingdom, the Kingdom of the priest has been established among us."[10]

If religion is for man, his betterment and happiness, it has to be humanistic and cherish certain human values. It has been rightly said that "Religion is nothing more than the consciousness of the highest social values." When this consciousness will be there, a man will be patient and tolerant enough to understand others' view, respect other faith than his own. Good character is the very essence of religion. In Qran Sharif it is said, "If you wish to be lived by God, be faithful when trusted and honest in your speech; and be a good neighbour to others." For a variety of reasons at times we become very intolerant and do not want to show any concern to the faith or religion of others. It leads to a gap in cross-cultural communication.

Once a qazi asked Guru Nanak: "How darė you disparage my faith?" Nanak answered in his forthright style : "It is far too easy to call oneself a Muslim; but far too hard to become one." On query Nanak highlighted his understanding of a Muslim through the following words :

"If compassion be the mosque, and faith the prayer mat
and honest living one's Quran,
and Humility one's circumcision,
and continence one's fasting,
then, verily one may be called Musalman.
If virtuous deeds make-up one's pilgrimage to the Kaaba,
And truth be the guide of one's spirit,
And one's prayer be for the Lord's Grace,
And the rosary be of His Will, the God will."

The Qazi then asked him to say his prayers in the mosque with him and see for himself the difference. Nanak replied : "There are five times in the day that you offer your prayer, so do I. My first prayer is of truth, the second of honest living, the third of the Grace of God, the fourth of clean mind, and the fifth of the remembrance of God." But, Nanak added, he would not disappoint the qazi and would accompany him to Mosque for saying the prayers.

Such type of secular attitude can definitely make any religion a humanistic one thus render better service towards human beings.

**Assimilative Process in America : The Process**

America, alike India, has cultural pluralism, where Irish Americans, Jewish Americans, Native Americans, Black Americans, Maxican Americans, Japanese Americans, Indian Americans (Amerindians), Hispanics, Asians, Pacific Islanders etc. are living. The sources and causes for cultural diversity in America are in multitude. But one of the prominent reasons was nations's inclination to the theory of cultural assimilation or melting-pot theory, which stands as in contrast to the theme of cultural pluralism, for which America, having gained experience through hoary past of herself and from the history of other countries, is now leading to cultural pluralism.

In fact, cultural pluralism is an ideal state of social conditions characterized by equity and mutual respect among existing cultural groups. It contrasts with the popular theory of melting-pot in which ethnic minorities were expected to abandon their traditions and get assimilated in the host society or macroculture. "In a pluralistic society members of the ethnic minority groups are permitted to retain many of their cultural ways, as long as they confirm to those practices deemed necessary for harmonious co-existence within the society as a whole". In other words it is a process of compromise characterised by mutual appreciation and respect by two or more ethnic groups; whereas the theme of melting-pot sounds forced assimilation. But according to some scholars the theme of melting pot still holds good, particularly in the field of education and the same should not be taken as endoctrination in the strict sense of the term.

Education historian cubberly vividly expresses the process: "Everywhere these people (immigrants) tend to settle in groups or settlements and to set-up their own national manners, customs, and observances. One task is to break their groups and settlements, to assimilate or amalgamate these people as a part of the American race, and to implant in their children, so far as can be done, the Anglo-Saxon conception of righteousness, law, order and popular government and to awaken in them reverence for our democratic institutions and for those things which we as people hold to be of abiding worth".[11] No doubt, in America as well as in India where the society is characterized by ethnic pluralism, this notion is accepted by teachers. But in the institutions run by minority group the fear of indoctrination of to their ethnic identity cannot be ruled out.

According to Stills1[12], "The true test of assimilation is when members of an ethnic group experience the following conditions :

Change of cultural patterns to those of the host society.
Large-scale entrance into cliques, clubs, and institutions of the host society on the primary group level
Large-scale intermarriage
Development of a sense of peoplehood based exclusively on the host society.
Absence of prejudice
Absence of discrimination
Absence of value and power conflict.

## Cultural Diversity

Policies of genocide, resettlement on reservation, subordination through force or bonded labour (or slavery prior to its abolition in 1865) – these were a few prominent factors leading to cultural diversity in America and falsifying the myth of melting pot. According to Binnett, "The most blantant evidence against the melting pot myth is the oppression of Black Americans is under slavery, and later under Jim Crow laws, which legalised the separation of blacks and Whites. With the 1896 U.S. Supreme Court decision in Plessy V. Ferguson, separate but equal facilities for blacks became the law of the land. For the next sixty years an extreme dual system pervaded all aspects of life in American South. Jim Crow Laws were passed to keep "Coloreds" separate from Whites in schools, public transportation, restaurants, theatre, baseball fields, public bathrooms, swimming pools, doctors offices and so on. Many court-rooms had separate bibles for giving oaths. Intermarriage was illegal in 38 states until the mid twentieth century, and Blacks were denied their right to vote through grandfather clauses, poll taxes, and outragious literacy tests until voting rights legislation was passed between 1964 and 1970".[13]

For certain white ethnic groups it was, of course, possible to melt their microcultures into the host Anglo-sexon culture, but it was rather difficult for the black ones including East Asian Americans, Native Americans, darker skined Mexican Americans etc. Moreover, these people were not given a favourable atmosphere; on the contrary, they were prevented from doing so. All this was done under the presumption that "isolated groups would retain certain aspects of their original culture and create a new culture, that is distinct from the Anglo-Western European core". Through one of the studies undertaken by Feagin it is concluded that "none of the ethnic groups he studied, with possible exception of Irish Americans, could be considered totally assimilated into the Anglo-saxon core culture". The whites also, other than natives, not welcome for melting purpose for the fear of mongrelisation of the "American Race", which was founded and developed by the Nordic race. The term "mongrelise" is derived from the word "mongrels", inhabitants of central America and southeast Europe, which are looked upon as inferior races as far as mental outlook and intellectual levels are concerned.

**Culture within Culture**

As presumed, rightly and foresightedly, by the Americans that various ethnic groups living in America, if segregated will retain their own cultural facets and, in due course, will come out with a new culture distinctly different from Ango-saxon; became a reality with gradual and steady evolution of their microcultures over the time. Among the blacks also we find lot of cultural diversity, which is but natural looking into their respective microcultures. While immigrating to America from their motherland in various capacities they certainly carried their customs, traditions, arts, value–system etc. A man cannot be totally changed as the lemon cannot be converted into an orange, whatever bio-chemical process we may adopt. Through various processes, of course, we can bring about tremendous changes in its size, shape, colour, taste etc. If so happened with the black immigrants in American world. Thus, through the processes of innovation, fabrication, synthesis and adoption etc. they have been able to form a new culture of their own, something in between their parent culture and the culture of the host society. S.W. Mintz writes,

> "The millions of enslaved Africans could only bring with them certain parts of their ancestral cultures-whatever they could carry in their minds. One includes here speech characteristics (Pitch, intonation, timbre), folklore heroes and motifs, religious beliefs or values, artistic skills and preference and the like. But the slaves had only harshly limited opportunities to maintain anything like the full content of their original cultures."[14]

These facts are applicable not only to Negroes but also to others having similar complexion, whether they immigrated into American as slaves, indentured labour or otherwise. They form very large percentage of the present American population. Today, African American comprise over 11 per cent of the population in the United States. It is estimated that between 10 and 14 of the Black population in the United States was free prior to the Civil War. Though socially the gap between the blacks and the whites has been bridged, by the enforcing various laws and social movements led by various negro leader including Nelson Mandela and prior to him King Martin Luther etc. but economically they still lag far behind. Referring to the massive migration of southern Black people to northern cities in the twentieth century, so well points out that "much of the later cultural contrast between the established Negro elite and underprepared black migrants to the cities had its origin in this difference between their respective ancestors. Many of the outstanding Negroes of the post-Civil War period and early twentieth century were descendants of the 'free persons of colour'. Whites who pointed to those individual successes and asked, 'Why can't the others do it?' Were usually unaware that the older blacks were at an entirely different point in their social evolution."[15]

**Asian Americans**

According to the census 1980 there are about 3.5 millions Asian Americans forming 1.5 per cent of American population. The Asian group includes Japanese, Chinese, Vietnamese, Cambodians, Amerindians (from India), Indo-Chinese, Koreans Fillipinos etc.

The Japanese entered America in the late 1800s as sugar-cane field workers; whereas the Japanese entered not as immigrants to work on the transcontinental rail-road in the mid 1800s. Japanese American are known as 'issei' and are settled in Hawaii and California. They were mostly engaged in Agriculture. Due to excessively owning of Land by Japanese in California US Government had to take immediate action in order to circumvent these acts of Japanese. In 1941, ultimately certain mandatory provisions were enforced to get evacuated the land. Under these provisions, (Executive order 9066) thousands of Japanese were affected. But, by the virtue of their hard work and sustained efforts they have aimed considerable social status in American society. Consequently acculturation of the Japanese is no more difficult. In this connection Binette, has rightly observed:

> "Japanese Americans are often regarded as a classic example of the American success story. Stereo-type earlier as the "yellow peril", now they are often stereotyped as the model minority. Japanese Americans have the highest literacy rate of any ethnic group in our (American) society, tend to be financially well off, and have been assimilated into the predominant language and religion. The similarity between traditional Japanese values and attitudes and the macroculture may be superficial mask hiding some deep cultural differences."[16]

Thus, we observe that the success of Japanese American is rooted in their value-system and family styles, and work-culture, in particular. Shinolosim, official religion of Japan, is greatly influenced by Chinese Taoism. In his book styled as 'why has Japan Succeeded', Michio Morishima, has carried out investigation into the subject and developed for the sake of comparison between China and Japan. He notices that:

> "whereas Chinese interpretation of Confucious doctrines as individualistic and humanistic and militaristic. The contrast arguably has existed ever since Confucianism first came to Japan in about the sixth century. This is not surprising because the Japanese have suffered at all times from a sense of inferiority vis-a-vis the powerful Chinese empire, leading them to be, throughout their history, closely banded together and aggressive."

After two centuries of isolation which lasted until 1859, Japan came under pressure from the West. In this crisis the intelligentia, who had been educated in the Japanese Confucian manner, succeeded in unifying the country and finally established a new, powerful modern government.

There are no ethnic divisions nor regional division due to rapid urbanization and the impact of powerful multi-media.

**Indian Americans**

The number of ethnic Indians in Substantial numbers is only in Guyana (5 per cent) and Surinam (37 per cent) and Trinidad and Tobago (40.4 per cent) among the various Carribbean countries. In other states the population of ethnic Indians is too low to have any impact on the social or political life of these countries. Geographically speaking West Indies and Carribbean Islands are often used interchangeable because of number of common features. According to Vidya Sagar, "In spite of the wide divergencies in size, ancestry, language, history, population density, and political organisation, the countries of the Carribbian share a common culture the result of their somewhat parallel experience as plantation colonies populated by African and Asian labourers dominated by distant European economic and political powers. Cut-off from their homelands and in most cases unable to attain the schooling that would have given them entry into the European ruling class, the Carribbian made a virtue of necessity by combining the desperate elements of their past and their new environment to produce a true new cultural manifestation that is best known as Creole culture, i.e., locally raised."[17]

In linguistic context 'Creole' means a language formed from the contact of a European language especially English, French or Portuguese with another language, an African or Indian or any other language of Afro-Asian core. Many Creoles aroused in Surinam, French Creole in at least three distinct dialects namely Duch, Hindi-Urdu and Chinese. The East Indians, as the persons of Indian origin are known, came predominantly as indentured labour from India to replace the Africans in plantation work. The indigenous peoples of Guyana are collectively known as Amerindians.

On Scriptural and linguistic basis it is proved that Indians sailed to Latin American where they established merchant's colonies and empires like the Inca and the Aztec. These Indians sailed to Latin America in the year 1835. In the year 1985 these settlers. Later on known as Amerindians, celebrated 150th Anniversary of their settlements, which was graced by a few scholars and also diplomats from India. The question of the identity of the Amerindians had been a matter of discussion some time past.[18] These East-Indian living in America are called. Amerindian, who went there as labour immigrants from various provinces indentured Labour was recruited in India and through various methods they were enticed to leave their Motherland. Facing lot of difficulties during Voyage they landed in British Guiana. In 1917, by a decision of Government of India, further emigration under the Indenture system was disallowed, as it was considered to be derogatory to India's self-respect as a nation and undesirable in the estimate of enlightened Indian public opinion. With the consent of West India Committee Chinese were also introduced in British Guiana on the same terms and conditions.

> "On the 17th May, 1879, 515 Chinese immigrants landed on colony and were favourably reported upon. This experiment of immigration, without contracts, excited much interest in the colony, but the results were not considered satisfactory to the planters, with the fatal consequence that the experiment was not further pursued and Chinese immigration came to a sudden and unceremonious end."

The idea of tapping India as a possible source of labour for overseas countries, was an experiment, undoubtedly, as regards British Guiana, but an idea not foreign to the India the emigration of labourers from India to other countries."[19]

It is true that initially in the nineteen century from various provinces of India people immigrated to other countries as labourers; but gradually they attain dominance, settled colonies and ultimately ruled the land. British Guiana and Mauritius are the glaring examples of this Historical facts. This was against the hope and expectations of the then administrators, as Peter Ruhomon has observed : "It is interesting here, to note, that Lord Glenelg saw no reason to believe that any natives of India would even look to the British transatlantic colonies as a permanent home or that they would be reconciled to the abandonment of their native country, except by the hope of returning, with whatever they may be able to save by their labour in distant land. Subsequent events, however, have proved these-fears to be groundless; The majority of Indians who have come to British Guiana have comfortably settled down and made the colony their homes."[20]

These people not only survived, but survived with grace rendering good services to their then masters, as it is recorded in the Lord Sanderson Committee Report. It reads : "There can be no doubt that in the manner, Indian indentured immigration has rendered valuable services to those of our colonies in which, on the emancipation of Negro Slaves, the sugar industry was threatened with ruin, or in which the supply of steady labour had been required for the development of the colony by methods of work to which the native population was averse."

They had also been able to preserve their ethnic entity by maintaining age-old customs and traditions, cultural tenets and metaphysical postulates and their own religion as a whole. That is why the local missionary's various attempts of conversion could not be materialised. Unlike Chinese, they proved to a very hard nut to crack. This is why one of the Christian missionaries found that after six years of preaching and teaching, he was rewarded with but only 16 converts which, no doubt, exercised a discouraging impression. The use of this failure Mr. Bronkhurst endeavoured to explain in the following words :

"Whatever might be the question of the wise men do our day, in regard to the conversion of the immigrants, experience has taught me that it is almost impossible to make any impression for good on the mind of the adult coolies; they look upon the Christian Missionaries with suspicion and merely as paid agents of the Government morally and spiritually, they are as hard as stone and cold as ice. "Your religion", they say, "Will do for you and your children born in the Colony provided they do not come with us to India. We have a religion as well as you and cannot forsake it for a new one".[21]

The Hindus and Muslims, on coming to the colony, brought their religions customs and beliefs with them, in the pursuit of which they were very devoted and from the practice of which they were not easily divorced. Thus, Guiana is in the process of evolving a distinct culture based in folk-traditions and the contribution of ethnic communities. Amerindian culture is important to music and dance, the landscape has long been central to painting and sculpture, and the literacy arts reflect Guiana's history and its path to independence. Cultural institutions are concentrated in Georgetown, the capital of Guiana.

These settlers, alike their counterparts forming ethnic minority in America, needs lot of boosting and encouragement through new tools and techniques, particularly in the field of education. To cater to the needs of these ethnic minority America has introduced the system of multicultural school. According to Benett, "Multicultural education is an approach to teaching and learning that is based upon democratic values and beliefs, and seek to foster cultural pluralism within culturally diversed societies and an interdependent world"[22] During Reagan's regime very challenging reports like "A nation at risk" attracted the attention of the government to focus on the national commitment to true excellence in education. In one of the surveys the following statistics on the nations drop-out rate is given :

| | |
|---|---|
| Americans Indians/Alaska Natives | 42% |
| Hispanic | 39.9% |
| Blacks | 24.7% |
| Whites | 14.3% |
| Asian/Pacific Islanders | 9.6% |

These figures confirm the fact that we have attained neither excellence nor equity in education due largely to our failure to educate the nation's ethnic minorities and the poor".[23]

The rise and fall, sorrow and agony, aspirations and ambitions, inward feeling and ethos of these Asian immigrants have nicely been depicted in the following lines of Martin Carter :

I come from bigger yard of yesterday.
Leaping from the oppressor's hate
and the scorn of myself.
I come to the world with scars upon my sole
wounds on my body, fury in my hands.
I turn to the histories of men and lives of the people.
I examine the shower of sparks the wealth of the dreams.
I am pleased with the glories and sad with the sorrows.
rich with the riches, poor with the loss.
From the nigger yard of yesterday I come with my burden.
To the world of tomorrow I turn with my strength.[24]

**The Navajo[25] Way**

To a Navajo, **time** is ever flowing; can't be broken; Exactness of time is of little importance.

To a non-Indian, time is of the utmost importance and must be used to its fullest extent.

To a Navajo, the **future** is uncertain. Nature, which is more important than man, may change anything. This life is what counts–there is no sense that life on earth is a preparation for another life.

Non-Indians prepare for the future. Such items as insurance, savings, and plans for trips and vacations show to what extent non-Indians hold this value.

**Patience** : Navajo. To have patience and to wait is considered a good quality.

**Non-Indian.** The man who is admired is the one who is quick to act.

**Age : Navajo.** Respect is for the elders. Experience is felt to bring knowledge. **Age** has priority though increasing power is going to those who speak English well. Knowledge is power.

**Non-Indian**. The great desire is to look younger and live longer. Much money is spent to pursue these efforts.

**Family : Navajo**. The Indian cultures consider many more individuals to be relatives than do non-Indians. Clan relationships are strong. The Navajo is wary of nonrelatives and foreigners.

**Non-Indian**. Biological **family** is of utmost importance, and relationships are limited within this group.

**Wealth : Navajo**. **Wealth** is to be consumed and used as security-always to be shared. Many Indians are suspicious of individuals who collect material possessions. Some tribes give love gifts and enjoy this practice.

**Non-Indian**. Non-Indian **cultures** have measured wealth in terms of material things. Many such possessions often constitute status symbols and are considered highly desirable.

**Nature** : Navajo. Humanity lives in perfect balance with nature. The earth is here to enjoy. Heed signals from nature-learn from animals. People are an integral part of this universe and must do their part to maintain harmony and balance among the parts of the cosmos.

**Non-Indian**. **Culture** here is a constant search for new ways for control and mastery of the elements around. Artificial lakes are made ; natural waters are controlled; electricity is generated and controlled. Such accomplishments are looked upon with pride.

Cultural premises among the Navajos may be summarized as follows :

1. The universe is orderly.
2. There is a basic quest for harmony.
3. The universe, though personalized, is full of dangers.
4. Evil and good are complementary and both are ever present in all things, thus human nature is neither basically good nor evil.
5. Everything exists in two parts, male and female, which belong together and complete each other.
6. The future is uncertain-nature (which is more powerful than people) might change anything.
7. This life is what counts-there is no sense that life on earth is a preparation for another existence.
8. Time and place are symbols of recapitulation.
9. Events, not actors or quality, are primary.
10. Time is ever flowing, can't be broken.
11. Concept of life as one whole–Navajos have a hard time thinking

in terms of social, economic, and political distinctions.

12. Like produces like . . . the part stands for the whole.

**Multiculturalism**

United States of America is a federation of 50 States. It was not known to the world upto 16th century. It was discovered by Columbus and John Cabbot. Originally it was inhabitated by Red Indian. During the first three quarters of the 17th Century an overselling majority of English settlers came to America with the Dutch, Sweds, Germans, French, Spaniards, Italians, and Portuguese, accounting for about 10%. After 1680 large numbers came from Germany, Ireland, Scotland, Switzerland and France for various reasons. Christine I. Benett has rightly observed: "We are a nation of immigrants. Between 1820 and 1970, more than 45 millions immigrants, mostly from European nations, entered the United States. The prevalent view was that the newly arrived ethnic groups would give up their unique cultural attributes and accept the Anglo-Saxon way of life. The school was expected to play the major role in this forced assimilation."[26]

But the view proved to be a misconception and the idea of forced assimilation was to be given up. In recent years, the theory of cultural pluralism has emerged as an alternative to the melting pot. Cultural pluralism is a process of compromise characterised by mutual appreciation and respect between two or more ethnic groups. The process has come out of historical experience of the nation. Two adult educators who have concerned themselves with the subject of multiculturalism in adult education are Horace M. Kallen and Robert A. Carlson. Carlon's recently revised work, also in this publication series, the Americanization Syndrome : A quest for Confirmity (1987) presents a controversial analysis of education for Americanization. He argues that most Americanisation programmes have been "no more and no less than attempts at cultural genocide (p.12). On the other hand, Kallen, writing in the early part of this century, looked to 'cultural pluralism' as the most democratic frame work for making newcomers at home in America. He is quoted by carlon on this "——. democracy involves, not the elimination of differences, but the perfection and conservation of differences. It aims through union not at uniformity, but at variety."[27]

As it has been mentioned that 'cultural pluralism', idealistically allows all groups to live and work together while maintaining their cultural identities, raises a problem of possible contradiction. Some people still hold that emphasis on cultural distrinctiveness works against allegiance to a common American culture and has the possibility of promoting divisiveness, and enhancing social segregation. Proponents, on the other hand, see 'cultural pluralism' as the only tenable basis for ensuring equality and human rights for all.

Both the above views regarding cultural pluralism are more idealistic and less practicable. Human behaviour is so flexible as well as complex that no such ideal can be candistined on the extreme hypothesis as somewhere, somehow they overlap. In this context the following view seems to be balanced and rational as well :

> "It's representative sample of the U.S. population were asked to indicate whether citizens should be expected to conform to cultural patterns, values and traits of the dominant culture or be allowed to maintain a separate cultural identity, they would probably indicate that neither end of the continuum is desirable, although responses are likely to favour Anglo-conformity. If we were to study the cultural patterns of individuals in United States, we would again find individuals across the continuum. Such findings would support the idea that ethnic attachments exist simultaneously with shared cultural trends. How culturally diverse we are does not seem to matter as long as we agree on certain basic values, one of which is respect for one another's cultural differences, we need to learn live together, not how to become alike."[28]

This type of understanding is very important as far as cross-cultural communication is concerned and goes a long way in bringing about peace and harmony in the society eliminating all petty barriers of cultural communication. At the same time, it is very pertinent to all the states wherever cultural pluralism exist among different ethnic groups.

For this purpose cultural consciousness is very essential, which comes out of awakened intelligence, Religious prejudices should not come in the way of smooth cultural communication. But the history of religions endorse a different evidence, as Bertrand Russel says : "Every step towards the better treatment of coloured races, or every mitigation of slavery, every moral progress there has been in the world, has been consistently opposed by the organised churches of the world."[29]

In the history of mankind it is found that the reformers, may it be Martin Luther King or Mahatma Gandhi, advocated dis-enchantment with such religion, organised religion, which created obstacles and hindrences in man's pursuit of higher and nobler values. Many theologists like Teilhard in many parts of the world rebelled against the tenets of organised church to bring them in line with the needs of healthy crosscultural communication. Many scholars have been tracing the latent unity behind the linguistic, ritualistic and environmental diversity and basic value-patterns enshrined in Hindu, Buddhist, Taoist, Sikh, and Zen Buddhist, Christian and Islamic systems. There has been a grand galaxy of such positive thinkers which includes Buddha, Tao, Confucious, Ashoka, Akbar, Ramkrishna, Vivekanand, Aurobindo and so on.

## Cultural Change and Biological Consideration

On the basis of good many researches is has been observed that cultural change is guided by biological considerations to a great extent. In one of the studies of the Mundas of Chhotanagpur it has been observed that Hindu Cultural Traits ceased to be absorbed with readiness after the tribe came under the influence of Christian missionaries. Christianity was attended by economic advantages, whereas Hinduism rather exercised a disintegrating influence upon Munda culture. N.K. Bose observes that "when a choice was offered between the old Munda, Christian and Hindu cultures, the second was chosen because of its higher economic or power potential. It was the same when the Juangs gave-up *jhum* cultivation and adopted the Hindu system of agriculture. This means that men select such traits and hold the promise of economic advantage or which happen for the time being to serve as symbols of power. The same truth is borne out by our study of the modern history of Bengal. When men thought that a surrender to western civilization was to their advantage, they allowed themselves to be biased in its favour. Again, as soon as they began to think in a different way, they resisted western influence, first by orthodoxy, and then by communalism or nationalism."[30]

## Science and Culture : A Pragmatic View

While discussing 'Lure of Philosophy' will Durant remarked "Perhaps if we desire stability of mind and soul we shall have to seek it Less in Science than in Philosophy"[31] It means that to resolve the human problem of survival and co-existence philosophy, a part of the culture, may be more useful. Contrary to the idea, Victor C. Ferkiss holds : "The idea that human culture is dependent on its technological foundations is at first startling or even offensive, yet reflection will show this to be as obvious as it is undeniable."[32] It is true that the scientific discoveries of the great scientists, brought about a lot of changes in living-styles of a man. They have made his life more convenient and comfortable; but

Science and technology is not all and all for man's happy and peaceful existence. That is why many historians have been inclined to regard technology as of only incidental importance and have ignored its impact and influence on culture. Will Durant is one of those, who consider philosophy as 'melting pot'. Scientific discoveries may be modified or refuted in course of time with the advance of new theory or idea; but the eternal values of life nurtured and advanced by the philosophy remains for ever. In a strong mood Will Durant asks :

> "To what distant has our famous Nebular Hypothesis flown? Does contemporary astronomy countenances it, or smile in its clouded face. Where are the Laws of great Newton now, when Einstein and Minkowski and other distinguished gentlemen have upset the universe with their unintelligible relativity. Where are indestructibility of matter and the conservation of energy in the chaos and dispute of contemporary physics?"[33]

In 1749 the Academy of Dijon offered a prize for an essay on the question, "Has the progress of sciences and the Arts contributed to corrupt or to Purify, Morals?" Rousseau's essay won the prize. Culture is much more of an evil than a good, he argued – with all the intensity and sincerity of one who, finding culture out of his reach, proposed to prove it worthless. "It was even a saying among the philosophers themselves that since learned men had appeared, honest men were nowhere to be found". "I venture to declare that a state of reflection is contrary to nature; and that a thinking man (an intellectual) is a depraved animal". It is need of the hour to have a sort of equilibrium between feeling and reason. It would be more healthier practice if the feelings of heart are also developed instead of shere reasoning. Many idealists believe that education does not make a man good; it only makes him clever – usually for mischief. Instinct and feeling are more trustworthy than reason. The feelings are more inclined towards idealism whereas reasoning leads to realism. With the decay of idealism reality comes out. At times the idealism and realism overlap each other, since in a social group many eristic tendencies work letently, which aim at winning rather than at reaching the truth. The balanced and precised work of Moore 'Principle Ethic' (1905) marks a new departure in philosophy, the birth of a New Realism. The "philosophy of common sense", which Moore initiated, of course, needed a medium of expression radically different from that of the idealists.

Since the time of Aristotle some philosophers and educators have been labouring under the delusion that it is enough to train an individual in certain techniques of reasoning to cultivate his ability to syllogise in strict conformity with the precepts of formal logic, and the individual would emerge as a full-fledged thinker. But in modern times due to rapid and violent strides of science and information technology various human faculties like memorising, thinking etc. have been considerably affected. Effectuous media like space technology, micro-electronics and talking computers have minimised the time of intervals between discovery and application of knowledge as will be revealed from the following facts and figures :

| Item | Discovery Year | Application Year |
|---|---|---|
| Photography | 1727 | 1839 (112 years) |
| Electric Motor | 1821 | 1886 (65 years) |
| Telephone | 1820 | 1887 (67 years) |
| Radar | 1925 | 1940 (15 years) |
| Atomic Bomb | 1939 | 1945 (6 years) |
| Transister | 1948 | 1951 (3 years) |
| Solar Battery | 1953 | 1955 (2 years) |

Explosion of knowledge has revolutionalised the ways and means of education, trade, commerce, communication etc. The inventors have been benefitted by the theories or principles discovered by their predecessors. It is well admitted fact. It was Darwin, like many others, who said that he stood on the shoulders of all his predecessors, and every other discoverer must admit the same. Even Einstein had his debts to pay for the "theory of relativity", and he did so very generously. Historical evidences are on record that at times religious taboos and authoritarian attitude of the rulers were great enemies of the discovers. Sir Thomas Browne, the author of Religio Medicine, said much the same: "The mortallest enemy unto knowledge, and that which hath done the greatest execution upon truth, hath been a peremptory adhesion unto authority". The example of Galileo is the historical testimony of this fact. He was nearly burnt alive because his discoveries about the solar system did not agree with the Bible; he only escaped by saying that the Bible was right and he was wrong. Jenner was attacked for introducing vaccination for small pox. Pasteur's discovery of germs was objected and questioned mainly because he did not possess any degree or diploma in medical science.

All inventors or discoverers were the believers in the world without borders. Many a time due to narrow concept of nationalism and vested interests of the rulers these people had to suffer a lot mentally as well as physically. Regarding catholic outlook of the scientists Patrick Pringle has aptly remarked; "There is a free-masonry in science, a spirit of free exchange of information, that often makes scientists to accept orders to keep their discoveries secret. Just as a doctor finds it hard to understand colour-bars, because he knows that under the skin we are physically all alike, so other scientists, dealing with forces that transcend manmade frontiers, are inclined to find it difficult to differentiate between what are called nations. They know that nations are not races, and that the lines on the map of the world are unscientifically drawn, and being scientists, they rarely evince any emotional response to songs and shouts about their fatherland. Most of them have habit of regarding the earth as one planet, and human beings as one species; and this sometimes get them into serious trouble."[34] This is exactly what happened to Oppenheimer, the discoverer of atomic bomb. Two such very powerful bombs were dropped on Hiroshima and Nagasaki (Japan) in 1945 which ended World War II. Shortly after the explosion of the bombs he was suspended while security charges against him were investigated. The board that carried out the investigation confirmed his loyalty but said that he should not be given access to the nation's atomic secrets.

In the disastrous tragedy of Hiroshima no one had been more instrumental than Robert Oppenheimer, director of the Los Alamos project. An observer who was watching him closely that morning has given the following account : "He grew tenser as the last second ticked off. He scarcely breathed. He held on to a post to steadily himself . . . . When the announcer shouted 'Now' And there came this tremendous burst of light, followed . . . . by the deep growling roar of the explosion, his face relaxed an expression of tremendous relief." This much from the outside. But what flashed through his mind during those moments, Mr. Oppenheimer recalled later, were two lines from the Bhagavad Geeta in which God is the spokesman:

I am become death, the shatterer of worlds; waiting that hour that ripens to their doom.[35]

This incident is not only symbolic instance of meeting the East and West but also that of culture and science. It is said that science is systematized knowledge, realized science is philosophy, and realized philosophy is religion. Thus religion and science are not opposed to each other; but they are suppliment to each other. Albert Einstein has rightly remarked, "Science without religion is lame and religion without science is blind". As we have already mentioned that religion is not any principle or doctrine, but it is an experience.

Experience is a personalised matter as such it does not imply intellectual ingredients only; but also one's feelings, emotions, values cherished and so on. In religious experience reason comes afterwards. The most important thing is the depth and solidity of experience, as Romain Rolland says, "Religious historians who seek only to discover the intellectual inter-dependence of systems forget the vital point : the knowledge that religions are not ordinary matter of intellectual dialectic, but facts of experience, and that although reason steps in afterwards to construct systems upon the facts, such systems would not hold good for an hour, if they were not based upon the solid foundation of experience."[36]

Indian mysties firmly believed in such religious experience to attain perfection. In their view religion is of no use if it does not teach the eternity of soul. Modern science has resolved the whole phenomenal universe into three states and has explained that those states are matter, energy and consciousness.[37]

To sum-up the topic we can say with Dr. Radha Krishnan : "Science reveals identical cosmic elements as the basis of human life. Philosophy visualizes a universal consciousness at the back of nature and humanity. Religion refers to our common spiritual struggles and aspirations".[38]

**Aryans' Love for Learning**

The system of education in ancient India was a unique one in many respects. Scores of unparalleled works on art, literature and positive sciences testify the testimony of its rational and unique character. The very importance of education was realised in India from early times, and utmost emphasis was laid upon the acquisition of knowledge. Knowledge was considered to be the third eye of a man and all the human acts were supposed to be merged in knowledge.[39] A man devoid of spiritual knowledge was considered as unwise and unfit for giving any worthwhile advice, howsoever, learned he may be. On the basis only a distinct line of demarcations laid down between 'Vidya' and 'Avidya'. Further it is said that true knowledge is the one, which leads to 'salvation' or 'Moksha' an ultimate aim of life "Sa Vidya Vimuktaye".[40]

Taking into account this uniqueness of ancient Indian education F.W. Thomas has very aptly remarked:

> "There has been no country where the love of learning had so early an origin or has.exercised so lasting and powerful influence. From the simple poets of vedic age to Bengali Philosopher of the present

day, there has been an uninterrupted succession of teachers and scholars."

The age of Mantras was followed by the age of Brahmanas, which was later on followed by Upnishads. But it should be remembered that these ages are not strictly successive in time. They overlap one another to a considerable extent. The hymns or mantras consisting of about ten thousand stanzas reveal some of the highest and noblest aspirations of the early Aryans. Being creative products of poetic minds they are not only of educational significance but also indicative of growth and evolution of the minds of the early Aryan thinkers. The attitude of devotion and reverence revealed by these mantras has a very sound ethical and moral significance. These mantras enable us to gauge "the unfolding of the human mind in the earliest stages of thought" and testify the growth of a civilization which was the product of centuries. According to Rabindranath Tagore they reflect the spontaneous expression of "a people of vigorous and unsophisticated imagination awakened at the very dawn of civilization to a sense of the inexhaustible mystery that is implicit in life." In fact the composers of these mantras had an abiding faith in the unknown which attributed not a casual relation but divinity to every element and force of nature, Vadas say that the earth is upheld by truth ("Satya") of which God is supreme exponent. They further hold that God reveals himself through "Rta"(eternal order). This great law of "Rta" and "Satya" has two-fold significance-cosmic and moral.

With the passage of time the main object of worshipping the Gods with piety and devotion was lost sight of and its place was taken by pompous ritualistic performances. Thus ritualism came into being. Upanishads stands for rationalism, which was a consequential development in the society.[41]

Memorisation was one of the earliest modes of ensuring the growth and continuity of human knowledge. It was of two types-mechanical memorization (without understanding) and memorisation with understanding. The latter was considered better, as it is now-a-days. The main-spring of spiritual knowledge would have dried up if the process of oral transmission had not been invigorated and enriched by ancillary knowledge. That is why the four Vedas (Rik, Yajur, Sam and Atharva) are called "Shruti" also. Six ancillary braches of these Vedas like prosody, grammar, phonetics astronomy, etc. are called Vedangas. These secular subjects enriched Vedic knowledge by revealing some of the higher and deeper truths of life.

The Vedic and subsequent literature presents a very glorious picture of the society with various fibres of social elevation and sublimation. The system of education is of course, a sub-system of the entire social system. Therefore, the over-all picture of the educational system also sounds very sublime trend. But the freedom and opportunity for higher learning available to women-folk during Vedic time is not visible in the epic period. According to A.S. Altekar "education of women was prevailing in the Vedic society. But by the time of Mahabharata the tradition of study of Vedas by women-folk was almost extinct.[42] The early marriages of girls and the rigidity of caste-system began to pose a challenge to the excessive hormic zeal of the reformers. Moreover, being a feudal society education was largely restricted to the priestly class, Education was mostly available to the members of royal family or to affluents. It was in the princely and noble families only that the children used to have the privilege of special tutors to teach them at home. Otherwise the students had to go to the hermitages in the farflung forest areas, where the safety problem generally persisted upon. Because of the problem of safety, it was not feasible for women-folk to go to these hermitages for their education. Therefore, the women-folk used to have their education at home itself by the elderly persons of the family or the guest visitors.

Faith in preceptor or sense of reverence towards Guru was considered to be the first and foremost condition for attaining knowledge in general and spiritual knowledge in particular. Eklavya is the glaring example of this age-old belief. By the virtue of his deep sense of devotion. Eklavya could excel even Arjuna in archery. The Mahabharata holds that "One who is full of faith and has fully controlled his senses attains knowledge.[43]

Inquisitiveness was considered to be a must for good studentship. The entire gamut of relations between the teacher and taught was governed and guided by the common belief that *Guru* is indispensable and nobody can learn the desired Lores (Vidyas) fruitfully without appearing and satisfying '*Guru*'.[44] An important place was given to discussion and debate particularly in higher studies and a man's ability was best judged by his power to vanquish opponents in debate or discussion. This very trend prevailed in Brahmanic as well as Jain-Bauddha system of education.

As far as aims of education are concerned it was not merely confined to three R's. A very multi-dimensional curriculum right from training in arms to the training in the science of medicine and surgery, different occupations and vocations also formed the part of the curriculum to prepare the useful and refined citizens for the society by inculcating in them various moral, social, cultural and spiritual values. Infusion of piety, righteousness, formation of character, development of personality inculcation of civic and social duties, promotion of social efficiencies and preservation of national culture may be prescribed as some of the objectives of educational system in Ancient India. According to Dr. R.C. Majumdar,

> "The object of this system of education was three-fold: the acquisition of knowledge, the inculcation of social duties and religious rites, and, aboveall, the formation of character. All the three aims were kept distinctly in the forefront, but the greatest emphasis was laid upon the last. Even the greatest champion of Brahmanism boldly laid down that neither the study of the Vedas, nor liberality, nor sacrifices, nor any self-imposed restraint, nor austerities ever procured the attainment of rewards to a man whose heart is contaminated by sensuality."[45]

In the Brahmanic system there was restriction on admission. Karna had to hide his real caste to be a disciple of Parshuram. There are many other examples. But Buddhist system paved the way for growth of a broad-based democratic system of education by admitting all castes to the monasteries (Viharas). In spite of this a great emphasis was laid on character formation in Buddhist educational system also.

The system of education as a whole was rather informal than formal because there were no fixed hours for teaching-learning nor there were definite prescribed textbooks. It was only verbal communication between the teachers and the taughts. Methods and modes of teaching also differed from person to person and place to place. There was no symmetry or harmony in the various methods of teaching applied at various places. Studies of Vedas, Vedangas, Political Science, trade and commerce – these were main branches of learning besides these, the study of various positive sciences like Materia Medica, Chemistry Botany etc. were also taught. Special training in arms and in physical fitness were provided to the princes. Education in military science was the nucleus of the entire system of education and various socio-religious traditions. These places played very vital role in bringing about national integration and propagation of Indian culture aboard.

In this way we see the most influential picture of the society in the system of education prevailing during that time. The basic concept on which the cordial teacher-taught relationship was based, was the concept of indispensability of teacher, in the process of education. That is why the relation between the pupil and the teacher was very harmonious and cordial. They were united by mutual confidence, respect and affection, though at times the teacher used to behave in a very vexing tone.

The most interesting character of educational system was that there was no fixed place of learning or teaching. Even the discussion on subtle topic like the self and the supreme can be visualized at market place, in a butchery or at the shop of the grocer. This is indicative of the fact that pomp and show was not favoured at all in the field of education. Simple living and high thinking was order of the day.

The essence of education lies in the inculcation of various human values through education. We find very critical analysis of our moral and social values interwoven in the various episodes. At times we find contradictory statements regarding various moral values. But, if we go into the deep philosophy of the values, we come to the conclusion that the view point of our ancient thinkers has been very practicable and appealing. Mbh. obviously holds that our various moral and social values are subject to changes from time to time and from place to place. Therefore, we find the mention of two sets of principles, which can easily be called as Yug-dharma and Sanatan-dharma. The former stands for the changeable set of values while the later stands for eternal set of values. We also find mention of various negative values. At places it has been advised that the individual must also know the nature of the negative values so that he may not be adversely affected by them.

Due respect was given to the low-ascendent persons if they were found to be of good moral character or of very high wisdom. Due respect was given to shudras in the Society. In the field of education we find many low descended persons enjoying high prestige in the society by the virtue of their learning and wisdom. Mahamati Vidur etc. were such individuals who commanded great respect in and outside the palace.

*Varnas* and *Ashramas*–these two were the most important social institutions. The students obtained their education at *Guru-Kul* during the period of celebacy, i.e., the first Ashrama. After having attained knowledge and taking permission of the preceptor, they used to come back in order to become house-holders. Number of students in *gurukul* was limited only, and as such there was no problem of discipline. The knowledge and skills acquired by the students were tested through different informal tools and techniques. At times the sacrifice, modesty, obedience and other Virtues were also tested by the respective preceptors. The women folk were provided good training in fine arts at their homes wherever facilities existed.

The teaching was mainly the job of Brahmins. But, in the are arena of knowledge, no differentiation was made on the basis of caste or creed. Therefore, in the Mahabharata we find the examples of may low-descended to command prestige and reputation in the society on the basis of their distinguished achievement in the field of knowledge as well as their personal conduct and attitude towards their mission and not by the virtue of their being simply Brahmins. Brahminhood was not the condition for commanding honour and reputation in the society. In the Mahabharata, we find god many examples of poor Brahmins who had to lead the life in distress and hardship. The teacher-taught relationship was just like father and son relationship. The students used to stay at the hermitages like the members of the family of the preceptor. Thus, they were influenced by the grand personalities of the preceptor. This very impact of *guru* went a long way in shaping their personality in future life. This very impact or influence is lacking very much these days. Nowadays teachers do impart knowledge but they are not able to influence the pupils under thier charge. This was not the case in the ancient system of education in India.

Royal patronage was one of the most powerful source for propagation of knowledge. That is why the system of education even being informal in character, it was very impressive and fruitful.

The centres of learning in Ancient India were very simple and mostly of informal type. During Vedic or Epic period we do not come across with any university like Nalanda or Takshashila. The main learning centres can be classified under the following five heads :

1. Hermitages (Acharyakul or Gurukul),
2. Parishads or Samiti,
3. Royal Assemblies,
4. Places of Pilgrimage, and
5. Sites of Sacrifice (Yajna Mandapas)

According to F.E. Keay these parishads were the nucleus of something corresponding to a university. Regarding the format of these parishads he observes that "The parishads were like judicial assemblies and in others like ecclesiastical synods, but as those who composed them were most of them also teachers, they correspond to a certain extent to the associations of teaches in the Middle ages of Europe, which developed into universities, but even a student was a member of the Parishad". As far as the size of the parishad is concerned ancient authorities have opined differently. According to Parashar "four or even three able men from amongst the Brahmanas in a village, who know the Veda and keep sacrificial fire, form a parishad."[46]

Dr. R.K. Mookerjee has given a very picturesque discription of such two famous hermitages mentioned in the Mbh. i.e., Hermitages of Shaunak and Kanva.

**Naimisha**

The most important of such hermitages was that of the Naimisha, a forest which was like a university. The presiding personality of the place was Saunaka, to whom was applied the designation of Kulapati, sometimes defined as the preceptor of 10,000 disciples. Saunaka attracted to Naimisha a vast concourse of learned men by his performance of a twelve years sacrifice, of which the most essential anga or accompaniment was the discourses and disputations of learned men on religious, philosophical and scientific topics. In one place (ix 37) we read of "ascetics living at Naimisharanya being engaged in a sacrifice lasting for twelve years", on completion of which they set out in large numbers for visiting the various sacred shrines of the country. In another place (ib, 14) we have the same reference with the interesting additional information that in the course of that twelve years' sacrifice, when a particular one called Visvajit had been completed, the Rishis started for the country of the panchalas, and reaching there, requested the king to give them twenty-one strong and healthy calves to be given away as dakshina for the sacrifice they had finished.[47]

The places of pilgrimage played very important role in propagation of knowledge. 'Vidur-Niti' is a part of Mbh. like that of Shrimat-Bhagavat-Gita. The former is the elaboration of the surmons given by Vidur to Dhritarashtra and the latter is the exhortion of Lord Krishna to the Arjuna when he was very much perplexed and frustrated on the battle field. Similarly Sanjay from charioteer class and Lomharshan enjoyed honour and respect in the royal family. The countribution of the warrior class towards the propagation of spiritual knowledge need not be over-emphasised. There were many scholar kings who patronised learning to the best of their ability. The detailed account of the royal patronage by such warrior class to spiritual knowledge is documented in Chhandogya Upnishad. Janak was one of the most celebrated patroniser of spiritual knowledge. He was himself a great scholar of yoga and other allied scriptures. But he mainly believed in rationalism.

Besides the scholar kings we find a galaxy of scholars in Mbh. who contributed substantially towards the propagation of various branches of learning. Among these scholars great sage Vyasa and his disciples, Kulpati Shaunak, Disciples of Shaunak, Lomharshan and Ugrashrava, Maharshi Narada, Uddhava, Bhishma, Dronacharya, Shuracharya, Mahamati Vidur, Kahod, Uddalak, Shwetketu Ashtavakra, Chyavan, Bharadwaj,

Vishwamitra, Kapil, Asit etc. are noteworthy.[48]

The priest class occupied a very prominent place in the field of learning and knowledge. However, because of their paramount supermacy later on they had to face opposition by warrior class. Various stories of struggle between warrior class and priest class for supermacy in the field of knowledge are depicted at various places in the epic.

From the critical survey of various educational ideals and istitutions depicted in Mbh. We come to the conclusion that it was a system of education national in character and appealing for the masses. The Principle and theories propounded during the epic period are even relevant these days with certain modification and innovations.

**Sumeridans and Their Contribution :**

L.A. Waddel in his monumental work ''The makers of Civilization in Race and History' opines that "Sumerians were the oldest known of all civilized peoples of the ancient world and the founders of civilization in Mesopotamia".[49] No doubt, in several aspects of life, Mesopotamia led the way and other civilization followed. It is land between two rivers Tigris and Euphrates. Sumer was the heart of Mesopotamia in ancient days. The regions to the north-east of sumer were called Babylonia and Akkad. Being a very fertile land having perennial irrigation system Mesopotamia flourished in leaps and bounds and by about 3000 B.C. it had reached a very high level of achievement in the field of agriculture and trade. The cities of the region appear to have started as centres for the control of irrigation in the area and soon became centres of commerce and industry also. The most important of these cities were Erech, Eridu, Lagash and Ur. Each was the capital or a small state.

They were always fighting among themselves. By about 2600 B.C. the kings of Ur. had become powerful. The people of Akkad in the north-east belonged to a different stock but had adopted much of sumerian culture about 200 B.C. a strong king combined Sumer and Akkad into one kingdom with its capital at Agade, which was soon destroyed by invaders. The important event in the History of Mesopotamia is the rule of a new dynasty at Babylon. Hammurabi, the greatest Babyloman ruler, united the whole of what is now called *Iraq*.

By 1600 B.C. this kingdom was also destroyed by the Hittites who came from Asia Minor, now *Turkey*. The Hittites were the first to make regular use of horses for war chariots and to make iron implement. Hammurabi provided his people a code or a system of Laws called Hammurabi's code of Law. One of the highlights of the code is that it made a crime against one citizen a crime against the whole state and the state fixed punishment for the offender. Sumerins believed in life after death as was common in ancient time. That is why they put food and other nencessities of daily life into graves. This practice appears to have been discontinued in summer and the dead were buried in the backyard of the houses.

The Mesopotamians used pielographic script for writing called Cuneiform script. The sumerians were the first people to evolve a proper system of writing. The people of Mesopotamia counted by sixties as we count by tens. Ours is the decimal system. Whereas their system was sexagesimal.

In the field of Astronomy Mesopotamians made astonishing progress. They could calcutate the length of the day and night, and the rising and setting of the sun and the moon. They divided the whole day into 24 hours, a time-system followed all over the world. They divided the sky into twelve parts and assigned each a name-Arics, Taurus, Gemini, Cancer, Leo, Virgo, Libra, Scorpio, Sagittarius, Capricorn, Aquarius, and libra. This has come down to us as the twelve signs of the Zodiac or rashis as they are called in India. Another remarkable achievement of the Mesopotamias was the invention of a calendar. Calendars can be calculated on the basis of the movements of the sun, or the moon. It may be solar or Lunar. The Mesopotamian calendar was Lunar, based on the moon, and like all Lunar calendars it was incorrect. A year is really a time that the earth takes in making a complete revolution around the sun – 365 days, 5 hours, 48 minutes and 46 seconds. The lunar year is about 11 days less than the solar year. But, inspite of this, it can be called as their contribution to the modern world.

After the conquest of Babylon and the fall of Damascus (750 B.C.) Assyrian empire came into existence. Senna-cherib was a great Assyrian conqueror, who made Nineveh, the finest city in western Asia. After a century later at the advent of nomads from the north and east-the Medes, the Caldians and the Iranians – Assyrian greatness came to an end. They destroyed Nineveh in the 7th and 6th century B.C. After Assyrians, Iranians (Indo-Europenas from Central Asia) built the empire, which was later on conquered first by Alexander (4th century) and by Arabs consecutively.

**Malayasia and India : Cultural Bonds**

Till the 19th Century the civilized races of Malay owed their religion, their political system, astronomy, medicine, literature, sculpture and everything to India. The arrival of Indians in the Malay region was neither sudden nor violent. An Indian trading ship would sail across the Bay of Bengal in the South-West monsoon to exchange beads, generally Indian but sometimes Roman, and clothes and articles of dress for gold, tin, ivory, camphor and other produce of Malayan forests.

## Teaching of Religions

Priests came and taughts the ritual of great religions, Hinduism and Buddhism, in Sanskrit that was awe-inspiring, because unintelligible to the crowd. The Indian pioneers counted among them Gunavarman, a Kashmiri prince, who perhaps visited Kedah in Northern Malay and certainly visited Java, where he made many converts to Hinayana Buddhism before he passed on to die in 431 A.D. at Nanking.

The centres of Indian influence and trade were Hinduized first kingdoms. For soon some of the Indian immigrants married into leading Indonesian families in Malay, Sumatra, Java and Borneo, injecting into primitive tribal organisations the Hindu conception of the divinity of kings and inaugurating little courts that came to be centres of the religions, the learning and the art of India of their day.

## Coronation Ceremony

For more than one thousand years the Malayan world was under Hindu influence and even after the acceptance of Islam much Hindu influence survived, especially at courts and in magical medicine and in the drama. To this day the enthronement ceremony of Malay Sultans, orthodox Muslims though they are, is Hindu with a Muslim Veneer. After lustration, the Malay ruler dons royal dress and in the headdress of one Sultan of the oldest descent is thrust a "lightning seal" whose handle is made of "thunderwood", clearly a survival in culture of India's vajra or thunderbold symbol so often represented in Javanese sculpture.

A coronation oath is read in corrupt Sanskrit praising the new ruler as a great king who ravishes the three world by the jewels or his crown and extolling his conquest of evil, his luck, his justice, his power of healing. A Malay ruler has to sit as immobile as possible during the enthronement ceremony, rigidity being evidence in Hindu ritual of incipient godhead.

In one Malay State, Negri Semblan, when the court herald proclaims a new ruler, he assumes a Brahmanical attitude, standing on one leg with the sole of his right foot resting against his left knee, the right hand shading his eyes and the tip of the fingers of his left hand pressed against his left cheek.

## Use of Symbols

Finally, part of the Malay enthronement ritual consists in the new ruler going in procession round his royal dominion. This Hindu circumambulation recalls how the oldest Malay dynasty was connected with Mt. Meru, the heaven of India, wielder of the thunderbolt and controller of weather. In Burma, Siam, Indo-China and Indonesia, the capitals of old kingdoms had a hill, a shrine, a temple or a palace identified with Mt. Meru. The owner of such a holy eminence was a receptacle or incarnation of Siva or Vishnu or Indra. And it was as a lord of the State's symbolic Meru that a Malay king guarded the fortunes of his people. The hill behind one Malay palace is still called the Mt. of Sri Indra. The Tamil poem Manimekali mentions two Malayan kings who claimed descent from Indra and the capital of more than one Malay State was styled Indrapura.

## Buddhist Shrine

As ancestor of one of the Sailendra Maharajas who by the ninth century ruled Sri Vijaya, conquered Central Java and was responsible for the erection of its most noble Buddhist shrines, including the world famous Borobodur. Many pieces of sculpture on Java's shrine rank with the sculputre of Indian temples like Belur and Khajuraho and are as supreme in the world of art as Kalidas in the world of poetry.

Trade and law and war came to the Malay world from India. In the relic chamber of a Kedah temple have been unearthed minature models of weapons, including swords and shields of types that occur in the Ajanta frescoes. A broad spatulate dagger is of the shape of a dagger associated with Shiva in his demon form of Bhairawa. Such a dagger was used in Tantric rites common in Sumatra and Malay in the 14th and 15th centuries.

## India's Great Gift

Hinduism began to give way before Islam in the 13th century of the Christian era, until in the end there was no part of the Malay world that was not Muslim except the small island of Bali.

From the cradle to the grave the Malay is surrounded by Hindu influences. Even the nursery tales many of them are derived from fables, the jataka tales and somadeva's Ocean of Story.

Weaving of silk and embroidery and work in gold, silver etc., were introduced by the Hindus.

**REFERENCES**


1. Wissler, Clark, *Man and Culture,* p. 264.
2. *Ibid*, p. 269.
3. Christine L. Binnett : *Comprehensive Multicultural Education*, p.15.
4. *Comprehensive Multicultural Education*, p.17.
5. Ratna Naidu : *The Communal edge to Plural Societies,p.*78.
6. Shalina Mehra : *The Eternal Web,* p. 34.
7. Gail M. Inlow, *Values in Transition*, p. 3.
8. Hall : *Beyond Culture*, p. 58.
9. Dr. S. Radhakrishnan, *Towards a New World*, pp.67-68.
10. Quoted in Chamberlan, J. Kant. Vol.. I, p. 510.
11. E.P. Cubberly, *Changing Concept of Education,* p. 16.
12. Stills, Assimilation, p.438.
13. *Comprehensive Multicultural Education* p. 88.
14. S.W. Mintz, "Creating Culture in the Americas" in *Readings in Anthropology* 75/76., p. 202.
15. Sowell, *Ethnic America*, p.10.
16. *Comprehensive Multicultural Education*, p.106.
17. Vidya Sagar, "The Carribbian" in *Mother India*, Children Abroad, Jan. 1988, p. 5.
18. For details readers are referred to the book named *The Indians and the Amerindians* authored by B. Chakravary.
19. Peter Ruhomon, *Centenary History of the East Indians in British Guiana, p.23.*
20. *Ibid,* P. 25.
21. Peter Ruhomon, *Centenary History of East Indians in British Guiana,* p. 215.
22. Christine I. Bennett, *Comprehensive Multicultural Education*, p.11.
23. *Ibid;* pp. 13-14.
24. Quoted in the booklet by M. Shahabuddeen on *Slavery and Historiographical Rectification*, p. 3.
25. Navajo is a member of an American Indian people native to New Maxic and Arizona.
26. *Comprehensive Multicultural Education.* p. 86.
27. Robert A. Carlson, *The Americanisation Syndrome* : A Quest for Confirmity (1987) p. 97.
28. *Multicultural Education in a Pluralistic Society*, p. 26.
29. Bertrand Russell, Why I am not a Christian, pp. 24–25.
30. N.K. Bose, *Cultural Anthropology*, p. 89.
31. *The Pleasures of Philosophy*, p.10.
32. Victor C Ferkiss : *Technological Man : The Myth and the Reality*, p. 28.
33. Will Durant, *The Pleasures of Philosophy*, pp.9-10.
34. Patrick Pringley, *Great Discoveries in Modern Science*, p. 12.
35. Histon Smith, *The Religions of Man* p. 23.
36. Romain Rolland, *The Life of Vivekananda,* p. 346.

37. In fact matter and energy are inseparable. They are different states of the same substance. The idealists try to divorce matter and force from mind or consciousness.
38. Dr. Radhakrishnan, *Religion and Society*. p. 13.
39.. सर्व कर्माखिलं पार्थ ज्ञाने परिसमाप्यते। *Bhagavadgita* 4.33.
40. श्रद्धावाँल्लभते ज्ञानं तत्परः संयतेन्द्रियः। ज्ञानं लब्ध्वा परां शान्तिमचिरेणाधिगच्छति।। *Ibid* 4. 39.
41. Thomas F.W. , *The History and Prospects of British Education in India*. p.1.
42. Dr. A.S. Altekar : *Position of Women in Ancient India*, p.10.
43. तद्विद्धि प्रणिपातेन परिप्रश्नेन सेवया।
उपदेक्ष्यन्ति ते ज्ञानं ज्ञानिनस्तत्त्वदर्शिनः।।
— *The Mahabharata, Bhishma Parvan* 27.34.
44. न बिना गुरुसम्बन्धः ज्ञानस्याधिगमः। Shanti 32.622 Compare — आचार्याद्धैव विद्या विदिता साधिष्टं प्रापयति। *Chhandogya* 4.9.3.
45. Dr. R.C. Majumdar, *Ancient India*, p. 451.
46. F.E. Keay : *History of Education in India and Pakistan*, p. 45.
47. Dr. R.K. Mukherjee : *Indian Education*, pp. 333-34.
48. For detailed account of these ancient scholars pl. see *Education And Values in Mahabharata* by Dr. N.L. Gupta.
49. *The Makers of Civilization in Race and History*, preface, p. IX.

# 3

# CROSSCULTURAL COMMUNICATION
## Multireligious Perspective

What is religion–Eastern thoughts on religion, Western thoughts on religion, five dimensions of Religions, Religious Pluralism, Religions of the Asian Countries–Spiritualism, Transcultural Communications; Religious Fibres; Indian Perspective–Multidimension, Microcultures of Islam, Fundamentalism Vs Liberalism, Composite Faith of Akbar, Brotherhood of Islam, Golden Mean, Shankara and Budha, Shadows of Advaitism, Buddhism and Christianity, Buddhism and Taoism, Cross-cultural Communication Through Buddhism, Religions in India, Secularism; Indian Context, Western Concept of Secularism, Wars of Religions in France, Communalism, Majority Vs Minority, Minorityism; Religion in America–Contribution to Christianity, Assimiliation in America, Turky; Christianity to Islam; Hinduism and Zoroastrianism, Religion in Japan, Shintoism: Japanese Version of Taoism, Trans-religions Communication, Inter-religious Dialogue. Revival and growth of Judaism, Indian Gods and Deities Equality of Religions.

### What is Religion?

### Eastern Thought

"That which brings both earthly good as well as the supreme good in the form of salvation (*Moksha*) is *Dharma*"[1] – *Kanad*

"Salutations to that glorious *Dharma*, as it sustains mankind. Such laws as sustain all, are verily called *Dharma*"[2] –*The Mahabharata*

"There are four-fold indices of *Dharma* like the Veda, the Smriti, *Sadachar* (good conduct) and what is pleasing to one's Conscience." –*Manu*

"Patience, forgiveness, restraint, unstealing, purity, control over sense-organs, talent, knowledge, truthfulness and absence of anger–these are ten characteristics of *Dharma*"[3] – *Manu*

"Man is identical with a beast so far as food, sleep, fear and sex are concerned; but the additional quality he possesses with him is *Dharma*. Those who are devoid of a sense of *Dharma* are veritable beasts."[4]

– *Bhartrihari*

"O brother, there is no virtue equal to doing good to other, and nothing so mean as to inflict pain on others."[5] – *Tulsidas*

The real is in your home within
Why wander you from forest to forest;
Go where you will to Kashi or to Mathura,
You will not find him.
Except in your soul within. – *Kabir*

Religion does not consist in mere words...caste is nonsense. Those who love God, love everybody. – *Nanak*

He who has faith has all, and who lacks faith lacks all. It is faith in the name of the Lord that works wonders, for faith is life and doubt is death. – *Ramakrishna Paramhansa.*

Despondency is not religion, whatever else it may be. By being pleasant always and smiling, it takes you nearer to God, nearer than any prayer. – *Vivekananda.*

Religion reflects both God and man. As religion is a life to be lived, not a theory to be accepted for a belief to be adhered to, it allows scope and validity to varied approaches to the devine; but they are all forms of the supreme. – *Dr. S. Radhakrishnan*

*Dharma* came to mean peculiar duties and privileges for a person as a member of the community, as a member of the varnas or as in a particular stage of life. – *P.V. Kane* (History of Dharmshastra)

Multiplicity of religions has led to much unhappiness and great discord. It is the duty of wise men to find means to end it. May God sow in our minds the seed of true religion that false religions may disappear, and wise men may give-up their hostilities and increase happiness. It is an established fact that five thousand years ago, there was no other religion except the vedic. – *Swami Dayanand*

It (Hinduism) is not a religion but a system. It is not creed but a mode of thought. It allows an amount of individual freedom in thought, the like of which is not known to many other religious system of the world. It gives absolute freedom of worship of every individual, according to his own taste, belief and development. — *Lala Lajpat Rai*

"The whole gamut of man's activities today constitutes an indivisible whole. You cannot divide social, political and purely religious work into water-tight compartments. It (Religion) provides a moral basis to all other activities, which they would otherwise lack, reducing life to a thing of sound and fury signifying nothing." — *Mahatama Gandhi*

"Religion fulfils the spiritual urges of man and channelizes them towards an effort to attain the goal of self or God-realization. It links the soul of man with the ultimate reality in god and enables man to attain the knowledge of the self which means complete identity with the supreme being." — *Vinoba Bhave*

"The world union will be based on spiritual religion of humanity. Spiritual collectivism would subdue social and political chaos of the modern world. A spiritual society alone could build the future richness and good life". — *Sri Aurbindo*

**Western Thoughts**

Love your enemies, bless them that curse you, do good to them that hate you, and pray for them which despitefully use you, and persecute you.

It is written that man shall not live by bread alone, but by every word of God. — *Jesus Christ*

Religion is the virtue by which men show God due worship and reverence. — *St. Thomas Aquinas*

Faith is to believe, on the word of God, what we do not see and enjoy what we believe. — *St. Augustine*

The very word "God" suggests care, kindness, goodness; and the idea of God in his infinite care, infinite kindness, infinite goodness–we give God the name of good: it is only by shortening it that it becomes God. — *Henry Ward Beecher*

It is only religion, the great bond of love and duty to God, that makes any existence valuable or even tolerable. — *Horace Bushnell*

A man who puts aside his religion because he is going into society is like one taking off his shoes because he is about to walk on thorns.

The joy of religion is an exorcist to the mind; it expels the demons of carnal mirth and madness. — *Richard Cecil*

Religion is life, philosophy is thought; religion looks up, friendship looks in. We need both thoughts and life, and we need that the two shall be in harmony. — *Clarke James F.*

God hates those who praise themselves.
Faith is the ear of the soul.
Prayer is conversation with God. — *Saint Clement*

Religion's home is the conscience. It's watchword is the word 'ought' – It's highest joy is in doing God's will.

— *Theodore Ledyard Cuyler*

Piety and morality are but the same spirit differently manifested. Piety is religion with its face towards God; morality is religion with its face toward the world.

Religion, in its purity, is not so much a pursuit as a temper; or rather it is a temper, leading to the pursuit of all that is high and holy. Its foundation is faith; its action, works; its temper, holiness; its aim, obedience to God in improvement of self and benevolence to men.

— *Tryon Edwards*

Religion, like music, is not in need of defence, but rendition–Religion is the appreciation of life's spiritual values and the interpretation of life, its origin, its purpose, and its density, in terms of them.

— *H.E. Fosdick.*

It is the glory of the true religion that it inculcates and inspires a spirit of benevolence.

No man's Religion ever survives his Morals. — *Thomas Fuller*

Religion is the final centre of repose; the goal to which all things tend; apart from which man is a shadow, his very existence a riddle, and the stupendous scenes of nature which surround him as unmeaning as the leaves which the sibyl scattered in the wind. — *Robert Hall*

Religion is not a dogma, nor an emotion, but a service is not of the head alone, nor of the heart alone, but pre-eminently of the life, as the only infallible criterion of what we really are.

— *Roswell Dwight Hitchcock*

Men are not made religious by performing certain actions which are extremely good, but they must first have righteous principles, and then they will not fail to perform virtuous actions. — *Martin Luther*

Religion is nothing else but love of God and man.

Religion is the fear and love of God; its demonstration is good works; and faith is the root of both, for without faith we cannot please God; nor can we fear and love what we do not believe. — *William Penn*

Men will wrangle for religion, write for it, die for it; anything but live for it. — *Charles Colton*

All religions must be tolerated ... for ... every men must get to heaven his own way. — *Frederick the Great*

Religion may be the most immoral thing in the world. It is, when it is a religion which brings comfort without rebuke, when it gives satisfaction without conviction of sin. — *H.E. Luccock*

Religion is inner side of Civilisation. — *H.D. Majar*

To be furious in religion is to be irreligious — *William Penn*

You must make your own religion, and it is only what you make yourself which will be of any use to you. — *Mark Rutherford*

The religious behaviour is learnt as a normal part of the socialization pattern. For effective cross-cultural communication understanding of religious differences are very significant since it is not merely theory or principle but a way of life for many people. Wilson[6] has rightly observed on this core:

> "Religion is much more than a voluntary association of people with a common hobby or pastime. A denomination, sect, or church is also a community of people who intermarry, worship together as a family, choose their friends along religious lines, and socialize their children according to the teachings their faith. Each faith, even each denomination, is a separate, subcommunity as well as a voluntary association. It is a way of life, with social clubs, athletic leagnes, insurance companies, professional societies publishing houses, veterans groups, and even innovating committees."

In Indian society this type broad-based socialization or religion has been prevailing over the centuries; but in certain groups it was taken as individual concern and its rituals were considered to be tods for self-emancipation. But, broadly speaking entire life circle was pervaded with religions web, right from the brooming of courtyard to officering oblations, from birth-ceremony to the last ritual. But here one distinct point of difference must not be ignored that the East has been preferring path of Renunciation to the path of desires. At the face-meaning renunciation sounds negation of life also; but in deep sense it is not so. In Bhagvadgeeta we come across with a very practical viewpoint. Krishna says – "Since it is not possible for embodied beings to renounce all action completely, hence it is said that he who renounces the fruit of action has truly renounced."[7]

**Five Dimensions of Religion**

Stark and Glock (1969) outline five dimensions of religion on which religious groups place different emphasis:

1. *Belief*: a certain theological outlook whose tenets the religions will acknowledge.
2. *Religious practice* : worship and devotion that people follow to carry out their religious commitment.
3. *Experience* : the feelings, perceptions, and sensations that assure some contact with ultimate reality that is a supernatural agency.
4. *Knowledge* : information about the basic tenets of one's faith, scriptures, and traditions.
5. *Consequences* : the effects of religious belief, practice, experience and knowledge on the person's daily life.

In these five dimensions there is a sort of linkage. Impact of these dimensions on the particular religious group will depend upon values, cultural or religious, cherished by the group concerned.

**Religious Pluralism**

In India religious pluralism had its origin right from the Vedic times. In Rigved it is said, "Supreme being is one, learned people call him by different names".[8] Alike religion there are number of forms of worship. This multiplicity of form of worship also is not only in India but in other countries also. Hopkins has rightly observed :

"Man has worshipped everything on earth, including himself, stones, hills, flowers, trees, streams, wells, ocean and animals. He has worshipped everything he could think of beneath the earth, metals, caves, serpents and underworld ghasts. Finally, he has worshipped everything between earth and heaven and everything in the heavens above, mist wind cloud, rainbow, stars, moon, sun, the sky itself, though only in part has he worshipped the spirits of all these objects".[9]

Idealists have been trying to establish the unity and harmony in various forms of worship by promoting the transcendental thinking that all the forms are the same or have the same result. It is only the liking, taste and inclination which make a difference. Just as all rivers fall into the same ocean, similarly, all worships are acceptable to God.[10] But the propounders, supporters and followers of these various forms, due to superiority complexes or allied vested interests, most of them failed to hold the view that other forms are as good as theirs. Right from the inception of the cut they started quarelling and establishing the superiority of the forms to which they were adherent.

Some naturalists like Lucretius, Bertrand Russell etc. hold that religion is like a disease born of fear and as a source of untold misery to the human race. The views of these naturalists quoted by Dr. Radhakrishnan are noteworthy :

> "In the spirit of Lucretius, Bertrand Russell exhorts us to give-up the gorgeous consolation of religion and those dreadful thought of the invisible which had incited men to kill themselves and kill others. According to him, the future religion will consist of two parts : a worship of the ideal conceived merely as the ideal, and a worship of the actual merely as actual or existent. The first involves the goodness, but not the existence, of its object, and the second involves the existence, but not the goodness of its object. We must accept the universe as it is and expect nothing from it. It is more manly to believe in the actual and suffer it than reveal in the absurd".[11]

**Idolatry**

Idolatry is one of the most popular forms of worship, which have been prevailing in India as well as many other countries including the developed ones. We worship idle or various forms taking it a symbol of a God or deity in order to appease the God so that we may be saved from the wrath of God. After close scrutiny of the ways of the worshippers we find that many, who claim to be the professed denouncers of idol-worship indulge in this. Fetish-worship, astrolatry (star-worship), zoolatry (animal-worship including the snake), tree-worship are obviously different forms of idolatry. Similarly, man-worship, tomb-worship also come under the same category.

Various images consecrated in various temples of India and other countries have one or the other historical or mythological ground, which stands elaborated in the holy books of the religious concerned.

**Religions of the Asian Countries**

> "It was in the refined pessimist solution of the world that the soul of Asia was born and found its expression. In India with its metaphysical sense of the divine, the invisible is more real than visible. Realization of the divine is only possible through relaxation of tension and not its intensification.
>
> "The intensification, the complication and centralization of scientific and development processes is one of the ultimate stages in the advancement of man and is a natural prelude to spiritualization before his arrival at the ultimate and self-subsistence pole of consciousness, which would perhaps also be the Buddhist Nirvana or Hindu Brahmin." — *Teilhard de Chardin.*[12]

**Spiritualism**

In the above statement we observe that materialistically. Teilhard, like many of his counterparts, holds that material advancement is a natural prelude to spiritualization, whereas the Eastern, particularly Indian, viewpoint is quite different. Tielhard himself says that "through centuries the East stood for spirit and the West for matter." Historically speaking centuries ago the East, particularly India, had decided, quite emphatically and convincingly, his path, i.e., of spiritualism. Swamy Rangnathan and making these two viewpoints clearly says :

> "Broadly speaking these differences reduce themselves to two viewpoints. One of which holds that matter or outer nature is the focus of all values and the other which affairs man as that focus. The first leads to undue emphasis on the creations, possession and enjoyment of material wealth and the search for organic satisfactions, whereas the second, while putting due emphasis on the above, leads to the pursuit of values and satisfaction lying behind the sensate level of life, and to the experience by man of spiritual freedom and

dignity."[13]

**Transcultural Communication**

For the proper transcultural communication through a balanced mind a sort of synthesise of these two viewpoints seems to be very necessary. There had been a galaxy of thinkers in Asian Countries, who tried to synthesis within themselves the oriental concept and way of life. Such individuals, sages and seers, emperors and kings, teachers, innovators, poets scholars and host of others, who shone like a beacon through out the East and world. There had not been a restriction of caste, creed or colour, as far as the imparting or receiving of true knowledge is concerned. In the Mahabharata we find even Chandal or Butcher exhorting the sage Gautam. Manu says that "a good thought should be obtained even from a child" ("Baladapi Subhashitam Grahyam"). Due to such sublime and universally appealing thinking the Asian Countries could maintain and preserve their repository of knowledge and could influence the Greeks and other Europeans. Will Durant has truly remarked in this context:

> "This subtle infusion of an Asiatic mould into the wearied body of the master Greek was followed rapidly by the pouring of oriental cults and faiths into Greece along those very times of communication which the young those very times of communication which the young conqueror had opened up: the broken dykes let in the ocean of Eastern upon the lowlands of the still adolescent European mind. The mystic and superstitiously faiths which had taken root among the poorer people of Hellas were reinforced and spread about and the Oriental spirit of apathy and resignation found a ready soil in the decadent and despondent Greece."[14]

In fact, when Socrates (399 B.C.) was put to death for truth-speaking, the soul of Athens died with him. With this subtle departure from the truth the Athenians' freedom of thought was destroyed irrevocably. The death of Alexander (322 B.C.) quickened this process of fall of Greek starature. Macedonian Aristotle, a worthy disciple of worthy master (Socrates) and preceptor of Alemander, had to mirror the political subjection of Greece. Here we may recall that the introduction of the stoic philosophy into Athens by the phoenician merchant Zano (About 310 B.C.) was just an example of oriential infiltration. This was the period when Mauryan rulers were ruling in India. Chandragupta Maurya, the founder of Mauryan empire, met Alexander's forces in 327 B.C. after the defeat of porus and the capture of the Punjab, and teamed up with them for the capture of Magatha. This can be termed as first "Indo-European treaty."

Even after the fall of Athens cross-cultural communication, particularly in the areas of art and literature, continued. Sir John Marshall observes," Indian ideas in expression and in execution, the statue of Parkham falls naturally into line with other products of indigenous art and affords a valuable starting point for the study of its evolution. These two works represent the alpha and omega of early Indian art, between which all the sculptures known to us take their place, approximating to the one or the other extreme according as the Indian or Perso-Hellenic spirit prevailed in them". It is different matter that all the scholars do not opine identically as far as foreign origin of Mauryan art is concerned. Many scholars including Dr. Smith do not ascribe foreign origin to the art of Ashoka's period.

**Religious Fibres : Indian Perspectives**

**Multidimension**

The religious traditions of India have been grand, gracious and multi-dimensional. Its polytheism was so grand and pervasive that it made a significant contribution to the evolution of theological thoughts of the western countries including the Greeks, particularly in ancient time. From the dawn of civilization, from vedic period, India has taken a lead in the religious world and proved to be a bed-rock for all major religions of the world. There had been a continuous process of refining religion for the noble cause of humanity, though on this count there had been several disputes, duals and rivalry which can be very well found on scriptural records. The sixth century (B.C.) may be treated as landmark in the history of religions, when two great religions-Buddhism and Jainism–came into existence. These two were heterodox and revolutionary in character, though, in fact, they are considered as off shoots of Hinduism only; but they infused a new religious spirit among the countrymen by removing the barriers of caste and creed and thus democratising the domain of religion. Dr. R.C. Majumdar has rightly observed :

"The old vedic religion had gradually ceased to be a strong living force since the upnishads had initiated freedom of speculation into the fundamental problems of life. Discontent with the existing state of things, brooding over the ills and sorrows of life, a passionate desire to remove them by finding out a new mode of salvation, and an earnest endeavour to discover the ultimate reality became the order of the day. It created a ferment of new ideas and theosophical principles, leading to the establishment of numerous religious sects, such as never occurred in India before or since."[15]

Since these two religions were just off-shoots of Hinduism, though heterodox in character, were assimilated by an Indian culture in a course of time. In the sixth century (A.D.), i.e., approximately after ten centuries, Islam came into existence in Arab. Arab contacts with Indian were pre-Islamic and entirely peaceful before their conquest of Sind and Multan in the eighth century (712 A.D.) Monism of Islam was found to be akin to monism of Vedanta, one of the six systems of Indian philosophy. Due to enterprising nature of Arabs they soon became the dashing force in Indian scenario, as Dr. Abid Hussain writes :

"In the seventh century when Islam infused the Arabs with a new spirit of adventure and enterprise, their foreign trade increased by leaps and bounds and the conquest of Iran gave them monopoly of Indo-Iranian maritime trade. Soon they had their settlements in Sri Lanka and on the coast of Malabar. Since they had come as peaceful traders they were welcomed by Hindu rajas and their subjects, and were given full freedom not only to profess and practise their religion but also to preach and propagate it and they made full use of their freedom. No wonder that their zeal rekindled in the minds of their Hindu neighbours the dormant divine fire caused a stir in their religious life."[16]

Initially, in fact, Arabs came, like the Britishers to Indian as traders. Later on they became invaders and subsequently indulged in active politics of the country. Propogation of Islam was their secondary aim. Qutub-ud-Din Aibak, a slave of Mohammad-bin-Quasim, conquered Delhi in 1193, but could become an independent ruler only after the death of Ibn-Sam. This can be said as the starting point of Muslim rule in India. Prior to the great conquest of Babar (1526) and establishment of Moghul rule in India many dynansties, viz. Khilji Dynasty (1290–1320 A.D.), Tughlaque (1320–1412 A.D.), Syed (1414–1451 A.D.) and Lodhi

(1451–1526 A.D.) ruled over India. During this large span of period Islam saw many ups and downs. Lastly, Babar defeated Ibrahim Lodhi and laid the foundation of Mogul empire, which had gradually great kings like Humayun, Akbar (1556–1605), Jahangir (1605–1627), Shah Jahan (1628–1658). Aurangzab (1658–1706) etc. of these Akbar was very famous for his religious tolerance and his outlook. G. Hocking in ''Living Religion and World Faith" very aptly said that''. . . Akbar quite deliberately experimented with a common syncretic religion in order to reconcile the conflicting ideological positions of Islam, Hinduism and Christinaity".

During Moghul period we find a galaxy of such nationalist Muslims, who were not only inclined to Hinduism but also adopted Hindus lifestyles keeping their own religion intact. Besides Akbar we can quote the names of Dara Shikoh, Amir Khusarau, Abdul Rahim Khankhana, Rashkhan etc. The last two composed poems also on various Hindu themes, whereas Khusarau called himself "a parrot of India" and felt pride in conversing and composing poems in Hindi Language. Similarly, there were many Hindus adopted muslim lifestyles. There are also certain interesting examples of persons following the rituals of muslims but had reservations in taking tea or food with muslims.

## Microcultures of Islam

There are also examples indicating rivalry to the extent of hostility among the micro-cultures of Islam. Aurangzeb, being sunni, hated Shia Musalmans and being a fanatic Muslim, he persecuted the Hindus and Sikhs. The Rajputs, who had served the Moghul Empire for more than a hundred years, rose up in arms to save their religion and their prestige. Aurangzeb revived the Zezia (religious tax levied on Hindus), encouraged the plunder of temples and denied employment to Hindus in military and civil services. The Rajputs retaliated by desecrating the mosques and burning Koran. The Sikhs continued the struggle to death with the Moghals in Punjab, while in Deccan, the Marathas, under the leadership of Shivaji, were determined to overthrow the Moghal yoke.

## Fundamentalism Vs Liberalism

Among fundamentalists there was a group of liberals who believed in brotherhood, a central value of Islam, in real sense. The cult of Sufism symbolizes the liberalism of Islam. During the initial centuries liberalism was a general character of Islam, which continued upto 11th century. till such period Islam was very inquisitive for internalising many good ideals and lores from Greeks, Romans and Indians. But, in 13th Century after occupying the throne in India, its trend of thought was changed and the basic value of universal brotherhood waned from its core. With the passage of time many countries in middle Asia adopted Islam and they moulded its tenets suiting to their convenience. Reactionary forces started playing their role harburing over material prosperity following negative values.

The sufies, though from the Muslim community, were quite liberal and believed in social harmony. "The sufis originated in Muslim community, but they developed a secular faith in God who belonged neither to the Muslims, nor to the Hindus alone, but to the entire humanity. Their visionary doctrines appear to have been flourished in Hindustan in the early ages where they were accepted by Hindu mystics, hermits and monks for the propensity to a similar life of austerity."[17]

**Composite Faith of Akbar**

Akbar, the great, set an example of composite faith in the composite culture of India. Akbar's conciliation of the Hindus and his interest in their Literature and religion made him many enemies among the pious Musalmans or the fundamentalists. Jodha Bai, his favorite queen was a Rajput princess; another of his wives is said to have been a Christian. So the festivals and ceremonies of these faiths were observed in the royal palace with zeal and zest. On every Friday he loved to collect professors of religions around him and listened impartially the arguments of the leaders of various religions. Akbar-namah (Biography of Akbar) records such a conference. He was so deeply engrossed in various faiths that someone call him Parsee, the other jain, somebody Hindu and the other Christian. He got the Bible translated into Persian language and allowed the missionaries to propagate Christianity in his state. He allowed Muslims to be converted in any other faith, if they desired so. In this way we see that he extended all his cooperation to other religions so generously that a few fundamentalists called him kafeer (an idolator).

Akbar promulgated a new state religion "Deen-E-Ilahi" (The Devine faith), based upon natural theology, and comprising the best practices of all known forms of belief. Akbar himself was the prophet of this creed. Every morning he used to worship Sun, which animates the universe. During his life-time he was worshipped by the ignorant multitude. This new faith, unique in character, could not gain popularity and didnot survive after the death of Akbar.

**Brotherhood of Islam**

The ideal of universal brotherhood of Islam was so humanistic and appealing that it attracted the attention of many reformers of the modern age including Swami Vivekanand. As many Hindus became the disciples of muslim saints and fakeers, many muslims also became the followers of Hindu Saints and social reformers. Swami Vivekananda's admirers included some Muslims also. One of them was Mohammed Sarfaraz Hussain of Nainital, an Advaitist at heart. After meeting Swamiji in May, 1898, the latter started calling himself Mohammedanananda. The Swami has great admiration for the Islamic ideal of universal brotherhood, but wanted it to be made applicable to all human beings, not just among the Muslims alone. In a letter written to Mohammedanananda from Almora on 18 June 1898, Vivekanand wrote :

> Whether we call it Vedantism or any ism, the truth is that the last word of religion and thought, and the only position from which one can look upon all religious seats with love. I believe it is the religion of the future enlightened humanity . . . . I am firmly persuaded that without the help of practical Islam, theories of Vedantism, however, fine and wonderful they may be are entirelaps valueless to the vast mass of mankind . . . . . For our motherland a junction of the two great systems. Hinduism and Islam – Vedanta brain and Islam body – is the only hope.[18]

Vivekanand used to quote Prophet Mohammad's message, said to be the last before passing away.

> "And hearken, O mankind ! An Arab has no superiority over a non-Arab and is not superior to an Arab : a white man is not superior to black man nor a black man superior to a white man, except by virtue of his conduct. The noblest in the right of Allah is he who is noblest in conduct".

Hindu scriptures have repeatedly established the superiority of deeds and conduct over the source of birth or lineage. From the history, it is established that many low-born persons rose to the zenith of excellence by the virtue of their noble conduct and sustained efforts. When Karna, being born of low caste, was insulted and humiliated and debarred from participating in the tournament.

Duryodhana very proudly and emphatically spoke :

Noble deeds proclaim the warrier,
And we question not their source !
Teacher Drona priest and warrior
Owns a poor and humble birth.
Krip, noblest of Gautamas,
Springeth from the lowly earth
Known to me thy lineage Bhima,
Thine and thy brothers four
Amorous gods your birth imparted
So they say in days of yore ! [19]

## Golden Mean

As we have already mentioned that common points of contact among the various religions are more than the points of difference. Compassion is the central value of the value-system of Buddhism as brotherhood is for Islam. Both Mahavir and Buddha lord great stress on 'ahinsa' (non-violence), but Mahavira was more doctrinaire and rigid in his theory as well as practice. Gautam Buddha and Mahavira went through the same discipline of self-denial and mortification and realised ultimately that moderate or the middle path was more commendable, as he said :

*The string overstretched breaks,*
*and the music flies;*
*The string overslack is dumb,*
*and music dies;*
*Tune us the sitar*
*neither low nor high.*

It was the wisdom of this golden mean and the wonderful compassion that attracted and still attract millions to the way and love inculcated by him. Due to rigidity in doctrines Jainism could not become as popular as Buddhism.

## Shankar and Buddha

A great master mind and exponent of Hinduism, Shankar appeared on religious scenario of Indian in seventh century. Born in Kerala, brahmin by birth was a propounder of Vedantik school of philosophy. His genius and works, were many-sided. He found his Guru on the banks of the Narmada, in Govindpad, a disciple of the famous gaudpada, who had written a famous Karika on *Mandukya Upnishad*. By the age of 16 his studies were over. Guru sent him to Banaras to expound the pure and simple Hinduism of Vedanta.

He got recognition at Benaras, where his famous commentaries on the Gita, Upnishad and Brahmasutra of Vyas were written and studies by his pupils. It is said that right comprehension is the father of right practice. Similarly, for right communication also right comprehension is necessary. Though in principle he differed from Buddhism, but he had also equally compassionate heart. It was the misery of man caused by his ignorance that moved him, made him wander to all the four corners of India. Man did not know the invaluable mind of bliss in himself but was, in utter ignorance. Due to ignorance he goes on making frantic efforts to clutch at bliss from outside, thinking that wealth, woman, name and fame or a imaginary heaven will give him happiness. Shankar found that he was himself the fountain of bliss and this was an inheritance to be claimed by all.

Striding on the foot-prints of Shankar Swami Vivekanand tried his best to convince man of his rich inheritance in himself. There are certain similarities in the lives of these two great spiritual leaders. Some facts are as under :

1. Both of them were short-lived. Shanker died at the age of 32 and Vivekanand at the age of 42.
2. Shankar spent the last 8 years of his life wandering all over India from Kashmir and Badri in the north to Kerala and Kanchi in the south and from Assam in the east to Dwarka in the West. Vivekananda too spent the last eight years of his life travelling all over America, Europe and India with the same precious message.
3. Preaching of both the leaders were based on Vedanta (Monism). Order of Ramkrishna Mission calls the latter as "Practical Vedanta".
4. Besides formal gurus, i.e., Shankar's Govindpad and Vivekananda's Ramkrishna, they had informal and unique gurus. Once Shankar called on a Chandala to move off his path. The Chandala asked him whom he was calling of to move, the body or the soul ! This opened the eyes of Shankar and he fell at once at the feet of the Chandala as if he was his guru. And composed the famous 'Manisha Panchaka' of 5 verses the gist of which is like this : "he who has learnt to look upon all as Brahman, is really my Guru . . .be he a Chandala or a Brahmin".

Similarly, Vivekananda's eye-opener was a lady dancer giving her performance at the palace of Jodhpur, where Vivekananda was staying as state-guest before his maiden journey to Cicago for participating in the world conference on religion. Soon after the dance started he shut the windows of his room facing to the dancing hall lest he should get disturbed by the glimpses of the postures of on-going dance. After the dance was over the damsel came to the room of Vivekananda and asked him in a rebuking tone : "What type of Samnyasi you are, who gets disturbed with such trifle matter ! How will you accomplish the enlightenment of high order ?" This opened the eye of Vivekananda and he said instantly: "thanks, I take you as my guru". Both of them opposed rituals; but at the same time advocated the supreme importance of ethical values and laid stress on the character-formation.

In fact, like Shankar no other teacher in the world has been so emphatic in discarding rituals and advocating the supreme importance of ethics, a base of spiritualism. At the surface it will seem to be contradictory to note that Shankar also composed various stotras, which evidence his deep sense of devotion. Here we should remember that Shankar calls Jnana Nishtha as the highest form of Bhakti (devotion).[20] For him Jnana Nishtha is not a cold and heartless process, but the extremely concentrated passion for Atman. Thus, Bhakti and jnana Nishtha are one and the same in essence for him.

**Shadows of Advaitism**

According to Shankar "the realisation that there is but on self (in all) is the supreme aim of discipline of Jnana (knowledge).[21] The proposition established by all Upnishads is that final release results from knowledge.[22] Shankar goes so far as to say that this is the only teaching of all Upnishads. Other matters found therein are by the way. Some interesting similar quotes are given as under, which is eloquent of common thread in various religions :

| | | |
|---|---|---|
| Gita | — | There is nothing else besides Me, Arjuna. Like clusters of yarn-beads formed knots on a thread, all this is threaded on Me.[23] |
| Quran | (1) | I am in you, but you see Me not. |
| (Mohammed) | (2) | There is no God other than (the) I. |
| Christ | (1) | I am the Way, the Truth, the Life. |

| | | |
|---|---|---|
| | (2) | I am the light, which lighteth every man who comes to this world. |
| | (3) | Without Me thou can't do nothing |
| Guru Nanak | — | Wherever I amness is there thou art not, when thou art within me, then 'I' am not.[24] |
| St. Paul ! | — | "I live, not I, but the Christ Live in me." |
| St. John's Gospel | — | "I can of mine own self do nothing : as I hear, I judge; and my judgment is just; because I seek not mine own will, but the will of the father which hath sent me." (New Testament) |

Similar idea has been expressed by Thomson, a mystically inclined western Poet :

*The angels keep their ancient places.*
*Turn but a stone and start a wing*
*'Tis ye, 'tis your estranges faces*
*That miss many splendoured Things.*
*Does the fish soar to find the ocean*
*The age plunge to find the air,*
*That we ask of the stars in motion*
*If they have rumour of thee there ?*

Saint poet Kabir calls Brahma the Primal Principle or the Essence. It is beyond to me space, qualities and attributes. According to Kabir Brahma is neither in temple nor in mosque, neither in Kaba nor in Kailas. He is not in any ritual or rite, neither in yoga nor in renunciation. If you are a true seeker, you will find Him in a moment in yourself only. Though Kabir was monotheist but he did not deny the existence of the Hindu deities; but he considered that their worship was not necessary; and thus he can be said as anti-idolatrous in his views.

**Buddhism and Christianity**

Compassion and service–these two are central values of Buddhism and Christianity respectively. Compassion is a feeling and service is an action. When compassion is translated into action it becomes service. Thus, as far as Central value is concerned both the religions are same in essence, whatever their outer forms, i.e, ritual etc. may be. Both of these religions initially arose against the costly rites and rituals, but later on the followers infused various ritual practices into the natural systems of these religions.

If we turn over the pages of history we will find that both these religions arose in favour of the poor, down-trodden and exploited ones paving the path of democratic values in religion. According to Will Durant, "Christianity arose out of two great complexes of historical conditions: first the growth of a helpless and hopeless proletariat, and of industrial and commercial exploitation in Jerusalem, Alexandria, Antioch, Athens and Rome; and second, the contact and mingling of the moral ideas of jews, so well described by Esther, with the philosophical and theological ideas of the Greeks."[25]

Amongst the Chinese religions these three are main-Buddhism, Confucianism and the religion of Lao-tse. All these religious are describe as oriental. Will Durant says : "It would be difficult even to describe them as Oriental, unless you wish to describe Christ and Socrates as orientals. For the religion of Lao-tse is almost the same, in essence with that of Christ; and so called religion of confucius (for it is better described as a philosophy) is strangely like the thought of the Greek."

Contribution of Confucious to the growth of Chinese culture and civilization was tremendous. His preachings were more for intellectual than for a common man. He provided aristocratic moral code – "The Way of Superior Man". For many year his code of conduct was used in giving training to the government officials in China. Buddha did not have any such privilege, nor it was desired one on his part. The central tenet in the teaching of confucious was that being moral has nothing to do with self-interest. Whereever self-interest is involved moral behaviour does not come under the purview of the any moral value. Suppose someone is very punctual in taking meal or doing his routine personal work, such punctuality aiming at self-preservation or safe-guard cannot be called value.

There are many Christ saying which resemble the sayings of Buddha and confucious. Once confucious said:

"What you do not wish others to do unto you, do no unto them."

This very saying is found not only in Christianity and Buddhism, but in Hindu[26] scriptures also. According to Will Durant. "he (Confucious) resembles far more Socrates, Aristotle and Goethe; he identifies morality with intelligence and preaches not humility and gentleness, but the full development of personality.[27]

Confucious, like Lord Buddha believed in ethico-political system which is believed to have existed in the early part of the Chau Dynasty, which is known as the Way (Tao). Tao is a very important word in ancient Chinese literature. Confucious has no where defined what he means by

Tao. According to Raymond Dawson, "It (Tao) is a model of political order which can be best understood by studying the way of the ancients, a model to be studied and followed just as moral training consisted of the study and imitation of model individuals. It meant a society in which all the highest moral and political ideas were followed. To devote oneself to the study of the Way and to attempt to bring it into being for one's own generation was the highest calling of the gentlemen."[28]

Huston Smith has rightly remarked : "No civilisation is monochrome. In china the classical tones of Confucianism have been balanced not only by the spiritual shades of Buddhism but also by romantic hues of Taoism."[29]

### Buddhism and Taoism

As we have mentioned that no authentic reference, except various legends, is found regarding the term 'Tao'. However, after the term 'Tao', Taoism came into being, which is said to be the model of political order, whereas Huston Smith[30] identifies this term (Tao) with a man name LaoTzu, said to have been born about 604 B.C., which has the following shades of meaning : "Old Boy", "the Old Fellow", or "the Grand Old Master". Some scholars doubt whether any such man ever lived. If at all he did we do not have any account but 'mosaic of Legends'. We can say that this legendrical name appears to be Shrouded in Mystery, when we come across with the various philosophical tributes describing uniqueness of Tao. To quote a few:

1. Tao is the way of ultimate reality,
2. It exceeds all thoughts and imagings,
3. Words cannot describe nor define Tao,
4. The two which can be conceived is not the real Tao,
5. Tao is the ground of all Existence,
6. Tao is ultimately transcendent, immanent and the way of universe.[31]

Tao's model for politics was ethico-political, what Buddha also preached, Buddha's follower kings included a galaxy of great rulers; but Ashoka stands as a guiding star for the ethico-political order, which he adopted soon after his agony after the victory of Kalinga, stained with blood-shed and lot of disasters. He became the follower of Buddhism and Buddhist Way in his administration. The following maxims of Tao resemble very much with the contents of rock-edicts of Ashoka the great:

One who would guide a leader of man in the uses of life.
Will warn him against the use of arms for conquest
Even the finest arms area instrument of evil
An Army's harvest is a waste of thorns.

In time of war men civilized in peace
Turn from their higher to their lower nature
But triumph is not beautiful
Is one with a will to kill
The death of a multitude is cause of mourning :
Conduct your triumph as a funeral.[32]

**Crosscultural Communication Through Buddhism**

We have already mentioned that Buddhism did not start as a new and independent religion. It was an offspring of Hinduism. Therefore, Buddha protested against certain practices contrary to humanitarianism, particularly slaughter of cattle, caste-system. Vedic ceremonialism etc., while other fundamentals of metaphysics were inherited from the ancient faith of Hindus. After Kalinga War Ashoka stood as first great patron of Buddhism after having decided to undertake no further military campaigns. Instead he began to think of religious conquests (Dhammavijaya). Comparing the Taoism, Confucianism and Buddhism P.V. Bapat Writes :

"... . Throughout the Han period (65-220A.D.), although a number of scholars had come to china, worked among Chinese and translated a fairly large number of texts into Chinese, Buddhism had a hard struggle with the indigenous religious systems. Confucianism, with its traditional prestige at the court and its hold on the nobility, looked down upon Buddhism as a barbarian religion. In the Han Period attempts were made to transform Confucianism into a religion but its religious character was much less developed than Buddhism. Taoism was more firmly established as a religion but its philosophical background was much weaker than that of Buddhism. This gave Buddhism certain advantages over the indigenous religions."[33]

Thus, Buddhism was a much richer, than Confucianism and it had a profounder philosophy than Taoism and as such the Chinese elites themselves started pleading Buddhism. Mou-tseu of the Han period wrote a treatise, in which he compared the doctrines of Buddhism with Confucianism and Taoism and established the superiority of the former.

With the earnest and enthusiastic patronage of Ashoka Buddhism spread over many other countries including Korea, Japan, Tibet, Siam (Thialand), Indonesia and other countries of South-East Asia. With the passage of time, as it happens with other religions, Buddhism was divided into two branches–Hinayana and Mahayana.

According to Kosambi "Buddhism appeared as the great civilizing influence in Mongolia. It was mainstay of feudalism (though leading to peace between Barons) in China. The whole of both church and state in thinly settled, inaccessible Tibet were based upon the Buddhist canon. It has left us with the most beautiful of cave art from Tun Huan to Ajanta, Superb temples, in Thailand, Burma, Indo-China, the colossal sculptures of the Bamian chief in Afghanistan. Its legends induced parallel stories of Christ walking on water, the Christian saint's tale of Barlaam and Josaphat. The Essenian "Teacher of Righteousness" deduced by scholars from the Qumran (Dead Sea) scrolls bears a title precisely equivalent to that of Buddha (Shasta or dhamma. chakka-pavatakka)- surely not by accident. The doctrines of Manicheism were certainly influenced by it, while the Lukman of the Mohammedans may ultimately be the Buddha. The Barmecide minister whose empty feast in the Arabian Nights made the name into an adjective, apparently came from a family of Buddhist abbots (paramaka) in persia."[34]

### Religions in India

India is such a country where almost all the religions of the world are flourishing such as Hinduism, Islam, Christianity, Sikkhism, Jainism, Buddhism, and Zoroastrianism with their various microreligious trends. As per the census of 1971 the percentage of the followers of various religions existing in India is as under :

| Religion | Percentage of the followers |
|---|---|
| Hindus | 82.72 |
| Musalmans | 11.20 |
| Christian | 2.60 |
| Sikkhs | 1.39 |
| Bauddha | 0.71 |
| Jains | 0.78 |
| Others | 0.40 |

This census (1971) was the last one where the statistics based on religion and caste has been given. Later on, it was realized that in a secular country like India such caste or religion based statistics should not be given since many individuals donot prefer to be labelled as "minority" because the term connotes inferior or lesser status vis-a-vis the majority. Therefore, in the census reports of 1981 and 1991 such statistics were omitted. In Indian society there are various ethnic groups but for the people in general, ethnicity is not so important as they are in United States of America.

## Majority Vs Minority

When various ethnic groups meet in a macroculture various processes start depending upon various socio-political phenomena prevailing at the time. In the process of assimilation macroculture accepts other ethnic identity. Generally it happens so with a few exception. View-points of other cultural groups are accepted, if they are not a threat to social harmony or national unity.

In a culturally plural society of India ethnic diversities are appreciated and they are given proper place in the society provided they do not cause a threat to the national unity and integrity. India did not believe in the featureless unity and as such many of the traditions of microcultural groups are kept alive with all possible efforts.

In a process of suppression it is not fact that it is majority only which can suppress the minority. At times minority may also suppress the majority as it happened in British India, as it is happening in South African countries. For example in America white slave owners, were a numerical minotiy on the large southern plantations, but they hold political and economic control despite the large number of Black or Mexican American citizens. So the case is with the numerical minority of white South African government and society. In various colonies of the Britishers in Asian and African countries this phenomena was in hogue.; Under such circumstances the process of segregation starts and the minority group is debarred from their common human right *i.e.* taking job, house, or a membership of certain club or society.

## Secularism : Indian Context

Whatever the history of secularism may conclude, whatever the politicians may deliberate, whatever the dictum of various dictionaries may sound the domain of Indian secularism is so complex and widespread that neither of these can confine it within its fold. Prof. J.N. Nanda has tried to streamline it. He says : "In India secularism has a wider meaning.

Secularism here means seperation of religion and politics, *i.e.*, political parties must not attract people in the name of particular religion or religious acts. A secular belonging to any political party or religious persuasion shows equal respect to all religions. No religious act obnoxious to others is to be publicly performed where others can take offence. Almost every religion now in India has this secular kernel. Innumerable gods and goddesses in different climes and cultures basically manifest the same reality. The middle path and right path as preached by the Jains, the Buddha and the Vedantists became the universal common thread of all Indian religion."[35]

Indian secularism is a unique one. According to the Western concept, secularism means a tendency or a system of beliefs which rejects all forms of religious faith or worship. It means something the present world or to things which are not spiritual or sacred. But in the Indian context, secularism means comprehensiveness in which all religions receive equal protection, treatment, regard and respect; and in which there is a place for everyone whether he belongs to one religion or another or to no religion. As per the Indian constitution a secular state does not mean that citizens cannot practice their religion. But no religion is given preference over other. Accordingly article Twenty-five of Indian constitution gives a right to freedom of religion to all Indian citizens. All citizens can practice their religion. Religious communities can also set-up charitable institutions of their own. That is why in India there are hundreds of charitable trusts carrying on various socio-religious activities quite freely.

Moreover, there is freedom for the propagation of each religion without hindrance or bar and there is also the freedom to promote and propagate synthesis of religions. At the same time, Indian secularism insists on the promotion of moral, ethical and spiritual values which are common to all religions. Secularism so defined is uniquely Indian. K.N. Pannikkar holds that "The notion of 'Hindu', 'Christian', or Parsi' communities which has come to stay with us, is not the reality neither in the past nor in the present. An alternative notion or community on the basis of secular and material conditions of life will not automatically come into being through objective social transformation, economic development, operation of the market etc. They have to be created through local level and secular activities."[36]

With T.N. Madan we may say that:

> "It has become an intellectually fashionable practice now in Indian to say that the capacity of some sections of the Indian people to

harbour secular and nationalist sentiments and the incapacity of others to rise above a narrow, communal outlook, can be traced to their socio-economic development. Secularisation is thus seen as one aspect of modernization. Nationalism is judged as not merely good and progressive but historically valid, in the sense that it is forward looking, and therefore, true per contra communalism is judged as not mere bad and retrogressive but also as untrue in the sense of false consciousness. Religious conflict is seen as an expression of an immature class-conflict."[37]

**Western Concept of Secularism**

Indian concept of Secularism is totally different from the Western concept. The former encompasses all the religions within its fold with equal concern without making any of the religions prominent or significant. For this purpose, as illustrated earlier, codal provisions have also been enshrined in Indian constitution. Western concept of secularism is anti-religion or anti-church which is the result of series of historical events sounding antagonism against the church of various kings and humanistic scholars. In the medieval period particularly in 15-16th century the rulers of Europe cast their envious looks on the growing power and wealth of the Church. The wealth of the church could not be taxed whereas they were amassing huge wealth in the form of "peter's pence" and "tithe" ( one-tenth of income) from each Christian. Some of the methods the Pope and his agents adopted were highly questionable according to conscientious Christians. In Germany, the sale of indulgences by the Pope's agent, John Tetzel, provoked Martin Luther to revolt in 1517.

All the Lutheran states and towns in Germany joined the protest against the Emperor Charles in 1529, who was safeguarding the prestige of the Catholic Church led by the Pope. A strong reaction to Luther's religious revolution came in the form of bloody religious conflict dividing Germany into Catholic led by Emperor Charles V and protestant led by Protestant ruler of Germany.

The Popes and the Prieists lived in luxury and did not strictly conform to the ethics such as celibacy, chastity and exemplary conduct. There was a general laxity in carrying out the ecclesiastical duties. In their struggle for power and pelf they forgot all about the service to be rendered to God and mankind. They established their own courts to punish those guilty of religious offences. It frequently interfered in state matters. Therefore, such type of interference was obviously to be boycotted and to bring about the desired reforms. Thus the rise of secular outlook was an important feature of the pre-reformation period.

Here we must remember that in England as compared to Germany the antagonism between religion and state entered late. Moreover, Religious persecution in England, though not in Ireland, was on a smaller scale and less ferocious than in continental Europe. The first step in the English Reformation, which was carried through by Parliament, was characteristically, an attack on the fees of Church Courts for the probate of wills. Henry himself began his assertion of the royal supremacy in matters ecclesiasical by a piece of chicanery. He had already confiscated Wolsey's property on the plea that the exercise of authority as papal legate was a breach of a statute of 1393 forbidding any transaction with the court of Rome which were against the interests of nation and mankind at large. E.L. Woodward has rightly observed :

> "The conflict between Church and State, or between Church and society, had begun in Germany before the first phase opened in England. The dispute over ecclesiastical jurisdiction was intolerably sordid. The dispute over Church property was not less sordid; greed or need or both against vested interests. Once the breach with Rome had been made, doctrinal changes were bound to follow. They were accepted by the English people, not easily but with less opposition than might have been anticipated. Such acceptance does not show either cynicism or religious indifference. It would be impossible to explain the intensity of religious feeling in the seventeenth century if religion in the latter half of the sixteenth century had been something irksome or unwanted in English life."[38]

## Wars of Religion in France

If we turn over the pages of European History it will be clear that after every religions war the aim was material prosperity rather than spiritual pursuits. According to H.A.L. Fisher in Europe crusade "was not to bring Christ nearer to man but to found the commercial empire of Venice in Levant"[39]. Wars of Religion in France was not an exception to this phenomena. The struggles between Catholics and Protestants became more prominent in the later half of the sixteenth century which proved to be disastrous to the country. These wars of religion very nearly broke-up the hard-won unity of France, inflicting evils which cannot be measured by battle losses alone. During this period religious fanaticism and resultant violence became the order of the day.

Some murders were committed out of religious fanaticism, others in pursuit of private vengeance, others, as in all times when the hideous taint of espionage infects the body politic, out of senseless terror. The morality of the Huguenot saint was embarked upon a struggle which was largely carried on by the methods of the Irish gunmen. The wise French humanist stood aloof, like Montaigue, whose essays, published during the savage tyranny of the Catholic League, express the gospel of an englightened Epicurean and charitable scepticism.

According to H.A.L. Fisher :

> "the position of France when Henry II died in 1559 was roughly as follows : the Genevan or Huguenot propaganda had made great progress. It had found friends in the army and in the Parliament of Paris, and in many country towns had secured a large following of devout adherents. Several persecutions had not checked the movement. Though the price of heresy was burning at the stake and eighty-eight humbling Protestants had paid that price under Henry II, the new faith continued to make converts. Little French Bibles and psalm-books circulated surreptitiously and were read in the privacy of household gatherings. Teachers, trained in the fortifying school of Geneva, travelled about with their incitements to heroism and endurance. Nor were the French Huguenots kept in ignorance of the fate of their co-religionists in other lands. They learnt how protestant women were buried alive in the Netherlands, how Queen Mary sent Protestant bishops to the stake in England, and how John Knox had raised his Genevan flag among the Scots. The congregations of the faithful were knit together in a confraternity of martyrdom. A body of heretical opinion, still imperfectly organised, but anxious, and inflamed, and strengthened by a sense of solidarity with Protestant communities in other countries, confronted the weak and impecunious government of France."[40]

## Communalism

There are a variety of definitions of 'communalism'. It has been defined through various phrases–'an ideology' 'a false consciousness' of "a struggle for scarce resources". Wilfred Cantwell Smith has defined it as "that ideology which has emphasised as the social political and economic unit the group of adherents of each religion and has emphasised the distinction, even the antagonism, between such groups."[41]

A social phenomenon like communalism or so cannot be defined within set group of words since it is very complex, heterogenous and dynamic one. It differs from place to place, country to country and moreover from time to time. History tells us that the USA, Spain, Russia, many nations of Africa had civil wars. In these cases one of the prominent reasons was discrimination and 'scarce resources'. When minority is discontent with the existing set-up there is always a possibility of communal disturbances. During the last few decades the minority issue has loomed large in Ireland, Somalia, China, Pakistan, Sri Lanka etc. Any authoritative creed obeying a single authority like the Vatican or a Mao leads to opposition, silent and suffering or vociferous and rebellious. Therefore, to ease the tension among various groups democratic ways can go a long way in cementing the communication gaps. Dictatorial attitude entails the possibility of communal conflicts.

Tracing the history of communalism in India, J.N. Nanda remarks :

> "The communal virus was transplanted from Europe into India partly because of the imperial policy and partly because of the misinterpretation of India's multi-religious reality enrichment. The only way to rid ourselves of communalism is by a massive inculcation of secularism and practice of democratic consensus."[42]

If we turn over the page of world history we will observe that the cases of destruction of places of worship are found in many countries including India and Latin America. In Mexico, Guatemala, Costa Rica, the Mayan and Aztec pyramids were the places of worship. The worship was performed at the top of these pyramids. The Spanish conquerors, in most of these places, destroyed the top portion of pyramids and constructed churches for assertion of power. It may also be taken as an appropriation of cultural symbols for the exercise of political superiority. In India during Mughul period, particularly in Aurangzeb's regime many Hindu places of worship were demolished and mosques were erected with this very purpose. The fundamentalists take such incident like demolition of Babri Masjid in Ayodhya (6th December, 1992) as "correcting the mistakes committed in the past". Thus justifying it they do not take it as any wrongful gesture.

Highlighting such acts as parts of the political culture of the medieval times, K.N. Panikkar cites number of instances from the Indian history; According to him:

"In India such destructions were not limited to Hindu temples by the 'muslim' rulers. There are several cases of Hindus destroying Buddhist Viharas. More importantly the instance of Hindu rulers destroying and looting Hindu and jain temples are not wanting. Harshadeva, an eleventh century king of Kashmir, defiled and looted temples in order to replenish his treasury. He even went to the extent of appointing a special officer whose function was to seize the images and wealth of temple. In the twelfth century. Subhatavarman, the Paramara ruler, plundered a large number of jain temples in Gujarat. In medieval times most temples had wealth stored in them and therefore, they were obvious targets of plunder. If the Hindu rulers themselves could not resist the temptation of plundering temples in their won territory, it is not surprising that invaders like Mahmud of Gazni plundered and destroyed temples."[43]

**Minorityism**

The UN Human Rights Commission appointed a special subcommittee for protection of minorities in 1946. This subcommittee, after protracted discussions, adopted the following definition of minorities in its resolution of January, 1950. "The term 'minority' includes only these non-dormant groups in a population which possess and wish to preserve stable ethnic religious or linguistic traditions and characteristics markedly different from those of the rest of the population. Such minorities should properly include a number of persons sufficient by themselves to develop such characteristics and the member of such minorities must be loyal to the State of which they are nationals."

According to this definition, the Ladakhis, nagas and Mizos can be considered ethnic minorities and the followers of Islam and Christianity religious minorities in India. With the formation of linguistic States, there have emerged small linguistic monorities living in the border areas of some States. Such people are generally bilingual. For example, the Kannada-speaking people in the southern part of Maharashtra generally known Marathi as well.

**According to Balraj Madhok**

"There is no Urdu-speaking minority in India because Urdu is not the mothertongue of the people of any region of India. Even in Jammu and Kashmir where Urdu has been given the status of State language, only about 3,000 people declared Urdu as their mothertongue in 1991 according to the purport of the Linguistic Commission of India.

Muslims of foreign origin who constituted less than five per cent of the population of united India were considered to be Urdu-speaking. Most of them migrated to Pakishtan in 1947. They are now the Urdu-speaking "Mohajir" minority in Pakistan.[44]

Indian Muslims have the same mothertongues as other people living in different regions or States of the country. They cannot be considered a linguistic minority in any part of India."

The Constitution of India has given some special rights to religious and linguistic minorities in the matter of running educational institutions denied to the majority of the Indian population. Some segments of Hindu society have been trying to secure a minority status to take advantage of these special rights. Thus a vested interest has been created in minorityism.

The international minorities are in desperate situation. Kurds find themselves in Iran, Iraq. Syria and Tukey. The Ewe people are divided between Ghana, Togo, Burkina Faso and Nigeria. Somalis and Malians are internationally scattered.

Population movements disturb the demographic balance. The Indians have overwhelmed the Polynesians in Fiji Islands. Recently Tripura has been taken over by outsiders. That is why Article 6 of the Draft International Convention on Protection of National or Ethnic Group Minorities says :"the physical character as well as the demographic composition of a territory in which national or ethnic groups or minorities are living must not be changed without legitimate cause and the consent of those concerned".

Liberal ideology has a blind spot for minorities. International law is as impoverished in many ways as the legal theory. Consociational theory, a Dutch inspiration, going back to Althusius, modifies the individualism of the contract and makes it a compact between "cities, provinces and regions".

"It seems that minorities whatever depredation are inflicted on them must attempt to find justice within the boundaries of existing states and be reconciled with them. Self-determination is not a right of minorities. They must look instead of human rights : those which are not the rights of 'people'."

**Religion in America**

Dr. Reinhold Niebuhar calls United States "the most religious and the most secular of Western nations" Norman Birndaum remarks that "the typical American today is in fact, a Calvinist with neither fear of hell nor hope for heaven." These remarks seem to be paradoxical; but at the same time they sound a transitional mood of the American in term of their inclination towards the religion they cherish. Historically speaking the United States is a young nation, but with a rich history and it has been called on to become world leader. There is a uniqueness about American Christendom, about religious life in America.

**Contribution to Christainity**

When the question was posed to an American Theologist (Niebuhr) by a British journalist (Henery Brandon) "What is its contribution to Christianity" ? On this the remarks of Niebuhr are notweorthy :

"The unique element in American religious life comes primarily form the degree of our pluralism we don't have a state church or anything approaching a State Church. We have separation of Church and state, we have multiplicity of Protestant sects that Europe did not have; significantly, have a greater Jewish population.

I also think it is significant that American religious life has been at least organisationally–more vital than European religious life. This has developed through two sources–this is essentially a lay church – and immigrant church, which was torn out of its intimate relation to this culture into a new culture, and therefore, had to provide communities, integral communities, which were as integral as the sectarian community. So, the Late Bishop Bergraf, when he visited the Norwegian churches, said these Norwegian churches are quite different from what we have in Norway because they all run their own affairs and the laymen are very active.

America may be so religious because it is so secular, that is, it is highly technical civilization and its communities are bound together. We are a more urban civilization in those than you are in England, for instance. In England everyone tries to spend at least a weekend in the country, but we are urban people. We have these Urban centres, and they are essentially inhuman. And the religious communities have established communities in which, to use a high sounding phrase, "Men are completely known and all forgiven" — at least "Completely known". and that has view vitality to the religious life of America, which is, may be not ultimately significance in terms of the history of Christianity, the history of Western civilization, but certainly it accounts for the degree of vitality of our religious life."[45]

In America Jewish influence is stronger than in any place. Some fantastic and irrelevant expression, one may call them superfluously and superstitious, prevail in American society as – "If you bow your head and give your life to Christ he will make you a new creature and then you will be colour blind, there won't be a race problem etc. Such expressions can be easily traced in almost all the religious faiths particularly in folk-religion. With the passage of time they also filture sown in urban phenomena. So the case is with some Western civilization and America is not an exception to this trend. But by the virtue of sustained efforts of revivalists and reformers such superfluous faiths are swayed away. In the 19th Century it happened in India. When a galaxy of revivalists including Raja Ram Mohan Roy, Ramkrishan, Vivekanand etc. gave a rational base to Hinduism.

**Assimilation in America**

We have explained in Indian context that there had been a centuries long process of assimilation of microcultures in India through which many races like Non-Aryan, Dravids, Sakas, Huns, Mangols, etc. were assimilated in the melting pot of Indian composite culture. The degree of pluralism in United States had also been almost the same except the chronological anthropological aspect. Therefore, in United States the process of assimilation was a socio-cultural need. In fact, "Assimilation is the process by which microcultures become synonymous with the macroculture. Either cultural patterns that distinguished them from the macroculture have disappeared, or their distinctive cultural pattern have been adopted by the macro-culture so that there is no longer a distinct and separate culture, or them combination of the two has occurred. In the United States the middle-class microculture reflects this process, In fact, the values and traits of this cultural group are often defined as the national culture or macroculture. However, some of the values and traints of the middle-class microculture are not universally accepted by all members of the macroculture."[46]

In United Nations there had been a great revival of religion. According to one of these surveys in the early nineteenth century only 30 per cent of the population was in the church, whereas by the mid-twentieth century the population was above 60 per cent. Earnest Troeltsch, whose thesis was that religion grows in simple attitudes of the countryside and withers in the sophistication of the urban life. But, in United States just opposite has occurred. It has withered in countryside, but flourished more in urban areas due to various socio-religious reasons. Actually, city-life has more frustration, suffering and multiplicity of horrors, terrors and deaths too, wherein pure rational coherences do not work or give people any sort of consolation and thus religion and only religious commandments stand as a rescue. However, Christianity is not to be interpreted as an ultimate moral idea universally. But it has its vitality to impress and attract the non-religious or atheist mind.

## Turkey : Christianity to Islam

The Hittite period was Turkey's earliest known civilisation; long believed to be a purely mythical people they actually had power over much of Anatolia, Asian Turkey, from 2000 to 1200 BC. The stupendous size of the ruins of Hattatusas gauges the power of their culture. Even before that time people are known to have lived in Turkey and traces have been dated right back to 6000 BC.

With the collapse of the Hittites, Turkey broke up into a number of small states and not until the Graeco-Roman period were parts of the country united again. Later Christianity spread through Turkey carried by people such as Paul the Apostle who operated from Tarsus in southern Turkey. In 330 AD the Emperior Constantine transferred the capital of the Roman Empire to Byzantium which he renamed Constantinople, for a thousand years it was the centre of the Byzantine Empire.

The rise of the Moslem Arab states, plus the arrival of the Turkish people from the east, spelt the end for the decrepit Byzantine Empire. Adopting Islam as they moved west, the first great Turkish empire of the Seljuks captured Constantinople in 1452. Within a hundred years the empire spread far into Europe under the leadership of Suleyman the Magnificent.

At the time the Turkish empire was modern and aggressive in comparison with feudal Europe. The Janissaries, the first modern standing army, gave the Turks a military power unknown amongst the European nations who had to raise an army from scratch each time a war started. The Turks treated minority groups, including Christians and Jews, with consideration but their success was based on expansion not industry or agriculture. When their march westward was halted at Vienna in 1683 the delcine soon set in and Turkey became the sick man of Europe. As the nationalist ideal swept through Europe after the French revolution, Turkey found itself with unruly possessions in the Balkans and Greece. Harsh attempts to crush the popular risings with cruelty only hastened the decline. Finally, the unfortunate Truks picked the wrong side in World War I and emerged with the country shrunk back to its present borders.

At this Nadir of Turkish history Mustafa Kemal, the father of modern Turkey, came to the fore. Ataturk, as he chose to be called, had made his name by repelling the Anzacs at Gallipoli. Rallying the army after Turkey's defeat he overthrew the final weak rulers of the Ottoman empire and pushed back the allied forces which were preparing to divide up Turkey. Especially the Greeks. Ataturk then proceeded on a rapid modernisation course, the essence of which was a separation of religion from politics, introduction of the western alphabet and western dress and moving the capital from European Istambul to Asian Ankara.

Naturally such sweeping changes did not come easily, progress has been slow and much of the country is still desperately poor. Hampered by its cold war pawn position and facing periodic confrontation with Greece. Turkey has only achieved limited political stability. Although there has been some back pedaling on his limitations to religion, Ataturk remains the symbol of modern Turkey.

## Hinduism and Zoroastrianism

Hinduism and Zoroastrianism—these two are the offsprings of the Sanatan Dharma of Aryan, which has a twofold development—one in Iran and another in India. In Iran, it received the leadership of Zarathustra, one of the greatest teachers, that come to teach our race. Fortunately his teachings are preserved in the 'Gathas'. His teachings and main tenets of Zoroastrianism are collected in "Zend-Avesta, which is ancient religious book like Rigveda, main deity of this religion is 'Agni' (fire-god). In Rigved, we find various hymns in invocation of Lord 'Agni' alongwith Indra, Varuna, Usha etc.

After the advent of Islam in Iran the followers of Zarthushtra came to the western shore of India, initially they got settled nearby Bombay and Surat. Gradually they got acclamatised in India and now they (more than one Lac) form the part of Indian population. They; are famous for their enterprising nature and sound character, because of common background and philosophy there is a great resemblance in the teachings of Zoroastrianism and Hinduism. Some prominent Preechings are as under :

1. There is only one supreme being, who is the creator of all the universe. He is given the name of Ahuramazda.

2. In the beginning of all manifestation there were two primareval spirits created by Mazda called – The good spirit and the Evil sport – and both of them are essential for the fulfilment of God's Plan. In Sankhya philosophy they are called Purush (spirit) and Prakriti (matter).
3. Zarathustra says, "Listen with your ears the good teaching I bring, think over it with a clear mind and then each man decide for himself the choice between the two paths." Such unassuming and rational piece of advice was given Buddha also.[47]
4. The Law of Karma – Like Buddha Zarthustra also said that a man is the maker of his fortune or misfortune as he is responsible for his good or evil deeds. Man has freedom of choice which entails natural consequence – his full responsibility man forges his own chains and he alone can break them. This "he is his own friend or his own foe".[48]

   Hinduism also invariably declares inevitability of Karmite Laws. Failure after failure may come, but ultimately success is certain. Every soul is promised that for him there is "the resurrection", the life eternal without any bondage. The Christ has very rightly seed : Every Saint has his past and every sinner has his future". Therefore, the greatest sinner on the earth has the hope of liberation (Mukti) as soon as he learns his lesson and makes the right choice. Zarthustra says that the freedom of choice is always with him provided he "thinks it over with clear mind".
5. The path of eternal peace shown by Zarthustra is that of trinity of virtues–knowledge, love and service. For perfection full harmonious growth of all the three is needed, without which there can not be the realization of the true beauty of the triple sat-chit-anand, in human being. These correspond respectively with head, heart and hand, which respectively represent-Jnan, Bhakti and Karma.

Thus we can say that Zaroastrian ideals have been always inspiring its followers to live in the world and realize god through doing their respective duties.

### Shintoism : Japanese Version of Taoism

Taoism is said to have originated with a man named Lao Tzu born about 604 B.C. Lao Tzu is one of the legendry figures of China, as we have very little information about his authentic date and place. In spite of this Taoism has a tremendous impact on Chinese culture. Truly speaking in China "the classical tones of Confucianism have been balanced not only by the spiritual shades of Buddhism but also by romantic hues of Taoism." According to the tradition Confucious, intrigued by what he had heard of Lao Tzu, onced visited him. His description suggests that he was very much baffled by the strange man, yet came away respecting him. He writes :

> "I know that they have wings to fly with, of fins that they have fins to swim with, of wild beasts that they have feet to run with. For feet there are traps, for fins nets, for wings arrows. But who knows how dragons surmount wind and cloud into heaven. This day I have seen Lao. Today I have seen a dragon".[49]

At times it is said that Confucianism is one of three religions of China, the other two being Taoism and Buddhism. In fact, these are three doctrines, from which China has been deriving spiritual and social guidance and inspiration. The Chinese equivalent of 'Confucianism' is 'ju chiao', which means 'the doctrine of the literati'. So Taoism, alike confucianism, was one of the doctrines followed in China and Japan.

Literally 'Tao' means 'path' or 'way'. This tao cannot be perceived as it exceeds the reach of the senses. It exceeds all thoughts and imaginations as well. Hence words cannot describe or define it. It is eneffable and transcendent. Thus, we can say that it is a symbol of supreme being, a cosmic soul. When we say that it is a ground of all existence and it is behind all and beneath all, it resembles with 'Brahman' of Vedantic philosophy. It bears a resemblance to Bergson's 'elan vital' and parallels to some extent the 'Lex creterna' of the classical West. In the practical sence Tao refers to the way man should order his life to gear in wit the way the universe operates. 'Tao Te Ching' (The way and its power) is the basic text of Taoism. The 'Way' can be taken in the following three senses:

1. The one way to approach the basic power of universe if through magic. From this approach to the power of Tao comes popular Taoism, the Taoism of the masses. Any such type of doctrine does not and cannot stand with the test of time and it happened so with this type of approach, as Huston Smith has rightly remarked : "To pass from the lofty heights of the 'Tao Te Ching'

to the priestcraft of popular Taoism is like passing from a crystal mountain spring to the thic, fetid waters of a stagnant canal Mysticism becomes mystification and religion is perverted into Necromancy and sorcery. There have been long epochs in China's history when Taoism in its popular form could be characterised as little more than a funeral racket".[50]

2. *Esoteric Taoism* This second approach to the power of universe is mystical. It was more or less the conveyer doctrine, which "barely survived into the Christain era and left little mark on the Chinese culture as a whole.
3. The third approach to the power of universe is of ethical and social character, which is common in other religious traditions of Asia including Hinduism, Confucianism etc. It is the power that holds society together.[51] According to smith "The natural phenomenon which the Taoists saw as bearing the closest resemblace to Tao itself. was water. They were struck by the way it would support objects and carry them effortlessly on its side. The chinese characters for swimmer deciphered, mean literally "one who knows the nature of water". Similarly, one who knows the nature of the basic life force knows that it will sustain him if he will only stop this thrashing and flailing and trust it to buoy him and carry him gently forward.[52]

> Those who flow as life flows know
> They need no other force :
> They feel no wear, they feel no tear,
> They need no mending, no repair

The Taoist rejected all forms of self-assertiveness and dominance of man and believed in humility, moral Character and creative quitude, which can be created through following the calculated directives of the consciousness. Confucious says "Mannerism and dominating personality have nothing to do with the man-at-his best".[53]

Confucious was not a 'sage' nor a political thinker, he was predominantly a social philosopher to Him man's upright and moral character is the basic for the well-being of the state. Confucious says "Wishing to order well their states, they first regulated their families. Wishing to regulate their families, they first cultivated their persons. Wishing to cultivate their persons, they first rectified their hearts. Wishing to rectify their hearts, they first sought to be sincere in their thoughts".[54]

Sincerity stands as neuculus of all moral and ethical values, which has eloquently influenced the work-culture of China and Japna. This is main virtue behind their unparalleled success. It has been rightly said, "Sincerity is that whereby self-completion is effected, and its way is that by which man must direct himself. Sincerity is the end and beginning of things, without sincerity there could be nothing ....... The possessor of sincerity does not merely accomplish the self-completion of himself. With this quality he complete other man and things also.[55]

Taoism has great influence on Shinooism. The former is Japanese and the later has its roots in China. Shintoism is an official religion of Japan incorporating the worship of ancestors and nature-spirits. It is derived from the Chinese phrase 'Shen Dao' meaning 'way of the gods. It is a Shamanistic system of belief. Shaman is a central feature in any tribal group. According to oxford dictionary shaman is "a witch-doctor or priest claiming to commutate with gods etc. Michio Morishima, taking into consideration the historical background of Shintoism and Taoism elaborate the resembling characteristics of these two religions. In his opinion "China and Japan there is prima facie no significant difference in ideological lay-out. They are primarily Confucianist countries. Buddhism came to Japan not directly from India but always through China, and Shinto which is generally thought of as religion truly indigenous to Japan, was, even in its primitive form, deeply influenced by Chinese Taoism. Indeed, it has been suggested that Shinto might even be nothing other than a Japanese version of Taoism. Japan succeeded in easily assimilating modern capitalism, while China continued to be exploited by imperialists from West and Japan. This paradoxical situation can be resolved only by viewing it in the light of instability theory."[56]

**Religion in Japan**

In the primitive stage the religion in Japan was a simple nature-worship as in India we find the invocational verses in Rig Ved for deities of nature including Varun, Agni, Usha etc. Later on under Chinese influence some concepts of ancestor-worship came into existence. This religion was called shinto, "The way of the gods", as it came to be known in the sixth century to distinguish it from Buddhism, which by that time had reached Japan through China. Though the material culture of early Japan was crude; but its religious and social life were of comparatively high order, for shinto was based on "Appreciation rather than fear". Clyde and Beers have rightly remarked:

> "In this "religion of love and gratitude rather than of fear," man's religious nature expressed itself through simple sentiments of awe in the presence of the wonders of nature. Anything in nature prompting this emotion of wonder was called kami. This word, usually translated into English as "good", actually means "above" and thus "superior." Kami stood for the simple shinto idea of deity, and it is obviously important to remember this when attempting to understand the deification of living emperors in modern Japan and also of Japanese soldiers who died for their country. In this Shinto reverence for nature the Sun Goddess occupied a central position. She was not only the central deity of early Shinto, but she also became the mythological ancestress of the Imperial Japanese House. Purity, the chief virtue among the concepts of this early religion, was expressed in the first instance in physical cleanliness."[57]

Besides Shinto, Confucianism and Buddhism also played very vital role in shaping social and cultural patterns of Japanese life. Buddhism acquired tremendous influence in eighth century. It was one of the Chief instruments through which the young bureaucratic government sought to strengthen its control by appointing the "right" men as Chief abbots of the growing and powerful monasteries. Later on during Heian period (794-1185) Buddhism was adopted and developed by Japan in its own way and thus it became Japanese Buddhism in real sense, different from Indian or Chinese Buddhism. With a significant emergence of great religious leaders in Japan during Hojo Regency (1205-1333) Buddhism caught-up new heights. This was a period of spiritual vigour.

Great religious leaders such as Honen (1132-1212), Shenran (1173-1262), and Nichiren (1222-1282) gave new impetus to the intellectual and spiritual life of the Japanese and contributed a lot to make Buddhism a popular religion in Japan. Hojo regents repelled the Mongol armies and defeated Kublai Khan, who had become Emperor of China in 1263.

## Transreligious Communication

There is an interesting study of two religions. Neoplatonism has many points of contact with Buddhism, especially in enjoining the abstention from sacrifices and animal food.

Buddhism was well known to Clement of Alexandria (A.D. 150-218). He repeatedly refers to the presence of Buddhists in Alexandria, and declares that 'the Greeks stole their philosophy from the barbarians'.

He is the first Greek writer to mention Buddha by name. 'There are', he says, 'some Indians who follow the precepts of Boutta, whom by an excessive reverence they have exalted into a god.' He knows that Buddhists believed in transmigration and 'worship a kind of pyramid (stupa) beneath which they think the bones of some divinity lie buried'. Perhaps these facts throw some light on the curious resemblances between the Gospel story and the life of Buddha as told in late Buddhist works like the Lalita Vistara. Some of those are the Buddha's miraculous conception and birth; the star over his birthplace; the prophecy of the sage Asita, the Buddist Simeon; the temptation by Mara; the twelve disciples with the 'beloved disciple', Ananda; and the miracles, coupled with the Buddha's disapproval of these as proofs of his Buddhahood.

More startling still are the points of similarity between the Buddhist and Christian parables and miracles. Thus in Jataka 190 we read of the pious disciple who walks on the water while he is full of faith in the Buddha, but begins to sink when his ecstasy subsides. On his arrival the Master inquires how he has fared. 'Oh, his arrival the Master inquires how he has fared. 'Oh, Sir, he replies, 'I was so absorbed in thoughts of the Buddha, that I walked over the water of the river as though it had been dry ground !' As Max Muller remarks, mere walking upon the water is not an uncommon story; but walking by faith, and sinking for want of it, can only be accounted for by some historical contact and transference, and the Jatakas are centuries older than the Gospels. In Jataka 78 the Buddha feeds his five hundred brethren with a single cake which has been put into his begging-bowl, and there is so much over that what is left has to be thrown away. In a late Buddhist work, the Saddharma Pundarika, there is a parable which bears a close resemblance to that of the Prodigal Son.

During this period, 'nascent Christianity met full-grown Buddhism in the Academies and markets of Asia and Egypt, while both religions were exposed to the influences of surrounding Paganism in many forms, and of the countless works of art which gave expression to the forms of polytheism. The ancient religion of Persia contributed to the ferment for international communication, and by the incessant clash of rival civilizations.'

It is possible that the rosary, the veneration of relics, and the exaggerated forms of asceticism which were such a striking feature of Alexandrian Christianity, may be traced to Indian sources. When the French missionary travellers, Huc and Gabet, visited Lhassa in 1842, they were deeply shocked at the close resemblance between Catholic and

Llamaistic ritual.

Max Muller traces these to the contact between Tibetan and Nestorian monks in China between A.D. 635 and 841, when both were suppressed. At the famous monastery of Hsian-Fu they actually collaborated. Gnosticism was a deliberate effort to fuse Christian, Platonic, and Oriental ideas at a time when syncretism was particularly fashionable at Alexandria. Gnosticism has been described as 'Orientalism in a Hellenic mask'. The great Gnostic teacher Basilides, a Hellenized Egyptian who was a contemporary of Hadrian (A.D. 117-38), definitely borrowed his philosophy from the wisdom of the East, which he interweaves in an ingenious fashion into the framework of Christianity. Like Buddha, he is a pessimist. 'Pain and fear are inherent in human affairs.' He has a remarkable explanation of the reason why God permits His saints to suffer martyrdom, which is evidently based on the Buddhist doctrine of Karma. 'The theory of Basilides', says Clement, 'is that the soul has previously sinned in another life and endures its punishment here, the elect with the honour of martyrdom, and the rest purified by appropriate punishment.' Basilides was a firm believer in transmigration, and cited texts such as St. John ix. 2 and Romans vii. 9 in support. Basilides' theory of personality has strong Buddhist affinities.

**Inter-Religious Dialogue**

For inter-religious dialogue very open and sincere efforts are required. According to Michael Amaladoss, "Christians in Asia, reflecting on their mission have to take account of other major religions like Hinduism, Buddhism and Islam that are part of the asian scene. This encounter with other religions has been the object of reflection and comment in various meetings of the Asian Bishops, starting with their first meeting in Manila in 1970, in which they resolved :

> We pledge ourselves to an open, sincere, and continuing dialogue with our brothers of other great religions of Asia, that we may learn from one another how to enrich ourselves spiritually and how to work more effectively together on our common task of total human development.[58]

For general orientation to this type of inter-religious dialogue he puts forth his remarks as following :

1. Dialogue takes place, not in the abstract between ideas, beliefs and practices, but between two groups of people, often sharing

the same life situation and facing the same problems — in this case Hindus and Christians.

2. This dialogue between two groups of people, who share a common divine call to build up a new humanity, covers all dimension of life; economic, socio-political, psychological, cultural and religious.
3. Religion, as the ultimate guarantor of a world-view, of values and attitudes, is basic and influences and is influenced by the other dimensions. We can not reflect adequately on inter-religious dialogue without taking into account the other dimensions of human life.
4. Dialogue supposes an open attitude to receive as well as to give, to change as well as to challenge, to set out on a path of co-operation and convergence rather than confrontation to mutual fecundation.
5. All communities are painfully aware of the continuing gap between idea's and life. However, in any serious dialogue both aspects will have to be taken into account.

It is within the framework of these remarks that I would like to continue my reflection, focusing on the various dimensions of life – economic, socio-political, psychological, cultural and religious – successively. Some overlapping is inevitable.

## Revival and Regrowth of Judaism

"People are coming out of woodwork and announcing they are Jewish" says David Lerner, a British educator who helped found a sabbath school in Minsk. He further adds: "Six years age, Jews were still beaten up in Minsk. Now there are three religious congregations, the sabbath school, a youth movement and a voluntary welfare organization." If we go through the annals of history we find that jews were the most sufferers through the ages whereas it has been estimated that one-third of the western civilization bears the marks of its Jewish acestry. The Westerners have been feeling its force while naming their children. Huston Smith has rightly noted; "Michael angle felt it when he chiseled his David and painted the 'Sistine Ceiling' : Dante when he wrote 'Divine Comedy' and milton, 'Paradise Lost the United States Carries the indelible stamp of its Jewish heritage in its collective life : the phrase *by their creator* in the Declaration of Independence, the words "Proclaim Liberty throughout the Land" on the liberty Bell. The real impact of the ancient Jews, however, lies in the extent to which Western civilization took over their angle of vision on the deepest questions life poses."[59]

In the modern times also many Jewish scholars left tremendous impact not only on social sciences but also on the modern science and technology. It will suffice to quote a few of them. Baruch Spinoza, the greatest philosopher of modern times, was Jew. Peenliar Odyssey of the Jews filled the back ground of spinoza's mind, and made him irrevocable, however, ex-communicate, a Jew. He was a brilliant scholar, and the elders looked upon him as future light of their community and their faith, though his father was a successful merchant. Karl Marx, who propounded the theory of communism in the field of social sciences, was a Jew. His theory, till very recent time, was considered as panacea in the socialist world. Due to collapse of USSR, of course, it has now lost its charm. But during the last few decades it enjoyed a tremendous impact on the functionaries of the socialist world. Sigmund Freud, propounder of the theory of Psycho-analysis, was a Jew. The theory of Psychoanalysis made a landmark not only in the history of modern psychology, but left a great impact on the contemporary world literature. The *theory of relativity* was propounded by a great scientist Albert Einstine, who was the greatest Jew of modern times. Thus in the galaxy of modern scholars there had been many Jews, who influnced the modern world by the virtue of their substantial contribution in one area or the other.

The first five books of the bible, the Pentateuch are styled as the *Books of Moses* under the assumption that he wrote them. Ancestors of moses were born in Israel (old name-Cannan) but due to famine they had to migrate to Egypt under the shelter of the king named Pharaoh. At first they had been welcome in their adopted country, had been accepted by the Egyptian King, the Pharaoh, as hard-working and valuable immigrant. But as the years went by and the *Israelites* prepossessed and grew in number, the Egytians grew less enthusiastic. As bible puts it into the mouth of pharaoh, "Behold, the people of the children of Israel are more and mightier than we : come on, let us deal wisely with them; Lest they multiply, and it come to pass, that when there falletch out any war, they join also out enemies and fight against us," With this very fear Esraelites became sore of the eye in egypt and consequently humiliated and tortured. Under such circumstances Moses (name given by the King's daughter) was born and reared. He grew safely to man's estate; but was aware that he was an Israelite.

Years later, with devine guidance but with great difficulties and obstacles Moses could bring back the children of Israel to the promised Land crossing the river Jordan. Lord said; "This is the Land which I swore unto Ibraham, unto Issac and unto Jacob."

Following World War I, Britain was given the Mandate of Palestine, for centuries under Turkish control. The British had promised Zionists that in Palestine would be established a homeland for the scattered Jewry of the world. At the same time Arab population Living there was assured that its rights could be protected. After a number of international meetings and conferences to discuss the question of Palestine, the independent Republic of Israel came into existence in 1948. This, unfortunately, could not take place without a mass displacement of Arabs, and thus was born a feeling of deep hostility between Arab and Jew, which worsened over the years."[60]

In Budapest, Prague, Warsaw, Moscow, Bratislawa, Berlin, in hundreds of towns and villages from the battle to the black sea, Jewish communities are re-emerging and coming together in a kind of continental minyan, synagogues and schools are coming on the foundations of Jewish institutions. Jews once more reviving traditions and cultures long buried in the ashes of Hitler's ovens or under the weight of communist oppression. No doubt, it is an historic change.

When Nazi Germany fell into ruins in the spring of 1945 there were many desperate men anxious to avoid capture by the allies, for they knew the civilized world word would not forgive them for their heinous acts committed during world War II. It is believed by Allied Intelligence that Eichmann and many other ex-Nazis were assisted in their escape from Europe by" a system of underground railways operated by authoritarian members of some of the Roman Catholic monastic orders."[61] The most notorious of them was Adolf Eichmann, the man who was personally responsible under Hitler for the extermination of millions of Jews. According to his own estimate, five million Jews were killed on his direct orders.

In 1946 Eichmann escaped from an American prisioner-of-war camp. He is regarded as the masskiller of Jews. In disguise he lived in Argentine for some years. Ultimately he was located early in 1960. He was brought to trial in Israel on 11 April, 1961 and sentenced to death on 15th December, Although Israel does not normally employ the death sentence. He was hanged on Ist June, 1962. His crime was one of the greatest in the history of mankind. Bormann and Mueller-these two were his counterparts and were also located by Israeli secret service at the instance of David Ben-Gurion, Israeli's then Prime Minister.

The regrowth of Judaism is not unprecedented. The Jews of Persia survived the violence under the regime of Ahasuerus, the Jews of Europe outlasted the Inquisition, and programs failed to wipe out the Jews of

Russian Empire. Yet cruel as generations of persecutions were, all stopped short of the Nazi attempt at genocide. According to one of the estimates there were 8.3 million Jews in Eastern and Central Europe before the rise of Hitler. Some 450,000 fled the Nazis before World War II. More than 5 million died in the Holocaust. After the war a few hundred thousand of the survivors left immediately for Israel, Western Europe or the U.S. ; an additional 265,000 managed to emigrate from the Soviet Union between the mid-'68s and the early' 80s, and still more headed towards West when communism collapsed in 1989.

Auschwitz was by far the worst of the Nazi concentration camps, containing the bones and ashes of the estimated 1.5 million of Hitler's victims who died there-1.1 million Jews, 75,000 Poles and thousands of others including Gypsies, homosexuals and communists, targeted for annihilation by Hitler's minions. Kurt Goldstein, a Berlin member of the international Auschwitz Committee has aptly remarked :

> "The camp is at once the world's largest crematory and most gruesome industrial artifact." It was an experiment in how to kill the most people in the smallest area, in the least time, for the cheapest price ....... ..... It was a killing machine. Persecutions are part of history. But the factory—like systematic extermination of entire peoples, the Jews and Gypsies, is unique.

It was hoped that what happen at Auschwitz in 1944 would give a good lesson to the world community but proved to be an illusion. Let us ask ourselves how little we have learnt from such horrible experience of millions and how much is still to be done for the dignity of mankind and what should be done to open the door of humanism, the religion supreme, being at the threshold of natural or revealed religion. Renewed interest in Judaism should be taken as part of a broad search for spirituality, more particularly dignity of man and humanistic spirit inherently dwelling in him.

**Indian Gods and Deities Abroad**

Referring to the Indian Goddess Maya from whom the Mexican race derived its name, Mr. Poindexter[62] says, "This same 'Mother of Gods" was carried to America and appeared in the Maya theogony of Yucatan under the name – Maya – in this same functions she performed in India". She was characterised in Mexico, by the same emblem of the Lotus as in

India. In Indian vernacular Laxmi is called as Goddess of wealth whereas wealth, in a light philosophical waive, is called 'Maya', because of unstable existence. Almost all the Hindu Gods were known to the ancient inhabitants of South America. Triloknath (Lord of trinity of worlds), was known to the Maxican by the same name, until the Spanish conquerors mistakenly changed the name into Tlogue Nahuaque. Triloknath was acknowledged by the Mexicans as their supreme God and creator.

In this connection the version of Chamanlal is noteworthy. He writes: "In a temple in Gautemala is a statue of an incarnation of Vishnu as Kurma, the tortoise. The sculpture is richly detailed and strongly suggests that it might have been wrought by Hindu hands. At Copan I found no fewer than three images of Hanuman, the monkey-faced and celebrated in the Indian Ramayana epic.

The biggest temple in Mexico housed an image of Siva, and museums throughout South American countries have several figurines of Siva and Ganesha, his elephant-headed son. Surya, the Hindu sun god was the supreme deity of the South and Central American people and his image is frequently found on monuments, particularly in Bolivia and Peru. In the Palenque Temple of the Sun in Mexico Surya occupies the place of honour.

Even Yama, the god of death of Hindu mythology, has found his way to Mexico and Peru, while typically Hindu lotus and chakra motifs adorn the temples."[63] America still preserves Vamana, Siva, Ganesh, Indra in the museums of Central America.

American scholar E.C. Squire wrote nearly a hundred years ago : "a proper examination of these monuments would disclose the fact that in their interior as well in their exterior form and obvious purposes, these building (temples in Palenque, Mexico) correspond with great exactness to those of Hindustan.." Sir Stamford Raffles, the British historian, expressed a similar view when he wrote; "the great temple of Borobudur in Java might readily be mistaken for a Central American temple."

For centuries the whole of Eastern Asia from Burma to Japan was united with India in the closest ties of friendship. There was a living communication of hearts through common religion, philosophy and thought. A famous Japanese scholar once said, "If I were to write the history of Japanese thought it would be the history of Indian thought. This is equally true of our gods and pagodas from the Himalayans to Horyuja." Factually speaking Japan is a treasure-house of Hindu gods and Buddhist deities. Some of the Vedic gods that have almost vanished in India are referred in every corner of Japan, such as – Brahma, Indra,

Shiva, Ganesh, Sarswati, Rudra, Prithivi, Surya, Soma, Kartikeya, Sahasra Bahu, Kuvera and Yama are household names in Japan. Gautam Buddha is the presiding deity in most of the temples but almost everywhere the Indian gods either keep him company at the main alter or sit behind the gallery of gods. Out of all the Hindu gods Siva is the most popular in Japan as in certain parts of North America. Chamanlal has quoted two legends regarding miracles of Lord Shiva prevailing in Japan. He writes:

> "We begin our pilgrimage with the Achala in the temple known as Fudo-do at Koya San, the Kashi (Varanasi) of Japan. Its architectural style is unique and pleasing to the eye. It was built by a priest Gyosho, in the year 1198. Achala is from the chisel of the priest himself. Here Siva is attended by eight young gods carved by Unkei, the master sculptor of early Kamakura period.
>
> Next we visit the famous Namikiri Achala (Siva) enshrined in the Nan-in Temple at Koya. This image was carved by great sage Kobo Kaishi who founded this hill monastery. He carved it in China and brought the image with him. When his boat was caught in a terrible storm out in the China Sea, he prayed to Siva for a safe passage to Japan, Presently the sea calmed down. Therefore, it is called Namikiri – sea-subsiding Achala.
>
> Such a miracle was repeated by Siva when Kublai Khan's Mongolian army threatened to invade the Japanese Island of Kyushu in 1281. This image was carried to the coast, and no sooner did their prayers to Siva for victory commence than the sea began to rage so terribly that Kublai Khan's whole army was destroyed by it. Only three persons survived".[64]

**Equality of Religions**

Kazi Nazrul Islam, a noted poet of Bangladesh, has impressed upon the equality of religions and religious scriptures in his poem "On Equality". According to him man's heart is the universal temple of all the Gods of men. There is no temple or Kaaba greater than the heart of man. The only need is to search the almighty within. Therefore, he says:
"Of Equality I sing :

> *Where all barriers and differences*
> *between man and man have vanished,*
> *where Hindus, Muslims, Buddhists and Christians*
> *have mingled together. Of Equality I sing.*

*What are you – a Parsi, a Jain, a Jew ?*
*Or a Santal, Bhil or Garo ?*
*A confucian or a follower or Charvak the atheist ?*
*Go on, say more.*
*Yet, friends, be whatever you may please,*
*whatever books and manuscripts you may carry*
*in your insides or on your back or shoulders*
*be it the Quran, the Puranas, the Vedas, Vedanta,*
*the Bible, Tripitaka, Zendavesta, Granthsahib-*
*and Whatever you may read of these as you please,*
*yet why this vain labour,*
*this driving of an auger into your brain ?*
*Why this haggling as in a shop ?*
*Fresh flowers are blooming along the way !*
*Within you are all the books, the wisdom of all ages*
*and you need only to open wide your soul*
*to find all the scriptures there."*

## REFERENCES


1. यतोऽभ्युदयनिः श्रेयससिद्धि : स धर्मः – *Maharshi Kanad*
2. नमो धर्माय महते धर्मो धारयते प्रजाः।
   यत् स्याद् धारणायुक्त स धर्म इत्युदाहृतः।।–*Mahabharata*
3. वेदः स्मृतिः सदाचारः स्वस्य च प्रियमात्मनः।
   एतच्चतुर्विधं प्राहुः साक्षाध्यर्मस्य लक्षणम्। Manu II.12
   धृतिः क्षमा दमोऽस्तेयं शौचमिन्द्रियनिग्रहः।
   धीर्विद्या सत्यमक्रोधो दशकं धर्मलक्षणम्।। — *Manu Smriti-VI-92*
4. आहार निद्राभयमैथुनं च समानमेतत् पशुभिर्नराणाम्।
   धर्मो हि तेषामधिको विशेषो धर्मेणहीनाः पशुभिः समानाः।।–*Niti Shataka*
5. परहित सरिस धर्म नहिं भाई।
   परपीड़ा सम नहिं अधमाई।। — *Ramcharitamanasa Compare* –
   अष्टादशपुराणेषु व्यासस्य वचनद्वयम्।
   परोपकारः पुण्याय पापाय परपीडनम्।। — *Maharshi Vyas*
6. Wilson, J., Religion in American Society: *The Effective presence*, p. 278.
7. न हि देहभृतां शक्यं त्यक्तुं कर्माण्यशेषतः।
   यस्तु कर्मफलत्यागी स त्यागीत्यभिधीयते।। — *The Bhagvadgita* XVIII. II
8. एकं सद्विप्राः बहुधा वदन्ति। – Rigved
9. Hopkins, *Origin and Evolution of Religion*. p.13.
10. रुचीनां वैचित्र्याद् नानाऋजुकुटिलपथजुषाम्।
    नृणां गम्यस्त्वमसि पयसामिवार्णवः।। — *Pushpdanto , Shiv Mahimna Stotra*
11. *An Idealistic view of life*, p. 41.

12. Teilhard de Chardin : *Towards the future*, p. 9.
13. Swami Rangnathanand : *Eternal Values for a Changing society*, p. 540
14. Will Durant : *Story of Philosophy*, p. 97.
15. R.C. Majumdar, *Ancient India*, p. 160.
16. Dr. Abid Hussain, *National Culture of India*, p. 70.
17. Dr. Pranab Bandyopadhyay, *Yogis and Mystics*, p.104.
18. R.S. Rambadran : *Vivekanand – Divinity on Earth*, pp. 61-62.
19. Condensed versical translation of the Mahabharta, by R.C. Dutt, p.12.
20. ज्ञाननिष्ठा परा भक्तिरित्युच्यते। – *Comentary on Gita p.* 18-55.
21. ज्ञानस्य हि एषा परा निष्ठा यदात्मैकत्वविज्ञानम्।
22. ज्ञानात् मोक्ष इति च सर्वोपनिषदां सिद्धान्तः। — *Chhandogya* p. 2-23
23. मत्तः परतरं नान्यत्किंचिदस्ति धनंजय।,
    मयि सर्वमिदं प्रोतं सूत्रे मणिगणा इव ।। *Geeta* .3.7.
24. Shloka M.I. Var. of Maru M. 3.
25. Will Durant : *The Pleasures of Philosophy*, p. 361.
26. आत्मनः प्रतिकूलानि परेषां न समाचरेत्। — *Mahabharata*
27. *Pleasures of Philosophy*, p. 353.
28. Confucious, p.78.
29. *Huston Smith* : *The Religious of Man,* p.183.
30. *Ibid*, p.183.
31. *Ibid*; pp.184-85.
32. Quoted in *Religions of Man* pp.197-98
33. *2500 years of Buddhism*, P.V. Bapat's article on' Ashoka and the Expansion of Buddhism, p. 59.
34. Damodar Dharmanand Kosambi : An Indroduction to the study of Indian History, pp.162-63.
35. J.N. Nanda, *Conflicts and Co-existence India*, p. 95.
36. K.N. Panikkar, *Communalism in India*, p. 23.
37. Madan's article titled "The Historical significance of Secularism in India", in the book *Secularisation in Multi-Religious Societies,*" edited by S.C. Dube and V.N. Basilov, p.13.
38. E.L. Woodward, *A History of England,* p. 74.
39. H.A.L. Fisher, *A History of Europe,* p. 249.
40. H.A.L. Fisher, *A History of Europe*, Volume I, p. 573.
41. W.C. Smith, *Islam in India : A. Social analysis*, p. 187.
42. J.N. Nanda, *Conflicts and Co-existence India*, pp. 102-3.
43. Communalism in India, p.13.
44. Letter to the editor, *The Hindustan Times*, 1-11-94.
45. Henry Brandon, As We Are, p.142.
46. Multicultural education in pluralistic society, p.22.
47. Compare – "But, whatsoever, after due examination and analysis, you find to be conducive to the good, the benefit, the welfare of all being – that doctrine believe and cling to and take it as your guide" – Alarkalamsutta, Gautam Buddha
48. Compare आत्मैव आत्मनो बन्धु : आत्मैव रिपुरात्मनः। – Bhagvadgeeta VI.6
49. *Regions of Man*, pp.183-4.
50. *Religions of Maun* p.186.
51. Compare – "धारणाद्धर्म इत्याहुः धर्मो धारयति प्रजाः"।
52. *Religions of Man* p.191.

53. Alfred Doeblin, *The Living Thoughts of Confucious*, p.40
54. *Ibid.*, p.59
55. Confucious and Capitalism, The Currier, December, Michio Morishamia, 1987, p. 36.
56. Clyde and Bears, *The Far East*, p. 39.
57. V.A. Smith, *Oxford History of India*, p.134.
58. Michael Amaladoss, *Faith Culture and Inter-religious Dialogue*. p. 26.
59. Huston Smith, *Religions of Man*, p. 233.
60. Walter C. Langsam & Otis C. Mitchell, *The World Since 1919*, p. 681.
61. Charles Wighton, *Eichman, His Career and Crimes* (Odham, 1961), p. 239.
62. Ambassador Miles Poindexter of the United States spent several years in Peru and made personal investigation from the descendants of the Inca rulers and proved that the founders of the Inca dynasty were four "Ayar" brahmins.
63. Chamanlal, India : *A Cradle Cultures*, pp. 98-99.
64. Chamanlal, *ibid*; pp.100-101.

# 4

# RELIGION AND POLITICS

Personal Ethics Vs State Ethics, Indian Perspective, Present Scenario, Gandhi's Ram Rajya', the concept of 'Ram Rajya uniqueness of polity, secularism and Gandhiji, Muhammad Iqbal : Two Views, Indian Nationalism and Unity of Mankind.

For good or bad cross-cultural communication religion and politics have a very vital role to play. As revealed from the history of various sects and religions and micro-cultures and macro-cultures that it was politics which used faith and religion of the people to accomplish their vested interests, may it be religion-state like Iran or a secular like India. Therefore, in the context of cross cultural communication it is necessary to discuss the coverage and scope of the relationship between religion and politics alongwith its various characteristics in the international perspective.

## Personal Ethics Vs State Ehics

Ethics teaches the whole duty of man. It is the sole mistress of life, whereas politics is concerned with political life of a man which includes political views, activities, associations etc. Ethics may be divided into two sections: (1) Personal Ethics, which deals with the individual and the family;[1] (2) State Ethics, which treats of the state and its institutions. Har Dayal observes that "these two sections of ethics are inseparable and inter-dependent like a pair of scissors. Personal Ethics rises and falls with state Ethics and state Ethics also varies with personal Ethics. Virtuous individuals create and maintain good political and economic institutions; and good institutions produce virtuous citizens. Personal ethics cannot flourish under evil institutions; and noble institutions cannot exist among a corrupt and degraded people". Thus, we can say that personal Ethics and state Ethics rise and fall together. Most of the religions lay stress on personal ethics only. They do not discuss politics;

but there are nations which discuss politics taking very base of their respective religions.

The Greek and Chinese philosophers recognised the fundamental relation between personal Ethics and State Ethics. Greek philosophers maintained that politics and ethics were not separable from each other. The problems of state, politics and citizen etc. were solved on moral basis. If need be, politics was sacrificed for the sake of ethics. State was considered as community of communties or association of associations. Aristotle, in his famous treatise said : "The state is a union of families and villages having for its end perfect and self-sufficient life." Greek philosophers were mainly concerned with 'ideals' rather than with reality'. F. Pollock says: Plato's *The Republic* must be considered as a brilliant exercise in philosophical imagination not as a contribution to political science". For Greek thinker politics was the total study of man, society state, morality etc. It was Machiavelli who separated politics with ethics.

In modern times some "Political scientists" of America are trying to separate politics and political study from values and they are bent upon making it an empirical discipline by founding it merely on facts. They declare "end of ideology" in politics by pleading for a value-free science of politics. Various idealistic philosophers including Plato, Rosusseau, Kant, Hegel, Green, Bosanquet, Bradley have accepted the state as ethical institution, whereas many others like anarchists have regarded it as an unethical institution. Idealists maintain that the function of state are to create conditions for the full and best possible development of human personality or to create the external conditions necessary for the inner development of man.

Amongst the ancient thinkers of India Brahspati declared that "the time-honoured institutions of each country, caste and family should be preserved intact."[2] Speaking of a newly conquered country, Yajnayalkya[3] says: "whatever the custom, laws and usages those should be observed and followed by the king as before. But the custom should not be immoral or opposed to public interests. It must be based on good conduct (Sadachar). Gautam[4] observes that rules of conduct for countries, races and families are authoritative, if they are not opposed to the vedic injections (Shruti).

In Hindu Stripture wherever the word religion is associated with the king or kingdom, it means good conduct and an ideal administration respectively. While elaborating the characteristic of a religious king in Mahabharata it is said: "The king is for the religion (righteous conduct) and not to fulfil his own desire. That is why Lord Indra says to Mandhata:

the king is the protector of the religion. The one who rules over the state righteously, he is considered as divine king and the one who is unrighteous goes to hell. The one who embodies the religion (Ṛighteousness), that only is called king."[5]

Here 'religion' means just welfare of the subject. Through a simile it is rightly explained: "As the pregnant woman keeping aside her likes and dislikes always keep in mind the welfare of the child developing in her womb, so the king should away keep the welfare of his subject in his mind refraining from the arbitrary deeds and performing those only which are meant for the good of his subject."[6]

Due to narrowmindedness of the religious leaders, with the passage of time, they failed to visualise the true meaning and spirit of religion and care for the good of the mankind in a broad perspective. Consequently the clergy gradually lost its credibility. E.A. Wodehouse has aptly observed :

> "Rightly or wrongly, people today have ceased to expect guidance and illumination on secular matters from the clergy. It is felt that the clergyman is, by virtue of his office, and of the dogmas to which he has to subscribe on ordination precluded from the larger and more unprejudiced purview of life which provides the only light in which the world's affairs can profitably be studied."[7]

**Indian Perspective**

In a few quarters it is opined that religion and politics should not be allowed to be mingled with each other since each has its own arena. This sort of idea is generated, perhaps, due to vitiated social atmosphere caused by communal and sectarian forces for their vested interests. But if we turn over the pages of our history we would find that polity had always some sort of religious base, not in the rigid and ritual sense, but in the sense of socio-cultural values. While religion or religions were also patronized by the kings. Ashoka the great, Chandragupta Maurya, Samundragupta, Chandra Gupta and Harsha from the ancient period and Akbar, Dara-Shikoh etc. from the medieval period can be enumerated in the glaxy of secular kings, who repected and patronized the faiths and religions other than their own.

From the Vedic times downwards, the king has been regarded as the patronizer and upholder of the moral order, an integral part of the religion. The Vedic society enjoined that the ideal king was to be 'dhritavrata', dedicated to law and piety. The king may be divine (divinity of Indian king was different from Egyptian or Greek Kings), but the laws are still more. Therefore, the laws must be respected by him. The essence of rulership lies in 'dharma' and the king should realise that there is nothing higher than 'dharma' and always abide by it.[8] The first king Vena had to take the oath that he would scrupulously follow the dharma prescribed in the authoritative works on the subject and never act wilfully.[9] Shukracharya describes the king both as a master and a servant of the people.[10] The Dharmashahstra literature is particularly emphatic in pointing out that it is the king's duty to enforce the 'dharma', as determined by the sacred texts and accepted customs, and not to enunciate it on the authority of himself or any state organization.

Expressing deep concern over the deterioration in the communal situation in the country during the last few years the resolution said, "every one must make efforts to desist from words or deeds that are likely to inflame communal passions or give encouragement to disruptive forces".

* * *

> 'Prime Minister, P.V. Narsimha Rao, announced setting-up of a standing committee to initiate a national debate on secularism'.

* * *

> 'The BJP Leaders criticised other political parties accusing them of trying to politicise the Ayodhya issue for electoral gains.'

The above-quoted excerpts of a newspaper are indicative of the fact that in order to maintain peace and harmony in the society the state, constitutionally committed to secularism, has to control and monitor the affairs pertaining to religious matters. At times, as one of the fanatic writers has said in his autobiography — "intolerance is of the very essence of true faith or faith believed to be true appears to be true, though it is not so. Any individual experience, idea or impression cannot be taken as truth, it cannot be generalised; because the fundamental values like peace, love, non-violence, righteous conduct, truth etc. are found invariably in all the religions of the world. We cannot ignore the historical fact that :

> "The stability of Indian life, for centuries past, has rested on the firm foundation of 'Dharma'. Though the inculcation of the spirit of 'Dharma' high standards of ethics, clear-cut codes of behaviour, and a widespread acceptance of non-material values as of high importance that possessions, have come to be the expression in ordinary society of true Indian culture."

## Present Scenario

But now-a-days scenario stands changed. It is rather politics and not 'Dharma' which is the fountain source responsible for any substantial change. In other words we can say that these days the politicians furnish the philosophy – the entire direction of the nation's life. Our constitution mainly enshrines political and economic values and also the fundamental rights of the citizens. Our national values include various moral, social, cultural, aesthetic and spiritual values. Various religions prevailing in India are good conservators of these national values symbolizing an identity of the nation. These national values are the real indicators of our identity, otherwise politico-economical structures, rights etc. are common to many other democratic countries. India has adopted these things in her constitution from others only. Therefore, in order to manifests her identity through various human values in all its aspects very vital decisions are taken by politicians only. Whatsoever party may be in power, it is our moral obligation that we should design the frame of our political, economical, social and educational policies in conformity with our fundamental national values.

## Gandhi's 'Ram Rajya'

As a staunch believer in the theories enumerated in 'Ramcharitamanas', Mahatma Gandhi reposed faith in a benevolent monarchy, which he called 'Ram Rajya'. The basic concept of 'Ram Rajya' was that of a welfare State. But Gandhiji did not elaborate the concept and left it vague just saying that–it would fulfil the aspirations and yearnings of deprived, disinherited and downtrodden classes of Indian society, it would be superior to any other social system devised by man and known to humanity in historical age, it would excel the democratic system evolved by philosophers and scientists in the West since Magna Charta was forced from King John of England. Thus in the absence of precise connotation of the concept the builders of free India could not derive any concrete guidance. It has given rise to various concepts of the ideal state and created 'a virtual babel'.

## The Concept of Ram Rajya

Tulsi's concept of Ram Rajya was that of a benevolent monarchy. In Uttarkand of Ramcharitmanas, he has given elaborate description of Ram Rajya, salient points of which are as following :

— Nobody dies in young age; nobody suffers from any pain. Everyone's body is beautiful and afflicted by no sickness. No one is poor or miserable; none is dependent or foolish or without good qualities.
— All are without hypocrisy, devoted to duty and virtue. Both men and women are clever and possess good qualities. All admire virtuous men, scholars and enlightened. All are grateful and no one plays frauds.
— In Ram Rajya all sentient and non-sentient beings are above the consequences of Time Action and Nature.
— In Ram Rajya no one commits sins, so there is no need to use rod to punish; the environments are congenial and favourable; therefore, there is no need to divide and rule the people.
— In forests trees grow and blossom; elephants and lion live together and birds and animals, forgetting enemity, live with love.
— Creepers and trees offer coveted honey, cows give desired milk, the earth grows abundant needs of society.

Goswami Tulsidas was a supporter of autocratic, authoritarian and dictatorial rule in which the ruler transcends humanity which exists merely to make him happy. He instructs the people to docitely bow before his firmans, right or wrong. However, certain political values, contained in the above description of Ram Rajya are noteworthy. Justice, health, happiness, brotherhood, doing good to others, concern for countrymen, patriotism – these are central values of Ram Rajya. Tulsi's concept of an ideal citizen was that he should be free, not only from ignorance and ill-will but also from disease and want. That means according to him political freedom and equality is incomplete, without economic freedom. He realized from the core of his heart that no duty is higher than doing good to others – "Parhit Saris dharam nahi bhai". Thus we see that total happiness of the people was the sole aim of Ram Rajya. Our seers too have been aspiring to see all persons in society in a healthy, happy and good condition – "Serve Bhavantu Sukhinah". Merely achieving 'the greatest good of the greatest number' is a western out look, not ours.

**Uniqueness of Polity**

The uniqueness of time-honoured Hindu polity has been the delinking of the political power from the economic power and vice-versa and both of them from the legislative power, that is why our three wings (legislative, executive and judiciary) of the government are having an independent identity and functions. This is said to be an ideal condition, where the deadly combination of any of these two or three (as in communist states) powers getting concentrated in the same hands is eliminated. Thus is our constitution the judiciary under the direction of the supreme court, is independent and free of any influence of the executive and legislature. The fundamental rights of a citizen had been clearly defined and declared inviolable. These rights, among others, include complete freedom of expression and right to form associations, caste – distinctions had been annulled throughout in the provisions of the constitution and untouchability had been abolished and its practice in any form forbidden under articles 15(2) and 16(2).

**Secularism and Mahatma Gandhi**

On the Indian Scenario, Gopal Krishan Gokhale, the moderate leader, whom Gandhiji haled as his 'political mentor' first talked of 'spiritualising politics' but he was not a man of religion, but a secularminded person. But, his commitment to the national cause was praiseworthy. He contended that India's dire need then was of men who could devote all their time and talents to the service of the country. Therefore, he established 'Servant of India Society. B.R. Nanda observes that "this idea of 'spiritualising politics', of evoking abnegation and self-denial for secular causes, which inspired Gokhale to establish the servants of India society, also appealed to Gandhi; he applied it to the various ashrams he set up in South Africa and India. But he went further, and extended the application of this idea to the political field. Satyagrah, his method of resolving conflicts, drew it dynamic from his deeply-held religious and philosophical belief, which were not exclusively Hindu. He acknowledged his debt not only to Gita and the upnished, but to 'the Sermon of the Mount', and the writings of Tolstoy and Thoreau. One can be atheist or agnostic, and still practice *Satyagraha*. But it is easier for a man of religion to accept the assumptions on which Satyagraha rests. That it is worthwhile fighting, and even dying. For causes which transcend one's personal interests, that the body perishes, but the soul lives, that no oppressor can crush the imperishable spirit of man, that every human being, however, wicked he may appear to be, has a hidden nobility, a 'divine spark' which can be 'ignited'.[11]

In fact Gandhi, in modern times, was the first leader who associated spiritual values like truth and non-violence with practical political affairs very graciously and successfully. For him politics devoid of religion is like a noose for the nation, which may stangle and ultimately destroy it. He himself writes "..... my devotion to truth has drawn me into field of politics and I can say without the slightest hesitation and yet in all humility that those who say that religion has nothing to do with politics do not know what religion means". For Gandhi religion is identical with morality and truth is the substance of morality. According to Kriplani "Gandhi's religion and morality were the same. They were identical terms."

His religious basis of politics did not mean injecting religious bigotry or fanaticism in politics. He did not also mean political exploitation of religion. For example, he supported to Khilafat movement in 1920-21 on humanitarian ground rather than bargaining considerations. In fact, he was neither a communalist nor a revivalist. He stood for unity of all human beings and was crucified for the sake of fostering unity and brotherhood between the two major communities of India (Hindus and Muslims). The concept of religion he wanted to be the basis of politics is not to be identified with any credal dogmatic theology; He stood for a religious cleaning of the structure of society subsequently resulting in the elimination of gross superstitions and customs that usurped the true spirit of religion. A true religion was to blind man to God and subsequently man to man as he himself says, "I am endeavouring to see God through service of humanity for I know that God is neither in heaven nor down below but in everyone."

Gandhi's spiritualisation of politics left two prominent problems for the country. Ravindra Kumar writes, ".... yet the success of orthodox pluralism, a success confined to the sphere of political mobilization, left two problems, as a legacy for politics in India after 1947. First, Gandhi's belief that religious cleavages could be healed by using religious loyalties as the basis for nationhood proved to be a miscalculation. With the British Government anxious to exploit every division within society in India, the ideology of orthodox pluralism heightened instead of reducing the gulf between different religious communties. Even in the decades after 1947, therefore, religious and communitarian solidarities continue to plague politics in India, though it is important to remember that such solidarities often provide a mask for the promotion of class interests. Secondly, the device of drawing the rich and powerful into the national struggle, often through policies which more than protected their interests, ensured that these classes would assume a dominating position in politics after independence. Neither of these consequences, we would emphasise, was Gandhi's seeking. Yet their presence in the structure of contemporary politics in India is a fact which cannot be easily denied."[12]

Thus, we can say that like Plato, Cicero and Kant he gave priority to moral values in social and political life. He believed in the piety of the resources while accomplishing the aim, just contrary to Kautilya and Machiavelly, whose prime concern was the interests of the State rather than piety of the resources. The Protagonist of Pakistan rediculed the phrase 'Ram Rajya' which Gandhi occasionally employed to describe the goal of Indian Freedom Struggle. This was Gandhi's equivalent for the English term 'utopia'. The great saint Tulsidas used the term 'Ram Rajya' in the context of monarchial form of government. But what Gandhi meant by this 'saintly idiom' was an ideal polity firmly founded on the noble principles of justice, equality and free from exploitation. That is why he broke laws that were unjust. He believed that it was wrong to tax salt which even the poorest people use. Therefore, after having duly informed the then Viceroy he broke such law through 'Dandi March' (Namak Satyagraha). Very violent events like 'Chauri Chaura' (Feb 1922) Noakhali and others were faced firmly and reconciled by the virtue of his absolute commitment to the eternal values like truth and non-violence.

The moral influence of his personality and his gospel and technique of non-violence cannot be weighed on any material scale, nor its value is confined to any particular creed or country. It is imperishable gift to the entire humanity. Though he was deeply religious in his person; but advocated for a secular state. Louis Fischer[13] noted the strange paradox that "Jinnah, who had grown up as a secular nationalist in his younger days, and who apparently had little interest in religion founded a state based on religion, while Gandhi, wholly religious, worked to establish a secular state. Gandhi said, "He did not believe in state religion even though the whole community had one religion. The state interference would probably always be unwelcome. Religion was purely a personal matter . . . . . " Therefore, he opposed to state-aid, partly or wholly, to religious institution. He was against the inculcation of denominational and sectarian religious teachings in state institution. Therefore, he did not include religion in the curriculum of 'Basic Education' propounded by him in 1937 at Sweagram (Wardha-Maharashtra); as he was afraid that religions as they are taught and practised today may lead to conflict rather than unity.

He wanted religious education to be the exclusive concern of the religions associations as he regarded it as a matter of personal experience and private judgment. He did not like the organised agencies of the state to meddle with religious considerations of the people. Thus, Gandhi's religious-mindedness did not detract a bit from his concept of secularism, be it politics, education or any other social phenomena. Dr. Verma has rightly observed, "this theory of divided allegiance implying the superiority of the obligation to obey God or the inner conscience is a monumental contribution of Gandhi to political philosophy."[14]

## Muhmmad Iqbal : Two Views

Dr. Muhmmad Iqbal (1873-1938) was a notable poet, religious philosopher and a political ideologist. He was a too complex personality to be understood easily. Once he himself said, "Even Iqbal does not know Iqbal". When understanding himself is such a complicated task for a poet, how much more difficult for others. Mohmmad Hasan has rightly said, "Iqbal has often been painted in black and white. To many he is a hero–a poet-philosopher whose poetry and thought remain flawless expressions of the Bergsonian Life force. To other he remains a nodding Homer, whose erratic thinking led to the partition of Indian sub-continent. — Iqbal was much too complex a personality for such simplifications."[15]

Prior to his visit to Europe, the young Iqbal was an ardent nationalist. He adored his country and composed poems of Love and unity. In 1904 he wrote his famous poem "Taranah-i-Hindi", which became almost Indian anthem. In this poem he eulogised India – the land of his dream in these lives :

"The best in the world is our Hindustan
We are her nightingales: She is our rose garden.
The lofty mountain that almost touches the sky,
Is our guard and is our sentry.
Religion does not teach us mutual hatred
All are Indians – our home is Hindustan.[16]

A visit to Europe brought a tremendous change in his views. His earlier assertion, "We are Indians and India is our home" was changed to altogether contrary version. He began to write, "China, Arabia and India are ours", "We are Muslims and the whole world is ours. Thus progressive Iqbal was changed to Iqbal–reactionary. His earlier nationalism vanished. He became an ardent "Khilafatist and Pan-Islamist", In his famous poem "Shikwah aur Jawabe-i-Shikwash" (complaint and answer) he clearly stated : "Nation (quwm) is created and sustained by religion, if religion expired, there will be no nation." To him "Pan-Islamism" meant union of Muslim States.

He condemned patriotism as a 'Subtle form of idolatory', which Islam could not tolerate in any form. Hence he suggested its replacement by

Islam. To him, Islam was no longer just a religion. It was a race-making force and the Muslims had become a race. He left that the slogan of all Indian nationalism, if realized, might lead to perpetual political ascendancy of the Hindus, who were in majority in India. Such a Hindu dominated policy may unpede the cultural and religious development of the Muslim community. He considered Indian National Congress as Bourgeoise association. Further he apprehended that the concept of Nationalism might develop separalist feelings in the Islamic brotherhood.

Iqbal, due to his changed view towards nationalism, was one of the instrumentals for partition of India (1947). Badshah Khan, popularly known as Frientier Gandhi, in his autobiography, has rightly said: "Pakistan was founded on hatred. She was born not of love but of hatred and she grew-up on hatred, on malice, on spite and hostility. Pakistan was created by the grace of the British in order that the Hindus and Muslims might forever be at war and forget that they were brothers."[17]

Iqbal's ethical approach to politics induced him to think of a theocratic state governed by the Laws of the 'Shariat'. He could not reconcile to the ideas of a secular state as according to him "Islam, is only an effort to realize the spiritual in a human organisation." But in the theocratic state of his vision the ruler could not abuse authority and become a dictator.

**Indian Nationalism and Unity of Mankind**

During the renaissance period all eminent Indian national leaders contributed to the growth of nationalism and the struggle for freedom. These leaders were men of thought and action. They gave new concepts to the masses of this land and inspired them in rising to the highest sublime level of patriotic fervour as they had imbibed in themselves noble national values like love for country, freedom, equality, patriotism. They were magnanimous people, and it would be sheer blasphemy to attribute any narrowness of mind or sectarianism to any one of them. Yet, unconsciously and inadvertently they have a start to the Indian nationalist movement which aroused the deepest apprehensions in the minds of the largest minority community in the country, i.e., the Muslims. Their efforts to elevate the Indian nation were closely linked with the upliftment of the Hindu religion and society.

The Arya Samaj, Paradoxically, represents the blending of the progressive and reactionary elements. It was progressive in the sense that it repudiated the authority of the priest and denounced the meaningless dogmas condemned forthrightly the divisive tendencies prevailing in Hindu society. It set in motion and educational movement which was inspired by the urge to kindle national pride and national consciousness. It strove to knit Hindu society into a homogeneous and self-respecting body. It championed the upliftment of the depressed and untouchable classes. All these activities of the Samaj were very commendable for which its founder Swami Dayanand Saraswati got all praise and applauds from all the quarters because all these activities were inspired by the spirit of constructive reform, racial solidarity and nationalism. But, other side of the activities of the Arya Samaj was not progressive; rather it was reactionary. The programme of *Shuddhi* (reclamation and reconversion) was started by the Samaj in order to check the going out of the Hindus to other religious denominations. It was also meant to win non-hindus to the Hindu-fold. Thus, he made Hinduism a full-fledged proselytizing religion. Other organisations like Hindu Mahasabha, RSS etc. sanctioned it. V.D. Savarkar took it as one of the major premises of Hindu Sangathan. The impact of 'Shuddhi' was two-fold: positively, it prevented the Hindus from becoming non-Hindus: negatively, antagonised other proselytizing religion. The Programme of 'Shuddhi' inflicted a wound on Muslim sentiment. To counteract this the Muslim resorted to 'Tabliqh'.

Many contemporary leaders were not in favour of 'Shuddhi' Lala Lajpat Rai says : "The Shuddhi was undoubtedly one of the basic causes which produced the atmosphere leading to riots and other exhibitions of violence."[18] Still it cannot be overruled that the pre-requisites of nationalism, like the unity of race, culture, history, traditions etc. were provided by the Arya Samaj in the earlier phase of the evolution of Indian Nationalism. Dayanand expressed his various socio-biological-religious views in *Satyartha Prakash*, a comprehensive treatise embodying details governing a Hindu's life. His slogan was "Back to Vedas". He also used to say, "Our only object is that mankind may progress and prosper." He believed that political slavery was a national curse. For India his ideal was *Swaraj*. He rightly diagnosed the disease of the body-politic of India and sought to prescribe its remedy. Despite the meritorious services he could not escape certain unavoidable limitations. The diversities of Indian national life demanded an ideology and a programme which could inspire all the communities to sink their differences and rally round a national focus; but his ideas paved the way for the emergence of the ideology of Hindu Nation and Hindu Nationalism.

While paying tribute to Rabindra Nath Tagore, Pt. Jawaharlal Nehru rightly remarked, "Nationals, specially when it urges us to fight for freedom, is noble and life-giving. But, often it becomes a narrow creed, and limits and encompasses its votaries and makes them forget the many sidedness of life. But Rabindra Nath Tagore has given to our nationalism the outlook of inter-nationalism and has enriched it with art and music and the magic of his words, so that it has become the full blooded emblem of India's awakened spirit."[19]

The above remarks on nationalism of a secularist Nehru don't conform with the overall view of the revivalist. The revivalist did not view nationalism as a mere civic, economic or political ideal. Nationalism itself was a religion for them. Civic, economic and political Ideals were just its manifestations. Aurobindo Ghosh would say, Nationalism is a divinely appointed shakti of the eternal and must do its God-given work before it returns to the bossom of universal energy."[20] Similarly, B.C. Pal views nationalism in India as a spiritual urge and Bankim saw in the country the image of 'Jagadhatri', as is obvious from his famous Bengla novel *Anandmath*. By blending religion and nationalism Bankim was pointing to a vital character of Hindus. Therefore, he preached patriotism as the highest religion. In the said novel he represented the country as Goddess Kali, black because of intense misery, naked became the country was no less than a vast burial ground. But, the future India would be like radiant Durga who will annihilate the 'demons' and usher in an era of plenty and prosperity. His sublime song *Bande Mataram* became a national slogan and creed an ideal and an embodiment of the national spirit, that which gave the vision of the mother. In this regard, the third stanza of the song is noteworthy —

> Terrible with the clamorous shouts of seventy million
> Throats, and the sharpness of swords raised in
> twice seventy million hands
> who sayeth to thee, mother, that thou ark weak ?
> Holder of multitudinous strength
> I bow to her who saves to her who drives from her
> armies of her foemen the mother

B.C. Pal and Shri Aurobindo took over bodily the doctrine of nationalism from Bankim. Thus, the forces of nationalism were spiritualised in Bengal. He must not forget that the ultimate aim of Aurbindo's thinking of unity of mankind', as Dr. Karan Singh has rightly observed: ". . . . an important factor in his thought was the conviction that India must be free not for herself alone, but for the benefit of entire mankind. He left that India had a spiritual message which was urgently needed in the world of the twentieth century, in fact she was destined to lead mankind up the next step of spiritual evolution, and one of the reasons why he was so adamant that the political goal should be nothing less than complete independence was his conviction that then alone could India fulfil her true destiny in the broader international community."[21]

In his political writings Shri Aurbindo laid great stress upon this broader aspect of Indian nationalism, At the time when India was firmly and securely under British rule, and the prospect of her becoming free appeared dim the credit goes to his vision that he was able to foresee clearly her destiny as a free nation, and to stress the importance of the contribution that she must make to the world community. Making this point clear in one of his letters he said "our ideal of patriotism proceeds on the basis of love and brotherhood and it looks beyond the unity of the nation and envisages the ultimate unity of mankind."[22]

**REFERENCES**

1. Hints for
self-culture, p.156.
2. II.29-31
compare देशधर्मान् जातिधर्मान् कुलधर्मांश्च शाश्वतम् ।
पाषण्डगणा धर्मांश्च शास्त्रेऽस्मिन् उक्तवान् मनुः ।। — Manu I.118
3. Yajnavalkya Smriti I.342.3.
4. देशजातिकुलधर्मांश्चाम्नायैरविरूद्धाः प्रमाणम् – गौतम स्मृति
5. धर्माय राजा भवति न कामकरणाय तु ।
मान्धातारिति जानीहि राजा लोकस्य रक्षिता ।।२ ।।
राजा चरति चेद्धर्मं देवत्वायैव कल्पते ।
स चेदधर्मं चरति नरकायैव गच्छति ।।३ ।।
यस्मिन् धर्मो विराजते तं राजानं प्रचक्षते ।।४ ।। — Mahabharata, Shanti, Ch. 90.
6. यथा हि गर्भिणी हित्वा स्वं प्रियं मनसोऽनुगम् ।
गर्भस्य हितमाधत्ते तथा राज्ञाप्यसंशयम् ।।४५ ।।
वर्तितव्यं कुरुश्रेष्ठ सदा धर्मानुवर्तिना ।
स्वं प्रियं च परित्यज्य यद्यल्लोकहितं भवेत् ।।४६ ।। *Ibid.*, Ch.56.
7. E.A. Wodehouse, Introduction to "Five Essay" by Dean Inge, p. 9.
8. तदेतत्क्षत्रस्य क्षत्रं यद्धर्मस्तस्माद्धर्मात्परं नास्ति । Br. Up. 1.4.14.
9. यश्चात्र धर्म इत्युक्तो धर्मनीतिव्यपाश्रयः ।
तमशंकः करिष्यामि स्ववशो न कदाचन ।। — Mbh XII 59.116.
10. स्वभागभृत्या दास्यत्वे प्रजानां तु नृपः कृतः ।
ब्रह्मणा स्वामिरूपस्तु पालनार्थं हि सर्वदा ।। — Mbh IV 2.137
11. B.R. Nanda : *Gandhi and His Critics*, p. 73.
12. Ravinder Kumar, "Secularism in a Multi-Religious Society" p.32 in *Seculariztion in Multi-Religious Societies* edited by S.C. Dube and V.N. Basilov.
13. Louis Fischer : *Life of Mahatama Gandhi*, p. 430.

14. V.P. Verma : *Modern Indian Political Thought*, p. 93.
15. Mohammad Hasan, *A New Approach to Iqbal*, preface.
16. Iqbal, *Bang-i-dara*, p. 82.
17. Badshah Khan, *My Life and Struggle*, p. 209-10.
18. Lala Lajpat Rai, *The Arya Samaj*, p. 254.
19. *The Golden Book of Tagore*, p. 183.
20. Aurobindo Ghosh : *Bande Mataram* (weekly) 19th April 1908.
21. Dr. Karan Singh : *Prophet of Indian Nationalism*, p.175.
22. Open Letter to My Countrymen' Written by Shri Aurbindo in 1909.

# 5

# INTERDEPENDENCE
## Socio-Economic Perspectives

### Introduction

Indian Context, Indian Approach, Trusteeship, Panch Sheel, Indonesia and Panch Sheel, China and Militarism, Science and Technology in New Nations, Dominance of America : Historical Perspective, India and Britain, Pollution : Global Phenomena, Population Increase Global Phenomena, Befriending of Earth, Family Welfare Movement, Dunkal Proposal, New China : On Communicative Wave, Inter-Gulf Cooperation, Regional Cooperation in South Africa, France in Global Economic Scenario.

### Indian Context

India is predominantly an agriculturist country, where 70 per cent of the people leave in villages. That is why Lyndon Johnson, the president of United States, is reported to have said once : "To see India, you must visit villages. To understand India you must read Tagore. But to know India you must have a teacher like Indira Gandhi. I was lucky because I had all three."[1] Because of about two centuries exploitation by the Britishers it had an improvised state of economy. Before freedom (1947) millions of people were living below poverty line. Similarly, the condition was that of Hungary before her liberation. Until the middle of the thirties, agricultural labourers in Hungary live like dogs and there were three millions beggars.

Before independence India's mainstay of economy was agriculture only contributing the bulk of GDP, but after independence there had been rapid industrialization in every field in collaboration with developed countries like Russia, United States, Germany, Poland, Holland and others. In the roots of development technology has a great role to play. As far as technology is concerned India has taken all possible help, but at her own terms without any sting to her foreign policy. India had lot of transfer technology from friendly countries like Russia, Hungary, Japan, Holland etc. in various fields-war-planes, ship-building, telecommunication, electrical appliances, hydraulic machinery, detonator production, steel industry, petroleum industry, deep mining fertiliser industry, aluminium production, space-research, automobile industry etc.

But there are certain problems due to strategic restrictions in technology imposed by America and other developed capitalist countries since it has become a part of their politics. These restrictions are directed mainly against the socialist countries. Due to policy of non-alignment India has also to suffer, at times, However, India's stand in this context had been very candid, as observed by Smt. Indira Gandhi :

> "Recently, the Ministers of culture of 42 countries of Africa held a meeting where they said that they did not want industrialization that would ignore cultural development. But, many of these countries are dependent on other countries. It is all right for a smaller country; but India cannot be. We are too big for that. If ever we are in troubling whether it is a natural calamity or a man-made calamity, nobody can help us. Even a friendly person can help us marginally. Therefore, it is essential to be as self-reliant as possible. To some extent, all countries have to be interdependent; but I think that interdependence must be based on independence with each country and that can only be achieved when you are not dependent on other countries for essentials."[2]

**Indian Approach**

To live and earn is one of the fundamental urages in a man whenever and wherever by whatsoever means it is neglected or rather obstructed a sort of dissatisfaction is germinated in an individual and society at large. Here we must also remember the words of Christ : "Man does not live by bread alone." It simply means that food for physical body is not only necessary for a man; but food for his mind and soul is also necessary. Here lies the significance of moral, ethical and cultural values. Any system of Economics devoid of these value cannot survive and succeed for a long. The Gandhian approach to economic thought cannot be divorced from the basic postulate that man, his full development–morally, spiritually and economically—is essential for the growth of human society.

Therefore, we can say that his economic thought has basically two components – Decentralisation and Trusteeship. According to Mahatma

Gandhi "If India's economic policy is determined on these two basic factors, it would bring about the democratic order based on love, compassion, truth and non-violence. "He believed in decentralization, which lead, to even distribution of wealth and makes people tolerant. Better distribution of wealth better purchasing power; through which demand and supply of necessary commodities can be effectively regulated. He maintained that without decentralization of either wealth or power there can be no peace and harmony in the society.

As regards key industries and public enterprises there is no alternative to centralization; but this can be done either co-operatively or by state ownership of such industries. Here it will not be out of place to mention that Gandhiji was not against mechanization as such; but he did not like man to be used as a fodder for the machine. Tradition and modernity both are essential for the effective development of the society and nation at large. He was of the firm contention that technological development as adopted by the Western countries cannot become a role model for India. Everything taking place in the West or USA should not be taken for granted by the people here and considered to be perfectly alright.

## Trusteeship

About Trusteeship his secretary Pyarelal has given the following formula in his book entitled *The Last Phase* :

1. Trusteeship provides a means of transforming the present capitalist order society into an equalitarian one. It gives no quarters to capitalism, but gives the present owning class a chance of reforming itself. It is based on the faith that human nature is never beyond redemption.
2. It does not recognize any right of private ownership of property, except so far as it may be permitted by society for its own welfare.
3. It does not exclude legislative regulation of the ownership and use of wealth.
4. Thus, under State regulated trusteeship, an individual will not be free to hold or use his wealth for selfish satisfaction or in disregard to the interest of the society.
5. Just as it is proposed to fix a decent minimum wage, even so a limit should be fixed for the maximum income that could be

allowed to any person in society. The difference between such minimum and maximum incomes should be reasonable and equitable and variable from time to time, so much so that the tendency would be towards obliteration of the difference.

6. Under the Gandhian economic order, the character of production would be determined by social necessity and not by personal whim or greed.

For implementing this, both governmental apparatus and legal enactments would come into play. He did not contemplate violence nor did he intend that in the transition there would be chaos or anarchy. He wanted an organised, methodical and slow process of change. In 1947, he made it clear in the following words: if the rajas, the zamindars or the capitalists do not become trustees of their own accord, force of circumstances will compel reform, unless they court utter destruction. When panchayat raj is established, public opinion will do what violence can never do. The present power of the zamindars, the capitalists and the rajas can hold away only so long as the common people do not realize their strength. If the people non-cooperate with the evil of zamindari or capitalism, if must die of inanition.

Mr. Maurice strong, Secretary General of the UN Conference on "Environment and Development" held at Rio de Janeiro, who originated the concept of sustainable development once said: "India will be emerging soon as a major economic power, a role for which it was well prepared. Still the change could be a challenge, as Indian would also become the most populous country of the world, whereas its land and resources might not expand. But the issue was whether India was going to follow the Western model of uncontrolled consumption of resources. This model meant that agriculture would have only five per cent of population engaged in it . . . . The battle of making human species sustainable would be fought in Asia, and in Asia, India. Therefore, Indian would have to be careful how to choose its model." In nineties the consensus is being built-up in elite circles that a judicious mix of tradition and modernity must guide India's efforts for development as the pursuit of progress on western model would lead the country towards massive problems of joblessness and food shortages.

At the present phase the process of gradual liberalization is going on with certain improvisation. In spite of recent setback to the ruling congress party the investment are on increase. The foreign investors are quite aware of the eco-political signals and accordingly they are looking for ways to adjust to that process, if eventually it becomes a reality soon. The real issue is now the proper management, which will be feasible through an adequate scope for modifications and remodifications. In fact, 'Middlepath' seems to be keynote of the fresh reform measures.

## China and Militarism

China is not an affluent country like USA, UK or the Russia. Population-wise China tops the list of all the countries of the world. It is a multi-social state with about 50 minorities. About a dozen of them have a population of more than a million each. Non-Chinese races alone add up to more than 6 per cent of the country's population. Of these, there are more than one crore Muslims living mainly in North-West China, North China, South-West China, Tsinghai, Kansu and Sinkiang. Some time in 1963 there was a report regarding Muslim revolt in China, which is indicative of the fact that peking had not yet succeeded in its attempt to impose control over this sizeable minority.

Being a communist country religion is considered as the "Opium of the people", and cadres are instructed to remove this 'Vice' (Religion). As a sequel to this thinking Mao Tse-tung launched his campaign against theocratic authority which he described as "the system of gods and spirits, including the system of neither world ranging from the king of Hell to the city gods and local deities, and that of supernatural beings ranging from the Emperor or Heaven to all kinds of gods and spirits. Elaborating this Chinese Strategy Nadadur Shriniwasan[3] writes :

> "Ever since assumption of power in 1949 the makers of New China are busy experimenting the hold that religion has on the mind of the Chinese. In current official thinking religion is "an old superstructure left over from the old society, and is naturally at logger-heads with new socialist economic base". It can coexist only be serving the cause of party in power. "Democratic reforms of the religious systems" has become a new objective, which has touched Buddhism and Buddhists in China at many vital points. The Buddhists are being told that "participation in patriotic movements and efforts for world-peace are the sole foundation on which Buddhists may expect to become Buddhas".

Until 1950 the Buddhist monasteries of China were deriving. Most of their income from land-holdings which were received as gift from their patrons. But the Land Reform Act of June, 1950 Led to the confiscation of agricultural land belonging to Buddhist temples and monastries. The *wakf* Land also met the same fate. Mullas were deprived of livelihood. An observer reviewing the fate of Muslims wrote: "Islam has suffered an unremitting official hostility in China. Land, Livestock and other property belonging to mosques have disappeared into cooperatives and communes. Muslim religious leaders have been, so far as possible, seenlarised. The faithful have been exhorted, in the interest of production, not to fast during Ramzan, and forbidden to slaughter beasts for feasting after that ordeal; here and there they have been induced or compelled, it seems, to tolerate pig-raising. At school, Muslim Children may not learn Arabic"[4]

Outward propaganda is just contrary to the above statements. It is said that freedom of religious beliefs is a basic, long term policy of the Chinese Communist Party, and the Chinese Government, and it is protected by law. Its population is more than 100 crores, of which the Han nationality makes up approximately 94 per cent. Amongst the ethnic groups the Mongolian, Him, Tibetan, Uygur, Miao, Yi, Zhuang, Bouyei, Corean and Manchu are note-worthy, which have over a million people each.

Regarding rationalism in China Pt. Jawaharlal Nehru, first Prime Minister of India observed :

> "The Chinese have always been the least religious of people, and yet they have followed their system of an ethical and regulated life more strictly than any religious people. They tried to develop a rational society, but as they limited this within the four corners of the ancient classics, progress and necessary changes were prevented and there was stagnation and fossilization. We in India have much to learn from this Chinese rationalism, for we are still in the grip of caste and dogmatic religion and priest–craft and feudal ideas. The great Chinese sage confucious gave a warning to his people which is worthy of remembrance : "Never have anything to do with those who pretend to have to get a foothold in your country, the result would be a dreadful calamity."[5]

After liberation the social system has, particular education, undergone lot of changes. In the pre-liberation days over 80 per cent population was illiterate. After liberation the Government took over all the educational establishments, then made necessary structural changes to some of the universities or their departments, increased the number of science and engineering departments. Thus New China stands as quite changed. As per one of the surveys (1980) China had 2.8 million full-time doctors and medical workers in addition to some 1.57 million locally trained paramedicos and 3.5 million health workers in addition to some 1.57 million locally trained paramedics and 3.5 million health workers and mid-wives working part time. The Xinhua (New China) News Agency was established in January 1937 in Yan'an. At the end of 1948 the first branch outside the country was set-up in Prague. In October, 1949 after the founding of People's Republic of China, Xinhuo became the nation's official news agency. China had its first Radio Station on 5th Sept., 1945 known as Yan'an Xinhua Broad-casting Station. By the year 1980 the number increased to the tune of 105.

In the field of industry, transport, communication, aviation etc. China has taken very progressive strides. But as compared with developed countries China still lags behind particularly in economy, science and technology.

## Militarism

The majority of present day ruler in China have at one time or another served as military commanders. They are firm believers in military destiny of China. Their assumption of political authority has been largely due to successful military operations of Chinese revolutionary army. Mao Tse-tung makes no secret of it when he writes that "without armed struggle there would have been no place for the proletariat, no place for the people, no place for the Communist Party and no victory for the revolution". Thus being conditioned to the ways of war-tactics China made it an article of faith to militarise the people by enrolling immense numbers in the militia. Militia forms a second line of defence, a homeguard and a shadow reserve for the regular army. It also performs other essential functions, such as providing extra sentries, labour and intelligence. In 1959 Mao pronounced that militia should be universally popularised and predicted that militia would grow stronger with the passage of time. The very philosophy of militarism in China becomes very clear from the following version of Mao Tse-tung :

> "Political power grows out of the barrel of a gun . . . . . with guns at our disposal we can rear cadres and create school Culture and mass movements". "Everything", he observed, referring to his party's strength in Yenan, "has been built-up by means of the gun".

Peking authorities believe that peace too can be established by the virtue of barrel of gun. That is why they have been using gun in order to establish peace in their country. Chinese leaders never tire of proclaiming their desire for peace. Very confidently they call highly armed and well-equipped army units "peace brigades". Their warships are called "Peace No. 1", "Peace No. 2" and so on.

**Panch Sheel**

The term 'Panch Sheel (the five principles or rules of conduct) used in the context of India's diplomacy, was common to all religious sects in Ancient India, Brahmanical, Jain or Buddhist. Bauddha Acharyas prescribed the following five rules of conduct as obligatory for one and all baptised in the Buddhist order :

1. *Ahimsa* – Not to destroy any life.
2. *Asteya* – Not to take what was not given to one, *i.e.*, to abstain from stealing and robbery.
3. *Brahmacharya* - to lead a content life-to follow the principles of chastity and continence.
4. *Satya* – Not to tell a lie.
5. *Sadachar* – Not to indulge in any voice like intoxication etc.

India in ancient and modern times in Ceylon, Afganistan. In Iran, in Turkistan, in Central Asia, in Tibet, Mongolia, China, Korea, Japan, Burma, Siam (Thailand) etc. placed these ideals before them. The Panch Sheel thus at the outset was a great ideal and formula of moral re-armament, the oldest and one of the most potent in the world.

The term (Panch Sheela) was first incorporated in the communique on the trade and intercourse between India and China issued in Peking on April 29, 1954. This communique put forward the Principal as follows:

1. Mutual respect for each other's territorial integrity and sovereignty.
2. Mutual non-aggression.
3. Mutual non-interference in each others internal affairs.
4. Equality and mutual benefits.
5. Peaceful co-existence.

Since the signing of the 1954 argument India has signed similar agreements with a good many countries in Asia. It was hoped that promises to respect one another's territory and national inspirations would, in time, strengthen the likelihood of peace. The outbreak of conflicts between Panch Sheel nations especially after the seven point adaptation was affirmed at the 1955 Bandung Conference, was disappointing to India.

**Indonesia and Panch Sheel**

Towards the close of the second world war, during which the Japanese had conquered Indonesia form the Dutch, and, after their final defeat by America, were themselves being driven out, the Indonesian nationalists led by Dr. Sukarno, Dr. Hatta and others, declared their independence, and continued the final phases of the fight to establish themselves as a new independent country. What was formerly, officially known as Nederlandische India or 'the Dutch Indies', comprising most of the Islands of the Indian Archipelago, now rejoiced in the commonly accepted national name of Indonesia. The name, originally confined to the scholars of history and culture who conceived of the islands as a cultural extension of India, means 'India of the Islands', and is a modern creation of European scholarship, combing the two Greek words Indo or India and nesos, 'island', making the new name fall in line with other names like Micronesia, Melanesia and Polynesia. The Indonesian leaders, who value the association of their culture with that of India, eagerly took up this name. In 1945, when Indonesian guerrillas in Java and elsewhere were fighting both the Japanese and the Dutch who sought to come back again with the help of their European allies a committee was set up to find ways and means to establish the freedom they had proclaimed. This committee held some important meetings from May 29 to June 1, 1945, and again from July 10 to July 17. On June 1, 1945, Dr. Sukarno made a very significant speech before a gathering of Indonesian partiots and fighters pledged to win their independence, and in this speech he announced to the world the ideals which the free Republic of Indonesia had placed before itself-a conscious formulation of Indonesian *weltanschauung* or attitude to the world life (the German word was frequently used in this speech).

This great speech was made extempore, and was later officially published, after the principles enunciated in it had been enthusiastically accepted by the representatives of the Indonesian people. Dr. Sukarno began his speech by saying that all civilised nations at a critical stage of their history found it necessary to announce to the world what they stood for. Dr. Sukarno spoke of the Nazi Weltanschauung, proclaimed by Adolf Hitler; of the Japanese attitude which was based on a conception of the divine origin of the Mikado and the inherent superiority of the Japanese people; of the Soviet Russia communist attitude, and of the Sam Min Chu I or the three principles of the state propounded by Sun Yat Sen when he led the Chinese revolution against; Manchu Imperialism, the principles of nationalism, democracy and socialism. So Indonesia should also formulate her Weltanechauung, and on behalf of the nation, they were argued out and announced by Dr. Sukarno as follows:

1. *Faith in one's people* : Nationalism, without which no nation can achieve anything; and which alone can be the basis of national endeavour;
2. *Faith in humanity* : Universal humanity, which must be the basis of all international relations, considering the case of one's own people against the broad background of the universal brotherhood of men;
3. *Faith in freedom* : Freedom that is the basis of true democracy, freedom of mind, body and spirit;
4. *Faith in social justice* : Equal opportunity for all citizens of a democratic society, without any special privileges for anyone; and finally;
5. *Faith in God* : As the people of Indonesia, whether Muslims, or Christians, or Hindus or Buddhists, all believed in the existence of an ultimate Reality behind life.

According to S.K. Chatterji, "The Indonesian words which are used for these five great principles are interesting; three of them are based on Sanskrit, one on Arabic, and one on the native Indonesian speech, indicating the composite character of Indonesian civilisation. The words are: 1. Ka-bengsaan or nationalism : the Sanskrit word vamsa 'family', 'race', modified to bengsa in Indonesian, signifies 'nation' or 'people'; 2. Kemanusia-an or a sense of universal humanity, from Sanskrit Manushya : 'man' ; 3. Kemerdeka-an or freedom, the Indonesian word for freedom. Merdeka, is from Sanskrit mahariddhika which means 'great prosperity; 4. Keadil-an or justice, from Arabic 'adl' : justice; and 5. Ke-Tuhanan or faith in God, from than : 'Lord, Master, God, the native Indonesian word for the Divinity."

In the course of this speech of his, Dr. Sukarno said that five was a mystic number, and many things in both the physical, intellectual and spiritual domains went by fives. Thus, we have five fingers in the hand: there are the five elements in the physical world; Islam as a religion had its five pillars in ablutions, prayers, fasting, misgiving, and pilgrimage to Mecca; and as a member present in the meeting Dr. Sukarno, the

Pandava heroes of the Snaskrit epic, the Mahabharata who are honoured even now in Indonesia, were also five.

Dr, Sukarno said that he was anxious to give a single comprehensive name to these five principles. At first he thought of the Sanskrit expression pancha-dharma (in Indonesian, pantja-dharma), but dharma means both right conduct and duty as well as something more–the basis of all things. So at the suggestion of a friend, he selected the old expression panch-sila (Pantja-sila), sila meaning 'a guiding principle of conduct'.

It was in this way that just over ten years ago, the panch-sila of Indonesia was established both as an ideal and a way of life for an entire nation, and it was confined so are to that nation only, with full sympathetic appreciation from all right-thinking people. It was certainly a most remarkable contribution to modern political ideologies for a nation and this Indonesian pantja-sila shows President Sukarno in almost favourable light as an idealist and a contractive thought leader, not only for his own people but also for the whole of humanity. Incidentally, we Indians are happy to find that Dr. Sukarno has always had the greatest admiration for three of the noblest sons of India who also directed the thoughts of large masses of people throughout the entire civilised world : Swami Vivekananda, Rabindranath Tagore and Mahatma Gandhi.

**Science and Technology in New Nations**

Here the term "new nations" includes those states or countries who got the freedom approximately during the second half of the present century. For example the Republic of Congo (Brazzaville) was born on 15th August, 1960, another Republic of Congo (Leopoldville) got independence on 1st July 1960, exactly six weeks prior to the former. Nigeria (Eastern and Western), Nepal, Iran, Israel, Brazil and many others may be called new nations, that come under the second line of the developing countries; because of their different problems and priorities. The difference between the two is quite simple. The developing countries have by now, accomplished their basic necessities and now struggling for comforts and luxuries, whereas the new nations are still struggling for bare necessities. Chief Odebiyi of Western Nigeria once solemnly said that "there can be no peace when there is not enough food to eat, not enough clothing, nor enough shelter for everybody."

"Science will bring this land both peace and a renewal of its youth, creating here the springs of a new spiritual and material life" – these are Weizmann's words, emblazoned on a rock wall of Revovoth (Israel). Dr. Chain Weizmann was himself the chemist, who became Israel's first

President. Very aptly the institute, founded in 1934 has been named after his name. Advancement of science and technology in these new nations is a crying need for new path of progress. Fundamental research in science has been mainly responsible for the progress of mankind. It is a key to the economic future of all the countires of the world. All the discoveries in science have been made by scientists of developed states as they have the privilege of financing, fundamental research, whereas the new states have no research workers or scientists of their own. In this direction the developed countries must cooperate with the underdeveloped new countries. It is a very healthy sign that through various agencies, private and public, developed and developing countries are helping new nations in the field of scientific research and development as warranted by their mutual political relations and equations.

Every change in modern history has been preceded by an intellectual climate, French revolution (1879), Russian revolution (1917), independence of United States and of Latin America are the burning examples of the fact. Hence it is necessary to create intellectual environment in these new nations. For this purpose it is essential to depolitize the higher centres of learning. They should be free from ideological or political pressure. The idea of "free universities" should not lead of total privatisation of centres for higher learning, lest there is a fear of its identification with one or the other ethnic or religious group. In Latin America, "Private" means "belonging to the catholic Church". The universities must be given due autonomy in its functions and internal problems. After the revolution against the peron regime, Argentina has set a good example of "free universities".

High priority must be given to those disciplines responsible for the finding and development of natural resources. This is one of the vital task before the new countries, if they want to develop other branches of science and technology. In order to deliberate on various aspects of advances of science and technology in these new nations an International conference was convened by the Weizmann Institute of Science in Rehovoth, Israel, from August 15 to 25, 1960.

The conference was attended by ministers, high government officials, and leaders of educational and development institutions from many countries, including those recently established as sovereign states, as well as by leading scientists, scholars, and economists from all parts of the world. Specialised international agencies were also represented. The conference directed its attention to two processes which have deeply affected the life of this generation-the swift progress of science and technology and the change in the structure of the international community through the emergence of new states, mainly in Asia and Africa. The participants in the Conference expressed general agreement on the following points :

1. The new states have achieved political equality with other established states. But no such equality yet exists in economic and social progress. Most of the new states suffer from depressed living standards, low life-expectancy, slowness of development in agriculture and industry, and inadequate use of natural resources. The scientific thought and technical skills which could correct this situation are not yet being applied to the new states. Thus, the modern scientific movement is constantly increasing the strength and wealth of advanced countries. While having little corresponding effect in the less developed territories.
2. It is urgently necessary to reduce this disparity, both on human grounds and in order to further the welfare of peoples and states and create a more harmonious atmosphere of international relations.
3. The natural and social scientists participating in the Conference were agreed that science and technology are capable of bringing about swift improvements in the conditions of new states, through improved agricultural methods, water development, the prevention of disease and the promotion of health, improved nutritional techniques, the discovery and evaluation of resources, the adjustment of resources and population, and the stimulation of industrialization.
4. It was further agreed that in many areas of research and application, such as the utilization of nuclear and solar energy and the increased availability of fresh water by artificial processes, developments in he next decade may well have a positive effect on the economic conditions of developing states.
5. The representatives of new states revealed a strong desire to expand scientific education in their countries, to utilize the best scientific methods relevant to their development programs, and to maintain close contact with scientific though and action in scientifically advanced countries.
6. The following lines of thought and action were recommended at the Conference with a view to bringing science and technology

to bear more positively upon the problems of developing countries.

(a) The governments of developing states should regard the furtherance of science and technology as a major objective of their national politics and make appropriate provision for funds and opportunities to achieve this end.
(b) In the secondary and higher educational systems of new and developing states, accelerated programs should be undertaken with a view to establishing a body of scientific workers and technical experts.
(c) An early step in the activities of new states should be the undertaking of a thorough survey of natural and human resources as the basis for a development plan with a clear indication of priorities.
(d) Until such time as their own scientific manpower is adequate, new and developing states would be well advised to seek the help of scientific advisers and experts from friendly countries and international agencies to help them develop a scientific practice and tradition.
(e) Representatives of African states at the Conference pointed out the advantages of a regional approach. There may be cases in which projects of technical assistance and technical education can be applied with advantage by more than one state.
(f) States which have made advanced scientific progress should, as a matter of policy, be willing to expend scientific aid and advice to states less scientifically advanced.
(g) Scientific institutions and research workers in scientifically advanced countries should increase their preoccupation with those fields of research and application which are relevant to the problems of new and developing states.
(h) International agencies, governments, and foundations should carry out expanding programs of financial aid for developing states, with due emphasis on the transmission and diffusion of technical knowledge, the training of technicians, and the increase of technical and scientific equipments.
(i) The conference recognised that technical assistance will be provided by a growing number of international national, and private agencies. The development and coordination

of a technical assistance program from all these courses to support national development plans is a responsibility of the recipient governments. The Conference recommends that there be a study of the methods used by various agencies in providing assistance and by recipient countries in coordinating and utilizing assistance and that the results be used to increase the effectiveness of the program.

(j) It was generally agreed that the kind of contact developed at this Conference between the governments of developing states and leaders in various scientific and technological disciplines should be intensified and broadened to include the mutual elaboration of specific plans in furtherance of the objectives herein outlined.

7. To carry out the purposes and plans outlined under the preceding paragraph, the Conference decided to set up a Permanent Committee which will maintain contact with the participants into he Rehovoth Conference and with other governments and institutions supporting its general aims. The Permanent Committee will serve as a clearing-house and forwarding agency for requests and suggestions from developing states and from scientific workers and will try to promote fruitful contacts.

The permanent Committee will consider the convening of a second Conference at a suitable time, after consultation with governments, scientist, and international agencies, in order to review the progress made on the matters proposed under Section 6 of this declaration.

**Dominance of America : Historical Perspective**

United States of America, though a young nation, is at present leading the world particularly in the field of industries which include automobile, aerospace industries, telecommunication, chemicals, electronics and various kinds of other consumer goods. The economic system of any nation is the mechanism which brings together natural resources, the labour supply, technology, and the necessary entrepreneurial and managerial talents. Anticipating and subsequently meeting needs of the people of the land through production and distribution of goods and services is the ultimate aim of any economic system. As the saying goes "Flag follows the Trade", may not be true in all the cases and in all the ages, because in the modern world the type of economic system used by a nation is the result of political decision. For example, in nineties India introduced the policy of liberalisation in her financial strategy – it's obviously the result of her political decision. Such political decisions are the outcome of a historical experience. Any system or policy overlooking the history and cultural tradition of the land may not bear the desired fruit. A historical experience through social-system is modified and remodified and refined, that becomes a national culture.

*Society*

The USA consists of people of different languages, races and religions. In 1980 its population was about 23 crores. The people of United States mainly speak English and Christianity is the faith of bulk of people. There are 5.5 million Jews. Important religious organisations are – Protestant bodies, Roman Catholic Church, Old Catholic, Polish National Catholic, Armeman and Buddhists. The constitution of USA protects the freedom of each citizen to choose his or her faith and worship according to one's conscience. The first amendment of the constitution provides that the "Congress shall make no Law respecting and establishment of religion, or prohibiting the free exercise thereof". Educationally it is the most advanced country in the world and had been able to win the Noble Prize for number of times. Women enjoy perfect liberty and equality in American Society. Their number is more than the manfolk, they are 52 per cent as against 48 per cent men. They have every right to choose the directions in which they want to prosper. The progress made by the women is evident from the figures that from 1916 to 1976. 100 ladies have been elected in the congress, 5 have been elected as Governors and 6 have worked as ministers in the Cabinet of the President.

There are two major political parties – Republican and Democratic party. All other minor parties combined together could never gain more than two and a half per cent votes in the Presidential election. Though America has bi-party system; but their organisation, economic and political policies hardly differ. Both the parties support capitalism. It is said that if England is an example of rigid party system, America on the other hand follows loose party system. A member of a political party without resigning can vote for another political party. There is nothing like party discipline in America. It does not and should not mean that the political parties do not play any important role in the American political system. Ogg and Ray have rightly observed : "Today both the leading parties are notoriously conglomerate and disunited. Even so, they are not properly to be written off as merely two bottles carefully labelled but empty, as James Bryee asserted of the parties of forty years ago. By and large they still stand for some distinctive thing in traditions, attitudes, principles and policies. Cutting through all state of society, penetrating all geographical sections, enlisting in some degree all economic interests, they, however, must increasingly be all things to all men in order to hold, or hope to gain powers."

Richard N. Nixon, Ex-President of USA says: "As for as my economic policy is concerned, it has always been what I would call a conservative philosophy, conservative on fiscal matters, that, generally speaking, private enterprise can do more effective job than government enterprise in any particular field, although I recognise that there are some areas where private enterprise can't or won't do the job and where government enterprise must step in.

The philosophy of the democrats that the best what to assure social and economic progress was through increasing the Government participation in total economic effort and decreasing proportionately the private participation, I termed as 'radical'[6]

Nixon was Republican and had occupied the office of Vice-President also for number of years. During his regime there was a feeling among too a many Americans that Republican party works only in the interest of big business groups and against the interest of the wage-earners, whereas Democratic party is the party of the people.

Friedrich Baerwald has rightly observed :

> "A disregard of historically conditioned current situations has proved to be constantly in early experiment of development aid and planning. Mathematical model building has brought considerable sophistication to the methods of programming economic development. To a certain extent data of historical relevance can also be put into computerized systems. But altimately decisions dealing with economic development are not made in a laboratory setting. They are made by leaders who will not hand over the ultimate responsibility to specialized experts. Every concrete development process is therefore, based on interaction between technicians and leadership groups."[7]

If we go through the history of foreign policy of America we will see that the historical perspective has been there as under-current in the process of decision making. That is why with the exceptions of Vietnam War and recent Iraque War America's foreign policy for over forty-five years, as measured by the objectives she set for herself, was mostly a string of successes. By the early 1970 – America had passed the zenith of her power. It was not that she was becoming weaker absolutely, but rather that others were becoming stronger in relation to her and were thereby narrowing the gap between their power and hers. By 1972 the Soviet Union had effectively closed the gap between her strategic nuclear forces and those of United States. In this context Rober J. Art observes that.

> "In signing the strategic Arms Limitation Accords of 1972 America publicly accepted this fact and gave to the Russians something that had become central to their foreign policy objectives-official recognition by America of their co-equality in nuclear armaments. Although not yet possessing conventional forces as transportable and flexible as those of the United States, the Soviet Union was rapidly developing the sea and air transport capabilities that would enable her to act, not merely as a regional, but also as a global conventional power."[8]

Further, explaining the reasons for the decline of American predominance he says that it was America's very dominance that caused her influence to decline. He elaborates the reasons : First was the generosity that America exhibited towards Western Europe and Japan, Prostrate after World War II, these two were rebuilt through American aid, both direct and indirect. With respect to Western Europe, the United States not only poured in over 12 billion dollars in grant aid from 1948 through 1952, but also encouraged and aided the development of the European Economic Community that eventually became the world's largest free trade zone by population size. The EEC now rivals the United States for the world's trade. Through American benevolence Japan was given an access to sell in the American market such that by the early 1970s the United States took over one-third of Japans total annual exports, exports being the basis for Japan's postwar economic resurgence. For some twenty odd years, American businessman never had the same degree of access to sell and invest in the Japanese market that Japanese businessmen had in the American market. Moreover, both Western Europe and Japan were rebuilt and aided their economic flowering by America's bearing the major military burdens of protecting them. The fact that the United States derived significant economic and other benefits from these actions towards Europe and Japan is important to remember, but it does not alter the central point : the net effect of America's actions was to help fashion her words into her foremost competitors in the world's markets.[9]

Other congnizable factors responsible for the decline of American predominance were–here commitment to arms control, here entanglement in Vietnam and the recent conflict (28th August 1992) with Iraq and so on. As soon as Iraq, sent its troops into Kuwait, Mr. Bush, President of America, made-up his mind to go to war. His declared objective was to liberate Kuwait, but at the same time he aimed at the destruction of Iraq's capacity to strike at Israel and the over-throw of Mr. Saddam Hussain, President of Iraq.

In July, 1992 US. Britain and France prepared to resume air raids against Iraq of UN weapons inspectors were not granted access to all the sites they specified. In August, three Western coalition partners promoted the creation of a 'no-fly-zone' in Southern Iraq, in order to prevent Iraqi military aircraft attacking Iran-backed Shia rebels holed up in the marshes alongwith the Iran-Iraq border.

**India and Britain**

Britain is a parliamentary democracy with a constitutional democracy but not alike India. In Britain constitutional head is Queen Elizabeth II as head of the State, who acts on the advice of her ministers, whereas in India President is the constitutional head. Britain Parliament comprises the house of commons, the House of Lords and the Queen in her constitutional role. Indian Parliament consists of Lok Sabha and Rajya Sabha, headed by the speaker and Vice-President respectively. In Britain Crown holds the supreme command over the armed establishment, as in India President is the Commander-in-chief of all the three wings of defence establishments – Army, Navy and Airforce. Alike the President of India, in Britain, the Crown is also the fountain of honour. It bestows titles, honours and decorations. People realise and appreciates Crown's unifying, dignifying and establishing influence. In fact the institution of monarchy is something with which all Britons have grown up, it is a part of their heritage and culture.

On the basis of social status the people of England can be divided into Upper class, Medium class and Lower class. The prominent communities are the Jews, the West Indies, the Indians, the Australians, the Chinese etc. The British people have adopted either the Roman Catholic or the Protestant religion. The church of England is the official church. The British are basically conservative people, but they have adopted and incorporated socialist and democratic values in their habits and life-styles. Social status of women folk in Britain is far better as compared to women of Indian subcontinent. As in Britain, India is also following the fiscal policy of mixed economy. In both the countries the private and public enterprises are growing side by side.

Though England is a developed country, the problem of unemployment is faced by the government. India, being a developing country, facing problem of unemployment and poverty in larger extent. In the field of science and technology Britain is one of the most advanced country. As many as 70 British citizens have won the Noble prizes for science, a greater number for any other country apart from the United States. It is spending about 2.2 per cent of GDP on scientific research and development. It has the largest energy resources in the European Community. It is the world's eight largest oil producer, and fifth largest trading nation in the world. It's clothing industry is one of the largest in Europe. It is the Western World's largest producer of agricultural tractors.

London is major international centre for theatre, opera and dance. There are many important National Theatre Stages classical and modern plays. The Royal Shakespeare Company performs both at Stratford-upon-Avon, Shakespear's birthplace, and in London. The Royal Opera, Covent Garden, and the English National Opera– are the main London Opera Companies. Scotland, Wales and Northern Ireland have their own. British pop musicians and groups — some of them most popular being George Michael, Phil Collins, Wet and the Pet Shop Boys—have worldwide appeal and have set new trends. There are about 2,500 museums and art galleries, which include the major national museums, with world-famous artistic, archaeological, scientific and historical collection.

In India and Britain there are many similarities of national character, which have been cementing Indo-British relations. India is one of the prominent members of "Commonwealth of Nations". The term "Commonwealth of Nations" is of recent coinage, succeeding "British Commonwealth of Nations" as well as the still older "British Empire", Gradually "Commonwealth" has come to be used as most of the formerly imperial dependencies that have become self-governing member nations. Consequently the word 'British' was dropped as the prefatory adjective for a group of nations mostly Asian and African. One of the British ambition behind the theme seems to possess an imperical power through domination of huge Asian and African portions of the world. But with the rapid change in the global phenomena and liberation of most of the dependences including the recent South Africa, the ambition apparently got a set-back.

Moreover, the Commonwealth of Nations did not like to indulge in groups and adopted the policy of non-alignment as far as their political linkages were concerned, as it was necessitated on their part to be neutral in this regard and focus on socio-economic developments. Leon D. Epstein has aptly observed on this point : It has not been possible, however, for the commonwealth to present a united front on many of the most important international issues of concern to Britain. Not only have the African and Asian member nations been at odds with any seeming assertion by Britain of an imperialist role, as at Suez in 1956, but the established Afro-Asian position in cold war has been neutralist, under Indian leadership, and thus distinct from Britains alignment with United States. Broadly speaking, the new commonwealth nations have defined their global interests differently from Britains – no doubt because those interests are in fact different in many basic respects."[10]

Inspite of a few differences Indo-British relations have been cordial. These differences helped them to understand each other and explore the area of mutual interests. With John Grigg, we can say :

> "Indian and Britain have an historical link to which neither too much nor too little significant should be attached. But, above all, they have a similar traditions of tolerance, an approach to life which is more intuitive than strictly rational, and a respect for custom which is some times, in both countries, carried to excessive length. In India, as in Britain, the reformer has to contend with a stupefying power of inertia, which is the price that has to be paid for the blessing of stability."[11]

**Pollution : Global Phenomena**

Smog, a combination of smoke and fog, has become a dangerous problem in many parts of the world and more particularly in our part of the world. It reduces visibility and frequently irritates the eyes and the lungs. In extreme cases it has been resulted in death.

Scientists warn that you can't have both a big city and good clean air. And that, as a penalty for the desire of being big, we must accept the smog. The rulers as well as the ruled are still oblivious of the havoc being played by vehicle-emission.

Experts are of the opinion that the main reason for the increase in asthmatics and respiratory ailments is the presence of air-borne particles, smoke and sulphur dioxide and other lethal gasses, such as, carbon monoxide, hydro carbon, interzone oxide, deadly lead emission and tones of suspended particles in the air-borne dust and smoke because of exhaust fumes of vehicles which are increasing at an alarming rate.

They further state that the inhabitants share the responsibility with two climate in producing smog. Much of it comes from driving automobiles, buses and trucks, heating of houses and burning of trash.

Each person, by doing these things contributes a little to the over-all conditions. So also, each one of us is partly to blame for much that is wrong in our country. Often we complain about what is wrong but few of us do anything to make it right. Is it not better to light a candle than to curse the darkness.

The fields of government, such as education, labour relations and communications vitally affect us, no matter who we are and what we do. By improving these fields we can strengthen our country. In this context it is noteworthy that *I must do some thing* has solved more problems than merely saying that *something must be done*.

In relation to the enterprises and the Industry as a whole worker's participation in management will necessarily involve in the trade union adopting a positive role in relation to problems of production and actively intervening on issues such as :

1. Combating corruption and acts of sabotage including pilfering, arson and communal riots fostered by reactionary forces. Elimination of waste and improvisation of efficiency.
2. Effective and economic use of raw materials.
3. Concretely countering the monopolists' plans to infiltrate and undermine and weaken the specific role which the public sector has to play in an industry.
4. Democratic and correct pricing policies to combat pro-monopoly bias.
5. Full utilisation of installed capacity which necessarily means diversification of production as well as more state control over the monopolies in order to bring them within the orbit of centralised planning.
6. Establishment of machinery to co-ordinate effectively policies and the working of public sector enterprises which are closely linked with each other such as coal, steel and railways.
7. Radical changes in lending and credit policies of public sector financial institutions like nationalised banks, LIC etc.
8. Evolving a system for training suitable cadre for manning the public sector efficiently.[12]

## Befriending of Earth

The year 1972 can be called as a pointer to the environmental awareness at global level, when United Nations Conference on environment was held at Stockholm in Sweden. Subsequently, there were various small but significant movements, to quote a few :

1. *Chipko Movement*–which was started at the village Dashuli in UP under the leaders of Sunderlal Bahuguna, a noted environmentalist.
2. *Save Forest, Save Man Movement*
3. *Ganga Mukti Movement*
4. *Green Peace Protest in Europe*
5. *Brazilian Environment Movement*–Environmental activists in Brazil are working in unity to save rain forests.
6. *Save Tiger Movement*–To maintain the equilibrium in the environment this movement has been started in India.
7. *National Parks of India*–In spite of certain inherent managerial shortcoming India has a credit of maintaining in all 45 National Parks and 211 sanctuaries which occupy the area of 20 lacs hectors, 3 per cent of the total surface land of the country.
8. *Green Belt Movement in Kenia*–It is conducted by women under the able leadership of a women activist. Wangari Maathai, under this movement the women set-up plant nurseries in their villages and then persuade farmers to accept and raise the trees and they do not charge for it. Over ten million trees have been planted in Kenya's fast vanishing forest land.

But the gathering momentum was given support and global focus at the 1992 Earth Summit in Rio-de-Jenero in Brazil, and 'Agenda-21' was setout as a blueprint for action for the 21st century. In fact security no longer means only military or physical security. It increasingly includes social and economic security and a safe and healthy environment, security of human development through education, adequate nutrition, health care, clothing and shelter and the security of employment. In short it comprises everything that guarantees human dignity which implies human rights also. On 10th December, 1948 fifty-one nations including India adopted the Universal Declaration of Human Rights for assuring the dignity of human beings.

However, there are very serious ecological warning given by the experts. According to one of the opinions "The Modern Way of Life is productive of toxins to such an extent that the more advanced a country is economically the more dangerous it may be to live in it". Official reports indicate that more than 2,000 million ponds of toxic chemicals are being pumped into the U.S. air each year. This includes industrial and other emissions, but excludes automobile exhaust. Mr. Henery Waxman, Chairman of the U.S. Congressional Subcommittee on Health and Environment, has remarked : "Such high levels of toxic releases are sure to be accompanied by comparably high levels of human suffering". It is really horrifying to note that the United Nations Environment programme estimates that the industrialized nations generate about 90 per cent of the estimated 400 million tonnes of hazardous waste produced worldwide annually. Thus United States can be said to be the target producer and dumper of hazardous waste and unclaimed 'drums' in South America and Africa.

In this context Lester R. Brown has rightly said : "Nothing has underlined the common dilemma of all mankind so clearly as the environmental crisis now unfolding. Signs of stress on the ecosystem are everywhere today, reported daily in the press. The life-support system for man and other living things with which we share our earthly habitat are being threatened. The crisis affects everyone, the rich and poor, old and young, Asian and American, black and white, born and unborn".[13]

## Family Welfare Movement

UNO theme of the year 1994 was family. Family being a very important institution, the international community responded to the theme very promptly and positively. The cairo conference on population being one of its major highlights. Rapid rise in population is a universal problem causing serious concern for all; Family Welfare Programmes for child survival and safe motherhood are being implemented with enthusiasm and vigour through out the world. Gradually people are releasing the advantages of a small family. More and more couples are limiting the size of their families. Lester R. Brown holds that "the costs of continuing on the demographic and economic paths we are now rising and becoming unacceptable for a growing number of people throughout the world. This is reflected in such things as the emergence of the strong zero-population growth and technological assessment movements in the United States. Within many communities in the United States Europe and Japan there is already growing resistance to the further expansion of certain types of economic activity."[14]

China, a socialist country and Indonesia, and Islamic country could reduce their fertility in a comparatively short period of time. Both of these countries could do so because of their political commitment from top to bottom. Secondly, there was systematic and constant monitoring of the progress.

With confucious we can say that if the families will be happy entire world will be happy. Growing population is a matter of global concern. With the fall of death-rate and specticular increase in birth-rate the problem stands aggravated throughout the World, particularly in the developing countries. Of course, India was the first country in the world to have an official population programme; but in the field of its implementation, there is much to do to achieve the target. In 1993 the Government of India appointed an expert group on National Population Policy under the Chairmanship of Dr. M.S. Swaminathan which submitted its report on 22nd May 1994. The report suggested number of socio-demographic goals like complete elimination of marriage of girls below the age of 18, universal immunisation of children, reducing the infant mortality rate to 30 per 1000 live births or less etc. However, according to one of the surveys in India of the demographic dimensions by the end of the present century will be as following :

— One billion population
— Decrease of 5–14 age-group from 25.54 to 20 per cent
— Decrease from 54.07 to 60.79 per cent in the age group above 15–59.
— Labour force – 120 million will be added to the labour force over the next fifteen years.
— 60 per cent of the additional population will be in urban areas.
— Progressive decline of the size of the holding - per capita availability of cultivable land which was 0.94 hectare in 1951 will decline to 0.33 hectare.

**Happy Family**

For the happiness of any family the following considerations are very significant :

1. Family should provide love and emotional support to its members.
2. Family should provide adequate food and shelter.
3. The children should not be given unusual responsibilities which may hamper their growth, emotional and social.
4. Necessary exposures of opportunities must be given for the socialisation of the younger members.
5. In a family one may be rich or poor, the dignity of labour must be inculcated, particularly among the growing children.
6. Regarding values the principal of free choice should be implemented judiciously taking stock of various factors like peer-group, environment aptitude etc.
7. Feelings of mutual respect and ease among family-members must

be maintained and developed.

8. Authorisation attitude of the head of the family, if any, should be minimized and refined.
9. Delicate feelings and sensitiveness of the youngsters should not be hurt.
10. An adequate equilibrium between traditional and operational values should be maintained in the family, whenever and wheresoever needed.

Proverbially family is called eternal school of life. Therefore, to make the society happy and enlightened formal as well as informal education is a must. The concept of development of society and nation at large emerged shortly after the Second World War. The concept was used to refer to the instrumentalities whereby the poor nations of Asia, Africa, the middle–East and Latin America were to attain standards of living similar to those of the west. This westernized concept, later on, came to be known as modernization and consequently lot of ink has been spent to define and explain 'what is modernity' with reference to various areas like standard of living, family-norms, art, poetry, ways of thinking, believing etc. Some scholars took modernization as devoid of values, which may be said to be true in case of politics or mechanization; but not at all in case of family. In the East, at least in India the people have started to realise this fact. Underlining social features of the modern age, particularly that of the West, G.H. Bantock says :

> "The results in the spheres of private and family relationships were profound, especially during the twenties and thirties. Jealousies were recognized where no such imputations would previously have been made mothers, particularly were suspect as seeking to devour their sons; helmet was interpreted interims of an Oedipus situation. The theme of sexual renunciation practically disappeared as subject for a novel the dilemma of Israel Archer vis-a-vis Gilbert osmaond no longer appeared real. Interest in pervasion has grown. The relation between the generations has profoundly altered; and the Freudian phenomenon of infantile sexuality, though initially received with horror, has focussed attention on the importance of early development and given childhood a statues it had only previously had in the pages of Rousseau and the writings of other progressives."[15]

Before the First World War, male hegemony had suffered a reverse in the rise of new woman and suffragette movement. Bernard Shaw's analysis of feminity in Man, Superman and Candida implies and error in the 19th century assessment of the relative role of the sexes. It is not surprising that D.H. Lawrence, writing in 1913 found in the relations between man and woman the problems of today, the establishment of a new relation, or the readjustment of the old one . . . . ., and that, where parents and children were concerned, there was a break-up of the old authoritarian pattern. Post-war era was characterized by revolt of the new generation against authoritarian role of the parent, particularly in the West. Gradually with the passage of time its impact was observed in the Eastern world also.

**Dunkel Proposals**

The General Agreement of Tariffs and Trade (GATT) is a binding contract among about 123 countries which together account for 90 per cent of the world merchandise trade. The objective of the contract is to provide an appropriate international trading environment for the business community which can contribute to economic growth and development all over the world.

Since the end of the Second World War seven rounds of multilateral trade negotiations have been launched under the auspices of the GATT. The eighth, known as the Uruguay Round, was begun in September 1986 and ended with Dunkel Proposals signed by 117 countries in April 1994. The objective of the proposals is to promote growth and development through the removal of trade distortions and development or a more open multilateral trading system which is expected to generate about $ 200 billion a year as extra world income.

The Dunkel Proposals include, Trade in Services, Trade Related Aspects of Intellectual Property Rights, (TRIPs) and Trade Related Investment Measures (TRIMs). The objective of the proposals is also to make progress in liberalisation of trade in agriculture. Many difference arose during negotiations. Some of these were narrowed down while others remained outstanding, particularly in the crucial area of trade in agriculture, trade in textiles, rules of anti-dumping and TRIPs. Consequently Mr. Arthur Dunkel, Director General of GATT was assisgned the task preparing the final proposals in consultation with concerned parties. Mr. Dunkel, who is also the chairman of the Trade Negotiations Committee at the official level, drew up the proposals for the consideration of the governments known as the Dunkel Draft.

The seven broad areas, covered under the Dunkel Draft are :

1. Market Access
2. Agriculture
3. Textiles
4. GATT Rules Including TRIMs
5. TRIPs
6. Trade in Services
7. Institutional Matters.

*Market Access*

The objective here is to make the import and export among the countries as free as possible. Market access involves not only the reduction and elimination of tariff and non-tariff measures but also corresponding commitments at the level of domestic policies that distort trade and competition. India has offered a reduction by 30 per cent of its basic customs duty on raw materials, intermediates and capital goods with a few exceptions.

Many countries regulated their international trade for their own gain. For example, developing countries impose higher import duty and offer high subsidies to their exports to protect their own industries. Similarly, developed countries give very high subsidy to their farmers for giving them incentives to continue their agriculture production.

But now under Dunkel Proposals developed countries will have to reduce their tariffs by 36 per cent and developing countries by 25 per cent within six years. The signatory country would get the position of most favoured nations and it can import at less cost from the signatory countries than the country which has not signed the Dunkel Draft Text. (DDT). Thus, its goods will be more competitive as compared to those countries which have not signed the DDT.

China and Eastern European countries are not members of the GATT hence these are not included under the DDT. But these countries including China are trying hard to be included in GATT and China is even very keen to become a founder member of the World Trade Organisation which clearly shows that the Draft must have many plus points.

Any Change in its transitory phase has some teething problems but these can be solved if we really wish to be free from the *status quo*.

*Agriculture*

The Dunkel Draft provides proposals of two kinds-one, for general application and the other for developing countries to protect their interests.

**Proposals for General Application**

(i) All domestic support in favour of agricultural Products with the exception of certain measures shall be reduced by 20 per cent by the year 1999.

(ii) Export subsidies which are in the nature of direct subsidies shall be subject to commitments for reduction of budgeting outlays and quantities by 36 per cent and 24 per cent respectively from the year 1993 to the year 1999.

(iii) There shall be comprehensive tariffication, ordinary custom duty shall be reduced on a simple average basis of 36 per cent by the year 1999 with a maximum rate of reduction of 15 per cent for each tariff.

**Proposals for Developing Countries**

(i) Countries which have aggregate support levels of upto 10 per cent for individual agricultural products shall not require to make reductions (India gives subsidy of less than 10 per cent).

(ii) Investment subsidies provided to poor farmers have been exempted from the purview of reduction commitments.

(iii) The developing countries which have balance of payment restrictions (Such as India) have been exempted from the purview of tariffication of non-tariff measures. Further, they have also been given the facility of offering ceiling bindings of tariffs.

These provisions show that Indian farmers have not to be afraid of DDT. It will rather provide them good opportunities in global market.

For many years industrialised countries have been heavily subsidising and protecting their agriculture, completely destroying the world production and trade. Due to high subsidy to cereals, dairy products, meat, sugar, oilseeds etc. the world prices of these products have been depressed which have been reduced the market opportunities for the efficient producing countries. Now, according, to the Dunkel proposals the developed countries have to reduce their export subsidy on farm products by 36 per cent in value and 21 per cent in volume in the next six years. Consequently, the prices of certain temperate zone commodities are likely to increase due to the cut in agricultural subsidies on products like sugar, dairy products, etc., by developed countries. According to one estimate this will raise the prices of agricultural products by nearly 10 per cent in the world market. Due to the price advantage, India will get benefit in exports. This may have some adverse impact on certain poor food importing countries in the short run this but India definitely stands to gain from this. For example, higher sugar prices will directly benefit Indian farmers and it is true for other such products as well.

According to a study by the Food and Agriculture Organisation (FAO) benefits of DDT proposals to agriculture should not be measured merely in quantitative terms. Its greatest significance also lies in the radical change imposed on the future formulation of agricultural policy. Moreover, trade regimes in the future are likely to be much more transparent as a result of the conversion of most non-tariff barriers to tariffs.

India's large technical manpower which has the experience of interacting with farmers during the Green Revolution, can be utilised in the search for new varieties of seeds. And the labour intensity of seed production accentuates the advantage of low labour cost in India. Thus, India's future share of world seed trade may be sizable. India may also collaborate with foreign companies. Indian research could also be geared to meet the demands of rapidly changing scenario.

Thus under the DDT proposals developed countries have to reduce their subsidies and consequently India will be able to export more. Moreover under the GATT there is mandatory minimum access of the domestic markets of developed countries to farm produce from outside. Hence the European Union Countries, Japan, South Korea and others provide an opportunity for export of Indian agricultural products. India should make the best use of this opportunity. Thus in a very short period, India may find out large markets for its agricultural products in developed countries.

### *Textiles*

In textile and clothing, world trade was governed uptil now by the Multi Fibre Arrangement (MFA) which enables importing countries to deviate from the general Gatt rules and induce discriminatory restrictions on imports from countries which were able to export cheaper products by virtue of lower wages. Now under the Dunkel Proposals there is a provision to phase out the MFA under which textile exports from developing countries have been regulated by a rigid quota system for over 20 years. This offers an opportunity for India's exports to grow. Against this India's imports of textiles for industrial use like non-woven material, special woven fabrics etc. will rise to certain extent which is not a matter to be considered very serious. India's other textile exports including readymade garments and made ups will definitely increase.

*Trade Related Intellectual Property Rights (TRIPs)*

TRIPs is the most controversial issue which is aimed at creating a new uniform system of paternts all over the world. There is a provision for product patent in many areas instead of process patents which have till now being prevailing in most of the countries. A product patent prevents others from making the same products through any other process thus giving the patent holder an absolute monopoly. The patent period would also be almost double under the DDT.

The major steps relating to TRIPs as given in DDT that effect Indian Drug Industry are as under :

(i) The process patent gets replaced by the product patent.
(ii) The patent term gets extended to 20 years.
(iii) The import of patented product is considered equivalent to working of patent.
(iv) In case of alleged infringement of the patent, the burden of proof shifts to the accused.

There is an argument that due to these drug prices will increase and research and development will receive a hard blow in India.

Before 1970 India was also following the product patent system as it exists in USA and UK. Due to it India's production remained very low and India became a net importer of drugs and as observed by the Kefauver Committee of U.S. Senate in 1963, Indian drug prices were the highest in the world.

But the Indian Patent Act (IPA) 1970, changed the whole scenario. It helped in building a strong base and infrastructure for the production of drugs in India. India is now self-sufficient in 54 essential drugs and its varied formulations. National Laboratories and R & D Centres of India have invented cost effective methods and prices of drugs in India became among the lowest in the world and exports also shot up. Indian Pharmaceuticals industry grew from a mere Rs.300 crore to Rs.4500 crore and exports increased from Rs.12 crore to over Rs.1500 crore. Drug prices are 5 to 30 times lower than in the countries with product patents. For example, brand drugs in U.S. cost upto 250 times more than their generic cousins in India.

TRIPs regime will be applicable only to patent application filed after July 1, 1995. And generally it takes about 7 to 10 years for a patented drug to come into the world market from the date of the patent application. Thus, it is clear that the Indian drug industry if free to produce and sell all those drugs that are already in the world market.

Some of the other intellectual property rights are as under :

— Copyright protection will be given in accordance with the Berne convention. It shall extend to expression and not to ideas, procedures, methods of operation or mathematical concepts as such.
— Trade marks shall be made registrable whether on goods or services.
— Protection shall be provided for independently created industrial designs that are new or original.
— Patents shall be available for any invention whether products or processes in all fields of technology provided that they are new, involve an inventive strip and are capable of industrial application.
— The term of the patent has been for a uniform period of 20 years.

All countries have been given a transitional period of one year and developing countries an additional four years. To the extent that a developing country was not extending product patent protection to areas of technology on the general date of application of the agreement, it has been provided that the developing country may delay the application of the obligations in respect of patents to such areas of technology for an additional period of five years. Thus in respect of food, chemicals, pharmaceuticals, and biotechnological products, India will have the possibility of delaying the application of obligation under TRIPs till 1.1.2003.

*Trade in Services (GATS)*

The General Agreement on Trade in Services (GATS) sets out the frame work under which governments can have negotiations. The only thing required here is the most favoured nation treatment and transparency. There is no general obligation imposed on the need to provide access to foreign services enterprises or for granting them national treatment (the same treatment as to national enterprises). All these have been made subject to negotiations on a request and offer basis.

The framework also provides scope to participants to seek concession on movement of personnel as well as on investment's in the service sector. India and other developing countries can try to have favourable provision under this.

*Institutional Matters*

The Dunkel package contains an understanding on rules and procedure on dispute settlement whereby these rules have been time bound, automatic and judicial in approach. Specific provisions have been made on joining countries to follow the dispute settlement provisions in considering retaliation against other contracting parties. An important feature of the GATT. Rules on dispute settlement is that before any retaliatory step on dispute settlement is that before any retaliatory step is taken by a contacting party, it has to take authorisation from the full membership.

One of the important results of the negotiations on Dunkel package is the establishment of the Multilateral/World Trading Organisation (WTO) to provide the common institutional framework for the conduct of trade relations between the members of WTO in matters related to GATT, GATS and TRIPs agreement. WTO will be a successor agreement to GATT.

There is a mixed reaction against WTO. Indian opponents of the GATT believe that the WTO will strong then the U.S. Domination while the U.S. Congress is also worried about a loss of the U.S. Sovereignty to the WTO. American critics believe that the one country one vote principle alongwith the institutionalisation of voting will give the developing countries distinct edge in the WTO. Of course, these fears are not quite true because wit a bit of selective pressure on matters like aid, the U.S. may retain the support of a sufficient number of developing countries to safeguard its dominance. The U.S. President has also said that he will ask the WTO to look at social issues. Thus, alongwith social issues, aid, and even the use of Super 301 trade legislation, the U.S. will no doubt try to continue its dominance. But, at the same time it is to be noted that Uruguy Round Dunke Draft Text has no provision for unilateral action by any country and so sanctions imposed under Super 301 are liable to be struck down by the WTO.

## General Agreement on Tariff and Trade (GATT)

International Monetary Fund (IMF) has recently released a study entitled "International trade policies: The Uruguay Round and beyond" The study acknowledges that by disturbing the *status quo* and creating the need to adjust to a new marked structure, the implementation of Uruguay Round may involve transitional costs in specific areas for some countries. But given the fairly long implementation period of the round, the transition costs are expected to be felt gradually, providing time to exploit the opportunities unlocked by the round.

The study concludes by saying : "Indeed, the potential adverse impact in some developing countries is expected to be limited or outweighed by gains from the round as a whole".

The study points out that unilateral trade liberalizations was relatively limited among industrial countries, for whom trade relations among themselves and other countries deteriorated, owing to slow growth and high unemployment. But liberalisation was a hallmark of the reform efforts of many developing countries. According to N.C. Menon, "Under such difficult circumstances, the conclusion of Uruguay Round is a major achievement. It substantially improves the prospects for restoring confidence in and the credibility of the multilateral trade system".[16]

## New China : On Communicative Wave

China is a country famous for her geographical isolation as we find in western writings of the last two centuries. Geographical phenomena have played a tremendous role in shaping the history of any nation and China cannot be taken as exception to this universally acknowledged proposition. But it does not mean that there had not been developmental strides in the field of science and technology, religion and philosophy, statecraft and visual arts and so on. Montesquien, a noted social scientist, has rightly remarked: "A number of things given men: climate, religion, Laws, maxims of government, examples of past things, more, manners . . . . . .In each nation, in proportion as one of these causes acts with more force, the others yield to it by the same amount." He further adds that "In mechanics there are frictions which often change or halt the effects of theory : in politics (i.e., social science) they are as well."[17]

## Contribution of China

Recent researches prove that in the field of science and technology China's contribution has been tremendous one. Dr. Joseph Needham of

Cambridge University, who has spent over half a century investigating the history of Chinese science and technology, as through his outstanding research and writing, brought about the various new facts regarding the contribution of China towards science and technology. Dr. Needham and his colleagies, at the Needham Research Institute in Cambridge, have published various volumes under the title "Science and Civilisation in China". Similarly, Dr. Robert K.G. Temple in his book entitled. *Land of Discovery and Invention* has brought about so many new facts regarding the various inventions. Robert K.G. Temple says that "More than half of the basic inventions and discoveries upon which the "Modern World" rests come from China.

Without the importation from China of nautical and navigational improvements such as ships rudders, the compass and multiple masts, the great European Voyages of Discovery could never have been undertaken. Columbus would not have sailed to America, and Europeans would never have established colonial empires.

Without the importation from China of the stirrup, to enable them to their shining armour to aid damsels in distress; there would have been no Age of Chivalry. And without the importation from China of guns and gunpowder, the knights would not have been knocked from their horses by bullets which pierced the armour, bringing the Age of Chivalry to an end.

Explaining the isolation China Andrew L. March has referred to mainly two arguements: "First, that China has been handicapped by the absence of the specific and uniquely valuable elements ('contribution') making up western civilization : Christianity, Roman Law, Greek Philosophy etc. Second more Generally, that China has been without any comparable set of diverse, hence progress-generating elements and, deprived of the sort of fruitful interaction that Europe enjoyed, remained stagnant."[18] of these two argument the first one does hold good particularly in the light of new facts brought forth through intensive researched carried out in 'Needham Research Institute' in Cambridge.[19]

The second argument just suggests the geographical phenomena. It does not speak of anything about Chinese manners, economy, government, social structure or history. Thus we see that the argument enhanced regarding the isolation of China are loaded with Europocentrism. Because of our inclination towards the western elements we, at times, overvalue them. If China could not move fast towards diversion of his original cultural traits at the cost of material progress, it is a compliment on her part with spiritual point of view particularly when we visualize the slogans like "back to the roots", back to nature" and so on in the western world.

As far as diversity of religions in China is concerned Andrew L March has rightly observed : In the matter of religion for example, we assume that our heritage of Babylonian, Egyptian, Greek, Roman, Judaic, Christian, Drawidic and whatever other strands presents a richer and more stimulating array than what was available to China; Yet in China too, besides the native Taoism, Confucianism, and the old 'Classical' religion, there flourished at various times Judaism, Islam, Manichaeism, Nestorian Christianity, and many diverse schools of Buddhism. Again, a Chinese Scholar would be less likely than a European to know a 'Foreign' Language but he had to learn classical Chinese just as the European clergy learned Latin, and whatever familiarity he had with Chinese 'learned Latin, and whatever familiarity he had with Chinese 'dialects' acquainted him with Languages differing from each other as much as do many of the Indo-European idioms of Europe."[20]

Some writers have represented Chinese environment as deficient or crippling to the development of Chinese society. But in the great collection of writings on China edited by du Halde in 1735, a prime source for later writers, there is much about China's enormous fertility and productivity, its gold, silver, iron, coal, teeming fish, and medicinal herbs. Thus China is very rich in mineral resources. According to one of the estimates there is just twenty times as much coal in China as in the whole of Europe. "But with the deterioration of conditions in China after the late eighteenth and especially mid-nineteenth century, the acceleration of industrial development in Europe and America, and the writings of Malthus and other classical economists, a pessimistic estimate gradually came to prevail." It is also fact that due to tremendous increase in population searecity of land has been felt through the centuries. It has even been said that twice as much land could be required to support them in comfort.

Mao regime had tackled the problems of overpopulation in China very meticulously "by making an optimistic assessment of resources while at the some time minimising geographic determinism and stressing the humane-organizational and psychological-side of development, China has also for the most part followed the policy of sowing population growth through distribution of contraceptives, Legislation of abortion, and promotion of late marriages and small families."[21]

Long dominated by feudalism, China has undergone a sea-change during the Last hundred years. It is now changing in the direction a new China, Liberated and free. Its economic system was established after the Soviet model in the 1950s. In this system production become publicly owned in both town and countryside and thus there was an over centralization of authority. The Law of value and market forces were neglected, and absolute egalitarianism (Levelling) was rampant in distribution. Some changes were made in subsequent years, but the basic model remained unchanged till 1978.

The Third Plenary Session of the 11th Party Central Committee in 1978 corrected the "left" guideline, shifted the emphasis of national work to economic construction. Prior to this there were quite a few serious defects in the economic system of China, which Led to deterioration in the living standard and general satisfaction among the masses, though the assets of the government increased leaps and bound. Huan Xiang, a famous economist and an adviser to the Chinese Academy of Social Sciences, has described the economic scenario of China in the following words:

> There is no clear line of demarcation between the functions of the government and the functions of enterprises. The government intervenes directly in the management of enterprises. The enterprises are administered by the different agencies of the central government or the various local governments to which they belong, and formulate their development to which they belong, and formulate their development strategies in the light of their own needs. Thus the links inherent in economic development are severed.

There is excessive control by the various government agencies over enterprises, and the enterprises lack autonomy. Plans for the enterprises are handed down to them by the government, which also controls the transfer of raw materials, purchases all products and controls the distribution of all labour. Excessive administrative directive planning from the top down does not meet the needs of a complex economy.

There is disregard for the role of commodity production, the law of value and the market, resulting in dislocations between production and demand, and the inability of plans to meet changes in market demand.

There is excessive equalitarianism in the distribution of income. Most profits are remitted to the government, and all losses are covered by the government. The enterprises' and workers' rewards are not a function of their performance, resulting in enterprises "eating from the big pot of the government" and workers "eating from the big pot of the enterprise."

There is irrationality in the economic structure. The collective economy has not undergone due development, while the individual economy has been greatly super send. The modalities of operations are also rather uniform, something inconsistent with the existence of multiple levels of development in China.

These defects seriously hampered the initiative and creativity of the enterprises and workers, and to a great extent emasculated what would otherwise be a vigorous economy. The consequences of overcentralisation are : the more centralized, the more rigid; the more rigid the economy. The lazier the people; the poorer they are; and the poorer the people are, the greater the need for centralization, forming vicious circle. From 1953 to 1980, the value of China's fixed assets increased by 26 times, gross industrial and agricultural output by only eight times, national income by only four times and actual standards of living only doubled. In order to further emancipate productive forces, it is imperative to effect comprehensive and systematic reform to the economic structure.

New China has a unique system of *Think Tank* wherein intellectuals and experts from different fields are pooled into have expert opinion as and when required. One such 'Think Tank' is at Wuhan, where about one lac engineers, technicians, professors and teachers are concentrated. In order to help and advise the city government a 100-member 'Think Tank' was established. Prof. Li Conghuci, Vice-President of the economic management college at Wuhan University, was the first to suggest that Wuhan should focus on enliving economic interflow and transportation in the current urban reform.

Li compared industrial enterprises to the cell and funding to the blood. The cell cannot survive without blood, he said, so China should establish several financial centres. The developed financial system built in the capitalist world should not be dismissed as a unique product of capitalism, he said: Rather, it should be seen as a result of an advanced commodity economy. China has, in the past, made terrible mistakes in using money, he said. He added that China should study the capitalist financial markets and borrow the useful idea while dismissing the side effects.[22]

After a long period of study and discussion a set of new policies was formed in 1978. Since that time, the policies have brought important break-throughs to the country-side, where 800 million (about two-third of the entire population like that of India) Chines Live. In October 1984, the CPC Central Committee decided to shift the focus of the drive to the urban areas, and at the same time published its programme for overall economic reform. Of course, this was based on four cardinal principles–(1) keeping to the socialist road; (2) holding the peoples democratic dictatorship, (3) upholding leadership by the Communist Party, and (4) Upholding Marxism–Leninism and Mao Zedong though. Comrade Mao Zedong had rightly said

> "Mankind makes constant progress and nature undergoes constant change, they never remain at the same level. Therefore, man has constantly to sum up experience and go on discovering, inventing, creating and advancing. Ideas of stagnation, pessimism, inertia and complacency are all wrong. They are wrong because they agree neither with the historical facts of social development nor with the historical facts of nature so far known to us"[23]

Thus following dictum "Changes, the law of nature" China had taken a bold step in 1970s, both in theory and practice and is determined to press a head with the reform, despite all risks involved. The reform has brought about tremendous changes not only in people's economic life, but also in their mental outlook and why of life paving the path of material and cultural enrichment. That is why Chinese Leader, Deng Ziaping aptly called the reform *China's second revolution*. With the renewed mental out-look there had been various currents and cross-currents in and through China in socio-economic and cultural fields. Example of China is worth-emulating as far as control over the fast-increasing population is concerned.

**Inter-Gulf Cooperation**

Arab Gulf states are well-known for their affluence resulted by the production of oil, main and valuable product of the region. Historically they are bound by common religion and cultural heritage. There are natural linkage also among these countries. But in the modern times there are various sources of threats to these countries. The numerous islands that not the gulf are considered strategic targets of entry into the gold. Moreover, the discovery of oil has brought the region to the forefront of international conflict, being the main source of energy world over. It is also main base of gulf-economy. The day may come when the sources of oil may dry but being the natural phenomena it may take long years, a century or even more. They are depositing their oil wealth in foreign banks like U.S.A., Switzerland and so on, which cannot be called a sound and healthy practice economically.

Apart from the above potent sources of threat to the Gulf region, foreign interests in the Gulf are generally aimed at achieving the following objectives

- To obtain oil concessions with the maximum of profit.
- To benefit from the capital of the states in the region.
- To encourage differences and conflicts between the states in the region in order to prevent any cooperation and unity among them and consequently to keep them divided and weak.
- To encourage the migration of foreigners in the region in order to rob it of its Arab Character.
- To obtain special concessions to build military bases facilities for foreign troops.

The above mentioned alien interests in the region call for strategies that would neutralize the elements that breed tensions there. Certain steps are also necessary for the security of this strategically important area. The concepts of security applies to all fields of socio-economic affairs in the Gulf, for instance, social affairs food supplies, monetary and economic affairs, cultural, intellectual and spiritual matters and the media in addition to military security. The measures to ensure security in this region includes :

- The creation of a highly efficient transport and communications network between all the Gulf states.
- The prudent use of manpower in the region.
- The provision of strategic reserves of water and oil for local consumption and the guarantee of food and medical supplies and other requirements for domestic security.
- The establishment of a Gulf information bank
- The exchange of expertise between the Gulf states in all fields in order to reap maximum benefit from the manpower in the region.
- Enunciating a unified media strategy for the Gulf, aimed at increasing national awareness.
- The attraction of foreign investment to the states of the region.
- The development of education programmes in accordance with the new concepts and responsibilities imposed by recent events in and around the Gulf.
- The linking of Gulf security to that of the Red Sea and the Middle East in a single strategic entity.
- The establishment of maintenance and repair centres in all the Gulf states to form a technical basis for industrial and vocational development at the region.
- The production of spare parts for basic machinery and even the distribution of production and service centres for the use of the Gulf

states.

- The introduction of military service in all the states of the region with training programmes on the latest weapons which need time to master properly.
- The establishment of a special fund for Gulf security to which all the states concerned should contribute according to agreed principles.

Such measures will provide Gulf security by a collective strategy, that aims at preserving the security of the entire strategic belt rather than leaving this to be a responsibility of any single state.

**Regional Cooperation in South Africa**

'CONSAS'[24] was a South African Strategy in order to establish a regional co-operation particularly in the fields of economical affairs among the South African States. To monitor, enhance the Socio-economic progress among its members it played very important role. By the mid April 1994, the members of CONSAS included : South Africa, Transkei, Bophuthatswana, Venda and Ciskei. the idea of CONSAS was basically originated in the speech of R.F. Botha, Minister for Foreign Affairs and Information of South Africa delivered on 3rd April 1979, in a Parliamentary debate. It was based on the concept of "an equitable division of power and Land".

One of the objectives of the 'constellation' was to establish a confederation. In Parliamentary debates in 1980 and again in 1981 the Prime Minister, P.W. Botha, elaborated his government's view of the constellation of states and stated that the constellation could develop into a confederation. He also marked out four guidelines to this end, which were :

(i) sovereignty not to be affected;
(ii) equal status for member – states;
(iii) member states to have the right to withdraw from certain areas of co-operation or from the confederation itself; and
(iv) the confederation was not to inhibit bilateral contact.

The tough organization approached like, Customs Union, tight Integration, Economic Union, Common Market etc., were avoided by the 'CONSAS'. It adopted 'Functional Cooperation' model for regional organization which offered loose structure and gave priority to functions rather than structure (or institutions). Whatever institutions were established, these were only to facilitate the functions of the organization. There was another important feature of this model that it concentrated on coordination of mutually agreed plans and projects and did not seek to curtail national soverignty of the members.

The ultimate aim of CONSAS was political, to create a confederation, but it exhibited a functional typology. Functionalism, offered equality and sovereignty while recognising the forces of nationalism and did not need the signing of an appropriate multilateral treaty. CONSAS was basically a regional cooperation (no doubt dominated by South Africa). It was created by the will of its members but did not have the sanction of any treaty, while confederalism (one of its objectives) is a stage beyond functionalism and would have occurred only with the signing of an appropriate multilateral treaty. In the absence of such treaty the aim of confederalism was not realised.

**France in Global Economic Scenario**

The broad expansion of France's economic ties to the world has gone hand in hand with the development of Paris as a major, international financial center.

Liquid markets in stocks, bonds, futures and options have provided new ways for companies to raise capital, manage cash and hedge their currency and interest rate risks. Attracted by these innovations, foreign brokers, banks and asset managers, have established operations in Paris to participate in the development of the Capital's dynamic financial markets. Today, foreign investors own a third of French stocks and bonds, a percentage that has grown from a quarter in the past few years.

More than 800 French companies, with a total capitalization of $ 400 billion at December 1994. are listed on the Paris Bourse, which also quotes more than 200 foreign stocks. Efficient market operations are ensured by an electronic system that supplies market data in real time, computerized order routing, on-line trading and advanced clearing and settlement services.

According to Jean-Daniel Tordjman "France has enjoyed spectacular growth in foreign investment over the past decade. In 1980, inward stock totaled $21 billion. Today, it stands at $ 111 billion. This remarkable 500per cent increase means foreign investment is growing faster in France than in the U.S. or Britain.

The world's fourth largest economy has many strengths: a strategic location in the European market, a remarkable choice of sites, modern transport and telecommunications networks are but a few of them.

More importantly, France has made significant and continuous efforts to create the kind of pro-business climate sought by international investors everywhere. France's regulatory environment is one of the most liberal for foreign companies. Its labour and energy costs are competitive. The corporate tax rate has been cut steadily since 1985, and is now among the lowest in Europe".[25]

## REFERENCES

1. *My Truth* (Indira Gandhi's autobiography) presented by Emmanuel Pouchpadass, p.113
2. Indira Gandhi, *My Truth*, pp.179–80.
3. Nadadur Sriniwasan, *Inside Present-Day China*, p. 26.
4. *Far Eastern Economic Review*, 14 Sept., 1961.
5. J.L. Nehru, *Glimpses of World History*, p. 466.
6. As we are, compiled by Henry Brandon, p. 165.
7. Friedrich Baerald, History and Structure of Economic Development, Foreword.
8. Robert J. Art, "America's Foreign Policy : Historical Perspective" in '*Foreign Policy in World Politics*, edited by Roy C. Macridis, p. 340.
9. *Ibid*; p. 341.
10. Leon D. Epstein, "British Foreign Policy" in "*Foreign Policies in World Politics*", Ed. by Roy C, Macridis, p. 57.
11. John Grigg, "Twenty Years of India" in *Era of Rapid Change,* Publication Division, p. 12.
12. M. S. Krishnan, Democratisation of Public Sectors' in *Role of State Sector in Developing countries*, p. 240.
13. Lester R. Brown, *World Without Borders*, p.16.
14. Lester R. Brown, *World Without Borders*, Introduction, p. 9.
15. *The Modern Age*, Edited by Boris Ford, Part I,p.20.
16. N.C. Menon, *The Hindustan Times*, dated 19.11.94.
17. Quoted by Andres L. March in Idea of China, p. 51.
18. *Ibid*; p. 62.
19. For detailed study the following books can be referred to :
    (i) Various volumes of "Science and Civilization in China" brought out by the Institute.
    (ii) China, Land of Discovery and Invention.
20. *Ibid*; p. 63
21. *Ibid*; p. 109.
22. Han Baocheng, progress in urban Reform (China in focus) pp. 101-2.
23. Quoted in "Premier Zhou Enlai's Report on the Work of the Government to the First Session of the third National People's Congress of the People's Republic of China" (21-22 December 1964).
24. Expanded Form – Constellation of Southern African States. The name was chosen on the design of solar system. South Africa as a major economic and political power

in the region would act as sun in relation to other powerful states of the world, while the other Southern African States would act as planets of South Africa having fixed economic and political relations with it under 'CONSAS'.

25. *France Today*, preface.

# 6

# CROSSCURRENTS IN PHILOSOPHY, ART AND LITERATURE

Historical Perspective, Tradition, Universality of Crosscurrents, Oriental Thinking, East Meeting West Through Indology, Intercourse in religions, Hindu and Buddhist Missionary in USA, Differing Cultures and bridges of understanding, promoters of Transeen-dentalism, Polyglot sloven culture, Indian Cultural Suzerainty over Asia. Impact of Indian culture on South East Asian Countries. Confucianism entered Europe. Indo-French Artistic Exchanges, India's Impact on Western Thought and Literature.

**Historical Perspectives**

The oriental as well as oxidental thoughts have been making significant contribution through out the ages to human understanding pertaining to socio-cultural phenomena of one another by establishing currents and crosscurrents into various streams of thoughts. These currents are not only found in art and Literature but also in mythology, theology, myths, legends, religious effectiveness, cultural communications and so on. For example, the legend of annihilation is found in Islam (Kayamat) and Christianity also, though little different from that of 'Pralaya' of Hindu Mythology.

In a society or group ethnic culture remains as source culture forming basic structure of the macro-cultures but its evolution and further development becomes feasible through various currents of other cultures. Moving from one cultural world to another can be an enriching experience for the people of both the societies because of various common traits of mankind. These crosscurrents have been more apparent in science and religion. E.M. Forster, in his novel "A Passage to India", has rightly stressed the need to combine the success of western civilization with a new exploration of spiritual experience.

**Tradition**

The Irish poet Yeats, who had a great fascination for India and her philosophy, has rightly observed : "Tradition is always the same. The earliest poet of India and the Irish peasant in his hovel nod to each other across the ages, and are in perfect agreement"[1]

To Yeats the sense of tradition was not historical in time but that perennial flow of wisdom whose foundation is the invisible order of the soul's history. In 1885 he founded Dublin Hermetic Society, which met on June 16 under the chairmanship of Yeats" to discuss the wonder of "Eastern Philosophy", to make a study of the Vedas and the upnishads, Buddhist Sutras and Bhagvadgeeta, Kalidasa and Sanskrit drama etc. Yeat's occultism has been studied by many renowned scholars.[2]

Besides this spiritual heritage India has undergone the profound process of economic change and industrial development, which began in the west more than two centuries ago. It is said that the first general move of modernization occurred round the shores of the North Altantic Ocean, When the European minds turned from theology to natural sciences, from traditions to inventions and experiments in various branches of science and technology, when the communist took over power for the first time in Russia in the October Revolution, new ethusiasms and vigour was injected in the working class all over the world. There were great changes in political philosophy also. The communists including Marx, Lenin and others propounded their most persuasive theories for socio-economic developments, popularly called "Socialism".

On one other hand number of Afro-Asian colonies, at the same time were struggling hard for their liberation. Most of the world, outside the Atlantic area, was under one form or other of western colonial control. These Afro-Asian countries, even being under the colonial countries, tried their best to maintain their cultural legacy. The country like India fought his battle of freedom under the unique leadership of Mahatma Gandhi with the weapons of the truth and non-violence. It was a unique example in the world. Following the foot-prints of Mahatma Gandhi Nelson Mandela fought for liberation of South Africa and ultimately succeeded in it, though after a long time struggle. The same tools and techniques were adopted earlier in United States by Martin Luther King for the noble cause of the blacks. Thus we observe that there was a good deal of crosscurrents into the ideals of truth and non-violence as far as their use for political cause is concerned.

From the ancient times the searchers of truth have been looking to India. In the Old World India was the first country to conceive and practice metempsychosis. From 'Apuleius' we come to know how Pythagoras came to India and Learnt the doctrine from Brahmins over here. It was a cardinal tenet among the people of India, even in remote antiquity. Factually speaking thousands of years ago Indian seers and sages were pondering over the deepest problems while the Europeans were not even aware that such problems existed. The West has been content with the aim of fulfilment of human needs, desires, and aspirations whereas India believed that "Desire is never satisfied by the enjoyment of desire, it grows more and as does the fire to which fuel is added."[3]

But with passage of time a group in the Western world is also following the path of renuciation and there is a tremendous impact of ancient Indian Literature on such group. Ancient Indian Literature including Vedas, Upnishads, and Puranas etc. have made a mark in the literary traditions of the world.

The contribution of Vedas to the human thought has been summarised by Professor Max Muller in the his book Styled as "India; what it can teach us," in the following words :

> "The Vedic Literature opens to us a Chamber in the education of the human race to which we can find no parallel anywhere else. Whoever cares for his historical growth of our language and thought, whoever cares for intelli. Development of religion and mythology, whoever cares for the first cares for the first foundation of science, Astronomy, Metronomy, Grammer and Etymology, whoever cares for the first intimation of philosophical thoughts, for the first attempts at regulating family life, village life and state life as founded on religious ceremonials, traditions and contract, must, in future, pay full attention to the study of Vedic Literature."

Here the concept of renunciation requires supposition as at times it is misunderstood. It is not merely negation of life and world, but it is a negation of two negations of life – denial to be materialistic and refusal of ascetic. Here lies the *middle path* (Majhhim Patipada) of Buddha or "golden mean" of Aristotle. In other words renunciation is renouncing the "two extremes of life"–sensuous pleasures on the one hand and self-mortification on the other. On the philosophic basis responsibility arises in Indian thought when renouncing of the two extremes leads to the positive discovery and rediscovery of the middle path on the part of the individual or the nation.

**Universality of Crosscurrents**

Cultural currents and crosscurrents into various facets of culture is a global and natural phenomena. It is necessary also for enrichment of culture. Various nations have Geographical boundaries but human thought do not have any such limitations. "Mankind is unfortunately split-up into many "nations" at present, but it does not follow that this temporary sectionalism should also invade the domain of History. Kant's great idea of "Universal History" has been forgotten in the last century. Demented nationalism attempts to desecrate and disintegrate holy history, and to use its mangled and mutilated limbs as decorative emblishments for the bloodstained mansions and monuments of the warring nations. The nation-states must poison the young citizens, minds with the virulent virus of "patriotism" at a tender age, and history is, therefore, ruthlessly backed and broken into as many pieces as there are nations in the world. But what does the scientific historian says ? He gnashes his teeth in rage and cries: "You have murdered History, therefore, you shall sleep in peace no more. This shall be your doom, that like the house of Atreus, you shall destroy one another, because you have first destroyed history."[4] Without cross-cultural communication history, may it be of any nation, cannot claim to be intelligible and complete. Now-a-days History has been divided into many national sections to suit the political strife at different periods. But the fact is that nations have developed and progressed with the cooperation of many other nations irrespective of creed or colour. Swedish poet Tenger has rightly said, "Only Barbarism was indigenous in the beginning". It sounds that every nation has to pass through the stage in the early centuries.

If we go through the history of England and India we may easily find the threads of early Barbarism. Celtic and Iberian[5] invasions on England can easily compared, though not similar chronologically, with the invasions of Shakas and Huns on India. In these two countries many arts and crafts were learnt from the outsiders during the dawn of their respective civilizations. Describing the early man in Britain, G.M. Trevelyan says, "Iberian" blood probably flows in the veins of every Englishman, more in the average scot, most in the Welsh and Irish." Regarding cross-cultural, communication then prevailed he observes as under :

> "Many of these improvements, specially agriculture, metal work and long-ship buildings, were probably taught to the islanders by merchants from the distant south, or by continental tribes who had

learnt from those merchants. *The Levant was the cradle of European* civilization. The inhabitant of Mesopotania, Egypt and Crete, in days before Tyre, Athens or Rome, evolved agriculture, metal crafts, shipbuilding and many other of the arts of life".

The concept of the barbarian in early India was based on linguistic distinction. Aryans spoke Sanskrit whereas the indigenous people probably spoke Dravidian and Munda. Aryans were more civilized although they were unfamiliar with city civilization. As opposed to the Aryans the indigenous people were called non-Aryans (Anarya) *i.e.*, The Andhra, Tamil etc. In Hindu scriptures including Vedas they are called 'mlechha', 'vratya' 'dasyu' etc. Romila Thapar maintained that "The Aryans. . . . .did bring with them the central Asian horse and the light, spoke-sheeled chariot which gave them a military advantage over the local people still using horse-drawn carts. Further more it is also believed that the Aryans either brought with them, or else where instrumental in the dispersion of, iron technology, which again was superior to the existing copper technology. It is likely that the cities of the Harappa culture had already declined or at least were in the final stages of decline when the Aryans arrived."[6]

In Rigved[7] we find mention of two-footed and four-footed 'pashus' (cattle) and the Greeks also used 'andrapodon' for slaves compared to the beasts 'tetrapodon'. It is believed that *dasas* (slaves) were the descendants of the Indus cities, being pursuaded by some social phenomena like religion. This was the beginning of caste system in India. As in America the blacks were mostly occupied as slaves, so in India the dark-coloured indigenous people were called 'dasa' or 'dasyus'. The world 'Varna' means colour, but later on, Varna Vyavastha was popularly known as 'caste-system' and the Indian Society was divided into four Varnas — Brahman, Kshatriya, Vaishya and Shudra.

This categorization was not on the basis of birth, but on division of labour as we find in Rigveda that the members of one and the same family are occupied in different occupations befitting to their preferences and aptitudes. Now-a-days in politics also we find that the members of one and the same family hold affinity and loyalty to various political parties. D.D. Kosambi observed : "These Indian developments after the Aryan conquest would be all the more natural, if slavery in the Indus valley had been similar to that in Mesopotamia. There we find two classes of slaves. The first, "whether they were (originally) prisoners of war, defaulting debtors, or even born into slavery–could escape from their status and free themselves from chattlehood by three means : They could by their freedom with their peculium : they could be ransomed by their kin, or they could be adopted by their masters."[8] If such a slave of either sex married a free person, the offspring of the union were free.[9] This is precisely as we find it in the famous treatise on state-craft – Arthashastra[10], a monumental work of Kautilya, friend, philosopher and guide of Chandragupta Maurya. In Natya-Shastra[11] of Bharatacharya various tribal people like Kirata, Andhra, Dravida, Pulinda etc. are described as dark coloured only.

**Oriental Thinking**

According to Dr. Radhakrishnan "Neo-Platonists were convinced that logical knowledge alone was inadequate. Neo-Platonism, which originated in Alexandria, where Oriental modes of thought, were not unknown, presented a more organic view and grounded logical processes on the certainty of immediate experience. But the post-scholastic philosophers fell back upon a purely rationalistic approach to certainty, and the attempt to ground philosophy in science became more popular with the growth of natural sciences, which were actually engaged in pushing back the frontiers of knowledge through observation and experimental verification."[12] In fact, in the field of knowledge the eastern emphasis has been on creative intuition. It is rather a dominant feature of Eastern thought, whereas the Western system is generally characterised by a greater adherence to critical intelligence. There is no precise line of demarcations in the thinking of the East and the West. It just indicates to the tendencies, to which there are many exceptions also. It is universally held that Asians are more spiritual and less materialistic than Westerners. They believe in karmite laws and consequentially believe in other-world, reincarnation of soul. They have special respect for learning. Their attitude towards trees, river, mountain and total environment is pious, kind and spiritual one. Even before the discovery of pulsation theory in plants in modern times by Sir J.C. Bose and other botanists, they have been treating the plants as lively objects. Many plants like Beniyan, Peepal, Tulsi etc. have been objects of worship in India from the time immemorial. But the rigid social stratification (caste-system) and the callousness towards those in a lower social stratum, which are still vague in a few parts of the country – is a contradictory to their feeling and tradition of pan-theism. Gunnar Myradal has sharply pointed out this contradiction :

> "The widely accepted idea that Asians are bent on settling disputes peacefully and by mutual agreement, without resort to legal

procedures is refuted by the popularity of litigation in all South Asian countries once there is access to the courts. Against the claim that people in Asia are particularly spiritual and non-materialistic must be placed the common observation of a propensity for narrow materialism in all social strata – which is not surprising, considering the general poverty and the strains of social inequality. Outward austerity, even on the part of those who could afford luxury, was propagated and observed by Gandhi, and was certainly in agreement with his personal ideals. Clearly, however, the continued observance of simple, folksy dress, for example, which has become almost a uniform for popular leaders, is more a symbolic rite and a political device than a sign of a basic attitude."[13]

**East Meeting West Through Indology**

Charles Wilkins in 1785 translated the Bhagvadgita for the first time; Kalidisa's Shakuntala was translated by William Jones in 1789, followed by Manu's Laws a few years later. Finally, at the turn of the century, Colebrook and Horece Haymond Wilson were the scholars whose important essays and translations enabled all Europeans, including the Germans, to have their first comprehensive view of Sanskrit and its literature.

Johann Gottfried Herder was the first to follow up these efforts in Germany. Though he didn't know much about the country or the language, Herder has given an idealistic description of India which was for a long time predominant in the fantasy of German poets.

Within the system of his Philosophy of the History of Mankind, Herder gave an imaginative picture of India where according to him the origin of mankind is to be found : 'There, the human mind got the first shapes of wisdom and virtue with a simplicity, strength and sublimity which has–frankly spoken–nothing, nothing at all equivalent in our philosophical, cold European world,' The Childhood of Mankind meant for Herder the Golden Age, which he believed existed in the India of his time. He said :

> 'The Hindus are the most peaceful race of mankind. They do not like to offend any living being, they honour what brings life and eat the most innocent food, milk, rice, fruit of the trees, the healthy herbs which their ground offers them. (Their tongue) has never been enervated by the taste of fermented drinks or not dishes...Their stature is straight, slim and beautiful...Their way of walking and their way of bearing is highly graceful and charming. And as their stature is in

the same kind as their original shape of mind...moderation and calmness, a gentle mood and a calm deepness of their soul characterise their work and pleasure, their ethics and mythology, their arts and even their tolerance under the heaviest yoke. Happy lambs, why could you not pasture on your meadow without any disturbance and distress ?'

**Herder and Goethe**

Herder's idealising glorification of India then was taken up by the romantic movement and it is one of his great merits that the poetical picture of India given by him paved the way for the development of German Sanskrit philology.

Herder introduced the first Indian literary documents to Germany.

First of all Shakuntala by Kalidasa. In 1791 the first German translation of the drama was published by Georg Forster, who sent one copy to his friend Herder. Here are some sentences of his reply "I cannot easily find a product of the human mind more pleasant than this one : . . . . . a real blossom of the orient, and the first, most beautiful of its kind ! . . . . Something like that, of course, appears once every two thousand years...."

Herder published three letters on Shakuntala. He studied Kalidasa's play in the light of drama rules evolved by Aristotle : 'The Greek postulates a development of the events which is in each part natural; the Indian, however, aims right from the beginning to the end at a sacred, divine, miraculous correlation.'

Of course, Herder hurried to bring his discovery to Goethe's notice. His friend's enthusiasm about Kalidasa was not less exuberant. The instantaneous reaction of the poet after reading Forster's translations were penned in the following lines :

> Shall I embrace in a name the blossoms of spring, the fruits of the autumn. All that enchants and that charms, all that nurtures and fills,
> Shall I embrace in a name All Heaven and the whole of the Earth;
> Let me call, Shakuntala thee, and all is comprised in one name.

Nearly forty years later Antoine de Chezy, a friend of Friedrich Schlegel, published an edition de luxe of Shakuntala, and having sent it to Goethe, he received the poet's reply of October 9, 1830, as follows :

> 'The first time I became aware of this inexhaustible work, it produced such an enthusiasm in me, attracted me so much that I did not cease

from studying it and I even felt myself urged to try the impossible, namely, to adapt it for the German theatre. Through all these touch fruitless efforts I have become acquainted with this most valuable work to such an extent...that for the last thirty years I had not to read either the English or the German version...Only now I understand the enthusiastic impression which this work made upon me in former times. Here the poet appears in his supreme duty, as the representative of the most natural phase, of the finest way of life, of the purest ethical ideals, of the most dignified majesty and the most serious religion. But at the same time he remains the sovereign and master of his creation so that he may dare vulgar and ridiculous contrasts which, however, must be considered as necessary links of the whole organism.'

**Influence on Goethe**

Two years before his death Goethe thus confessed that 'Shakuntala' accompanied him throughout his lifetime.

And there is an interesting link between Kalidasa's masterpiece and Goethe's Faust. The plan for one of the three preludes, preceding the drama faust, the so-called 'prelude on the stage' where the theatre manager, the dramatic poet, and the actor discuss the problem of a good play, came to Goethe from the similar prelude in the Indian 'Shakuntala'.

Later on Goethe became acquainted with the Meghaduta, too, which was translated in 1813 by Horace Haymond Wilson. The poet mentions the small epos very often, sometimes calling it 'Kamarupa.' But let us investigate now where Indian impressions are bearing fruit in Goethe's poetical creations.

A few years later, the trilogy 'Pariah' was published. Goethe found the story for these three poems in his travel book. In the first part of Geothe's trilogy the despised Pariah prays to God :

For even to the dancing girls
You have given a goddess.
We others too want to hear of such a miracle
So that we can praise you.

The conclusion of the trilogy is the thanks of the Pariah to Brahma : Great Brahma ! Now I understand that you are the creator of the worlds ! I call you my sovereign for you approve of all.'

Between the prayer and thanks for the fulfilments, the central part of this trilogy gives the 'legend', the story of the inter-changed heads, which story was also told by Thomas Mann. Goethe narrates the story as follows: 'A Brahman kills his wife for unfaithfulness in thoughts. But then his son gets the order to re-connect the head and body of his mother. Because of his excitement, however, he makes a peculiar exchange, the head of the Brahmin wife is connected with the body of a Pariah woman. Thus she learns all that had been unknown to her as a Brahmin wife.' This means terrible suffering for her. But by enduring everything she becomes a goddess, whose duty is mediatorship, the goddess the Pariah was longing for.

It is always Kalidasa to whom Goethe turns time and again, full of admiration :

Kalidasa and others have attained their end;
They have with the neatness of the poet
Saved us from bad priests and grotesque images.
I would have lived in India myself
If there had not been any sculptors.
What can one imagine to be more pleasant,
Than Shakuntala and Nala, whom one must kiss,
And Megha-Duta, the cloud messenger.
Who would not like to send him to those with mental affinity !

Let us return to Herder and the Romantic movement. Herder had combined the hypothesis of the Golden Age of mankind and the idea that originally man had been the very image of God. Thus the longing of Herder was for the oldest documents of mankind to rediscover the purest revelation of God.

**Novalis and Schelling**

Novalis, the romantic poet par excellence, wanted to go back to Indian mythology. In his essay 'Christendom or Europe' he writes :

'The poetry full of charm and colour like a decorated India faces the cold dead peaks of this book-learning rationalism. In order to make India in the middle of the globe so full of warmness and beauty, a cold sea, dead cliffs, mist instead of a sky full of stars, and a long night, all this must make both ends of the globe desolate.

The famous romantic philosopher Schelling too grants India an important position in his Philosophy of Mythology. Max Mueller Writing about Schelling said that he was a great admirer of ancient Indian literature and he was especially delighted with the Upanishads...Schelling like

Schopenhauer thought the Upanishads to be the genuine wisdom of the Indians and of mankind.

The contrast between the poetical, idealised India and the facts determined the poet Friedrich Schlegel's Indian studies. In his Speech on Mythology, he explains the importance of mythology and its close connection with romantic poetry. 'Mythology and its poetry, both are one and inseparable.'

Friedrich Schlegel studied Sanskrit in Paris, the very first German to do so. He was able to read in this language and to translate from it. During that time, he wrote in one of his letters : 'But now everything else has been pushed away by Sanskrit. Here is the very source of all languages, of all thoughts, and of all poetry of the human mind; everything, originates in India, without any exception.'

The inspiring power of Schlegel's book stimulated Friedrich's brother, August Wilhelm Schlegel, who, in 1818, became the first professor in Sanskrit at a German university; inspired Franz Bopp, and last but not least, stimulated the linguistic genius of the poet Friedrich Rueckert to give the most congenial translations of Sanskrit literature.

**Poet Rueckert and Tamil**

Friedrich Rueckert was one of the few outstanding scholars in the field of philology who was able to master some dozens of languages. Like Heinrich Schliemann, who discovered Troy, Rueckert used to learn even the most difficult of languages within six to eight weeks.

One day in the summer of 1839, for instance, a missionary who was to be sent to South India requested Rueckert to teach him Tamil. Rueckert answered that he could not understand a single word of Tamil at the moment, but that he should come in October, then he would be able to teach him.

In the meantime, the poet took the Grammatical Damulica written by the missionary Ziegenbalg and published in Halle in 1716 and a Tamil translation of the Holy Bible, and then composed a Tamil grammar and a Tamil dictionary and taught this difficult language marvellously.

During those times, it was very difficult and expensive to get texts and dictionaries of Oriental languages, and Rueckert was a poor poet and professor. So he copied the Sanskrit dictionary containing 1,100 pages. This hand-written copy, corrected and enlarged by his own remarks, still exists.

The German scholar solved his problem in a similar way as the Indian pandit from Benaras who spoke fluent Sanskrit, but not a single word of English. One day he was persuaded to learn the despised language. Since he didn't like to look for every word in the dictionary, he learned the whole dictionary, page after page, by heart. And later in his lifetime, he was proud to discover that there were only two words which he didn't know.

The poet Friedrich Rueckert being at the same time professor of Oriental Languages at the University of Erlangen, 1827–1841, translated quite a lot of Sanskrit poetry. Nala and Damayanti, Savitri and others were introduced to German literature through masterly translations by Rueckert. And even Jayadeva's *Gitagovinda* lost nothing of its beauty in Rueckert's German version.

**Hermann Hesse**

During the 20th century many poets were touched by impressions and influences from the East. Even a separate book to deal with all of them would not be sufficient. Here we will mention only one, and in this connection pay homage to Hermann Hesse.

Rudolf von Ems, the knight and poet of the Middle Ages, did not even know that his Barlaam and Josaphat story was of Indian origin. The German poets of the 18th and 19th centuries could meet India and try to understand by means of original literature, Sanskrit poems or at least their translations. Now in the 20th century, we find poets who travelled to the romantic dreamland and learned by their own experience.

The most renowned of these Eastern wayfarers is Hermann Hesse.

After his journey to the East in 1911, he published his *Indian Diary* in 1913, but could not record his experiences in the form of poetry. He *confesses* :

> 'Then I learned-not for the first time, of course, but harder than ever-that it is nonsense to write down what you did not experience yourself and during the long interval when I had already abandoned the poetical work Siddhartha, I had to make up for practice of ascetic life and meditation before I could regain the sacred and congenial world of the Indian spirit : my true home-land !'

**Intercourse in Religions**

India has cultural relations with the west in ancient period. Indians reached central Asia via Hindukush, Afganistan and Bactria. Ptolemy regarded Eastern Afganistan as a part of India. Abul Fazal called Kabul and Gandhar as gates of India. Before the invasions of the Muslims, both Afganistan and Baluchistan were influenced by Brahmanism and Buddhism. But durng the time of the Gupta period the whole Turkeistan from Kasghar to the frontier of China had been transformed culturally into the greater India. According to B.N. Luniya, "Afganistan used to be a part of India in early times. It was included in Mauryan and Kushan empires. Being situated on the borders of India the ancient Indian culture extended there far and wide. Consequently there had developed famous centres of Indian culture like Bamiyan and Rudda". When Fahien and Hiuen Tsang visited India, during the regimes of Chandragupta Vikramaditya II and Harsha respectively, Buddhism and before the invasion of Subuktagin during the medieval period Hinduism was predominating in the valley of Kabul.

Prior to the conquest of Sind and Multan in 712 AD the relations between India and Arab were very friendly and cordial. Even after that for a long time there was a friendly intercourse with Baghdad, the capital of Caliphs. At Mansur and Harun Al-Rashid (754–809 A.D.) sent embassies to India, like the Chinese emperors, to procure Indian scholars, Al-Biruni, in the eleventh century, refers to the astronomical knowledge gained by Arabs through these sources. The Barmark family of Baghdad came from the Buddhist Vihar of Balkh.

During the intercourse with far-east and central Asia Hinduism took various new central forms making way to its further evolution. R.C. Majumdar has rightly observed: "In course of time the sectarian Brahmanical religion triumphed over Buddhism which for long played a dominant part in India. But although worsted in the struggle, Buddhism maintained its existence for centuries to come and was gradually assimilated to the Brahmanical religion. Thus the religious history of India during the first thousand years of the Christian era presented a new spectacle, the gradual rise of new sects and the corresponding decline of the once triumphant Buddhist religion".[14]

The Arabs had a very friendly relations with Indian rulers of South, especially Rashtrakutas. It is said that in the regime of Harunal Rashid Indian scholarship was held in high esteem in Bagdad. They borrowed a lot from many sanskrit books on Mathematics and Astrology. Large number of Arab students also used to come to Takshashila or Taxila University, which was a specialized centre for medicine during ancient period. Pt. Nehru has rightly observed :

> "Thus Arabs took much from the old Indo-Aryan culture. They also took much from the Aryan culture of Persia, and also something from Hellenic culture. They were almost a new race, in the prime of their vigour, and they took advantage of all the old cultures, they

saw around them, and learnt from them; and on the foundation they built something of their own — the Saracenic culture. This had comparatively a brief life, as cultures go, but it was a brilliant life, which shines against the dark background of the Middle Ages in Europe".[15]

Generally speaking religion acts as a tremendous force for social intertia. In South Asia religion has induced social change. But in a few cases, particularly in realization of values pertaining to modernity, it stands as an obstacles. But it can be overcome and in the West the people have overcome it by formulating suitable policies related to the religion. Gunnar Myrdal observes:

> "In particular, social and economic stratification is accorded the sanction of religion. The attitudes, institutions and modes of living and working that make-up this stratification do constitute very real inhibition and obstacles to planning. The strength of this stratification is evidenced by the unwillingness of the unprivileged and exploited lower strata to challenge them. Instead, they mostly accept them as a fate ordained by the gods and the whole paraphernalia of supernatural forces. It is this feeling, for instance, the restrains the untouchables in India from pressing into the temples and using the wells of the high castes".[16]

In the above estimate of the lower state of Indian society is, no doubt, the exaggerated one. Due to renaissance in the second part of the 19th century and by the virtue of sustained efforts of humanistic reformers like Vivekanand, Ramkrishna, Raja Ram Mohun Roy, Dayanand Saraswati etc. there had been sea-change in the Indian society. Moreover, untouchability has been declared as cognisable offence. Moreover, after the enforcement of Indian Constitution any sort of discrimination on the basis of caste, creed, colour or religion has been declared as illegal. One may argue that there is difference in theory and actual practice. It may be so to some extent but not so much so degenerated as described by Gunnar Myrdal in *Asian Drama*.

For survival of any faith or religion the active support of the masses and, at times, royal patronage is very essential. After the downfall of Palas, Buddhism passed into oblivion, as everywhere else, in the North-Eastern India also. By the 12th Century A.D. Buddhism in India was only confined to the small pocket in North-East India. Even there it was closetted within the monasteries. So when Muslim army advanced towards

Bihar; sacked the Buddhist establishments at Nalanda, Vikramshila and Odantpuri; massacred most of the monks residing in them. Thus rout of Buddhism was complete. The renaissance of Buddhism commenced in India towards the middle of the 18th Century when the British Civil servants started bringing to light its treasures hidden under dust and debris.

It may be administrator, a religious remormer, art-critic, artist or scientist, his main concern had been human-life. Therefore, constant target had been happy life. In a society harmony, happiness and peace can be brought about by minimising the differences at religious and sectarian level. This was realised as early as Ashokan period. Therefore, he laid down the principle : "One who reverenees his own religion and disparages that of another from devotion to one's own religion and glorifies it over all other religions does certainly injure one's own religion"[17]

Thus we see that over long cultural history of India, absence of religious persecution and tolerance to other faiths has been effective without the force of law or the authority of the state. India was secular long before it became an independent 'secular' state. Buddhism arose as a religion without proselytising and spread to Asia without the force of arms and disappeared from its land of origin; but Buddha still remains as an incarnation (*avatar*) in Hindu Mythology. Similarly, Mahavir, the founder of 'Jainism' finds a place in the galaxy of ten *avataras*. It proves the unique assimilating character of Hinduism. In this context the observation of W.J. Wilkins is noteworthy :

> "Both reject the divine origin and authority of Vedas; though when a Vedic Text agrees with his own belief, a learned Jain will not scruple to employ it to but tress his own teaching. Both may be regarded as heretical sects of Hinduism. Both reject the divine institutions of caste and profess to believe in the social and 'religious equality of man ! Though the Jains are not regarded as outside the pale of Hinduism. For when, as an orthodox Hindu, a place is found for him in the caste-system, he is not treated as an outcast. Both acknowledge in a general way the more common and modern of the Hindu deities, and very much of the worship of both is very similar to that which prevails among the Hindus."[18]

The Jain Saints (Tirthankar) belonging to the present age are twenty-four in number. The first and the last two of these are – Vrishabhadev, Parshwanatha and Mahavir. These are regarded as devine beings, we may take these three as fairly representatives of the whole. Like Buddha, Jesus also claimed no divinity, but both of these came to be worshipped as a God. It is general tendency among the peoples all over the world that they like to make gods of their great personalities. Kabir, a great saint poet of Bhakti movement was deadly against idolatory, but his followers idolized Kabir himself. That is why prophet Mohammed said clearly and repeatedly that he was human, and not devine. It has also been the tendency that instead of following the Preechings of these great noble souls, people have been fighting over the trifle matters like 'divinity' 'trinity' etc. as Jawaharlal Nehru has pointed out : "There was a great and violent controversy at one time among different Christian sects over a certain diphthong. One party said that the word 'Homo-Ousion' should be used in the prayer, the other wanted homoi-ousion – this defference had reference to the divinity of Jesus, Over this diphthong fierce war was waged and large number of people were slaughtered"[19]. This fact, and others in plenty, indicate that any religion was or even is not free from ritualism. The rite-element has harmed the society rather than benefitting it.

Today Christianity is politically the dominant religion as it is the religion of the dominant people of Europe. Historically speaking Christianity came to India long before it went to England or Western Europe. Christian missionaries came to South India by sea within 100 years or so of the death of Jesus.; On the Historicity of Christianity Thomas A Harris has suitably remarked :

> "If Christianity were simply an intellectual idea, it probably could not have survived, considering its fragile beginnings. It survived because its advent was an historical event, as was Abraham's leaving the land of Ur. as was Moses' exodus from Egypt, as was Paul's conversion on the road to Damascus. We may not understand religious experience, we may differ in its explanations, but we cannot, if we are honest, deny the report of such experiences by reputable men through the centruies[20].

The Sermon on the Mount and Modern European Christianity appear amazingly dissimilar, when we look at the race of armaments and series of wars within the continent. Surprisingly enough we find passages in the *Tao Te Ching* that read almost like the *Sermon on the Mount* :

> One who would guide a leader of men in the uses of life
> Will warn him against the use of arms for conquest
> Even the finest arms are an instrument of evil :
> An Army's harvest is a waste of thorns.

In time of war men civilized in peace.
Turn from their higher to their lower nature.
But triumph is not beautiful. He who thinks triumph beautiful.
Is one with a will to kill.
The death of a multitude is cause for mourning :
Conduct your triumph as a funeral.[21]

**Hindu and Buddhist Missionary in U.S.A.**

In India, no doubt, Hindus form a major part of the population *i.e.*, about 72 per cent. But right from the date of convention on world religions at Chicago in September 1893, when Swami Vivekanand made a historic debut through his enlightened and thought-provoking discourse for eighteen days. For Vivekanand religion is synonymous with "Universalism" spirit. This does not mean that he advocated for unity of religions. On the contrary he prayed that "they (sects) may multiply so that at last there will be as many sects as human beings . . . . Whirlpools and eddies occur only in rushing, living streams . . . . . It is a clash of thought that awakes thought . . . "

In United States he met several noted intellectuals like Professor Wright, the philosopher William James and great electrician Nicolas Tesla. It is believed that Vivekanand exercised some influence on the American philosophy (pragmatism). In his book titled as "The Variety of religious experience", William James has quoted Vivekanand on "Mysticism". Thus in the turning point of Western thought Vivekanand has played his definite role. Prof. Starbuck of California in his book "The Psychology of Religion" had also collected number of religious witnesses. Vivekanand also met in New York the highest representatives of Western Science — Sir William Thomson and professor Helmholtz.

During his second journey to the west he found Swami Abhedanand in United States who was doing lot of work on the theme of Vedantism. He settled Turiyanand down at Mont Clair near New York. He founded new Vedantic centres at San Francisco, Oakland, and Alameda. He received 160 acres of forest land as gift and created an Ashrama at Santa Clara district, where Turiyanand trained selected band of students in the monastic life. Since then Ramakrishna Mission was well established and a band of enlightened and devoted Swamis have been visiting United States for propagation of Hinduism. Vedantism in particular. Vivekanand delivered numerous lectures on the spiritual topics like "Christ the Messenger". "The message of Buddha, Christ and Krishna" and so on.

He firmly declared at that time : "Europe is on the edge of volcano. If the fire is not extinguished by a flood of spirituality, it will erupt". His intuition of the unity of the human race did not stop at the arbitrary divisions of races and nations. It made him say that he had seen in the West some of the best Hindu types, and in India the best Christian. Such best Hindu types still exist in European countries. Once narrating the experiences of United States Dr. Karan Singh said : "The enunciation of Sanskrit texts by the American monks could put many of our Panditas to shame". It proves that any faith or religion is not the heritage of a particular race or nation, but by the virtue of its appealing character it becomes universalised, a universal heritage for the largest good of the mankind.

The West is attracted towards Hinduism, not because of its ritual character but due to Vedantism *i.e.* universal manifestation of the great Cosmic Soul (Brahman), which is described in the *Mundakapnishad* in the following words :

> "The omniscient, the all-wise, whose glory is reflected here on earth, is the self-enthroned in the luminous city of Brahman, his etherical heaven. Firmly established in mind, seated in the heart, he controls life and body. The wise by the higher knowledge see him clearly as the radiant, blissful, immortal".[22]

Similarly, the west was attracted towards Buddhism because of its practical and transparent ideas particularly that of "Middle Path" (Majjhim Patipada). In the words of Aristotle we can term it as "Golden Mean" Hindu scriptures like *Bhagvadgeeta* speak of two paths in these words :

> "Two are thepaths, there is no third for man.
> Cleave to the self in yoga or loose yourself in matter".[23]

Buddhism establishes the third path negating these two extremes. Middle path is a sort of double negations–refusal to be an ascetic and gross involvement in materialism. Here lies the secret of Buddhism, which attracted not only south Asia, but also many European countries including United States. During last three decades the influence of these two religions in the Western countries has been tremendous. The receptivity of American towards Hindu and Buddhist teachings has been very substantial. Inspite of their spectacular economic and material success they are seeking refuge in the cults like *Hare Rama Hare Krishna* which clearly indicates the universal character of these religions.

As the time is passing by we find more and more number of American and European origin beptised in Ramakrishna order or in other similar organisation or religious bodies in the West. The pragmatic and secular approach of these monks has been one of the most fascinating factors. The words spoken in the last session of the Religious Parliament (27 Sept. 1893) at Chicago are note-worthy particularly with the point of view of trans-religious communication and understanding :

> "May he who is the Brahman of the Hindus, the Ahura Mazda of the Zoroastrians, the Buddha of the Buddhists, the Jevovah of the Jews, the Father in Heaven of the Christians, give strength to you . . . . The Christian is not to become a Hindu or a Buddhist, nor a Hindu or a Buddhist to become a Christian. But each must assimilate the spirit of the others and yet preserve his individuality and grow according to his own law of growth. The Parliament of Relgions...has proved...that holiness, purity, and charity are not the exclusive possessions of any church in the world, and that every system has produced men and women of the most exalted character ... Upon the banner of every religion will soon be written in spite of ... resistance : 'Help and not Fight', 'Assimilation and not Destruction 'Harmony and Peace and not Dissension".[24]

No doubt, Vivekanand left a deep mark upon United States. The Ramakrishna Mission established by him spread rapidly in many European countries of the West. Among his most devoted desciples we find scores of monk of American and European origin. Dr. Karan Singh has observed rightly : "While this is generally well known, it is not often realised in India that many of the leaders of Hindu and Buddhist missionary work in the United States are of American and European origin. We still seem to hold the quaint notion that India has a monopoly on Hinduism and tend to be somewhat condescending towards Western Hindus. As one travels, however, it becomes increasingly clear that Hinduism is now developing as a world religion; and although India will always enjoy a special position as the birth place of Hinduism and the home of largest number of Hindus, she will have to remember that the Hindu teaching have now become very much the property of the world."[25]

**Differing Cultures and Bridges of Understanding**

"Race itself has become the dominant loyality among many people, especially among fanatic advocates of "Aryanism" and among certain members of oppressed races. It seems today that the clash between the idea of race and of one World is shaping into an issue that may well be the most decisive in human history. The important question is, Can a loyality to mankind be fashioned before inter-racial warfare breaks out."

Garden Allport, the Nature of prejudice–

For positive and constructive crosscultural communication respect and co-operation among different groups is very much desirable. This sort of co-operation and understanding the following are essential :

1. Actualization or proper and positive evaluation of self.
2. Positive view of society
3. Positive view of other people (other than one's group)
4. Logical and objective thinking.

For actualization values like equality, democracy and justice are very essential. One should neither over-estimate oneself or underestimate. Over-estimation will lead to various superiority complexes whereas under-degradation is damaging to one's personality, as it has been advised in *Bhagvadgeeta*. Positive view of the society makes a man to realize that he is indebted to the society he is living in and he has certain obligation towards the society. By all means he should strive to maintain peace and harmony in the society by developing and promoting positive thinking and understanding. Positive thinking about the people implies that he should try to understand plus and minus points of the people and behave with them accordingly. But, basically he should believe in human dignity and should not overlook the worth of the people around him. Success or failure of this type of endeavour will considerably depend upon his actualization of his own self. For the first three logical thinking and reasoning ability which will help the individual in refraining from jumping to the conclusion without minute and meticulous observation. Any sort of superficial thinking is bound to lead to faulty conclusion.

Dr. Radhakrishnan has very rightly observed:

> "Today, all the people of the world form a close neighbourhood, thanks to the inventions of science and devices of technology. Transport and communication have resulted in the meeting of cultures, races, and religions. The only attitude that we can adopt in the present context is an attitude not of exclusiveness but of comprehension, not of intolerance but of understanding, no of hatred and fanaticism but

of appreciation and assimilation of whatever is valuable."[26] For proper comprehension and understanding knowledge of other races, cultures and religions is necessary. That is why the ideas like comparative religion, inter-cultural dialogue inter-racial relations etc. have come to the forefronts".

In this context the remarks of Romain Rolland are also noteworthy :

"The first result of an objective study of comparative Metaphysics and Mysticism would be to demonstrate the universality and perennial occurrence of the great facts of religious experience, their close resemblance under the diverse costumes of race and time, attesting to the persistent unity of the human spirit-or rather, for it goes deeper than the spirit, which is itself obliged to delve for it-to the identity of materials constituting humanity."[27]

Professor Rudolf otto of Marburg lived for fourteen years in India and having studied the comparative mysticism of India and Europe scientifically devoted a complete series of remarkable works to 'Asiatic mysticism'. His main thesis establishes the extraordinary likeness of the fundamental motives of humanity's spiritual experience, exclusive of race, age, climate. Similarly, Paul Brunton came to India in the quest of secret India. His quest for Mystic India forced him to travel through nook and corner of the land, from the holy rivers to the lofty ranges of the Himalaya, from the narrow lanes of Benara to the Magnificent palaces, from the solitary hermit to the old book-shops. In this quest he circled the country and after meeting and having first hand inter-action with them he recorded his experiences in the books entitled "A search in secret India."[28]

So far (w.e.f. 1934) about twenty impressions have been brought out, which itself is the indicative of the appealing theme of the work, in which he has successfully depicted the mystic experiences of Meher Baba, Hazarat Babajan (the woman faqueer), Upsani Maharaj, Shri Shankar (The spiritual head of south India), Brama (the Adyar Anchorite), Sarda Devi (the holy mother), Narsingah Swamy, Raman Maharshee and host of other yogis, mystics, Sadhus and miracle-men of India.

Alike Professor Rudolf Otto, Paul Brunton also tried to highlight the significance of spiritual experience and compared it with his own past experience of the material world and came to the following conclusion :

> "I did arrive at a new acceptance of the Divine. This may seem quite an insignificant and personal thing to do, but as a child of this modern generation, which realies on hard facts and cold reason, and which lacks enthusiasm for things religious, I regard it as quite an achievement. This faith was restored in the only way a sceptic could have it restored not by argument, but by the witness of an overwhelming experience. And it was a jungle sage, an unassuming hermit who had formerly lived for six years in a mountain cave, who promoted this vital change in my thinking. The production of such sages provides India with sufficient credentials to warrant attention from intelligent Westerners."[29]

With spiritual point of view and in conformity with the concept of omnipresence of the 'Cosmic Soul'[30] mysticism is always and everywhere the same. We can say that the profound unity of the human spirit is a fact. Once this very fact rooted in our heart of hearts the question of 'dualism' does not arise. Therefore, in all the religions it is enjoined that one should do unto others as one would like to be done to him.[31] In spite of the variations between different mystic personalities including our yogi's and saint-poets their mystic experiences were identical, to quote a few :

> "As I went to see God, my intellect stood motionless, and as I saw him, I became Himself. . . . . . As a dumb man cannot express the sweetness of nectar, so also I cannot express my internal bliss."
>
> – *Jnanadeva*

> "God's form can be see even by a blind man, and a dumb man can communicate even in a deaf man's ears the knowledge of God. An ant shall devour the whole universe by its mouth, says Namdeva, only we shall have to verify all these things in our own experience."
>
> "It is by their support that I move on the way. Thou bearest all my burden. Thou puttest meaning into my meaningless words. Thou has taken away my shame and put courage into me."
>
> – *Tukaram*

> The lamps are different, but the light is one: it comes from beyond
> If thou keepest looking at the lamp, thou are lost: for thence arises the appearance of number of plurality.
> Fix thy gaze upon the light, and thou art delivered from the dualism inherent in the finite body.
> O thou art the kernel of existence, the disagreement between Moslem, Zoroastrain and Jew depends on the stand point.
>
> — *Jalal-ud-Din Rumi*

Saint Kabir, a great exponent of Nirgun School of poetry and the brightest jwel of Nirgun Bhakti cult was a great mystic of his time. That is why he says:

> I am not religious, I am not irreligious
> Neither a monk nor a lecher
> I neither babblen nor listen
> Neither a master nor a slave am I,
> Neither bound, nor free,
> Neither non-attached nor attached
> Neither aloof nor involved,
> Neither do I go to hell
> Nor do I go to heaven
> All action is my doing
> And yet I am beyond all action
> Such a faith is rare indeed,
> One who has it is steadfast.
> Kabir neither founds a faith
> Nor destroys it.[32]

He used many mystic terms inherited from Nath sect. from Buddhists or Sunya-vadis. In his poetrry he describes his Supreme as a Void Nothingness. But his Shunya is different from the orthodox Buddhist position and more akin to Shankara's one, which is beyond speech. Kabir describes his god as the experience of sweetness enjoyed by a dumb person. It cannot be communicated, it is inexpressible, indescribable. The mystic trance, to which Kabir refers again and again, is something of this divine madness. Many a time Kabir takes recourse to the negative terminology on Upnishadic lines, such as 'not this, not that' (Neti Neti).

In Kathopnishad there are verses where God is described as a stage, where neither the eyes, nor the speech, nor the mind, nor knowledge can reach. Kabir also describes his Brahma as sans everything i.e., nothing:

> Beyond Vedas, beyond differences, beyond sin or virtue
> Beyond knowledge, beyond meditation beyond solid or void
> Beyond dress, beyond alms Beyond the snobbery and forms
> Kabir says, beyond the three worlds the essence unmatched is.[33]

The Atman is formless, boundless, beyond all change. It is like a drop in the ocean, it cannot be separated, the ocean-ness is in the dropness.[34] As a Boul poet Gangaram puts it:

You are ocean, I am a boat
you are also my boat-man
It is upto you, get me across or sink
whatever it is, I will be happy, not think
To sink in you is an act devine
or to get across is illusion of mine.[35]

Proverbially it is said that all great men think alike. Similarly, it can be said that all the mystic experiences are alike. Their may be certain variations, but those differences cannot be attributed to difference in race, caste, creed, age or sex; but something inexpressible and devine. Yogi Aurbindo observes:

> "At the gates of the Transcendent stands that mere and perfect spirit described in the Upnishads, Luminous, pure, sustaining the world . . . . without flaw of duality, without sear of devision and multiplicity, the pure self of the Advaitins, the inactive Brahmin, the Transcendent Silence. And the mind when it passes those gates suddenly . . . . receives the sense of unreality of the world and the sole reality of the silence which is one of the most perful convincing experiences of which the human mind is capable."[36]

The above-mentioned experience of Aurbindo can easily be condensed in the following lines of the Mother :

Without Him I exist not,
Without me He is unmanifest.
I am with you because I am you or you are I.

The Mother says "I am with you, that signifies a world of things because I am with you on all levels, in all planes, from the supreme consciousness down to the most physical. Here, at pondicherry, you cannot breathe without breathing my consciousness. It saturates the atmosphere almost materially, in the subtle physical. Farther my consciousness can be felt in the material vital, then on the mental plane and other higher planes everywhere. When I came here for the first time, I felt the atmosphere of Shri Aurbindo, felt materially, at a distance of ten miles, ten nautical miles, not kilometers. It was very sudden, very concrete, an atmosphere pure, luminous, light, so light that lifts you up."[37]

Thus we see that the mystic experiences of the noble souls had been alike. There might had been differences of variations due to individual reasons and not for any race, caste, creed, age or sex. Understanding of this fact help us the nature and character of spiritual communication, which leads to better mutual understanding. Emerson was very much influenced by Eastern mysticism. Although Emerson's mysticism has kinship with protestant, Occidental mysticism, it is also related to the oriental idea particularly that of transmigration of soul, the spirit of God etc. However, he did not exalt mystical experience for its own sake or draw the oriental conclusion that all other experiences are valueless. For him "the mystical experience was dynamically a means, rather than passively an end."

By the virtue of this very balanced view-point regarding mysticism Emerson's writings have been appreciated by the Indian intellectuals including Mahatma Gandhi. When Mahatma Gandhi was in South African jail because of his effort to end discrimination, he read some of Emerson's essays, and later advised his son to draw inspiration from them.

**Promoters of Transcendentalism**

In fact Ralph Waldo Emerson (1803-1882) was the best known 'Transcendentalist' and one of the famous authors of the western world to read and understand the magnificent wisdom of ancient Hindu scripture. Technically speaking 'Transcendentalism' is not a definable school of philosophy but a trend of idealistic thinking. Love of nature, belief in an essentially benevolent universe, and mysticism are main ingredients of Transcendentalism., Many of the Transcendentalists' ideas owe to Indian hereitage. He was acquainted to kant and von-schelling (German Idealist Philosophers) and through them knew some threads of oriental philosphy. He was fond of plato also. The very kinship is so great that it is difficult to distinguish his platonic idealism and the influence of Indian Philosophy.

Briefly speaking Emerson was influenced mainly in three dimensions of his broad spectrum of ideas, viz–

1. Hindu writings helped him to formulate his idea that God (or Brahma) is a cosmic, impersonal, disinterested force rather than an anthropomorphic, personal being.
2. As a consequence, Indian thought had a good deal to do with his concept of relativity of human values. About Indian classics once he said : *They are like rainbows to be thankfully received in their first impressions, and not examined and surveyed by*

*theodolite and chain.*

3. His mysticism has an apparent influence of oriental mysticism.

Henry David Thoreau (1817-1862) was another transcendentalist who surpassed many other transcendentalists of the west. His famous book "Walden" is an American Classic. His hypothesis is that a man must know "those principles which are inherent in his own nature," and act in accordance, with them. The 'Walden' was the result of this experiment. Secondly he believed, like Indian philosophers, that peace comes not from immersion in the business of the world, but from quiet and solitary meditation. Thirdly he was of the firm conviction that to obtain happiness man must free himself from the lusts of the flesh, inordinate desires and wants, presumptuous thoughts, and pride. Thoreau's life is an example of such striving.

In adequacy of the material prosperity is aptly streamlined in one of the dialogues of Aristotle:

> "Be assured that the good of man does not depend upon abundance of possession, but upon the right inner quality. Not even the body is regarded as in a happy condition, merely because it is backed out in resplendent robes, but only if, though wanting in finery, it is well developed and in good health likewise one should call only that man fortunate whose soul is ethically developed rather than the man who is rich in outward possessions and is worth nothing in himself. Even a horse is judged by its actual virtues. It is a poor horse. It is not rated higher because it has a gold bit in its mouth and a costly harness on its back."[38]

Thoreau was greatly influenced by Indian philosophy. He has also left a great impact on modern Indian thought through his writings. Mahatma Gandhi was very much inspired by his essay–"Civil Disobedience" at a very crucial phase of his life when he was in South Africa. Gandhi himself said that he had ". . . . translated a portion for the readers of 'Indian Opinion in South Africa, which I was then editing and I made copies extracts for the English part of the papers. The essay seemed to be so convincing and truthful that I felt the need of knowing more of thoreau and I came across your (Henry S. Salt's) life of him, his Walden, and other essays, all of which I read with great pleasure."[39]

It is said that all great men think alike. This was virtually true when we compare various facets of Mahatma Gandhi and Thoreau. These two resemble not only in thinking but in life-style also. Thoreau will be ever remembered in the history of cross-cultural communication for having made some outline of Indian thought known familiar to thousands of American readers.

Thomas A. Harris opines that "religious experience may be unique combination of a child (a feeling intimacy) and Adult (A reflection of ultimacy) with a total exclusion of parent. I believe the total exclusion of parent is what happens in Kenosis or self-emptying. This self-emptying is a common characteristic of all mystical experiences"[40] The state of Kenosis or self-emptying in said as "no mind" by St. Anguistinge. The self of such person touches the unconscious, the source of infinite possibilities. This state of mind has been nicely reflected in one of the poem; of Busan, the Zen master of seventeenth century :

While alive
Be a dead man,
Thoroughly dead
And act as you will
And all is good.[41]

It means to love God is to have no self, to be of no mind, to become "a dead man", to be free from constructive motivation of consciousness. "Such man's "Good morning" has no human element of any kind of vested interest he is addressed and he responds. He feels hungry and eats. Superficially, he is a natural man, coming right out of nature with no complicated ideologies of modern civilized man. But how rich his inward life is ! because he is in direct communion with the great unconscious."[42]

In Indian Philosophy such a person is called *Jeevan-Mukta* (The one liberated from life). This state can be attained through sense-restraints, moral observances, bodily posture, breath-control, withdraw of sense-organ from their objects, fixation of mind, meditation and trance. When the mind meditates on the self, and is observed in it, dissolves. This type of self-emptying is a common characteristic of all mystical experiences, as Bishop James Pike put it in his book named "If this be hersby" as following: "As we have seen there is a generic character to the mystical experience of, say, a Christian or Zen Buddhist, and in the experiential patterns of persons of both traditions can be observed common factors. This is illustrated by the fact that present day Zen Buddhist philosophers use the same Greek word as is used by both paul and Western theologians to describe a process which experience in East and in West – has been found to be a principal route to the consummation of personal fulfilments. The word is *kenosis*, that is, *self-emptying*." This kind of unconsciousness is also called "Cosmic consciousness". Ordinary consciousness is finite and thus have limitations. It is known, whereas unconsciousness is not so. Erich Fromm *et al.,* observe: "We can thus state that our Limited consciousness, in as much as we know its limitations, leads us to all sorts of worry, fear, unsteadiness. But as soon as it is realised that our consciousness comes out of something which, though not known in the way relative things are known, is intimately related to us, we are relieved of every form of tension and are thoroughly at rest and at peace with ourselves and with the world generally. May we not call this unknown the consmic unconsciousness, or the source of infinite creativity whereby not only artists of every description nourish their inspirations, but even we ordinary beings are enabled, each according to his natural endowments, to turn his life into something of genuine art."[43]

**Polyglot Slovene Culture**

The Nineteenth Century French Writer Charles Nodier, has pointed out elaborately how as a result of their cultural history all slovenes mastered two or three living languages in addition to their own. Alpine Slovenia on the Adreiatic was a stagine-post between the Roman and Germanic world of western Europe and the Slavic east, between Vinice and Vienna, Italy and St. Petersburg. Under these influences, an original Slovene culture took shape over more than a thousand year. Among its scores of creative talents the following are note-wrothy who contributed to cross-cultural communication over the world, particularly the western world :

1. *Herman Sclavus* — Heman Sclaus of Carinthia, a monk, astronomer and theologian who translated the quran into Latin in Twelfth century. He was the person who dreamt of bringing about a synthesis of Islam, Christianity and the Paganism of antiquity.
2. *Jacob Handl* — He was the great sixteenth century (1550–1591) polyphonist. He is also known as Jacob Carniolus Gallus.
3. *Anton Jansa* — He was an apiculturist existed in the eighteenth century (1743–1773). He is said to be one of the founders of European apiculture.
4. *Jurji Vega* — In the eighteenth century (1754–1802) he revised the logarithmic tables.
5. *Marko anton Plencic* — In the eighteenth century (1705–1786) he discovered the principle of microbial contamination.
6. *Friderik Jerrej* — He was a lingusit, missionary and Bishop of

nineteenth century (1797–1868) and was one of the first authors of grammars and dictionaries of amerindian languages of North America scattered around the world.

7. *Joze Plecnik* — He founded the school of architect in the nineteenth century (1872–1957).
8. *Anton Azbe* — He was an impressionist painter of the nineteenth century (1862–1905) founded a school of painting in Munich in 1891 at which almost all the leading Slav Impressionist studied.
9. *France Preseren* — He is one of the prominent figures of slovene literature having affinity with Byron and Puskin. He is considered to be the greatest Slovene poet of the nineteenths century (1876–1918).

The Slovenes proved their tenacity during the Second World War by mobilizing an army of partisans in their mountain fastnesses and maintaining backbone of national institutions. In the year 1945, after the Second World War was over, the republic of Slovenia was created within the socialist Federal Republic of Yugoslavia. As the emblem of their country they chose their highest mountain. Mount Triglav (Almost 2900 meters high). The three heads of this very mountain has nourished a host of their legends and beliefs.

**India's Cultural Suzerainty Over Asia**

India is a country which has been influencing many other countries over the centuries through her religio philosophical speculations and traditions of art, literature and value-system. India's history is a history of philosophical traditions and movement in metaphysics and religion that have influenced other lands. In this context, Radhakamal Mukherjee has observed as following :

> "The state was in fact cast into the shade by people who cared much more for their philosophies, patterns of worship and standards of morality, than for historical events. India's holy books that have shaped Asian culture comprised a good number. Those that were carried to Central Asia and China include the Brahmanical Vedas, Agamas and Ramayana and the Buddhist Tripitaka, Saddharm Pundarik, Mahyanika Vritti, Shriddhotpada, Ashokavandana, Abhidharmakosha, and Sutralamkar, while the *Mahabharata*, the *Ramayana*, Jatakas Milind Panha, Lalit Vistara, Manu Smriti, *Puranas*, *Agamas* and *Tantras* went to ceylon. Further, India and

Indonesia, as attested by many versions and representations in art. The apathy and misunderstanding, if not positive distaste of many Western Indologists have extended also to the realm of art. Like the epics and Sutras, Puranas, Agamas and Tantras, Indian Statues, bronzes and paintings, carried by generations of Indian and foreign monk pilgrims, had been chief vehicles of dissemination of India's culture in Central Asia, China, Tibet, Nepal, Further India and Japan."[44]

Long time back A.C. Das, in his famous book *Rigvedic India* observed that *Sapta Sindhu Sanatana Dharma* (Vedic Dharma) proliferated to far off lands thousands of years back. He says : "The real fact that when the whole world was steeped in utter darkness, the Rig Vedic Aryans on the bank of Sarswati and the Sindhu and in the beautiful valley of Kashmir, lighted-up the holy fire of civilization and spiritual culture and kept it burning and glowing for thousands of years for the benefit of humanity. In a much later age, a few faggots were taken from this sacred and burning pile to other countries where they burned and glowed spasmodically for some time till they were extinguished, removed as they were from their original source. The ancient civilization of Babylonia, Assyria, Phoenicia and Egypt are now mere names and things of the past beyond hopes of revival and resuscitation."[45]

On the basis of above statement it can be said that in the hoary past. Sanatan Dharma was the only Dharma, which was at one time practised by mankind all over the globe. There are four Vedas – *Rig Veda*, *Yajur Veda*, *Samaveda* and *Atharva Veda*. The first relates to ritual and worship and treats of first causes. The second treats of ceremonies observed in Sacrifices, and contains instructions respecting religious services, castes, feasts, purifications, ceremonies of at birth, marriage and death. *Sama Veda* contains odes or hymns in praise of the Supreme Being (Brahaman) and the subordinate deities. The fourth, or *Atharva Veda*. According to Dr. Radhakrishnan, "The explorers of the art, literature and thought of the world's varied cultures have a more decisive voice in shaping the minds and hearts of the people than even political leaders in the spirit of scholarship which knows frontiers, and which, if genuine, breeds humility and tolerance in the task of building a new world, in ridding ourselves of every trace of hatred, intolerance and fanaticism of every variety, in moving towards to a great meeting where we respect everyman, every race, every culture, every creed. The world craves for fellowship."[46] The spirit of this land, from the time of the *Rig Veda* till today, ask us to move together, to develop common ideals and proposes :

> Meet together, talk together :
> May your minds comprehend alike :
> Common be your action and achievement :
> Common be your thoughts and actions :
> Common be the wishes of your hearts
> So may there be union amongst you.[47]

In India, Vedas are regarded as fountain source of human thought and true religion. There are also certain subsequent writings called Brahmanas including Satpatha, Brahmana, Gopatha Brahmana etc. which illustrate and direct the ritualistic use of the old texts or hymns of the Vedas. The Upnishads, appended to bring out more fully and systematically the references in the earlier writing to the great problems of the universe and they are rightly mentioned as the fountain-head of all Indian Philosophy. Prof. R.D. Ranade says :

> "The Upnishads constitute that lofty eminence of philosphy, which from its various sides gives birth to rivulets of thought, which, as they progress onwards towards the sea of life gather strength by the inflow of innumerable tributaries of speculation which intermittently join these rivulets, so as to make a·huge expense of waters at the place where they meet the ocean of life."

The various exponents and commentators of life Vedanta right from Shankara, Ramanuj, Nimbarka, Madhava and Vallabha to the modern-time philosophers including Dr. S. Radhakrishnan–have always regarded upnishads as the sacred texts and have interpreted them in their own ways. Jain Acharyas have also taken idealsim and Karmite laws from upnishads. The Heterodox Buddhism derives its idealism, monism, absolutism, Shunyanavada, Kshanikvada (the theory of momentariness of all worldly things,) theory of Karma and the theory that of Ignorance (Avidya) is the root cause of the bondage and that Nirvana (salvation) can be attained by right knowledge alone, from Upnishads, being very much inspired from the Monistic thoughts of Upnishads, Schopenhauer, noted German philosopher, believed that "The Hindus were deeper than the thinkers of Europe, because their interpretation of the world was eternal and intuitive, not external and intellectual; the intellect devices everything; the Hindus saw that the "I" (Aham) is a delusion; that the individual is merely phenomenal, and that the only reality is infinite one – "That art Thou".[48]

**Concept of Avidya or Maya**

Many philosophers take these two terms—Maya and Avidya—as identical, as it has been expounded by Shankara, whereas there are others who explain them as two distinct entities. Refuting the elaboration of Shankara, Ramanuja take them as two different themes. He says that 'Maya' is the real power of God by which he creates the wonderful world. By 'Avida' he means the ignorance of Jiva by which he identifies himself wrongly with the material objects like the body, the senses, the mind etc. which are evolutes of Prakriti (matter). But like Shankara, he too, thinks that ignorance is the cause of bondage and that the immediate intutive knowledge of God is the cause of liberation. But the interpretations of ignorance and knowledge and the bondage and liberation given by Ramanuj are different from that of Shankara.

In fact, there are certain conceptual differences amongst all the expositions available on Vedanta, but the main base are Upnishads, which hold that a man forgets bondage for himself because of ignorance and only man can get rid of them, for which he is quite capable. Many scholars hold Shankara himself is the expounder of the concept of 'Maya' which does not hold good in the light of the Survey of Upnishads, Prof. R.D. Ranade has rightly pointed out the origin of this doctrine in the Upnishads on this comments, the following points mentioned in his famous work: "The Constructive Survey of Upnishadic Philosophy" are noteworthy:

1. Isha tells us that the veil that covers the truth is golden, so rich, gaudy and dazzling that it takes away the mind of the observer from the inner contents. (Isha 1, 5)
2. Katha says how people live in ignorance and thinking themselves wise, move about wandering, like blind men following the blind. (1, 2, 4–5)
3. Mundaka compares ignorance to a knot which a man has to untie before he gets possession of self in the recess of his own heart. (II, 1, 10)
4. Chhandogya tells us that knowledge is power and ignorance is impotence. (I 1,10)
5. Brhadaranyaka compares Unreality to Not-being, to Darkness and to Death. (I, 3, 28)
6. Prashna tells us that we cannot reach the world of Brahman unless we have shaken off the crookedness in us the false-hood, the illusion. (I, 16)
7. Brhadaranyaka tells us 'as if there were a duality' implying

thereby that there is really no duality. Maya is a semblance, an as-it-were, an appearance. (II, 4, 14)

8. Chhandogya tells us that Atman is the only Reality, everything else is merely a word, a mode and a name. (VI 1, 4)
9. Shvetashvatara describes God as a Mayin entity, who creates this world by his power." (IV, 9)

**Science and Technology**

Ancient Indian ideas of Physics were closely linked with religion and theology. Indian concept of element or Indian atomic theory etc. — these, atleast in their inceptional period, are not based not experiment but on intuition and logic. That is why they were not held universally and we find some sort of difference of opinion from sect to sect, from school (of philosophy) to school and so on. Accordingly to Prof. Basham, "Most schools believed that the elements other than ether (Akash) were atomic. India's atomism was certainly independent of Greek influence, for an atomic theory was taught by Pakudh Katyayan, an older contemporary of the Buddha, and was therefore earlier than that of Democritus. The Jainas believed that all atoms (anu) were identical, and that differences of the character of elements were due to manner in which the atoms were combined. Most schools, however, maintained that there were as many types of atom as there were elements."[49]

All schools admitted atleast four elements – earth, air, fire and water. To these orthodox Hindu schools and Jainism added a fifth i.e., 'akash' ('ether'). These five elements were thought of as the media of sense impressions – earth of smell, air of feeling, fire of vision, water of taste and ether of sound. Prof. Basham opines that "The Vaiseshika school, which specially elaborated its atomic doctrines and was the school of atomism *par excellence*, maintained that, before combining to form material objects, atoms made primary combinations of diads and triads. This doctrine of molecules was developed differently by Buddha and Ajeevikas, who taught that in normal conditions no atoms existed in a pure state, but only combined in different proportions in a molecule Samghat, Kalapa. Every molecule contained atleast one atom of all four types and obtained its character from the predominance of a given element. This hypothesis accounted for the fact that matter might show characteristics of more than one element; thus wax might melt and also burn, because its molecules contained proportions of water and fire. According to Buddhists the molecules coherred by virtue of the atoms of water in each, which acted as an adhesive."[50] According to

Vaisheshikas atoms cannot interpenetrate one another, for there is no intra-atomic space. They are inactive or motionless in themselves. These motion is due to an external agent. The later Vaisheshikas believe that God produces motion in the atoms, combine them into composite products with the aid of merits and demerits of individual souls for their enjoyments and sufferings. The physical order is subservient to the moral order. The world is not a fortuitous combination of atoms governed by mechanical law of causality. It is governed by the law of casuality subordinated to the Law of Karma (Karmite Law).

Two thousand years old Jain work describes a mercury turbine as engine for mechanically driven heavier-than-air flying machines; atomic theory was taught during the time of the Buddha; Indian scientists of 50 A.D. had known about nuclear fission and done considerable research for analysing the proper linking of atoms in the formation of different solids; plastic surgery was developed and practised in India as early as the first century of the Christian era; ancient Indian medical treatises had established the spread of malaria through mosquitos which was proved to the satisfaction of western medicine only at the end of the last century. The latest knowledge in the fields of anatomy and physiology only goes to confirm Sushruta's profound analyses of biology and organism. Modern medical science has yet to reach the depth of analysis of the abstract body explored to perfection by ancient Indian seers.

It was from India that the so-called Arabic numerals of nine digits and a zero with place value notations for the tens and hundreds went to Arabia, and from Arabia to north Africa and Europe. Professor Basham says: "The debt of the western world to India in this respect cannot be overestimated. Most of the great discoveries and inventions of which Europe is so proud would have been impossible if Europe had been shakcled by the unwieldy system of Roman numerals. The unknown man who devised the new system was from the world's point of view, after the Buddha, the most important son of India. The French astronomer and mathematician Pierre de Laplace who set forth a nebular hypothesis of cosmogony in 1796 has written : "It is India that gave us the ingenious methods of expressing all numbers by means of ten symbols. We shall appreciate the grandeur of this achievement when we remember that it escaped the genius of Archimedes and Apollonius, two of the greatest men produced by antiquity".

Astronomers and mathematicians talk of Pythagoras, Archimedes, Euclid, Ptolemy, Copernicus, Diaphantus, Galileo, Kepler, Newton, Euler, and a host of others who have, indeed, left the indelible impression of their greatness. But it is not generally known to what a great extent medieval and modern astronomers and mathematicians are indebted to the achievements of ancient Indians in these branches of science.

One of the sutras written before 600 B.C. clearly state what the Greek mathematician Pythagoras is said to have proved later–what is now known as the 47th proposition in the first book of Euclid. In the solution of the Pelican equation' Euler has not done anything so remarkable original as this solutions had been given by Indian mathematicians several centuries earlier. While the Greeks had no terminology for denominations above the myriad, and the Romans above the mile, ancient Indians had dealt freely with no less than eighteen denominations. The idea of alphabetic system of expressing numbers had originated in India even before the Greek civilization came into being.

Among the early Portuguese, Dutch and French adventurers who came to India in quest of trade, there were intellectuals who, fascinated by the country's ancient glory, took time off for extensive studies in the area of their interest. Early in the 17th century it was a Dutch commander, Baron Van Rheede, and the Carnallite monk Matthaeus who studied the flora of Malabar and compiled the Hortus Malabaricus, later published in twelve volumes at Amsterdam with 800 copper plate engravings, as a monumental encyclopaedia of trees and plants of the West Coast.

## Impact of the Indian Culture on South East Asian Countries

Like the countries of Western and Central Asia, the countries of South East Asia were also influenced by Indian Culture. Indian merchants and the followers of different Indian religions visited the countries of South East Asia. They established colonies and propagated their religion there. Indian culture and traditions also extended there along with the religion. These countries were quite backward before the advent of the Indians. The visits of the Hindus and Buddhists led to the mutual cultural contacts with these countries. Indians visited these countries for trade and for extracting minerals. Indian made many sea-voyages which are mentioned in Jatakas. Many Indian cultural remains have been found in Ceylon, Java, Sumatra, Burma, Kambuja etc.

### *Burma*

In early times Burma was called *Suvarn Bhumi* We do not know as to what were the relations between India and Burma in early times. Direct relations between Burma and India were established during the reign of Ashoka who sent missionaries for the spread of Buddhism. Buddhism spread rapidly far and wide in Burma. In the 6th Century B.C., two princes named Vimal and Shyamal founded the city of Pegu which later on became famous as Hansavarta. Regarding the expansion of Indian culture in Burma, B.N. Luniya writes, "The rise and growth of Buddhism in Burma was due to two Ashoka's missionaries, Sona and Uttara; but actually the apostle was Buddhaghosa, the famous Simhalese scholar, who went to Burma from Ceylon in 450 A.D. and established there the Hinayan form of Buddhism. Later on in the eleventh century the Chola king Rajendra I sailed over to Burma and conquered and annexed it. In the thirteenth century ceylonese Buddhism and Pali scriptures were introduced in Burma. During these centuries of close contact Indian thought and art influenced Burmese life." Again, "Even today a large number of Burmese are Buddhists and their language, script and religious rites and ceremonies have deep impression of Indian culture."

Many statues of Vishnu found in Burma indicate that Brahmanism also extended in Burma. On account of the close contact for a long time, Indian thought and art influenced the Burmese life. The language, script and religion of Burma bear clear Indian impact. Even today there are a large number of Buddhist monks in Burma. Indian influence is clearly visible in the Pagodas, statues of Lord Buddha and art of Burma.

*Ceylon (Sri Lanka)*

Contacts between India and Ceylon have existed from very early times. There are references of contacts between Ceylon and India in the *Ramayana*. Most of the Hindu believe that Indian culture penetrated in Ceylon for the first time when Shri Ram Chandra invaded Lanka. According to historical events, Kumar Vijay went Lanka near about 500 B.C. He married Yakshi Kuveni there and established an Indian colony. During the reign of Asoka, his son Mehendra and daughter Sanghmitra went to Lanka for the propagation of Buddhism. Even today Buddhism is widely prevalent in Lanka. A branch of Bodhi tree was planted in Lanka, still exists. Shunga king Duthgamini had built many Chaityas and Viharas. During his reign many Buddhist monks from Rajgriha, Sravasti, Vaisali and Pataliputra went to Lanka for the propagation of Buddhism.

India and Lanka had good trade relations, Tamrlipta, Sopara, Broach etc., were the ports from where the goods were exported to and imported from Lanka. The art of Lanka has been greatly influenced by Indian art. Indian art was freely used in the construction of the stupas and viharas of Anuradapur. The paintings of Sigria were influenced by the paintings of Ajanta. Thus, Indian culture had made a vast impact upon the life and culture of Lanka.

### *Siam*

In Siam or modern Thailand, there lived tribe known as Mons. These people had adopted Indian civilization and founded an Indian Kingdom named Dwaravati in the second or third century A.D. Later on Mahayan form of Buddhism extended in Siam from the neighbouring Hindu colony, Cambodia, several statues of Amravati style, have been found in Siam. The monuments of Siam bear the influence of Gupta art. A clear Indian impact is found on the administrative system of Siam.
According to B.G. Gokhale :

> "The influence of Indian ceremonial in Siamese Court of life is very extensive and even today the coronation of a Siamese prince can be performed only by a Brahman priest."

According to B.N. Luniya,

> "Many of the episodes and elements of the two famous Hindu epics, the Ramayana and the Mahabharat, have been freely taken over in Siamese literature. In the realm of art Siamese borrowed the conception of the Buddhist temples and Buddhist images from India – The names and the titles of the kings, people and towns of Siam even today reveal the traces of Hindu influence. They remained under the cultural influence of Indians till the sixteenth century A.D."

### *Java*

The ancient name of Java was 'Yavadvipa'. Fahien has described about the large number of Indian settlers in Java in the beginning of fifth century B.C. According to him, most of the Indian settlers were followers of Saivism. We know a good deal about the Indian cultural expansion in Java from the four inscriptions of king Purnavarma of 6th century B.C. Indian culture extended far and wide in Java during the reign of Avialangga and his successors.

We know from the description of Fahien that Brahmanism with its different branches existed in Java. Buddhism was not much prevalent. Vishnu was worshipped in Java. The statues of Sesasayi Vishnu, Krishan, Ram, Matsaya, Varah and Nar Simha have been discovered. Saivism was very much prevalent in Java. A king named Sanjaya had established Shiva Linga on a rock.

In the early literature of Java many 'Chandas' were composed on the basis of Sanskrit 'Chandas'. During the reign of Sailendra Empire, *Amarkosh* and *Amarmala* were written. Many books were written on the basis of Indian plots. The epics of *Ramayana* and the *Mahabharata* were popular in Java. As remarked by B.N. Luniya, "Indian art and literature flourished in Java to an extent unknown elsewhere."

The influence of Indian art may be seen in the many monuments of Brahmanism and Buddhism in Java. The monument of Barduda is the best example of the art of Java. Many statues of Lord Buddha and different gods and goddesses of Hinduism reveal the traces of the influence of Indian art. Like Sanchi and Bharhut, different incidents of the life of Lord Buddha have been painted here also. As remarked by Dr. R.C. Majumdar, ". . . . the general plan of the mouldings of the Japanese temples has its counter-part in Gupta style."

According to B.N. Luniya, "in fact India exercised its manysided influence in Java. The king of Malaya Peninsula and Indonesia bore Indian names. Their court customs and manners reflect Indian patterns. Their law codes were modelled on the Indian legal system. Saivism, Vaishnavism, Mahayan Buddhism and Tantrism gained popular favour and royal patronage. The Indo-Japanese art makes 'an extensive use of Indian motif the Kalamkar : a lion's head and a crocodile in decoration.'

### *Sumatra*

Sri Vijay Empire had been founded in Sumatra by the fourth century B.C. It was in a highly developed state in the seventh century B.C. Itsing, the Chinese traveller had visited Sumatra while coming to India. He had studied the texts of Pali and Sanskrit there. Near about 684 A.D. A Buddhist ruler named Sri Jananash ruled over there. The education of Buddhism was imparted in a beautiful way in the empire of Sri Vijay. In the eighth century A.D., Sailendra conquered this region. The rulers of this dynasty were the followers of Buddhism.

Like other islands, the traces of Indian religion and civilization are found in large number in Sumatra. The statues of Lord Buddha, Bodhisatvas etc., are found at Padang, Jambi and at other places. The statues of Shiva, Ganesh, Nandi, Bramha, etc. reveal the traces of Indian influence. Scholars are of the opinion that they are influenced by Gandhara art while others hold the view that they were influenced by Mathura style of art.

According to a scholar, "Krom traces its origin not to Gandhara school but to some Indian school of art in which the Graceo principles are found in modified Indianism form i.e., that of Amravati."

Dr. R.C. Majumdar holds the view that the statues of Lord Buddha, Avalokitesvara and Maitreya reveal the influence of Indian art" According to Dr. R.M. Majumdar, "Those images bear the closer affinity to Indian art, The style of the bronze image of Buddha is clearly reminiscent of the Gupta period, and that of Maitreya probably belongs to the same school."

### *Borneo*

Like Sumatra, Java, Siam etc., Indians had established their colony in Borneo also. Hindu kingdom was established "one of the kings of Borneo Maulvarman, son of Asvavarman and grandson King Kundunga (Kaundinya), performed the great sacrifice called Bahu Suvarnakam (large quantity of gold) and erected *Yupas* (sacrificial pillars) with Sanskrit inscriptions to commemorate it. The inscriptions are dated about 400 A.D, and record Mulvarman's rich donations and gifts of 20,000 cows to the Brahmans in the hold field of Vaprakesvara. In the eastern Borneo many antiquities have been discovered at many places especially in the cave of Kombeng. Twelve stone images of the Brahmanical gods Shiva, Ganesh, Agastya, Brahma, Mahakal, Mandishvar etc., have been found in the cave. Though indigenous elements are visible in the architectural art of Borneo, yet it is evolved on the Indian patterns of art. Hindu culture still flourishes there."

The Brahmans occupied prominent position in the Society in the empire of Maulvarman. Maulvarman used to perform all his works in accordance with Brahmanism. The statues of Shiva, Vishnu etc., found here seem to have been brought direct from India.

### *Bali*

The island of Bali is situated in the East of Java. Indian culture still flourishes in Bali. A Hindu Kingdom was established in Bali in the fourth century A.D. A Hindu Kingdom flourished in Bali in the sixth century A.D. under the Kaundinya Kshatriyas. Buddhism extended far and wide in Bali in the sixth century A.D. The names of the rulers of Bali such as Ugra Sen, Kesari resemble with Indian names. Saivism was prevalent in the island of Bali. The inhabitants were acquainted with Pauranic names such as Surya, Chandra, Durga Lakshmi etc. They observed fast at different occasions like the Indians. The worship of Pitras was done by them. The priests of the temples used to be the scholars of Sanskrit. The pillars of the temple were decorated by the stories of *Ramayana* and the *Mahabharat*. The art of Bali reveals the traces of the influence of Indian art. The statues of the period before the 10th century A.D. bear close affinity with Indian statues. The statue of 'Narasimha Avatar' is particularly beautiful from the point of view of sculptural art.

Bali was conquered by the Japanese rulers in the later half of the tenth century and for centuries it remained under their control. They established their supremacy over Bali in 1839 and the reign of last Hindu King of Bali ended in 1911. In the words of B.N. Luniya, "But it was the aggression of Islam in Java that forced its Hindu king to go to Bali. Henceforth the island of Bali became the seat of flourishing Indo-Javanese culture. Consequently, even today Hinduism with all its old traditions and practices flourishes there. Thus, while Hinduised Java succumbed to the raids of Islam, Bali retained its old and indigenous culture even to the present day. It is the last refuge of Brahmanical religion and Hindu culture in the Far-East."

### *Funan*

Funan was a province of the kingdom of Cambodia. The Hindus had the credit of ending the uncivilized state of this province. A brahman named, Kaudinya had established his kingdom in accordance with Indian laws and customs. In 484 A.D. Jaya Varman of Kaundinya dynasty sent a monk named Nagasena to China. The inscriptions of Kulaprabhavati, the queen of king Jayavarman and her son Rudra Verman indicate that the rulers of this dynasty were the followers of Saivism. Vaishnavism and Buddhism had also extended in Funan by the fifth and sixth centuries respectively. The inscriptions of these kings are in Sanksrit language. The inhabitants of Funan were fully aware of the Indian philosophical thoughts and religious beliefs. The temples of Funan were constructed on Indian style. The temples had square-shaped or rectangular-shaped garbhas of bricks and had steps. Thus, we see that Indian culture had extended far and wide in Funan.

### *Kambuj*

Kambuj was situated in the north of Cambodia. Matavarman was the king of Kambuj. He conquered and annexed Funan and incorporated in his empire. Most of the rulers of Kambuj were the worshippers of Saivism. Sri Matavarman had established the Linga of Trayambaka. The daughter of Viravarman is compared to Aradhanti in devotion to her husband and religion. Mahendravarman had established 'Shivapada' in Kambuj in the same manner as 'Vishnupada' was established in India. A rock inscription indicates the donation to God Shiva by the queen of Jayavarman II of Kambuj. The reign of Jayavarman is reckoned as the golden period of Kambuj. A ruler named Induvarman had conquered Champa. Ishanvarman had got constructed many Ashrama in Kambuj. He also got constructed a mixed statue of Shiva and Vishnu. King Jayavarman was the follower of Buddhism.

The inscriptions found in Kambuj indicate that the worship of Shiva, Vishnu, Durga etc., was widely prevalent here. The Ramayana and the Mahabharat were widely studied. The inhabitants of Kambuj were throughly acquainted with the names of Kailash, Udaigiriparvat, Suryavamsa, Chandravamasa, Manu etc. The Doctrine of Karma propounded in *Gita* was also fully known to them.

Art flourished in the state of Kambuj. The ruins of Angkorthom reveal the traces of Indian influence. King Suryavarman II had built a vast Vishnu temple in the form of Angakaurvata. This temple still exists in the form of a Buddhist Vihars. There was a Shiva temple in the middle of Angakorthom.

### *Champa*

Champa was an Indian colony in early times Shriman was the first Indian ruler of Champa. He was the follower of Saivaism. Sanskrit was probably the official language during his reign. Dharm Maharaj Shri Bhadra Varma (387–413 A.D.) and his successor Changraj are the famous kings among the early rulers of Champa. During the reign of Changraj, there were several disturbances and disorders. King Bhardravarma was a great scholar. He had studied all the four vedas, he was a worshipper of Lord Shiva and had constructed a Shiva temple in Myson. King Indravarman of Bhring dynasty was the worshipper of Lord Shiva and Saivism was the state religion during his reign. He also respected Buddhism. Jaya Parmeshvar Varmandeva Insvarmurti (1050–1060), Rudravarman (1061–1069). Harivarman (1070–1081), Maharadhiraja Shree Jaya Indravarman (1163–1180) and Jaya Simhavarman (1257–1287) were other famous rulers of Champa. The judicial system of Champa during the reign of Harvarman was based on Hindu principles. A inscription found at a place called Dang Duang in Champa refers the king as the God living upon the earth. Like the armies of India, the armies of Champa were defeated several times on account of the running away of the elephants. The Annamiles and the Mongolians had begun to attack Champa from the tenth century onwards.

Regarding the social condition of Champa, B.N. Luniya observes the following :

> "A Hindu society modelled on the orthodox Indian type developed in champa. The Brahmans occupied a high place, but the rank of the Kshtriyas was hardly inferior to theirs. Though Brahmanism dominated, Buddhism also enjoyed the patronage of several rulers. However, Brahmanism and Brahmanic cultural flourished and saturated life in Champa."

Marriages between Brahmans and Kshatriyas were prevalent in Champa. As a result of this, there existed a new caste known as Bramha-Kshatriya as it was in the case of India. The custom of bring the dead bodies was prevalent in Champa. After burning the dead bodies their ashes were kept in a pot. The ash of the dead body of a king was kept in a pot of gold and thereafter it was immersed in the sea. There were several means of amusements popular among the inhabitants of Champa. These means of amusements revealed the Indian influence. Indian 'Dhol' and 'Majira' were popular instruments of music in Champa. Women also participated in music and dancing Concerts.

The *Ramayana* and the *Mahabharata* were studied in Campa. Some of the inhabitants of Champa were scholars of Vedas.

Buddhism had received royal parentage in the State of Champa. The Buddhist rock inscription of Vechanha of Indo-China. Indicate that Buddhism was prevalent in the third century in Champa. In 605 A.D., a Chinese General had taken some Buddhist texts to China from Champa. Several monasteries were constructed by the kings of Champa. Vaishnavism was also prevalent in Champa. Several names of Vishnu such as Purshottam. Narayana, Govinda–Madhav, Vikrams etc. were prevalent. The four-handed form of Vishnu was worshipped. Different stories of the incarnations of Krishna were also prevalent.

Saivism was the main and dominant religion of Champa. Shiva was worshipped in many forms such as Mahesvara, Mahadeva Amaresh, Shambhu. Ishan etc. According to B.N. Luniya :

> "The native people were completely Hinduiesd. They worshipped Hindu gods and goddesses among whom Shiva, his Shakti or power,

his two sons, Ganesh and Skanda, were occupying predominant position. The object of Shiva worship was the Linga. One of the oldest of the Lingas placed in the Bhadreswara temple in Myson, was held to the national deity. Besides Shiva, Vishnu, Krishna, Buddha and other gods were also worshipped."

Regarding the art of Champa, B.N. Luniya writes, "As regards art, the people of Champa followed closely the Gupta art not only in subject matter but in technique also. The complicated stone foliation, celestial dancer poised on one toe, intent on pleasing the gods and a bronze status of Buddha discovered amongst the ruins of Champa reveal unmistakable influence of Indian art on the Champa art. A large number of temples were constructed in the whole country. In fact, the Champa art had attained a high level of excellence of in abundance of decoration and grogeous ornamentation in temples, toranas or main entrances and pillars."

*China, Korea, Japan and Philippine*

China was the main centre of Buddhism. Indian culture penetrated into Korea and Japan through China. In this connection, B.C. Gokhale writes :

> "Through China, Indian cultural influences spread into Korea and Japan and, wherever they spread they helped the indigenous cultures grow and manifest themselves through great philosophical, literary and artistic achievements."

Buddhism extended to China through Khotan in the first century A.D. Kashyapa, Matanga, Dharamratna etc., were the man Buddhist missions to China. A Buddhist monastery named Poma-See was constructed by the Chinese Mingati (57–76 A.D.) for these monks. According to Dr. R.C. Majumdar :

> Although original intercourse might have been inspired by commercial enterprise, it was soon overshadowed by missionary activity leading to more or less complete cultural conquest over extensive regions."

In the sixth century A.D., Chinese Emperor Nu-ti (502–594 A.D.) was a stauch supporter and patron of Buddhism like Ashoka. Buddhism was prevalent in China in almost every house during that period. There were about thirty thousand Buddhist temples and twenty lae Buddhist priests. The empire of Tang dynasty (618–907) was the golden period of Buddhism in China. Chinese were themselves inspired to adopt the new religion. Several Chinese travellers came to India to study the Principles, beliefs and customs of Buddhism. These travellers took hundreds of Buddhist texts of China. Sanskrit and Pali texts were translated by the Chinese. Fahien, Hiuen Tsang, Sung-yun and Itsing were the most prominent among the Chinese travellers who came to India to study Buddhist texts and to make a pilgrimage of Buddhist holy palaces. Many prominent Indian texts on literature and philosophy were translated in Chinese language. In the words of R.C. Majumdar :

> "Since then many other Buddhist missions are recorded to have visited China from time Most of these missionaries came from Central Asia. It should be noted that China paid a high compliment to Buddhism when they consented to learn ti from the monks of Central Asia, which was in her eyes a country of barbarians."

Buddhism made a great progress during the reign of Wei dynasty. About 47 big monasteries were constructed in Loyand and Changangan during this period. These were the main centres of propaganda of Buddhism. Shri P.C. Bagchi also writes :

> "Under the patronage of the Wei, Loyand and Changangan, became the greatest centres of Buddhist activities in China."

**Confucianism Entered Europe**

It is said that Buddhism entered Japan through China, with a mixture of Confucianism. Buddhism was first introduced in China in the first century B.C. and found gradually widespread acceptance in China, obviously not at the cost of Confucianism. Through the centuries the scholar-administrators continued to give expression to their analysis of man and universe in words and figures drawn from the old classics, even though the ideas they tried to express were clearly inspired by the abstractions of Buddhist philosophy. Eventually there gradually developed a more analytical presentation of orthodoxy, known as Neo-Confucianism.

The western world was very much fascinated towards this new knowledge. Soon after the discovery of the sea-route around the cape of Good Hope, Christain missionaries began to go to China. According to Ramond Dawson "The Jesuit missionaries reached China in 1583 and established themselves at Peking under the leadership of Matteo Ricci at the beginning of the 17th century. It was the general policy of Jesuit missions to try to secure the conversion of a country by winning the sympathy of its ruler, and Matteo Ricci and his colleagues soon became aware that, to gain the respect of the emperor, they had to make themselves congenial to the scholar-bureaucrats by whom he was surrounded. To achieve this they needed to become Chinese scholars themselves. So while steeping themselves in the classical literature,[51] they became strongly influenced by the attitude of the 'Chinese Literati', who thought of China as a country governed by philosophers, whose wisdom and virtue derived from the study of the ancient Confucian Literature which they had to master for the purpose of passing the civil service examinations."[52]

**Indo-French Artistic Exchanges**

Growing increase of French tourists to India and Indian tourists to France is reflective of the awareness of Cultures of France in India and India in France. Art has been playing an important role in promoting France-Indian Co-operation. Many French artists have drawn inspiration from India's wealth of myths and legends, while Indian artists have shaped new sensibilities from French creative effectiveness.

With the Festival of India held in France in 1985, the French were treated to a variety of Indian classical and traditional art forms ranging from the Pandavani epic songs to the Kathakali and the masterpieces of Indian Classical sculptures and paintings with the exhibition RASA, the nine faces of Indian Art at the "Grand Palais" in Paris. Peter Brook's play based on the Mahabharata was accelaimed as the most popular event of the festival.

Four years later, Indians were offered the best in French performing and visual arts. Various exhibitions, held at New Delhi, Bombay and Calculate, exposed various aspects of French Art: Sculptures from the Louvre Musoum (French Bronzes from Renaissances to Rodin) or works of famous artists in the exhibition "Birth and Life of Modernity", enabled the Indian public to discover the works of these artists, such as Paul Cezane, Vincent Van Gogh, Paul Gauguin or Pablo Picasso. Director Georges Lavaudant and Bharat Bhavan together produced Racine's play "Phedre" in Hindi for the Bhopal audience.

Since then, number of Indian artists have visited France, be it the Bharatnatyam exponent Guru V.S. Muthuswamy Pillai's visit to the International Dance Festival in Montpelier or be it the Dhrupad singers Ustad Nazir Zahirddin Dagar and Fayaz Wasifuddin Dagar to the Mira

Bai Festival in Paris. In 1994, a major exhibition of contemporary French art was held in Delhi and Bombay. Theatre groups from India are likely to take part in the Festival of Avignon and French director Jean-Pierre Vincent would co-produce a play with the National School of Drama. In this way, Indo-French artistic exchanges are poised for further development.

## India's Impact on Western Thought and Literature[53]

Eminent Indologists like Max Muller, Garbe and Winternitz agree that 'centuries before Christ there were in Persia, Asia Minor and Alexandria seats of learning which were visited, among others, by Greeks, and Brahmanas from India who played an important part in the intellectual fellowship promoted by these centres where Indian ideas were most popular.'

Garbe says that the doctrines of the Indian Sankhya philosophy exerted great influence on Greek thinkers like Heraclitus, Empedocles, Anaxagorus, Democritus and Epicures. He says that the theory of Heraclitus that "all bodies are transformations of fire" and of Empedocles of "the eternity and indestructibility of matter" are restatements of Sankhya ideas which were also the origin of the latter's belief in the transmigration of soul.

The Eleatic philosophers of Greece, says Huszar, were profoundly influenced by the Upanishads. Their view that God and the universe are eternal and unchangeable was distinctly Upanishadic. Says Erdmann: "The absorption of all separate existence in a single substance, as taught by the Eleatics seems rather on echo of Indian pantheism than a principle of Hellenic spirit."

Max Mueller and other European authorities take the view that Pythagoras had contact with Indian scholars in Persia, from whom he learnt the forty-seventh theorem of the Euclidean geometry, which is found in the Sulva Sutras of Baudhayana, his ideas of the science of music, the importance of numbers, his doctrine of reincarnation, as also the 'holy tetractyls' the meaning of which is found in the formula of diagrams for Vedic sacrifices to which again is traced the origin of the decimal system of notation. Colebrooke holds that the Pythagorians were indebted to their Indian instructors. Schrader declares that India is the birthplace of Pythagorian ideas.

### *Link with India*

Both Plato and Aristotle had contact with India through Persia when the

Achaemenian empire touched the borders of India and Greece. In the fifth century B.C., says Max Mueller, there were in Greece 'Brahmanas' from India. That they were in Athens in the time of socrates is corroborated by Eusebius, a Greek church historian of the third century A.D. He mentions the meeting of an Indian with Socrates who was asked by the former what was the scope of his philosophy. "An enquiry into human phenomena," replied Socrates. At this the Indian burst out laughing: "How can a man enquire into human phenomena when he is ignorant of divine ones ?"

Urwick is convinced that India is the birthplace of many of the ideas of Plato. "Plato is full of Sankhyan thought worked out by him but taken from Pythagoras," says Hopkins. Max Mueller says that "the similarity between Plato's language and that of the Upanishads is sometimes startling. Garbe holds that many of Plato's ideas were transferred from India to Greece. Gnosticism and neoplatonism are believed to have grown out of a synthesis of Christian and Indian ideas. The Gnostic idea of the plurality of heavens and spiritual worlds are regarded as distinctly Upanishadic.

There can be no doubt, says Erdmann, that Plotinus, the founder of neo-Platonist school which profoundly influenced European thought, had deep knowledge of Indian mysticism and himself led the life of a Yogi often rising into states of Samadhi, mentioned in the Yoga philosophy. His 'Universal Mind' and 'World-Soul' are clearly Vedantic. What he called 'Nature' is identified with Prakriti of the Sankhya whose influence is traced by Garbe in the explanation Plotinus gave of creation.

Indian influence in pre-Christian Asia Minor is attested by Zenob, a fourth-century writer of Armenia, who related how in the second century B.C. two Indian princes settled in Taron, west of lak van, and erected temples for the worship of Giasne, identified with Krishna. To this is traced the influence of the Bhagavata or Krishna cult on Christianity in those regions where a little later it had as many as five thousand followers.

### *Buddhism's Role*

Buddhism also had something to do with the growth of Christianity. In pre-Christian times there were Buddhists in Alexandria which had a number of them even in the second and third centuries A.C. Clement studied Buddhism with them. His tutor Pantaenus visited India as a Christian missionary. He is definite that 'the Greeks stole their philosophy from the barbarians' (Indians).

The Therapeutics of Alexandria were no other than followers of the

Buddha as their very name suggests. The Pali word there, derived from the Sanskrit word sthira meaning 'settled in peace' is a name of the Buddha, and the Pali word putta, derived from the Sanskrit word putra, means 'son', 'follower'. The essences of pre-Christian Palestine were also Buddhists. Historian Mahaffy says : "These Buddhist missionaries were the forerunners of the Christ."

Schelling, Schopenhauer, Mansel and Milman attribute the Buddhistic elements in Christianity to the Buddhist missionaries who came from India during the reign of Asoka. The parable style of the Bible is held to be an echo of the story-telling method of the Buddhist Jatakas, and, says Vincent Smith, "Some orthodox forms of Christian teaching we owe some debt to the lessons of Gautama".

Winternitz believes that "in the combination of the Jewish and the Greek ideas on which the teachings of the Christian Gospels are based, there was also some admixture of Buddhist thoughts and legends. Some undoubted borrowings from the Buddhist religious literature are also found in the Apocryphal Gospels".

The Gospel Story of the Bible bears striking resemblance to the account of the Buddha's life given in such Buddhist works as the Lalita Vistara, which describes the Buddha's miraculous conception and birth, the star over the birthplace, the prophecy of the aged and temptation by Mara and the twelve disciples.

Discussing the coincidence of the Jataka story of the pious disciple walking on the water with the similar story in the Gospels, Max Muller remarks that it can only be accounted for by some historical contact and transference, and the Jatakas are centuries older than the Gospels. The story of the Prodigal Son is found almost in the same form in the Buddhist work, the Suddhamma Pundarika.

Another fact which confirms the possibility of Indian influence on Christianity was revealed years ago in a book called the Unknown Life of Jesus Christ, translated from a manucript discovered in a monastery of Tibet by the Russian explorer, Lutovitch. The book fills up the gap of the Christ's absence from Jerusalem for Twelve years by describing his itinerary in northern India during that period when he visited India's well known cities and centres of learning and her great saints and scholars.

Indian knowledge was familiar to the Eastern churches of the Levant. A notable instance is furnished by the presence of Indian ideas in the writings of Origen (third century A.D.), who was one of the greatest of the Greek Fathers of the Eastern Church and a writer of many authoritative books on Christian theology. Origen believed in reincarnation and showed extreme eagerness to imbibe Indian wisdom, " those insights and illuminations from 'the christians that were before Christ". He was thrice punished, the last time to death, for holding 'un-christian' views, one of which must have been on reincarnation.

*Lofty Idealism*

An eminent Christian Thinker says that, had not in the fourth century the Council of Chalcedon condemned reincarnation then believed in by many Christian Fathers, the 'religion of love' would have been saved the disgrace of the cruel finality of everlasting punishment for the mistakes of this one life.

Many authorities have left that in India there is 'a sourcel and rich and constant enough in its yield of the water of Life to have fed all mankind's ecclesiastical channels.' They think that India influenced, directly or indirectly, that stream of lofty idealism and devotion which arose in the Rhine-land in the spring of the Middle Ages. Indian ideas were transmitted through a succession of teachers and disciples like the Arabian monk Bar Saudali, also known as Dionysius the Areopagite, whose doctrines were more Vedantic than 'Synoptic' Erigena, Echhart and his spiritual sons. This was as it were, a transplantation of Indian wisdom from the banks of the Ganga to those of the Rhine.

In his book the flowering of Mysticism, Refuse Jones has traced quite clearly this moment of Indian ideas through Persia, Alexandria, Cordoba, Padua and thence by Paris on to the Rhine, 'influencing and forming the thought and practice of the first great schools of Western mysticism. 'Scholarship', says Gerald Heard, 'has now proved as a fact of literature that the specific concepts which gave to Western religion its deepest insights and its most effective techniques were all imported from the Indian areas.'

It is well known that the stories of India form a substantial element in those of Europe, the Panchatantra, the Hitopadesha and the Buddhist Jatakas having played a most important part in this migration of stories from India. The famous Welsh story of Llewellyn and Gebert, many fables in La Fontaine's French work, a number of fairy-tales in Grimm and Hans Andersen, many stories in the Gesta Romanorum, the Decameron, and Chaucer's Canterbury Tales, not to speak of the fables of Aesop, are derived from India.

REFERENCES


1. 'Yeats and India' by Santosh Pall in *India and World Literature*, (Ed.) Abhay Maurya, p. 482.
2. To quote a few research work — "Yeats : The man and Mask by Richard Ellmann "*W.B. Yeats and Occultism*" by Harvansh Roy Bachhan. "W.B. Yeats : An Indian Approach" by Naresh Guha.
3. न जातु कामाः कामानामुपभोगेन शाम्यति।
   हविषा कृष्णवर्त्मेव भूयो एवाभिवर्धते।। — Manu 11. 94.
4. Har Dayal, *Hints for self-culture*, p. 32.
5. G.M. Trevelan, *History of England,* p. 7.
6. Romila Thapar, *Ancient Indian Social History*,pp.152. 53.
7. Rigved 3.62.14.
8. Damodar Dharmanand Kosambi, *An Introduction to the study of Indian History*, p. 98.
9. I. Mendelsohn, *Slavery in ancient Near-East*, p.104.
10. Arthshastra, 3.13
11. किरातबर्बरान्ध्राश्च द्रविडाः काशिकोसलाः।
    पुलिन्द्रा दाक्षिणात्याश्च प्रायेण त्वसिता समृताः।। — Natyashastra, 21/20/12.
12. *An Idealistic View of Life*, p.103.
13. Gunnar Myrdal, *Asian Drama*, p. 39.
14. R.C. Majumdar, *Hindu Colonies in the Far East*, p. 32.
15. J.L. Nehru, *Glimpses of World History*, p. 154.
16. Gunnar Myrdal, *Asia Drama*, p. 41.
17. Rock Edict XII.
18. W.J. Wilkins, *Hindu Mythology*, p. 488.
19. J.L. Nehru *Glimpses of World History*, (Fourth Impression) p. 87.
20. Thomas A Harris, *I am Ok you are Ok*, p. 271.
21. Quoted in "*The Religions of Man*"pp.197–98.
22. Mundakopnishad, 7th Shloka.
23. लोकेऽस्मिन् द्विविधा निष्ठा पुरा प्रोक्ता मयानघ।
    ज्ञानयोगेन सांख्यानां कर्मयोगेन योगिनाम्।। — Bhagvadgeeta 3.3.
24. Address at the Final Session (September 27, 1893).
25. Dr. Karan Singh, *Essays on Hinduism*, p.103.
26. Dr. S. Rakhakrishanan, *Our Heritage*, p.17.
27. Romain Rolland, *the Life of Vivekanand*, p. 348.
28. Rider and Company, Londor
29. A search in Secret India, p.13.
30. On the basis of this concept Swami Vivekanand calls all the beings as off-shoots of the 'Cosmic Soul.
31. आत्मनः प्रतिकूलानि परेषां न समाचरेत्। — महाभारत
32. Kabir, R.N. *Tagore*, p. 85.
33. *Kabir Granthawali* p. 103.
34. *Kabir Granthawali* p. 103.
35. Quoted in *Creative Art* (PB) by R.N. Tagore
36. Shri Aurbindo, *The Life Divine.*
37. Shri Aurbindo and *The Mother, on Themselves* Part II p. 17.
38. Quoted by Dr. S. Radhakrishnan, *An Idealistic view of Life*, p. 51.
39. Quoted in Bridges of Understanding, p. 21.
40. Thomas A. Harris, *I am Ok, you are Ok*, pp.207–28.

41. Quoted from Erich Fromm, DT Suzuhi and Richard de Martino, *Zen Buddhism and Psychoanalysis* , p.16.
42. *Ibid*; p.16.
43. Zen Buddhism and Psychoanalysis, p.17 Compare – "What is magic to our finite reason is the Logic of the infinite". — *Shri Aurbindo.*
44. Radhakamal Mukherjee, *a History of Indian Civilization* pp. 34–35.
45. A. C. Das, Rigvedic India (3rd ed.), p. 296.
46. Dr. S. Radhakrishnan Our Heritage (PB), p. 21.
47. सं गच्छध्वं सं वदध्वं सं वो मनांसि जानताम्।
    देवा भागं यथा पूर्वे संजनाना उपासते।। – ऋग्वेद 10.191.2
48. Will Durant, the story of Philosphy, p.339.
49. A.L. Basham, The Wonder that was India, p.499.
50. *Ibid.*
51. The four books formed part of much larger collection of ancient literature called Thirteen classics. In antiquity only five of these works had canonical status – (1) The book of Changes. (2) The Book of History, (3) The book of Songs, (4) The Ritual (which included the record of Rites), and (5) the Spring and Autumn.
52. Raymond Dawson, Confucious, p. 1.
53. Based on Chamlal's *India : Cradle of Culture*, p. 121-124.

# 7

# HUMAN VALUES AND CROSSCULTURAL UNDERSTANDING

What are values ? Communist Value-system, Present Day morality and American Morality, Microcultural Values of USA, Tips from Confucians, Taoist Values, Gandhian Values and school programmes, political Values, Negative or Demoniacal Values, National Integration Through Values Education, Towards the Age of Cultural Priorities, Concept of Progress and Cultural Values, Attitudinal change and values.

Cross-cultural values-brotherhood, courage, deeds, duty, family forgiveness, friendship, love, obedience, peace, sincerity.

## What are Values

Philosophically speaking values are those standards or a code for moral behaviour conditioned by one's cultural tenants and guarded by coñscience, according to which human being is supposed to conduct himself and shape his life-patterns by integrating his beliefs, ideas and attitudes to realize cherished ideals and aims of life. The 'good' of many or all should be taken as sole criterion for values. Psychologically in the context of instructional objectives 'valuing' falls under 'Affective Domain'. Affective domain has five major categories-receiving (attending), responding, valuing, organisation and characterization by value or value complex. The third category 'valuing' includes the individual's commitment to a certain goal, idea or belief. The fourth category builds up a value-system that includes his behaviour. The last category in this taxonomy is "characterization by value or value complex. At this stage of development, the individual acts assiduously and consistently in accordance with the values he has internalised.[1]

In fact, value lacks universal definition. According to Rokeach, "Values are beliefs about how one ought or ought not to behave, or about some end state of existence worth or not worth attaining. Values are abstract ideals, positive or negative, that represent a person's belief about ideal modes of conduct and ideal terminal goals."[2] A value is a standard we sue to influence the values, attitudes and actions of other; it is like yardstick we use to guide the actions, attitudes, comparisons, evaluations, and justifications of ourselves and other.[3]

**Communist Value-system**

As per the communist viewpoint "Morals are the models and standards of conduct people adher to. Morals as the actual being of good and evil in human behaviour are distinct from ideals as due to be. Morals taken as a whole bear on the morality of a social community. Morals differ in as much as there is difference between the being of difference between the being of different classes and social state, their place in the system of social production, and their cultural levels". Accordingly the following principles of communist morality make-up their moral code :

1. Devotion to the cause of communism,
2. Increase of social wealth by labour,
3. Collectivism,
4. Humanism,
5. Internationalism.

Prior to this proletarian moral principles morals of the exploiters were prevalent in Russia, which cannot be called universal nor the above mentioned morals can be called universal. Being a socialist pattern of society in Russia the main current trend in the development is the growing unity of its classes and social sections and consolidation of its social homogeneity. This is a stage on the way towards the supreme goal of the Soviet State, i.e., building of classless society in which, as Lenin Said "all must work". Article 19 of the Soviet Constitution defines the main ways leading to the goal as follows :

> "The state helps to enhance the social homogeneity of society, namely, the elimination of class differences and of the essential distinctions between town and country and between mental and physical labour, and the all round development and drawing together of all the nations and nationalities of the U.S.S.R."

Article 20 declares that "the free development of each is the condition of the free development of all." This serves to stress the humanistic orientation of the Soviet State's activities and the need to combine the vital interests of the individual organically with those of society. The article further adds: "The state is duty bound to ensure the realistic opportunities, and to develop the personalities in every way, this being an important pre-requisite for the intellectual and moral development of the individual."

Politically USSR, with its collapse, no more power-block. The very fallibility of Russian policies were predicted by various thinkers earlier. "The advocates of recent Western theories of "Industrial society" (Walt Rostow, Raymond Aron, John Galbraith). "Post-industrial society" (Daniel Bell, Alain, Touraine, Peter Drucker), "techetronic society" (Zbigniew Brzezinski and others) attack the maxist-tiniest theory of socio-economic formations and its conclusion that capitalism is historically transient in nature; they attempt to show that the capitalist system may be perfected and therefore, represents the future of the whole of mankind.

Referring to the enormous growth of the social significance of science, brogueis economists, philosophers, and futurologists insist that, owing to this fact, modern capitalism has undergone radical changes, that such Marxist categories as class-struggle are now inapplicable to it, that state regulated capitalism eliminates class-conflicts and easily overcome them. Substituting technological for social determinism, they allege that the use of nuclear energy, electronics and other scientific and technological achievements may result in a radical restructuring of the social political and intellectual life of capitalist society without the need for social revolution or class struggle".[4]

Thus, we observe that the above futurology regarding communism and its ideology came to be true. With the collapse of Soviet Union and end of the cold war, indications are that the world is now moving towards a unipolar world led by the United States, Recently on 3rd January 1993, the then US President, Mr. Geogrge Bush and the Russian President Mr. Boris Yeltsin, signed a landmark nuclear arms control treaty in Moscow, which will call for two-thirds reduction in the world's most terrifying weapons. Recently Sino-Russian summit was also held. Thus, the political equation, at the global level, are changing very rapidly. So, the case is for changeability of values in the Marxist world-view. Before and even after the collapse of USSR. the most important gesture was stress on humanism. They regarded freedom as the central value and posed their faith in 'New Humanism', as M.N. Roy puts is : "May is the archtype of society, co-operative social relationship contribute to develop individual potentialities. But the development of the individual is the measure of social progress collectively presupposes the existence of individuals......well being, if it is actual, is enjoyed by individual"[5] Elaborating further the tenets and axiology of 'New Humanism' M.N. Roy says: "The axiology of New Humanism deduces all values from the supreme values of freedom. Freedom is the supreme value of life, because the urge for freedom is the essence of human existence indeed, it can be traced all the way down the entire process of biological evolution. Since, all ethical values are derived from the biological heritage of man they require no sanction which transcends human existence. To be moral, one needs only to be human, it is not necessary to go in search of divine or mystic metaphysical sanction. Humanist morality is evolutionary"[6]

**National Integration Through Value Education**

In order to establish National and Emotional Integration the pattern of education should be based on the cultural and spiritual values of the country. If it is fulfilled, a sense of live, respect and reverence can be well imbibed in the young students. For this the proper teaching of arts, fine arts, history, etc. have its own importance. Apart from this, proper emphasis should be laid down on the inculcation of intrinsic values like-honesty, sacrifice, self-respect, etc. through various extra class-room programmes.

The education for the aesthetic values should be imparted through comparatively broader range of subjects. Under any superstition for this purpose the curriculum should not be confined to the selected few subjects viz., music, dancing, drawing, painting, modelling, poetry, etc. On this point John Dewey has very rightly stated that pupils can have intensified appreciation of geography and shop work just as well as of music and painting, the pupils can enjoy beauty in mathematics as well as in poetry. They should regard all arts as offering fulfilment. Young pupils' aesthetic yearnings, the use of arts alongwith the fine arts, in this sense the eustatic emphasis on school work is not a luxury but an emphatic expression and final embodiment of what makes education important and valuable. Therefore, aesthetic considerations must find a place in the school programmes.

The aim of National Integration can be achieved best through emotional integration. Patriotic sentiments can be profitably used to achieve national integration. Individual's identification with the interest and purpose of the nation is very essential. Therefore, it must be inculcated in the students. In order to form and develop national character, there should be proper understanding of the ideals of our composite culture. Therefore, salient features of this composites culture be directly or indirectly included in the curriculum. In the same way appreciation of this very culture be taught through the variety of extra-class room programmes. Emotional participation in nation-building activities, common modes of national interests, national discipline programmes and participation in national festivities may go a long way towards the establishment of emotional integration.

Keeping in view the fact that ours is a land of cultural diversities all curricular and co-curricular activities be chalked out and conducted so that there will be desired harmonious emotional development.

The fact should be emphatically brought to the notice of the youngsters that India had been multicultural since the dawn of civilization whereas the country like America became multicultural since the European settlers migrated to the land of the American Indian, who themselves did not share a monolithic culture. No doubt, today there are people from every country in the world living in U.S.A. but the condition is not very harmonious. Very often the problems of racism are confronted by the people. Thus we can say that cultural pluralism is not a new phenomena in India. Ravindra Nath Tagore has very rightly said :

> हेथाय आर्य, हेथा अनार्य हेथाय द्राविड़–चीन,
> शक–हूण–दल, पाठान–मोगल एक देहे होलो लीन।

> (Here in India, came, Aryans, non-Aryans, Dravidians, Chinese, band of invaders like Shakas, Hoonas, Pathans and Mughals also came; but ultimately they merged and formed the embodiment of India).

In the modern terminology this theory can be termed as "melting pot theory". In comparatively easier terms this process or phenomena can be called as 'assimilation' or 'acculturation'. A few decades ago this phenomena was considered to be ideal one and our aim had been 'unity in diversity'. But all precautions are needed to ensure that it should not be featureless unity. This type of unity of different races and religions was evolved basically under the assumptions that ethnica groups would surrender their various heritages in order to join the dominant culture (macroculture). The 'melting pot', while taken for granted earlier, has become controversial. However, it is a matter of great consolation that among various religions the points of difference are less than the points of contact and commonness as Mahatma Gandhi has rightly remarked.

Referring to contact points he says, "We may call ourselves Christians, Hindus or Mohammedans, whatever we may be, beneath that diversity there is oneness which is unmistakable and underneath many religions there is also one religion. As far as my experience goes, at one time or another, we the Mohammedans, Christians or Hindus, discover that there are many points of contacts and very few points of difference". (CWMG, Vol. 26, p. 396).

**Present Day Morality and American Morality**

Before we peep into the linkage between present day morality and American morality we should know what is morality ? It is a relative term, which differs in its shades of meaning from place to place, from time to time and from race to race. However, in broad sense, as Swami Vivekandand put it, "The only definition that can be given of morality is this: that which is selfish is immoral, and that which is unselfish is moral".

According to Will Durant–

> "Ultimately there are but three systems of ethics, three conceptions of the ideal character and the moral life. One is that of Buddha and Jesus, which stresses the feminine virtues, considers all men to be equally precious, resists evil only by returning good, identifies virtues with love and inclines in politics to unlimited democracy. Another is the ethic of Machiavelli and Nietzsche, which stresses the masculine virtuous, accepts the inequality of men, relishes the risks of combat and conquest and rule, identifies virtue with power, and exalts an hereditary aristocracy. A third, the ethic of Secretes, Plato and Aristotle, denies the universal applicability of either the feminine or the masculine virtues; considers that only the informed and mature mind can judge, according to diverse circumstances, when love should rule, and when power; identifies virtue, therefore, with intelligence; and advocates a varying mixture of aristocracy and democracy in government. It is the distinction of spinoza that his ethic unconsciously reconciles these apparently hostile philosophies, weaves them into a harmonious unity and gives us in consequence a system of morals which is the supreme achievement of modern thought".

William Peter interviewed eight outstanding men and women on the subject of American morality. Those interviewed were-Fairfax Cone, Margaret Mead, Agnes E. Meyer, Chase Smith, Learned Hand, Phyllis McGinley, Reinhold Niebuhr and Edward R Murrow. These people shed flood of light on the current moral scene of America reflecting various human values positive as well as negative being cherished by Americans. In the academic world 1958 study reported that 75 per cent of the college seniors questioned admitted cheating and that only 13 per cent felt a cheating student was basically dishonest. Further it is said that this knowledge may have prepared some Americans for the more recent expose of professional writers, who write examination papers for others for money.

Edward R Murrow felt too that the increased impersonality of American life has a good deal to do with present-day morality. "As the nation, our government, business, labour, the most of our cut off from the kind of individual relationships that used to pervade most areas of our lives," he said. "Employer-employee relationships are impersonal; a man can spend his whole life working for a company and never exchange a word with his boss". Often, he has no boss in the old sense but rather a board of directors and thousands of stockholders.

> "Even our attitude toward debt has changed under the impact of this new impersonality. Where we used to borrow from relatives or friends or from the banker whom we at least know slightly, we borrow, now from a credit institution. The man who has mortgaged his future for the next fifteen years to various faceless credit organizations has a different attitude towards meeting his debts with honour on a day-to-day basis".
>
> "More important, a feeling of impersonality leaves us feeling for more helpless than even before. We have lost a good deal of the sense that we as individuals can really do anything effective about the problems that threaten us. We've lost the feeling that national decisions can be influenced by individuals. The helpless feeling of the World War II draftee that he had suddenly been reduced to a cipher, a set of holds punched in an IBM card, that he could be sent anywhere, trained as anything, without regard to his education, experience or preference, by the simple mechanical shuffling of cards in a machine has become a peacetime nightmare for millions of Americans".

One probable result is that we tend to lash out against the system that has reduced us to this kind of importance. The knowledge that 'the

Bomb' hangs impersonally over all of us may have led to a permanent wartime philosophy of "let's take what we can get".

**Macroculture Values of United States**

Anthropologist Frances Hsu describes a series of postulates about the society of united states, based on his experience in both the United Stated and China, which give us an insight to understand the microcultural values in the united states. Nine such postulates given by him are as under :

1. An individuals most important concern is his self-interest, self-expression, self-development, self-gratification, and independence. This takes precedence overall group interest.
2. The privacy of the individual is the individual's inalienable right. Intrusion into it by others is permitted only by his permission.
3. Because the government exists for the benefit of the individual and not vice-versa, all forms of authority, including government, are suspect. But, the government and its symbols should be respected. Patriotism is good.
4. An individual's success in life depends upon his acceptance among his peers.
5. An individual should believe or acknowledge god and should belong to an organized church or other religious institution. Religion is good. Any religion is good than no religion.
6. Men and women are equal.
7. All human beings are equal.
8. Progress is good and inevitable. An individual must improve himself (minimize his efforts and maximize his returns); the government must be more efficient to tackle new problems; institutions such as churches must modernise to make themselves more attractive.
9. Being American is synonymous with being progressive and America is the utmost symbol of progress.[7]

Some of the macrocultural values that are predominant in United States society are : cleanliness, hard work, material comforts and material wealth, private property, health and youth, promptness, problem-solving and progress, formal education, being direct, and the right to dissent.

**Values Cherished by American Society**

Values that appear inherent in the microcultural depends upon the cultural tenets of the concerned macroculture. In United States of America, being basically a materialistic culture the following values prevail as mentioned by American Authors :

— Status based on occupation, education and financial worth.
— Achievement valued above–inheritance.
— Work ethnic.
— Comforts and rights to such amenities.
— Cleanliness as an absolute value.
— Achievement and success measured by quantity of material goods purchased.
— Equalitarianism as shown in the demand for political, economic and social equality and the belief that every individual has inalienable and god-given rights and has an equal right to self-government or choice of governors.
— Humanitarianism that is usually highly organized and often impersonal.
— New and modern as better than old and traditional.

**Tips From Confucianism**

— Do not wish for quick results, nor look for small advantages. If you seek quick results, you will not attain the ultimate goal. If you are led by small advantages, you will never accomplish great things.
— The nobler men first practices what he preaches and afterwards preaches according to the practice.
— If, when you look to your own heart, you find nothing wrong there, what is there to worry about, what is there to fear.
— When you know a thing to recognize that you know it, and when you do not, to know you do not know – that is knowledge.
— To go too far is as bad as to fall short.
— A man without virtue cannot long abide in adversity, nor can he long abide in happiness.
— When you see a man of worth, think of how your may emulate him. When you see one who is unworthy, examine your own character.
— Wealth and rank are what men desire, but unless they be

obtained in the right way they may not be possessed.

- Feel kindly toward everyone, but be intimate only with the virtuous.
- Hold faithfulness and sincerity as first principles.
- Benevolence is the tranquil habitation of man, and righteousness is his straight path.
- Virtue is not left to stand alone. He who practises it will have neighbours.
- The great end of learning is nothing else but to seek for the lost mind.
- A man can enlarge the principles which he follows : those principles do not enlarge the man.
- Virtue is the root, wealth is fruit.[8]

Exhorting the king once Confucious said : "To govern (Cheng) is to correct (cheng). If you set an example by being correct. Who would dare to remain incorrect."[9]

In Chinese language the word Cheng (to govern) and Cheng (to correct) are cognate. He further added, "Guide them by edicts, keep them in like by punishment, keep them in line by punishment and the common people will stay out of trouble but will have no sense of shame. The ultimate of government is the welfare of the common people. This the most basic principle in Confucianism. Example is better than precept. This is what he impressed upon the ruler.

"Moral example is far more effective than edicts, and where edicts contradict the example, it is the example that the common people will heed rather than the edicts. This point is most persuasively put by Confucious."

**Taoist Values**

Taoism negates all self-seeking and self-assertive processes and prefers inwardness of a man, and a man who is never forcing and never under strain. According to Tao the preliminaries to arriving at full self-knowledge are selflessness, cleanliness and emotional calm. By cleanliness he means perfect cleanliness of thought and body. He says:

> "Only where all is clean" will it reveal itself, therefore, put self aside". Perturbing emotions must likewise be quelled. Ruffling the surface of the mind they prevent introspection from seeing past them to the springs of consciousness beneath".[10]

The concepts of inwardness or emotional calm is not to be taken as identified with inaction, as it has been said in *Bhagwadgeeta* —

Only duty is thy concern
And not the fruits.
Don't stand for the fruit
Nor indulge in inaction.[11]

Emotional calm means to be the pure embodiment of suppleness, simplicity and freedom. Thus a kind of pure effectiveness will emerge in which no motion is wasted on outward show :

> One may move so well that a foot-print never shows speak so well that the tongue never slips Reckon so well that no counter is needed.[12]

Following the analogy of water, the Taoists rejected all forms of self-assertiveness and competition. The world is full of people who are determined to be 'somebody' or give trouble. They want to get ahead, to stand out. Taoism has little use for such ambition. Behind the 'success story' of Japan one of the prominent factors is that they discarded the ambition to be 'somebody', particularly in the industrial sector. Because there are no ethnic divisions in the Japanese society and regional divisions have disappeared as a result of rapid urbanization and the powerful impact of the mass-media, people are no longer conscious of a division between 'upper' and 'Lower class'. Everyone thinks himself or herself as middle-class. Therefore, following the ideology of Tao they prefer 'anybody' to 'somebody'.

There is always danger in being at the top. Chanakya (Kautilya) in his 'Neeti Shataka' says that "in the forest tall and straight trees are cut first". Similarly, Tao observes that "The axe falls first on the tallest tree".

Therefore, he alarms us :

Standing tiptoe a man looses balance,
Admiring himself he does so alone.,
At onetime in the world will a man,
Who is sane,
Over-reach himself,
Over-spend himself,
Over-rate himself.[13]

Thus we observe that there is a profound naturalism in Taoist value-system, but it is a naturalism of Rousseau, Wordworth, Thoreau rather than that of Galileo or Bacon.

**Gandhian Values and School Programmes**

In order to create new social order Gandhiji introduced Nai Talim in the year 1937 which is popularly known as Basic Education. This system of Education, which could not be continued for several socio-political reasons; as based on certain values cherished by him. He wanted that these values should be internalized by the younger generation also through new system of education evolved by him. The NCERT and Gandhi Peace Foundation had jointly sponsored studies in Gandhian Values at the school stage. These were the values which he practised himself in his personal and public life, experimented with them and suggested these values if we want to remodel the social set-up through education. Those values are as following:

1. Truth (Honesty) :
2. Non-violence (Love for mankind, service of humanity, satyagraha, compassion, universal love);
3. Freedom (Fearlessness);
4. Democracy (Rights, duties, responsibilities, national integration);
5. Sarva Dharma Samabhava (Composite culture, reverence for others beliefs, communal unity);
6. Equality (Removal of untouchability), social justice non-exploitation);
7. Self-realisation (Swadesh, dignity of labour);
8. Purity of ends and means (Integrity between thought and action);
9. Self-discipline (self-control);
10. Cleanliness (Suddhi, simplicity of life, non-consumerism, aesthetic life).

For the realisation of these values in the system of education, a properly planned curriculum, organisation of community life based on these values inside the educational institution and a programme of social service integrated to school life are very necessary.

Socially useful productive work (SUPW) should be integrated with the courses of study and participation in it should aim at developing dignity of labour, promotion of self-reliance, productive efficiency, cooperation, dutifulness, along with development of intellectual and aesthetic qualities such as sensitivity to beauty, spirit of inquiry problem solving capacity, productive skill, effective use of tools and implements.

**Political Values**

The political values in culture constitute an inseparable part of its total value–system. They are more important because of their pervasiveness, effectiveness, etc. These values affects the behaviour of all the citizens of the society during their life. Political values are visible in a country when citizens opt for one political party over another, when the president of India conveys his message on various occasions including those of national festivals etc. When the ruling party annex a bill into law, etc.

The very existence of government policies reveals that there are rules of one kind or another which are to be enforced if people were to lead a harmonious and peaceful life in the society. According to James Madison, government is, "the political and administrative machinery of an organized state". When the word government is used as a noun it refers to the institutions and persons who exercises authority in a cultural group. If it is used as a verb, it relates to the exercises of the authority, to the processes of control, etc. It has been rightly said that if people were angles, no government would be necessary. But people are not angles, they are persons who may have conflicting interests and desires. Therefore, some kind of government arrangement is necessary for every civilized group. Government can never be a static arrangement. In the words of Woodrow Wilson, it is an ever-living thing.

As far as government's policies are concerned, they are nothing but practical aspects of government in action as the values are political aspects of a religion. It embrasses such institutions of activities as political parties, the gaining and holding of political office, influencing public opinion and meeting may have other demands imposed on individuals by the institutions of government.

**Negative or Demoniacal Values**

Man is born with natural bliss of Love and compassion, but everywhere he is found to be victim of hatred, jealousy, anger, passion etc. From the dawn of civilization our social ethos has been disapproving these negative values. There vices weaken the human beings. That's what is prayed in Rigveda :

O Love-devine.
You offer us a wide defence.
Against hatred of alien.
That wastes and weaken us.[14]

Negative values are so-often spoken off a enemies of man that let him down in all activities of life. We are well aware of this fact. That is why we do not want others to be angry against us, we decry passion of all sorts when others succumb to this vice. We very often complain against them who are jealous of our rise and prosperity. We will never like that others hate us and despise on our heinest shortcomings. All these are common to mankind of all ages and places.

Mahabharata[15] has rightly enjoined. "Do unto others as you would like to be done to you". This is such a common thread that it is found in almost all the religions of the world.

Divine values are regarded as conducive to liberation, whereas negative or demoniacal values are supposed to be conducive to bondage. In Geeta hypocrisy, arrogance, pride, anger, harshness and ignorance—these are mentioned as demoniacal values. Men cherishing such type of values are not able to distinguish between good and bad. They do not know what is right activity and what is right cessation of activity. Therefore, they possess neither purity (internal or external) nor good conduct nor truth.

Possessed of hypocrisy, conceit and given to insatiable passion, and adopting false doctrines, they take to action with impure vows. Giving themselves over to endless cares terminating only death, and given to the enjoyment of sensuous pleasures, they believe the highest limit of joy to consist only in this. Held in bondage by a hundred ties of expectation, given over to passion and anger, they strive to enjoyment of sensuous pleasures.

### Towards the Age of Cultural Priorities*

The then Prime Minister of Japan, Mr. Masayoshi Ohira, in January, 1979, initiated several Study Groups in Japan with certain interesting term of reference. They were, "The Study Group on Economic Performance in the Cultural Age; "The Garden City State Concept Study Group", "The Age of Culture Study Group", "The Historical Evolution

* Based on the M.P. Biral Memorial Lecture delivered by the former Chief Justice of India at the London Kendra of Bhavan on October, 10, 1994.

of Science and Technology Study Group", etc. The reports of these groups are published by the "Foundation for Advanced Information and Research, Japan". The reports recognise that rapid industrialisation had produced what were referred to as the "advanced nations' deceases", in the societal structure. One of such is the "growth of individualisation". They create neurotic individualistic possessive tendencies, characteristic of an acquisitive society. These tendencies, the reports predicated; produce a conflict with the growing consensus for evolving a cultural society and fostering of inter-dependence. The Report on the Historical Evolution of Science and Technology says :

> "In the highly industrialized society isolated and alienated individuals have created the main cause of 'illness' of civilized countries which has reduced significantly the vitality of the society. It may be interpreted as an expansion of the living space of mankind being limited by the barrier of "finiteness of the globe".
>
> "..........Life, for instance, cannot be understood simply as an aggregate of elements but the concept of self-organization is the most important key to understand various life phenomena. It has been remarked in recent years that cells in a living body transform energy from one form to another directly and very efficiently, by the co-operation of the whole and individual elements. This is a subject to be studied in the context of 'holonic path' concept".

Speaking of the "Economic Management in the Age of Cultural Priorities" the Report says :

> "In order to secure existence with honour and vitality in the coming 21st century, what harmony should be realized between people, culture and economic principle and how should economic management be undertaken ? The following five basic philosophies may be sought after in economic management in the age of cultural priorities' :
>
> 1. Respect for humanity
> 2. Respect for Independence
> 3. Unblished Respect for creativity
> 4. Respect for originality
> 5. Respect for internationality".

Referring to what the values are, the Report says :

> "In any age and in any society, if a question is made to the people living therein, 'Are you happy?, not a few of them would answer, 'Yes'. There exist some fundamental life values, including the feeling of happiness and worthiness of life, which will not change, even if time elapses and the environment changed. They are something relating to the essence of people's desires. However, the latter assumes various forms in the current of times, diversifies the contents of life values' and thus appears as the change. It is, therefore, important in the study of 'life values' to grasp the essence of people's desires which does not vary with the lapse of time and then study the change of life values in the current of time".

Referring to modernisation in the West, the Report says:

> "The 'modern age' was ushered in with the industrial and civil revolutions in Europe. In science, this took the form of 'atomism'; in politics, economics, and society, it gave birth to 'individualism'. The Latin word 'individual' and the Greek work' atom' are identical in meaning".

Referring to the "Affluent Society at a Turning Point", the Report says :

> "Faced with a deteriorating natural and living environment, scientific and technological stagnation, resource and energy restrictions, and the worsening trade-off between demand control and welfare policies, the economic vitality of the developed countries has failed. In addition, they are plagued by the "developed nations' disease", symptoms of which are deep-rooted inflation, slowing economic growth, growing unemployment, loss of vitality in the private sector, the decline of business activity (loss of incentives to invest), government bankruptcy and huge fiscal deficits, balance of payments deficits, etc.
>
> Second is a cultural and social viewpoint. The affluent society has altered the desired, behavioral patterns and social structures of its people.
>
> These changes include the formation of a new middle class, the fragmentation of values, and the appearance of a social pathological

> phenomenon, the so-called "advanced nations' syndrome", in rich societies.
>
> The influence of centuries of modernization and industrialization on society has been the appearance of the 'British disease', or more generally, the "developed nations' disease" or the 'Civilization disease'. This malaise affects not only the economies of the countries involved, but its symptoms penetrate the political and social spheres as well. As a result, the advanced industrial societies are faced not only with declining economic vitality, but also with a variety of manifestations of anomie, such as decreasing political unity, terrorism, crime, juvenile delinquency, suicide, anxiety and depression, alcoholism, drug addiction, the loss of the will to work, and sexual confusion."

Does the ancient Indian tradition have any answers to these growing myths of modernity ? "No other country on our planet earth", said a well-known artists, "has nourished and integrated human aspirations and spiritual wisdom in an amazing continuity for more than four thousand years, than this continent called India. From the beginning of time, perhaps even further back than imagination can take us, there is evidence of a sophisticated culture with both a social and political order".

The artiste said : "The guru-shishya parampara emphasised the importance of learning and hermitages were their places of dwelling. Our civilization was born from nature, the greatest thoughts were nurtured amongst sylvan surroundings. Students came from far and wide away and were integrated into a highly intellectual approach to living". Gurudev Rabindranath Tagore said of India :

> "I love India, not because I cultivate the idolatry of geography, not because I have had the chance to be born in her soil, but because she has saved through tumultuous ages the living words that have been issued from the illuminated consciousness of her greater sons : Brahma is Truth, and the unity of all beings is in Brahma".

Without the development of the inner culture of man all our worldly possessions become the means of his own destruction, Science and technology, if recognised as ethic neutral, will surely destroy our great civilisation. Without a perception of the morality of the means and ends intellect becomes a self-stultifying instrument. The scornful impatience of the egoist wrecks his mission.

The ideals of the ancient Indian culture are not only 'Atmoddhara' but also 'Jagath hithaya'. Without respect for ethical principles, an acquisitive society cannot ensure happiness of its members. Indeed as Aldous Huxley points out :

> "The ethical doctrines taught in the Tao Te Ching, by Gautama Buddha and his followers on the Lesser and above all the Greater Vehicle, in the Sermon on the Mount and by the best of the Christian saints, are not dissimilar. Among human beings who have reached a certain level of civilisation and of personal freedom from passion and social prejudice there exists a real consensusgentium in regard to ethical first principles".

Indeed, happiness is the result of Indriya Jaya. If the leaders of the polity do not possess this attainment, the consequence will be that the political organisation will be corroded from within. Political power will then be perceived as an instrument of plunder and those exercising such power seek to perpetuate their own power irrespective of the morality of the means.

**Concept of Progress and Cultural Values**

The concepts of mass production, mass consumption and mass employment as enhanced by the social scientist like Karl Marx became the general creed of marxism, which subsequently resulted into the value of social equality. The whole gamut of process necessitated the education for the masses. Therefore, in most of the parts of the world universalization of education became the significant focal point of the educational process by the beginning of the twentieth century. Mass education was important not only to train employees for industrialism and the technology, but more importantly to teach the cultural values. Mass participation in the political process made universalization of education much more important as the time rolled by.

If we turn over the pages of History we find that aims of education in different civilizations have been highlighted as per there cultural tenets including the concept of development. Referring to the story of Yajnyavalkya, a great seer and exponent of *Brahmavidya* and preceptor of the King Janak, we find that the base of Indian culture and thus of education was spiritualism. Material progress was secondary. Yajnyavalkya wanted to partition his mundane belongings between his two wives Katyayani and Maitreyi, before leaving his home. Katyayani meekly accepted the proposal; but the spiritual-minded Maitreyi's reaction was strange. She said that material wealth was of no avail to her and that, therefore, she would prefer to be taught the ways and means as to how to attain immortality, which mere riches could not bring. The sage agreed with her that all that wealth could do was to make its possessor happy in the sense of enjoyment or worldly pleasures and comforts but that it could not give one immortality. At this Maitreyi became more insistent on learning about the means to attain immortality. The husband was pleased at this attitude of his wife. But in modern time due to misconception of notion of modernity and development the cultural values are deteriorated in India as in other parts of the world. It is a global crisis.

In fact cultural values vary from time to time and place to place and so from country to country depending upon the cultural postulates of the groups. The rate of change in cultural values very much depend upon various socio-economic phenomena prevailing at particular phase of the development as well as basic inclination of the group towards philosophical speculation. As per spellman, "The Concept of Development must be understood to be a projection, rather than a reality, based on identifiable Western images and stereotypes combined with a unique historical experience. The cultural values which arose from the dynamics of the nineteenth century industrial, technological, scientific, economic and social alternations are the basis for the criteria of today's development."[16]

In the Western context most significant of all cultural values is the concept of progress, which has been defined in many ways in various religious scriptures. In the Indian perspective there is no more significant value than Dharma. It has been the only yard-stick by which each and every aspect of life was measured. It may be compared in many respects to Chinese concept of the Tao and to some degree the Western idea of natural law. Dharma is the source of Law, the customs of the righteous, the order which unite the people and make the society harmonious provided it is understood and internalized in the right spirit, without much doctrinization.

There are various interpretations of the term "progress" Nineteenth century sociology was interpreted under the guidelines of the concept of progress of comet and Condottiere. Since the renaissance the idea of progress was interpreted in a different manner. A political, social and economic interpretation of progress was provided for the common man's benefit by Karl Marx. According to J.B. Bury, "This idea (Progress) means that civilization has moved, is moving and will move in a desirable direction."[17]

This definition, like many others does not cover the subtle aspects of the idea of progress. The criterion of desirability is based on one's value-system. Something, person or place desirable for 'A', may not be so for 'B'. It depends upon the cultural value of the individual or the group concerned.

In life problems are faced by the individuals or groups in all parts of the world and they have also their own ways and ways to solve various types of problems. They have different types of perceptions of the problems. Spellman observes that :

> "As a society oriented towards mass production and mass consumption it will emphasize the new as opposed to the old-two other time concepts perceived very differently in the cultural values of other societies. Products will be advertised as new, improved, recent, youthful; all terms culturally understood as highly desirable. Indeed, development itself is sometimes called modernization – suggesting the most recent is the best. To be 'ahead of the times' is considered highly complimentary, while being 'behind the times' is close to an insult. To be 'old-fashioned', 'archaic', or worse, or 'obsolete' is highly undesirable. Of course, cultural values are hardly ever so completely dominant as to annihilate all recessive cultural values. Such exclusive rigidity would be likely to result in the extinction of the culture through inability to adapt to changing environments. Some words such as 'senior', 'antique', 'venerated' still retain positive connotations. But essentially the lineal time perceptions of technological societies is an anti-age focus."[18]

Without the development of the inner culture of man all our worldly possessions become the means of his own destruction, Science and technology, if recognised as ethic neutral, will surely destroy our great civilisation ends intellect becomes a self-stultifying instrument. The scornful impatience of the egoist wrecks his mission.

The ideals of the ancient Indian culture are not only 'Atmoddhara' but also 'Jagath hithaya'. Without respect for ethical principles. An acquisitive society cannot ensure happiness of its members. Indeed as Aldous Huxley points out :

> "The ethical doctrines taught in the Tao Te Ching, by Gautama Buddha and his followers on the Lesser and above all the Greater Vehicle, in the Sermon on the Mount and by the best of the Christian saints, are not dissimilar. Among human beings who have reached a

certain level of civilisation and of personal freedom from passion and social prejudice there exists a real consensusgentium in regard to ethical first principles".

Indeed, happiness is the result of Indriya Jaya. If the leaders of the polity do not possess this attainment, the consequence will be that the political organisation will be corroded from within. Political power will then be perceived as an instrument of plunder and those exercising such power seek to perpetuate their own power irrespective of the morality of the means.

### Attitudinal Change and Values

For any improvement in the institutions Economic, Social or Political desired change in the attitude of the citizens and the concerned functionaries is very essential. It is the attitudinal change which leads increase in labour efficiency, effective competition, mobility, enterprising attitude etc., and ultimately make possible higher productivity and well-being of the Nation. A short of revolution can be brought out through the positive changes in the behaviour and attitude of the people.

Gunnar Myrdal has rightly observed :

> "The institutions invisoned the modernization ideals would imply a united and integrated national community within which there is solidarity and 'free competition' in a much wider sense than the term generally implies in economic analysis. In such a national community the social and cultural divisions would be swept away. There would be formed a nation with marked social and economic equality and mobility, where people were able to move from one area to another as well as from one economic level to another. The desire for such 'modernization' of institutions is most clearly expressed in India, where ironically, the barriers to free competition in the wider sense are strongest and most pervasive."[19]

There is no denying the fact that the Western countries have realised this ideal to the great extent. In the Communist countries in Europe, the standard of living is also growing day by day. Due to positive change in attitude, maintenance and upliftment of various institutions is healthy sign. Through the altitudinal change, an idea of social revolution can be materialised and the creation of the "new man" or the "modern man" is possible. For this, according to Gunnar Myrdal, the following values are very essential :

"1. efficiency;
2. diligence;
3. orderliness;
4. punctuality;
5. frugality;
6. scrupulous honesty (which pays in the long run and is a condition for raising efficiency in all social and economic relations);
7. rationality in decisions on actions (liberation from reliance on static customs, from group allegiances and favouritism, superstitious beliefs and prejudices, approaching the rationally calculating 'economic man' of Western liberal ideology);
8. preparedness for change (for experimentation along new lines, and for moving around spatially, economically, socially);
9. alertness to opportunities as they aries in a changing world;
10. energetic enterprise;
11. integrity and self-reliance;
12. cooperativeness (not limiting but redirecting egoistic striving in a socially beneficial channel; acceptance of responsibility for the welfare of the community and the nation);
13. willingness to take the long view (and to forego short-term profiteering; subordination of speculation to investment and of commerce and finance to production, etc.)"[20]

**Crosscultural Values**

About the significance, sagacity and vitality of religion Will Durant has rightly remarked "Religion has not only taken the sting out of death, it has beautified life with ceremony, with architecture, sculpture, painting, drama and music. It has lifted the routine events of human existence, from birth through marriage to death, to the level of sacraments, making these common things holy experiences, deepening them with feeling and transfiguring them with art, it has changed the sorbied tragedy of life into a poetic pilgrimage to an ennobled end. Without it, life is dull and mean, like a body without a soul."[21]

Hinduism lays special emphasis on courtesy and kindness and respect for all life and tolerance to all men. They are also pioneers in Bhakthimarga as it is called. The religion of Islam lays special emphasis on the Brotherhood of man. The Mahomedan faith has bound all it's members in a close bond of brotherhood and they are ready to help each other at all times. The Buddhist religion has taught us to respect and love all God's creatures and to hold fast to the doctrine of ahimsa. The Christian religion has taught us that God is a loving Father and that he loves us individually and cares for each one of us this fatherhood of God implies the brotherhood of man. Each one of us has a religion – we are born into a family which follows some religion or other. According to confucious it is our duty to find what beliefs our religion holds and to cling to it and fashion our conduct accordingly.

Besides these central values of the respective religions of the world there are many common values in the Eastern cultures which are found in almost all the religions. Here we would like to elaborate certain common values which are manifested in different religions, courage of the East particularly, such as – brotherhood, deeds, duty, faith, familial values, forgiveness, friendship, justice, love, obedience, peace and sincerity.

### *Brotherhood*

*Buddhism :* A friend is a great treasure and should be cherished as a brother. One should make good men his closest friends, his brothers.

*Christianity :* All men are brothers. If one has anything against one's brother, he should make his peace with him before attending to other religious duties. As one treats a brother, so does he treat God. To hate one's brother is evil. Brotherly love should rule the world.

*Confucianism :*Friendship and brotherhood are the cardinal virtues. One should gather about many friends and should love them as brother. The wise man will choose friends worthy of brotherly love.

*Hinduism :* The good man makes no distinction between friend and foe, brother and stranger, but regards them all with impartiality. A true friends will be sympathetic to you at all times.

*Jainism :* Be fair and impartial to all. Treat all men as brothers at all times. As one treats men, so should we treat all animals. They are also our brothers

*Judaism :* God has made all men brothers and they should live together as brothers at all times. It is good for men to act in unity as brothers. Such action will be blessed by God and will prosper.

*Mohammedanism :* All mankind is one family, one people. All men are brothers and should live a such. The Lord loves those who so live.

*Shinto :* Heaven is the father and earth the mother of all men. Therefore, all men are brothers and should sell together as such. By so living the country will be free from hate and sorrow.

*Sikhism :* Get together, my brethren,
And remove all misunderstandings through regard for each other.

*Taoism :* The spirit of brotherhood, kindness, is necessary if one would win friends. The spirit of the market, where men sell goods, should not be the spirit of the good man.

*Zoroastrianism :* One's friends, should be holy people. A holy man will radiate holiness to all his friends.

*Courage*

*Buddhism :* The wise man is not afraid. He knows his strength and does not fear. Likewise, he knows his weaknesses and does not attempt the impossible.

*Christianity :* God is strong, the helper of the good. Therefore, we should not fear, but face life with courage and confidence that the source of all power in the universe in on our side. God watches over the weakest of men.

*Confucianism :* The man of principle is courageous. He knows the right and will fight for it at all costs. God is on his side, and he takes courage from the knowledge of this fact.

*Hinduism :* To realize that God is all and all is God gives man courage. He does not shrink.

*Jainism :* A man may conquer thousands and thousands of invincible foes but that is one no real consequence; his greatest victory is when he conquers only his own self through indomitable courage.

*Judaism :* Be courageous, for God will not fail you. The Lord is on the side of the righteous man, whom then shall he fear? He will give you the strength you need when the time arrives for it.

*Mohammedanism :* God will guide the good. Therefore, they shall have no fear. He will lead them through all the rough spots of life.

*Sikhism* : Brave is he, who possessing strength displays it not, and lives in humble ways.
He is brave.
Who fight for the down-trodden.

*Taoism :* The philosopher is not influenced by praise or blame. He knows the truth and is not afraid, regardless of what happens to him in this world.

*Zoroastrianism* : Courage begets strength by struggle with hardships. Courage grows from fighting danger and overcoming obstacles. Develop the courage to act according to your convictions, to speak what is true, and to do what is right.

*Deeds*

*Buddhism* : Deeds determine one's place in society. One becomes an outcast or a highly placed person by his deeds. Evil deeds are easy to do; good deeds are difficult; but the good deeds pay the highest rewards.

*Christianity* : Man is known by his deeds, and is judged even so by God. God will reward good deeds and punish evil ones. The professed goodness is of no value; one must do good deeds or be condemned.

*Confucianism* : Reward will follow every good deed. Only by doing good deeds can a man know the true joy of living and have a long life.

*Hinduism* : One becomes what one does. The doer of good deeds will become good and the doer of evil deeds will become evil. Action, the doing of the good, is superior to renunciation. Thus, at all times one should be doing good.

*Jainism :* The good show the way to others by their good acts. Each day passes never to return. Therefore, do good at all times, for you can never call back a day to perform a good deed that was not done.

*Judaism* : Do good at all times, for man will be judged by his works.

*Mohammedanism* : On the Day of Judgement every soul shall be judged in accordance with his deeds. To do good drives out evil. God is the source of good deeds.

*Sikhism* : Man's deeds are recorded by the divine. He becomes good in the eyes of the divine by doing good deeds.

*Zorastrianism* : We come to the wise one through good deeds. It is important that we keep ourselves physically fit to do good deeds at all times.

*Duty*

*Buddhism* : One should be faithful to his duty at all times regardless of the situations. Faithfulness to duty brings the greatest of rewards.

*Christianity* : One has a duty to God and duties towards one's follows. One should take care to discharge one's duties.; it is one's duty at all times to do the will of God.

*Confucianism* : Man's duty comes from Heaven. Therefore, he fails in his duty at his peril. The wise man makes duty his aim at all times.

*Hinduism* : Never faulter in doing your duty. God has decreed man's duty, and to fail is to disobey God. It is through duty that a man reaches perfection.

*Jainism* : A wise man discovers his duty and does it at all costs. It is the duty of all to be impartial and to abstain from causing injury to all living things.

*Judaism* : The whole duty of man is to fear God and keep his commandments. This involves love and service to God with one's whole heart.

*Mohammedanism* : All men who do their duty will receive a fitting reward from the Lord.

*Shinto* : The path of duty is near at hand, men seek it in what is remote.

*Sikhism* : He alone is a householder who disciplines his sense desires. And begs from God Contemplation, Austerity and Self-control. And gives in charity all he can through his body.

*Taoism* : The middle way is the duty of man. He should avoid all excess. In this way he fulfills his duty toward man and God.

*Zoroastrianism* : The duty and good works which a son performs are as much the father's as though they had been done by his own hand.

*Faith*

*Buddhism* : Faith is necessary for the virtuous life. One's faith will not go unrewarded. Property follows upon faith.

*Christianity* : Faith is necessary, but it must be accompanied by works. One who is faithful even to death will receive a crown of life. He who asks in perfect faith shall receive. Faith is basic to full understanding.

*Confucianism* : He who lacks faith will not succeed. One must hold to faith at all times. Heaven makes great demands upon one's faith, but God is with man and he should never waver in his faith.

*Hinduism* : Faith is the pathway to wisdom. This faith will come if one years in his heart for it. The most prized of God is the man of faith.

*Jainism* : The man of faith has chosen the right pathway. He should practise his faith at all times.

*Judaism* : God is faithful and will preserve the faithful. The man of faith can expect great rewards from God.

*Mohammedanism* : Man should have faith in God, for God will always prove faithful. But God has no patience with the unfaithful.

*Shinto* : Even the slightest yielding to doubt is a departing from the

nature of man. Faith is fundamental to human beings.
*Taoism* : To have less than enough faith is to have no faith at all. The divine will repay with faith and faithlessness with faithlessness.

*Sikhism* : Good life and immortality are the rereads of the faithful. The religion of the Wise One will cleanse the faithful from all sin.

*Zoroastrianism* : Those who believe,
Their minds awaken to higher conspicuousness,
And to the inner knowledge of all spheres.

*Family*

*Buddhism* : The aged should be respected and reverred. He who does this will receive great rewards and will prosper. Children should give support to their parents.
Always honour one's parents.

*Christianity* : Children must respect and obey their parents, but the parents must also respect their children. There is to be mutual understanding and appreciation within the family.

*Confucianism* : Filial piety is highly respected. The virtuous man will never neglect his parents. Love and respect for relations and elders is the beginning of live and respect for all members of the state.

*Hinduism* : love and respect must reign in the home. This is commended because every member of the household is a soul and as a soul he is worthy of live and respect. Faithfulness must mark the relationship of husband and wife.

*Jainism* : The child should support his parents when he is able to do so. Although the family should work together to aid each other, each one must suffer for his own deeds. One's family is of no use to him at the time of judgment. Then he shall be judged in accordance with his deeds.

*Judaism* : Family love and solidarity is basic to Jewish life. The child must honour and respect his parents and obey them at all times. The parents must teach the child and rear him in the ways of the Lord.

*Mohammedanism* : A child should be grateful both to God and to his

parents. The family is a unit, and should beseech God as one.
*Sikhism* : Son, why do you quarrel with your father, due to him you have grown to this age ?
It is a sin to argue with him.
Always look up to the Highest, living among your kith and kin,
Like the lotus that stands above its roots which are in mud.

*Zoroastrianism* : Obedience, peace, charity, humility, truth, and righteousness should prevail in every home and the children should respect the parents at all times.

*Forgiveness*

*Buddhism* : Whatsoever may be the cause of your suffering, do not woulnd another, forgive him.

*Christianity* : Man should be forgiving. As he forgives his fellow beings so God will forgive him. God is forgiving and is ready and anxious to forgive those who ask for his forgiveness.

*Confucianism* : One should forgive if the act is unintentional, but should punish the intended evil act.

*Hinduism* : God will forgive the sinner, if he earnestly casts away his sin. Human forgiveness is the way to happiness among men. A wise man will always be ready to forgive.

*Jainism* : I forgive all the living beings. All living beings may forgive me. I cherish friendly feelings towards all. I do not hold any ill will towards man, beast or plant.

*Judaism* : The Lord forgives all sins. He is forgiving at all times, if the wicked ones will forsake their ways.

*Mohammedanism* : God lives those who forgive their fellow beings. God is forgiving and is anxious to forgive all those who will come to him with conrite hearts.

*Shinto* : Forgive others but yourself never.

*Sikhism* : Countless people have perished.

Without the spirit of forgiveness.
Remove malice from you own heart,
And behold ! The whole world is your friends.

*Friendship*

*Buddhism* : One should pick one's associates from among the wise and the good. Evil associates will corrupt a man. A man who reproves intelligently should be sought out since his words are the advice one needs.

*Christinaity* : "Evil companions corrupt good morals." Shun those who are not good. The wise man will seek out those who will help him to become better and attain greater sanctity. Shun the idle and the unproductive and week out the industrious and the creative.

*Confucianism* : Seek out the company of those who can give good advice and whose example is good. One may be friendly to all men, but one should be discriminating in one's choice of associates. Good associates will do good to you good, therefore cling to the best.

*Hinduism* : Look upon all the living beings as your bosom friends, for in all of them there resides one soul. All are but a part of that Universal Soul. A person who believes that all are his soul-mates and loves them all alike never feels lonely.

*Jainism* : Do not allow yourself to be deluded by evil associates. Make friends with those who are considerate both towards other people and towards animals.

*Judaism* : Do not follow the path of the wicked, or associate with those who are evil. Good friends are best.

*Mohammedanism* : Avoid those who do wrong. To associate with the wicked is to cast suspicion upon oneself. Therefore, avoid such suspicion by seeking out only the good men as associates.

*Sikhism* : Friend, if you possess some good, let us be friends
Let us be partners for doing good,
And let us ignore each other's flaws

*Zoroastrianism* : The good should associate with those whom they can help. A virtuous man will radiate his virtue far and wide. One is fortunate to be the associate of such a good man.

*Justice*

*Buddhism* : The wise man will weigh matters carefully so that he may judge justly. Hasty judgment shows a man to be a fool.

*Christianity* : All judgments should be made justly. Beware lest you fall into evil judgments. God is just and will judge all men justly, according to their deeds.

*Confucianism* : The man of honour desires justice and will seek after it in all his actions. Only the fool is unjust.

*Hinduism* : The one who hurts pious men falls victim to his own designs. This is divine justice.

*Jainism* : God, let me not stray away from the path of justice. I may remain ever steadfast against the denunciation by others, should ever be unmindful of the prospects of immediate death or life through millenniums, keeping my equanimity in poverty and plenty.

*Judaism* : The Lord loves justice and has erected his throne upon it. The man who deals justly with his fellow beings at all times shall truly live.

*Mohammedanism* : Live a just and honest life. God does not do injustice, and he expects his followers to be just. Act justly at all times and under all conditions.

*Shinto* : Injustice shall be overcome by justice. If one has made a promise, he must fulfil it justly even though it be made with the unrighteous. Man should think and act justly at all times.

*Sikhism* : Our acts, right and wrong,
At thy Court shall come to judgment;
Some be seated near
Thy seat, Some ever kept distant;
The toils have ended of those,
That have worshipped Thee;

O Nanak, their faces are lit with joyful radiance,
And many others they set free.
We are saved not,
If thou judgest according to our actions,
Forgive us. O Thou Forgiver of all,
And lead Nanak across this ocean of life.

*Zoroastrianism* : To see justice and fail to do it is an act of cowardice.

*Love*

*Buddhism* : One act of pure love in saving life is greater than spending the whole of one's time in religious offerings to the gods, sacrificing elephants and horses.

*Christianity* : Love is supreme in Christianity. It is the heart of religion. God's love for man and man's love for God, the love of man for man, and the love of the Christian for all others are central themes of Christian teaching.

*Confucianism* : Love makes a spot beautiful; who chooses not to dwell in love, has he got wisdom? Love is the high nobility of Heaven, the peaceful home of man, To lack love, when nothing hinders us, is to lack wisdom. Lack of love and wisdom lead to lack of courtesy and right and without these man is a slave.

*Hinduism* : The Lord is the lover of all beings, but he especially loves those who keep his laws and are devoted to him. One can best worship the Lord through love.

*Mohammedanism* : Abu Dharr said : God's messenger came out to us and said: "Do you know which action is dearest to God most high ?" When one man suggested prayer and Zakat and another Jihad, the Prophet said : "The action dearest to god most high is love for God's sake."

*Jainism* : One should show compassion to all creatures, and obey the Law at all times.

*Judaism* : One should love God with all one's heart. And one should love his his neighbour. The stranger has a cliam on one's love. God loves the good man, the righteous. He also loves the sinner and seeks to

draw him from his sin and to himself.
*Shinto* : The Lord will visit the home where love reigns.
Love is the representative of the Lord.

*Sikhism* : One who loves God truly will be cleansed of all his impurities. We obtain salvation by loving our fellow beings and God.

*Taoism* : God's love is for the good man at all times. The wise one taught universal love towards one's fellow beings and his followers should follow his teaching.

*Zoroastrianism* : Everyone should love virtue. Man is the beloved of the Lord and should love him in return.

*Obedience*

*Buddhism* : Those who obey the law and follow studiously the commandments shall have serenity of mind, joy, and prosperity. Obedience is the way to the good things of this life and of the life to come.

*Christianity* : The true Christian is known by the fact that he obeys the Commandments of God. If one desire true life here and hereafter, he should keep the commandments. The Christian will obey God at all times rather than man. If one keep God's commandments, God will dwell in him and act through him.

*Confucianism* : To obtain the favour of heaven, one should observe all the statues of heaven. Those who reverently observe these statues and are obedient to the will of heaven shall have happiness and shall become men superior.

*Hinduism* : The laws of God are eternal, lofty, and deep. The man who is obedient to them will be happy and, after death, will experience joy unsurpassable.

*Jainism* : The fool refuses to obey the Law and is sorry when he reaches the hour of death. Man is created to fulfil the law of God. The wise and pious are always obedient to the law of God.

*Judaism* : The commandments of the Lord are just and should be obeyed.

To disobey God will result in punishment, to obey will result in happiness and blessedness. God will show no mercy to those people or nations who refuse to obey.

*Mohammedanism* : All shall be well with the believer who hears the word of the lord and obeys. The law of the Lord has been set down for men to read and obey. The punishment for disobedience is severe.

*Sikhism* : Man is to God what a servant is to his master. Thus, he should obey at all times. If he obeys, he will have honour and happiness and will eventually meet his master.

*Taoism* : The complete and perfect man is the one who obeys the will of the Lord at all times.

*Zoroastrianism* : The Lord is wise. Thus, what he orders is good for his followers and his commandments should be obeyed. Immortality is the reward he offers to the obedient.

*Peace*

*Buddhism* : True happiness comes to those who live at peace with their fellow beings. The aim of all should be to learn peace and live peacefully with all men.

*Christianity* : Jesus is the Prince of Peace. He came to this earth to bring peace to all men. The peacemaker is blessed and shall be a child of God. We should seek the way of peace and finally come to peace with God.

*Confucianism* : Seek to live in harmony with all your neighbours and at peace with the brethren. Peace and love should reign throughout the world. The most high god seeks peace among his people.

*Hinduism* : If one would find happiness and security, one must seek for peace. The peaceful mind will become established in wisdom. God is a god of peace and desired peace for all people.

*Jainism* : The enlightened will make peaceful the foundation of their lives. All men should live in peace with their fellow beings. This is the Lord's desire.

*Judaism* : Judaism looks forward to an ideal time when peace shall reign throughout the world. God commends peace and urges all his followers to work for peace. The peaceful life offers the greatest opportunity for happiness and prosperity.

*Mohammedanism* : God will guide men to peace. If they will heed him, he will lead them from the darkness of war to the light of peace.

*Shinto* : The earth shall be free from trouble and men shall live at peace under the protection of the divine.

*Sikhism* : The True Nam is my support;
It is my food and drink;
By it my hunger of every kind is satisfied.
By saturating my mind, it had satisfied all my longings,
And given me peace and happiness.

*Taoism* : The wise esteem peace and quiet above all else. The good ruler seeks peace and not war, and he rules by persuasion rather than by force.

*Zoroastrianism* : All men and women should mutually love one another and live in peace as brothers and sisters bound by the indestructible hand of Humanity.

*Sincerity*

*Buddhism* : Be not slothful or flippant, but be earnest at all times. Goodness comes from earnestness. God lives the earnest, sincere man.

*Christinaity* :One's religious actions should not be for showing but should be done in earnestness. At all times the true Christian is sincere and earnest. He is never the hypocrite who acts merely for show.

*Confucianism* : Whatever you do, you should do with all your heart. Heaven will help the man who is sincere, and one's fellowmen will trust him if he is sincere and earnest.

*Hinduism* : The Lord does not favour those who are not sincere and honest.

*Jainism* : Clear thinking comes through sincere and earnest effort. One can be proficient in religious practices only to the degree that one is earnest and sincere. Through sincere actions one becomes pure.
*Judaism* : The Lord will help those who are earnest. He is near to the sincere and known man's inner being. He is not fooled by outward appearances.

*Mohammedanism* : God is not to be fooled. He knows whether or not a man is earnest in his professions and will deal with all men according to this knowledge. One who reprints in earnestness will be forgiven.

*Shinto :* Sincerity is the single virtue that binds divinity and man in one

*Sikhism* : To pretend religion is of no avail. Earnestness is the only basis for true religious acts.

*Taoism* : The manner of heaven is earnestness. If one is sincere and earnest is one's acts, one will attain to the truest sainthood.

*Zoroastrianism* : As long as a man is earnest, his reward will be great.

*Work*

*Buddhism* : Works, and not birth, determine one's place in the world. At all times one should work diligently and with earnestness. Hard work is praised.

*Christianity* : God works, and so man should work. The Christian will be diligent in good works all the time, for a man is to be judged by his works. As man works for the good, it is God who works in and through him.

*Confucianism* : Not ease, but work is the mark of a good man. The superior individual does not indulge in luxurious ease, but works constantly for the good. He is superior in that he does things which the base cannot understand or appreciate.

*Hinduism* : One becomes what he does. The man who does good becomes good, and the man who does evil becomes evil. The motive of one's works should not be the consequences. One should do good despite the results. No one who does good will come to an evil end.

*Jainism* : A day once goes will never return. Therefore, one should be diligent each moment to do good. We reach the goal of the good life by pious works.

*Judaism* : God will judge each man according to his works. All men shall be known by their works. Whatever one undertakes to do, one should do it with all his might. God commands men to work and promises that he will be with them in all good works.

*Mohammedanism* : Everyone should strive to excel in good works. Work constantly. God will observe your works and judge you according to whether they are good or evil.

*Sikhism* : God has determined from the beginning the works man must do. No man can escape this determination. Men become saints or sinners by their works only, not by their professions. Good works bring men to a clearer knowledge of the divine.

*Zoroastrianism* : We come to the divine through our good works. Thus, at all times man should strive to work well so that he may gain recognition in the sight of the Wise Lord.

## REFERENCES

1. For details the author's following books are worth-referring — *Value Education* : Theory and Practice (1986), *A Search for Human Values* (1992).
2. Rokeach, Beliefs, *Attitudes and Values*, p.124.
3. *Ibid*; p.160.
4. Philosophy in the USSR, pp.18–19.
5. M.N. Roy, *New Humanism*, p. 53.
6. M.N. Roy, *Reason, Romanticism and Revolution*, p. 496.
7. L.K. Hsu, *The study of Literate civilization*, pp.78–82.
8. Based on *The living thoughts of Confucious*' by Alfred Doeblin.
9. Confucius, *The Analects with Introduction* by D.C. Lau, p. 34.
10. *Religions of Man*, p.187.
11. कर्मण्येवाधिकारस्ते मा फलेषु कदाचन।
    मा कर्मफलहेतुर्भूः मा ते संगोऽस्त्वकर्मणि।।
12. Quoted in *Religions of Man*, p.190.
13. Quoted bin *Religions of Man*, p.192.
14. त्वं सोम तनूकृद्भ्यो
    द्वेषोभ्योऽन्यकृतेभ्यः।
    उरु यन्तासि वरुथम्।। Rgived 8/79/3.

15. आत्मनः प्रतिकूलानि परेषां न समाचरेत् । — Mahabharata.
16. J.W. Spellman, Development and Indian Cultural values, in *India–History and Thought* by S.N. Mukherjee, p. 207.
17. J.B. Bury, *The Idea of Progress* (Oxford, 1920), p. 3.
18. J.W. Spellman, *Op. Cit.*, p. 209.
19. Gunnar Myrdal, *Asian Drama*, p. 31.
20. Gunnar Myrdal, *Asian Drama*, p. 33.
21. Will Durant, *The Pleasures of Philosophy*, p. 387.

# 8

# TOWARDS NEW WORLD ORDER

Human Manifesto, Historical Background, UN Charter, UNESCO, Persestroica: An Epoch-making move, Practical Aspect, Indian Context, Combating Racism, Prejudice and discrimination, International Terrorism, Combating International Terrorism and Illicit trafficking in drug and arms, New World Order.

## Human Manifesto

For free, frank and harmonious new world order the following democratic values incorporated in the universal Declaration of Human Rights adopted in the United Nations General Assembly in 1948, are very essential :

1. acceptance and appreciation of cultural diversity,
2. respect for human dignity and universal human rights,
3. responsibility to the world community, and
4. reverence for the earth.

The declaration has been designed to serve "as a common standard of achievement for all peoples and all nations". The declaration states that all persons are born free and equal in dignity and expresses basic civil, economic, political and social rights of all humans. It is a statement of moral standards, to be followed by all nations. It stresses the fact that every one has the right to life, liberty and security of person, equality before law, freedom of movement, etc. irrespective of caste, creed, clour, sex or language. The Human Manifesto is as under :

Human life on our plant is in jeopardy.
It is in jeopardy from war that could pulverize the human habitat. It is in jeopardy from preparations for war that destroy or diminish the prospects of decent existence.

It is in jeopardy because of the denial of human rights.
It is in jeopardy because the air is being fouled and the waters and soil are being poisoned.
If these dangers are to be removed and if human development is to be assured, we the people of this planet must accept obligations to each other and to the generations of human beings to come.
We have the obligation to free our world of war by creating an enduring basis for worldwide peace.
We have the obligation to safeguard the delicate balance of the natural environment and to develop the world's resources for the human good.
We have the obligation to make human rights the primary concern of society.
We have the obligation to create a world order in which man neither has to kill or to be killed.

In order to carry out these obligations, we the people of this world assert our primary allegiance to each other in the family of man. We declare our individual citizenship in the world community and our support for a United Nations capable of governing our planet in the common human interest.

Life in the universe is unimaginably rare. It must be protected, respected, cherished.

We pledge our energies and resources of spirit to the preservation of the human habitat and to the infinite possibilities of human betterment in our time.[1]

**Historical Background**

Since the dawn of civilization, the mankind has been struggling hard against tyranny, injustice and inequality and for the protection of human rights and fundamental freedoms. The rulers have always endeavoured to keep the human beings divided on the basis of artificial barriers such as religion, race, caste, creed, colour and the like. A large number of human beings have been kept in bondage only to serve the interest of the rulers. The political, social and economic bondages have deprived the men of the opportunities for their free and full development. The struggle for freedom from such bondages has been continued.

The history reminds of the struggle of the people for the achievement of human rights and fundamental freedoms. The struggle of the patricians and plebisians in Ancient Rome, of the Barons of England against the tyranny of King John in England which resulted in the grant of Magna Charta in 1215, of the English Parliament against the arbitrary exercise of powers by the Stuart Kings which resulted in the execution of Charles I in 1649, expulsion of James II in 1688 and acceptance of the Bill of Rights in 1689, of the French Revolution of 1789, against the crimes of Louis XVI, which resulted in the French Declaration of the Rights of Man, of American Revolution against the exploitation by Britain which gave birth to the American Declaration of Independence, and of the Russian Revolution in 1917 which successfully overthrew the tyrant Tsars.

These struggles were limited to the section of the people and were regional in character. Nevertheless they had a far-reaching effect of great significance in the history of struggle of mankind in the field of human rights and fundamental freedoms and served the cause of advancement of mankind. The invention of Atom Bomb which was used in the Second World War and caused indiscriminate death of innocent persons in Hiroshima and Nagasaki has threatened the very existence of humanity and has changed the outlook of the peoples to the international relations and the problems of war. The peoples could no longer rely on the wisdom of the rulers in the matters of international intercourse. They became conscious of the fact that the incorrect policy and decision of war could land them in trouble and it would cause not only heavy economic pressure on them but also it would risk their lives in war as the wars have now ceased to be between the professional soldiers. Even the civilians are to sure of their lives being save once the war breaks.

This awakening of the peoples exercised a great pressure on the rulers of the Sıates, who had all along been exploiting the peoples for their petty selfish purposes, and satisfaction of distructive impulses. They realised the mood of the public which wanted the problem of human rights and fundamental freedoms to be made a concern of the world organisation. The peoples brought home to the rulers that there could be no permanent peace unless there was guarantee of human rights and fundamental freedoms at the global level. The peoples wished the Charter of the United Nations to be strong in its provisions for guaranteeing the human rights and fundamental freedoms as they had seen the origin of the war grow out of the violation of these freedoms by the rulers.

To meet the demands of the peoples before which the rulers were compelled to bow, the provisions were made in the Charter of the United Nations for the declaration, enforcement and protection of the human rights and fundamental freedoms. The second paragraph of the preamble of the Charter of the United Nations pledges the Nations "to reaffirm faith in fundamental human rights, in the dignity of and worth of the human person, in the equal rights of men and women and of nations large and small". The third purpose stated in Chapter I of the Charter is "To achieve international co-operation in solving international problems of an economic, social, cultural, or humanitarian character, and in promoting and encouraging respect for human rights and for fundamental freedoms for all without discrimination as to race, sex, language of religion."

The United Nations Organization has two distinct aspects. In the first place it is a political and security organisation primarily concerned with the prevention of war and maintenance of peace in the world. In the second place it is a welfare organisation striving hard to promote the Welfare of men everywhere through various social, economic and cultural projects and thus strengthening the foundation of peace.

The Principal organs of the United Nations competent to implement the provisions of the Charter concerning human rights are the General Assembly and the Economic and Social Council, acting either by itself or through the commission on human rights. Art. 68 of the Charter *Inter alia* authorises the Economic and Social Council to set up a commission on human rights. The Economic and Social Council decided in February 1946 to establish a Commission on Human Rights charged with submitting proposals, recommendations and reports to the Council concerning :

(a) an international bill of rights;
(b) international declarations or conventions on Civil Liberties, the status of women, freedom of information and similar matters;
(c) the protection of minorities; and
(d) prevention of discrimination on grounds of race, sex, language, or religion.

**UN Charter**

The Preamble to the UN Charter expresses the ideals and common aims of all the peoples whose Governments joined together to form the United Nations:

We the people of the United Nations determined

— To save succeeding generation from the scourage of war, which twice in our lifetime has brought untold sorrow to making, and

— To re-affirm faith in fundamental human rights, in the dignity, and worth of the human person, in the equal rights of men and women and of nations, large and small, and
— To establish conditions under which justice and respect for the obligations arising from treaties and other sources of international law can be maintained, and
— to promote social progress and better standards of life in larger freedom

and for those ends.

— to practice tolerance and living together in peace with one another as good neighbours, and
— to unite our strength to maintain international peace and security, and
— to ensure, by the acceptance of principles and the institution of methods, that armed force shall not be used, save in the common interest, and
— to employ international machinery for the promotion of the economic and social advancement of all peoples.

Have resolved to combine our efforts to accomplish these aims.

Accordingly, our respective governments through representatives assembles in the city of San Francisco, who have exhibited their full powers found to be in good and due from, have agreed to the present Charger of the United Nations and do hereby establish an international organisation to be known as the United Nations.

**UNESCO**

UNESCO through its recommendations and activities has played an important role in promoting Human Rights Education. In this context, UNESCO's 1974 Recommendation Concerning Education for International Understanding, Cooperation and Peace and Education relating to Human Rights and Fundamental Freedoms has been particularly important. Some of the specific elements of the Recommendation which are important in this context are : Understanding and respect for all peoples, cultures, civilizations, values and ways of life, including domestic ethnic cultures and cultures of other nations, stress on the inadmissibility of recourse to the use of force and violence, strengthening the struggle against all forms and varieties of racialism, fascism and apartheid as well as other ideologies which breed national and racial hatred, study of different cultures and their reciprocal influences, study of the major problems of mankind· such as equality of rights of peoples, exercise and observance of human rights, etc. The components relating to Human Rights which generally find a place in the curricula and text books at various stages include the study of the following :

— Basic features of the Indian political system and Indian Constitution, particularly the Preamble, and Parts III, IV & IV A which have a direct bearing on Human Rights.
— Problems and challenges of contemporary Indian Life – polity, economy, society, culture – which have a direct or indirect bearing on Human Rights.
— Diversity and variety of Indian culture, its composite and non-monolithic character.
— Indian social system and dynamics of social change.
— Major events in the history of India and the world relating to the struggle for political and civil rights as well as economic and social rights, and the role played by common people and outstanding leaders in these struggles.
— Human Rights situation in the world, particularly with regard to gross violations in the form of colonialism, racialism and apartheid.
— Literary works which reflect Human Rights concerns and quest for freedoms and rights.
— Biological unity of human species.
— Major historical documents such as the Declaration of Independence, Declaration of the Rights of Man and Citizen, United Nations Charter, Universal Declaration of Human Rights, etc.
— References to major historical documents such as the Declarations of the Rights of Man and Citizen.
— The United Nations Charter.
— The Universal Declaration of Human Rights.
— The Indian Constitution, etc.
— Major events in the history of India and the world.
— Major events in the history of India and the world.
— Relating to the struggles for political and civil rights as well as economic and social rights.
— The role played by outstanding leaders, Indian and non-Indian, in these struggles.

- — The problems and challenges of contemporary India and the world
- — Literary works which reflects human rights concerns and the quest for freedoms and rights, etc.
- — focus on human rights situation in the world, gross violation in the form of racism, etc. (particular attention needed).
- — The various kinds of human rights related questions in contemporary Indian situation, etc.
- — Popularizing international documents on human rights while celebrating the United Nations Day.
- — Promoting awareness about oppressive systems such as apartheid (occasional effort seen).

**Perestroika in USSR : An Epoch-making Move**

Main architect of the thinking–Perestroika was the then Supreme of USSR Mikhail Gorbachev. Of late, it was realized in the USSR that one can no longer live a secluded life, reteating into one's shell. Nothing happening on earth, here or there, this way or that way, bypasses an individual in one way or another, everything nowadays is everybody's concern. Addressing the French Parliament in late 1985, Mikhail Gorbachev said: "We have started a re-thinking and on adjusting in full conformity with the new realities on many customary problems including the military and political spheres.

The result of this re-thinking has been the elaboration of a new Soviet foreign-policy concept, which was based on mainly three components – traditions, self-criticism, and innovation. Traditionally it was based on "Leninist approaches to world affairs." According to Gorbachev : "This concept does not spring from thin air, but stems from Lenin's legacy and that of all successive periods in the development of Soviet foreign policy. It can be said that our present platform of actions in world affairs is a continuation and development of the sum total of ideas contained in Lenin's Decree on Peace, with due regard for all that has occurred since 1917".[2]

**Action Plan**

"You shall not murder" – this ancient maxim, which became one of the fundamental principles of Christianity, can be translated today as also meaning to renounce war, to disarm and secure normal, civilized relations between countries. With regard to today international life the ancient principle "You shall not steel" – means stop plundering others, and that nations should establish equal and mutually beneficial relations. Today ensuring humanity's survival implies age-old socio-moral values. On this issue all religious faiths, all schools of ethics have to contribute substantially one thing or the other.

The one which holds the mankind is called religion, according to Hindu scriptures. With Dr. Karan Singh, we can say: "Humankind today is living in a unique situation. Science and technology are transforming human civilisation before our very eyes, and in our own life-times we have witnessed incredible breakthroughs in numerous fields. Man has broken away from the confines of earth, reached the moon and begun his exploration into the planets and even the stars far beyond. Agriculture and industry, medicines and communications, all have benefitted tremendously from the efflorescence of human creativity expressed through science and technology. And yet the destructive potential of humankind also grows space, with tens of thousand of nuclear was heads of such potency that even a fraction of them can destroy not only the human race but probably all life on this planet. Thus, is the dilemma of man in the nuclear age."[3]

In order to remove this type of dilemma the 27th congress of the CPSU unanimously approved the programme for a nuclear-free and more secure world. The resolution of the 27th Congress of the Communist Party of the Soviet Union on the political Report of the CPSU Central Committee pointed out : "Fulfilment of this programme, which is epochmaking in its scope and significance, would open for humanity a fundamentally new period development the possibility of concentrating constructive work alone." The 27th Congress of the CPSU did not confine itself to approving and endorsing the proposition set forth in Mikhail Gorbachev's statement of January 15, 1986. Basing itself on the main ideas of the CPSU's new foreign policy concept the congress advanced a plan for building the foundations of a comprehensive system of international security.

Prior to this, *i.e*, in earlier congresses the Soviet authorities concentrated their efforts on solving major concrete problems, the problem of reducing this or that type of weapon, regional conflicts and so on. But they did not come up with a general long-term programme embracing all spheres of international security, which is exactly what was advanced by the 27th Congress. Its primary goal was to remove the threat of nuclear war and to propose a comprehensive system of international security by creating the type of conditions in which the revival of the war danger be averted. For this purpose 27th Party Congress incorporated certain basic provisions in its report which are as under :

1. *In the Military Sphere*

— renunciation by the nuclear powers of war – both nuclear and conventional – against each other or against third countries;
— prevention of an arms race in outer space, cessation of all nuclear weapons tests and the total destruction of such weapons, a ban on the destruction of chemical weapons. And renunciation of the development of other means of mass annihilation;
— a strictly controlled lowering of the levels of military capabilities of countries to limits of reasonable adequacy;
— disbandment of military alliances, and as a stage towards this – renunciation of their enlargement and of the formation of new ones; and
— balanced and proportionate reduction of military budgets.

2. *In the Political Sphere*

— strict respect in international practice for the right of each people to choose the ways and forms of its development independently;
— a just political settlement of international crises and regional conflicts;
— elaboration of a set of measures aimed at building confidence between states and the creation of effective guarantees against attacks from without and of the inviolability of their frontiers; and
— elaboration of effective methods of preventing international terrorism, including those ensuring the safety of international land, air and communications.

3. *In the Economic Sphere*

— exclusion of all forms of discrimination from international practice; renunciation of the policy of economic blockades and sanctions of this is not directly envisaged in the recommendations of the world community;
— joint quest for ways for a just settlement of the problem of debts;
— establishment of a new world economic order guaranteeing equal economic security to all countries;
— elaboration of principles for utilizing part of the funds released as a result of a reduction of military budgets for the good of the world community, of developing nations in the first place; and
— the pooling of efforts in exploring and making peaceful use of outer space and in resolving global problems on which the destinies of civilization depend.

4. *In the Humanitarian Sphere*

- cooperation in the dissemination of the ideas of peace, disarmament, and international security; greater flow of general objective information and broader contact between peoples for the purpose of learning about one another, reinforcement of the spirit of mutual understanding and concord in relations between them;
- extrication of genocide, apartheid advocacy of fascism and every other form of racial, national or religious exclusiveness, and also of discrimination against people on this basis;
- extension–while respecting the laws of each country–of international cooperation in the implementation of the political social, and personal rights of people;
- decision in a humane and positive spirit of questions related to the reuniting of families, marriage, and the promotion of contacts between people and between organisations; and
- strengthening of and quests for new forms of cooperation in culture, art, science, education, and medicine."

**Practical Aspect**

The programme detailed above appears to be too broad and too ambitious. Post-history of various politics-social circumstances in USSR did not allow the programme to be materialized due to collapse of communism in 1989 and disintegration of USSR. All the aims are not accomplished in any system, may it be that of UN Charter or human rights charter or a new thinking like Perestroika. But the ingredients of the theme were, no doubt, quite befitting to meet the requirements of the survival of the human race, as it has been rightly said by the advocates of the new thought: "It is needness to say that the Soviet Union cannot remake the world, it is and it will be changing on its own. But we do want to change the relations between members of the world community, and we propose that we all engage in this endeavour together–We are convinced that the realities of the nuclear age urgently require new rules governing the international life on our unique planet earth".

In the wake of recent (1994) cut-throat conflicts between Russians and Chechenyans the above Principal (Perestroika) does not appear to be practical. Thus it appears that with the collapse of USSR the said high worded ideology has also collapsed. Under such circumstances the doubt is raised-has the UN thrown up its hands in despair and resorted to ritual resolutions of peace and harmony and tolerance in place of any active involvement in world affairs ? Tolerance is an abstract concept implying a policy of live and let live, of co-existence which has been one of the cherished value of UNO. For this purpose more concerted efforts are required. As Pope John Paul said in his message for work for peace cannot be concerned merely with the external conditions of co-existence, rather it must effect people's heart and appeal to a new awareness of human dignity. Every human being is a person endowed with intelligence and free will and precisely because he is a person, he has rights and obligations which flow directly and immediately from his very nature. And these rights and obligations are universal, inviolable and inalienable. The truth about man is the keystone in the resolutions of all the problems involved in promoting peace to teach people. This is one of the most fruitful and lasting ways to affirm the value of peace".

**Indian Context**

Peace in India is not for one, but for many and for all. That is why from the dawn of Indian civilization we find, unlike any other land, a universal prayer, wherein peace is prayed not only for fellow-beings but also for all sentient creatures, even for earth, water and heaven, in fact for the cosmos as a whole :

> "Peace be unto the heaven. Peace be unto the upper ether, peace be into the earth. Peace be unto herbs. Peace be unto great trees. Peace be unto the God of the universe. Peace be unto Brahman. Peace be unto all. Peace be unto Peace itself."[4]

As Kant says, "The civil constitution of every shall be republican, and war shall not be declared except by a plebiscite of all the citizens. When those who must do the fighting have the right to decide between war and peace, history will no longer be written in blood. On the other hand, in a constitution where the subject is not a voting member of the state, and which is not republican, the resolution to go to war is a matter of the smallest concern in the world."[5]

**Combating Racism, Prejudice and Discrimination**

For healthy and productive crosscultural communication combating of racism, prejudices and discriminatory attitudes is necessary. To accomplish this objective we have to minimize negative attitude and behaviour and instil positive view toward the people, society and nation at large. Negative attitudes are originated by negative values. What are negative values ? Fear, hatred, jealousy, doubt, greed, deceit, inferiority, fault-finding, egoism, insistence, aversion etc. may be termed as negative values, which influence individual's conduct and behaviour negatively. These negative values are derived from various misconception and lack of self-actualization, No doubt, heredity and harmones do play their role in the gamut of entire phenomena. It is psychological fact that fearing persons are found to be cruel, jealous, harsh and so on.

The stereotypes prevailing in the society also cause prejudices, due to generalization and, at times, overgeneralization. Therefore, there is a great need for clearing myths and stereotypes associated with different races and ethnic groups. In order to achieve this goal a few assumption must be kept in view, particularly by teachers or those who are in a position to surmonize the people :

1. The very nature of negative values must be properly explained.
2. Language is not only vital source of communication but it is a heart of the culture.
3. People's effectiveness in multicultural communication can be improved by developing their cultural self-awareness. In other words their abilities and aptitudes to recognize cultural differences must be developed.
4. There are various tools and techniques of human communication, that should be used very meticulously and rationally for transcending cultural barriers.
5. Differing cultures in a society have certain dimensions. Some time they are obvious but in a few cases they are ambiguous. For example, the black experience in USA are obvious ones, that can be easily identified, defined and taught.
6. One can achieve a psychological balance between cultural pride and identity on the one hand and appreciation of cultures other than their own.

To facilitiate the streamlining of above facts it is necessary to undertake a crusade against sham knowledge and beliefs. Radhakrishnan has rightly observed: "People, therefore, who believe in religion as an experience of truth, as an encounter of the Reality, will never quarrel about the names which they give to God. They will never quarrel about the approaches by which one gets to God. They will tell us that God is there in our inmost heart. He is the secret of our being.; He is the Lord of our inner chamber. There he is if we have the perception to see that he dwells there, hidden."[6]

Socretes had rightly said that phibsophy starts when an individual starts doubting the things. But there should be certain logic behind the doubt. Eternal truths should not be doubted. Many thinkers and reformers were atheists; but they were humanists they doubted many things except the dignity of man. As Mahatma Gandhi said, "man is the supreme consideration. They also believed in this dictum though they were not religious like Mahatma Gandhi. "We develop a throw-away mentality to match our throw-away products," Says Alvin Toffler. We will be committing blunders if we equate the modes of cultural awareness with throw-away products. Will Durant cautions, "You do not remind him of the bitterness which religion brought into human life; the families broken apart by hard dogmatism and petty differences; the nations produced into war to determine the victory of creeds, the men and women killed in autos-da-fe for fear some little private heresy would upset an inspired Book and rock-founded infallible Church. You remind me of a sentence in spengler: Atheism, he says is entirely compatible with a wistful desire for real religiousness–therein resembling Romanticism, which likewise would recall that which has irrevocably gone. The first decades of our century were full of religious atheist. Like Anatole France, George Moore, George Santayana—romantic mourners for their dead faith."

Gudykunst and Ki, in their book *Communicating with Strangers* describe the multicultural person as "one who has achieved an advanced level in process of becoming intercultural and whose cognitive, affective, and behavioral characteristics are not limited but are open to growth beyond the psychological parameters of any one culture. . . . The intercultural person possesses an intellectual and emotional commitment to the fundamental unity of all humans and, at the same time, accepts and appreciates the differences that lie between people of different cultures."

Multicultural persons are facilitators and catalysts for intercultural contacts. They accept and appreciates the differences existing in macroculture as well as microcultures. They can understand cultural diversities among the nations as well as within a single nation without any bias or prejudices. Such type of international understanding goes a long way in creating the atmosphere of harmony and peace in society and nation at large by removing various racial, communal and linguistic barriers and inhibitions.

**International Terrorism**

As compared to criminal offences terrorism is quite different type of phenomenon as its seeds or germs lie not in economic misery or frustration but in political ambitions and designs of expansionist state. Terrorists are financed and patronized by such states due to their vested interests my it be Pakistan or Palestine, Punjab or North-Eastern states of India. Media play a great role in highlighting the terror. Tracing the history of International terrorism Maj. Gen. S. Mohindra observes :

> "International Terrorism has been a canse of worry the world over. But it cannot be allowed to continue and plague the lives of nations and also threaten innocents. It started and had begun its growth on the international horizon in the 1960s. It was sparked and fuelled by the early successes of the PLO which introduced airline hijacking as an international weapon to further their cause. This was followed by kidnapping, assassinations and so on, by groups the Iranian Mujaheed, Armenian A S A L A, the German Bader, Meinhof, Italian Red Brigade, the Japanese Red Army and others who had forged links and alliances to become a kind of Terrorist International. A net work of professional terrorists sought to weaken and demoralise democratic societies by attacking their citizens, their institutions disrupting their way of life and sapping their political will." (Maj. Gen. S. Mohindra. *Terrorist Games Nations Play*, Preface).

Terrorists Paralises all police forces judicatory process, but they are afraid of military intervention, which had been trued out successfully by Israel, which suffered the most from terrorist attacks. During last two decades there had been number of hostage taking, hijacking of planes, seizing of schools, apartments, hotels and buses, but Israel refused to yield to their demands and faced them with firm determination. Consequentially attacks were gradually minimised. In India terrorism is not a home-product, but it has been planted and nurtured by external agencies for certain political gains. By now it is proved, beyond doubt, that Pakistan is the one amongst such external agencies.

Such phenomenon occurs because of assumptions like "One country's terrorists are another country's heroes" or "Our Terrorists are their freedom fighters". Because of such attitude and the multifarious interests of the terrorists universally acknowledged definition could not be finalised, though once it was attempted by UNO. Therefore, terrorists are known by different nomenclatures like–resistance fighters, insurgents, guerrillas, partisans, revolution Aries and so on. Yasser Arafat flatly refused to be called 'terrorist'. In of the interviews (Time, 7Nov. 1988) he said: 'I cannot accept your saying if George Washington was called a terrorist by the British. De Ganlle was called terrorist by the Nazis What can they say about the P.L.O., except to repeat this slogan? We are freedom fithers, and we are proud of it. According to Internaitonal law and United Nations Charter, I have the right to resist Israel occupation. I do not want to harm anybody."

The last sentence of this statement is noteworthy. In India during the period of freedom struggle many freedom fighters like sardar Bhagat Singh, Ramprasad Bismit, Ashfaculla Khan, etc. were called terrorists by the British and were sentenced to death; but they were proud of their acts and we too feel proud of their sacrifice. In the annals of History their acts are glorified and they are called 'martyrs', as they suffered for the noble cause, i.e., freedom of their motherland. Yasser Arafat was also on the matching plane. In both of these example one thing is common i.e., they did not do any harm to the community or the innocents. They fought with the government for their legitimate right and succeeded also later on. This can be taken as a line of demarcation between freedom fighters and terrorists.

For combating terrorism collective and cooperative efforts are warranted so that proper strategies may be planned to curve it so that peace and harmony may be established in free societies.

## Combating International Terrorism and Illicit Trafficking in Drugs and Arms

Illicit drug trafficking, violent crimes including internaitonal terrorism, hijacking, illegal trafficking in arms and explosives, economic and financial crimes, defalcation, environmental crime — these have been of express concern for all the countries, big and small, irrespective of their form of government and fiscal structures. Thorstein Sallin, eminent American sociologist and criminologist has observed that : "Organised crime is synonymous with economic enterprises, orgnaised for the purpose of conducting illegal activities and when they operate legitimate ventures, do so by illegal means."[7] The main objective of such well organised crimes is substantial financial gain.

## Organised Crimes

To operate organised crime various crime-syndicates are formed. They operate at national as well as international level separately. In our country also we very often read in news papers about coal-Mafia, opium-Mafia etc. Such orgnaised crime come under a specific category, which is very different from professionally executed group-crimes, generally covered under article 400 of Indian Penel Code. Mafia is different from such cases. Mafia crimes are well-organised well-executed, and have continuing and strictly operated entrepreneurial style. In the most cases they have very respectable front-line.

**Historical Background**

The pattern of organised crime started first in Sicily and Italy as Mafia, which in its expanded form reads as "Morte Alla Francia Italia Anila." In English it means "Death to the French is Italy's cry". It is inferred that Mafia-trend might have originated as back as in 1282, as a resistance movement against french occupation of Italy and Sicily. Palermo and Naples were their original centres. The *Mahabharata* maintains affirmatively that the empire cannot be established without crime and violence. If we go through this dictum we may believe that the pursuit of politico-military ends by revolution or any uncovering means is a phenomenon as old as the history of man. The term Guerrilla, however, dates back to the Peninsula war of 1808-1814 and gained currency in use in the period following the French Revolution; but the term 'terrorism' got impetus from the activities of PLO. Kautilaya, in his *Artha Shastra* calls such activities as "Tusnim Yuddha" (Silent War).

Tracing the heritage of terrorism Maj. Gen. S. Mohindra has rightly observed : "Every period in history has had its terrorists. Even before first World War, a typical violent political act, which today we would probably term an act of international terrorism, involved attempts on the political leaders. Szar Allexander II was murdered in 1881, Empress Elizabeth of Austria in 1891, Archduke Franze Ferdinand in 1914 and so on. However, the technique to apply terror as a means to intimidate a large segment of population was perfected by the Russians during the Bolshevik Revolution."[8]

According to nature and character of an objective in modes and methods of terror have been changing through the ages. Well-planned international endeavours and firm determination is essential to compact such terrorism in our modern times. Without international understanding and cooperation it is not possible. With this view recently (13-16 Dec. 1994) India hosted Asian Regional Conference at New Delhi. It was, in fact, thirteenth Asian Regional Conference of International Criminal Police

Orgnaisation (ICPO) – Interpol. At present 176 countries are members of ICPO – Interpol, including India.

110 Delegates from 30 countires, viz., Australia, Armenia, Bahrain, Bangladesh, Brunei, China, India, Indonesia, Iran, Iraq, Israel, Japan, Kazakhistan, Korea, Loas, Mangolia, Malaysia, Nepal, New Zealand, Oman, Pakistan, Portugal (Macao), Qatar, Russian Federation Saudi Arabia, Sri Lanka, Thailand, UAE, UK (Hong Kong) and Uzbekistan participated in the conference.

15 observers from Frnace, Italy, Netherlands, Sweden, USA, Canada, Norway and Denmark and 3 Internaitonal orgnaisations, viz., Columbo Plan; Bureau, Sri Lanka, European Commission, Brussels, Belgium and United National Drug Control Programme (UNDCP) participated in this conference.

The conference put-forth the following recommendations and suggestions in order to combat international terrorism and illicit trafficking in drugs and arms :

1. Recognising the benefits to be gained form the speedy transfer and analysis of information relating to drug trafficking activities, member-countires in the region strive to improve the flow of information bilaterally and to the General Secretariat. Those in receipt of such information are urged to report any action taken and the result of enquiries to the source country so as to encourage further interaction.
2. Acknowledging the success and great potential of the technique referred to in he Vienna Convention (1988) as "Controlled Delivery", member countries in the region consider using this technique and that those not having the legal framework within which the technique may be utilised hereby bring to the attention of their legislative authorities the need for enabling legislation to be enacted. The availability of a draft model legislation is noted. For the benefit of member-countires the IPSO should maintain a list of all countries allowing such operations as well as all notable operations undertaken.
3. The potential value of the Interpol Weapons and Explosives Tracking System (IWETS) be fully exploited by member-countires in the region by routinely forwarding to the General Secretarial information relating to the use of firearms and explosives in terrorist acts and other violent crimes. The dependence of a comprehensive collection of data and a successful comparison of information on a willingness to do so

is noted.

4. Member-countires in the region should pay attention to cases of maritime pollution amounting to crime and caused by large vessels or oil tankers and also to illegal traffic in species of wild flora and fauna keeping the General Secretariat informed so that the overall situation can be monitored.
5. Member-countries in the region inform the General Secretarial of all known illegal cross border movements of radio-active materials using the "Ecapsmessage format". The General Secretariat is asked to keep member-countries informed of the overall situation after a study and analysis of the information received.
6. The financial and economic environment, in particular "unconventional" money-transfer systems be studied further by the General Secretariat which should provide the necessary information to encourage member-countires to adopt coordinated legislation to regulate such systems, where necessary.
7. Member-countries in the region encourage their respective passport issuing authorities to adopt security features on passports to prevent counterfeiting or alteration. Those countries that have already adopted such measures are urged to provide samples to requesting countries or the General Secretariat[9] upon request.
8. Efforts to locate and recover the regrettably large quantity of cultural property stolen and exported from within the Asian region should include up-to-date reporting of all cases of the losses to Interpol General Secretariat using the agreed procedure. The essential need for NCBs to circulate relevant information beyond police authorities (i.e. to museums, dealers etc. and the likelihood that this will increase the chances of recovery were noted. Also the need for the signature and ratification of the 1970 UNESCO Convention on cultural property by all the member-countires was noted.
9. Efforts on developing regional or sub-regional structures or systems to improve the quality of international police cooperation should be concentrated on issues other than the creation of a Regional Bureau, there being no consensus on the need to create such an entity. To this end, the Asian Working Party on Regionalisation is asked to meet at least once each year in addition to tis meetings held at the time of Asian Regional

Conferences and Sessions of the General Assembly. Individual members of the Working Party are asked to take the lead responsibility for studying and reporting on subjects including training and telecommunications as well as others which may be allocated by the Working Party for their attention.

10. Each Asian NCB[10] nominates a Contact Officer to improve the quality of co-operation between NCBs. The Contact Officer, who should preferably be able to communicate in English should be ready and able to provide a focal point for urgent request made personally by other Contact Officers and to intervene in particular cases upon request. The responsibilities should include the speedy transmission of police information and providing assistance in particular cases to ensure that investigations to obtain information or evidence in criminal or judicial procedures are executed as rapidly and as far as possible. Nominations of Contact Officers (and, if considered appropriate, their alternatives) including full particulars-languages spoken, telephone and fax numbers and usual hours of duty may be provided as early as possible, together with a passport-size photograph, to the Regional Co-ordinator without delay.
11. Member-countries in the region promptly take all appropriate action to ensure that their NCBs are able to reach the Service Standards set for NCBs during the 63rd Session of the General Assembly. The increased use of formatted messages by NCBs be encouraged to that all appropriate information may be contained therein unnecessary delay may be avoided.
12. The General Secretariat should study how the procedures of mutual assistance and extradition might be improved by the development of multilateral tools through, for example the offices of the United Nations.
13. The General Secretariat should continue to explore all possible avenues for organizing training courses on important aspects of crime on a regional basis and in this regard enter into immediate consultation with the UNDCP,[11] WCO and other international organizations as well as member-countries which have adequate training facilities and developed training programmes.

**New World Order**

The new world order, I believe, will be dominated by essentially rational and technical arrangements. That order will lack substantive values, and it will operate in accordance with procedural, that is to say, instrumental values. The emergent social system will not function in response to any set of specifically religious conceptions of human or social purpose. Religious organzations will surely continue, and some of their representatives may well be publicly conspicuous, but it is difficult to envisage the social system accepting the primacy of spiritual values or being significantly influenced by religious concern. The strength of the emerging rational and technical social order will lie in its transcendence of national, cultural, and religious differences, and in the objectivity of the criteria that will be established for a wide range of international, social and political activities.[12]

Such a presumption of Wilson is more applicable to the West than in the East. Such type of social order lacking salient psychological supports for man's emotional awareness, it will have only a limited capacity to motivate men. The East, particularly Indian traditions have been confidently depending upon the intrinsic values of human beings, rather than sentimental ones for any type of commitment, may it be moral, social or cultural. As far as primacy of spiritual values are concerned it may not be visualized in certain groups over-rational people of the East depending more inmaterial world, but it cannot be generalized for the entire gamut of the Eastern World since spiritualism has been the main nerve of the Eastern civilization which include tens of thousands of tribes and sub-tribes, that are still to be baptised into new technological order, which more insistently depend upon external agencies of control as if men were 'automatic pilots' of their own lives, whereas this phenomena may be predicted in case of the developed world only. Prof. J.N. Nanda observes : "Unity in diversity is the best goal for any nation or for the entire world. Each mind is complex and itself is a unity in diversity. Scientific approach, secularism and co-existence are the values that can guide people to happiness in the complex modern world. Social justice is the contribution of the materialist philosophy to world culture while secularism and humanistic approach is the contribution of ancient philosophies, both theist and atheist. Present-day thinking is approaching the same values by an objective examination of the universe".[13]

To accomplish the aim of social justice and co-existence, the problem is not only to "stop war" as a fire brigade might examine means of putting out fires, but also to discover what motives stand in the way of creating and internationally workable world, a world free from stress and strain, a world of peace and harmony. Then only we will be able to move towards new world order.

Dr. S. Radhakrishnan has confidently said, "The old order, the order which is the parent of Hitlers, Mussolinis and Tajos, is doomed. Those who fight against them must realize that they are laying the foundations here and now the new order of liberty. Our enemies are to be put down simply because they still cling to the old and do not help us to clear the path for the new. The cowardly inertness of the human mind must be checked if we wish to win the peace and prevent planting seeds of future disasters. To secure an enduring peace, we must eliminate the conditions which make for wars and be earnest about new way of life which will mean the sacrifice of cherished idols."[14]

Socio-political scenario of the world is changing very fast. These days are gone when sovereign states used to manage their relations with each other through their ambassadors and through diplomatic channels. Now it is not sufficient at all since transactional or multinational economic and military organizations and arrangements are emerging very fast creating more confidence among the nations concerned. But material progress should not neglect the cognitive aspects of human beings. For bright future of the mankind Dean Inge's these words are noteworthy. He says, "The Gemran savant sees the remedy in more perfect organization; in other words, our conquest of our environment is to be made more complete. The Englishman advocates the practice of eugenics and of the simple life for those who are willing to submit to this discipline; he has, apparently, no hope that the mechanization of life can ever be turned to the real improvement and happiness of mankind. It may be that as the German, writing before the cataclysm, under-estimates the disruptive forces in society and proposes to "heal too slightly" the wounds to modern life, so the Englishmen is too ready to assume that the disorders which have followed the war indicate a final break-up of our whole social order. The future will show whether civilization, as we know it, can be mended or must be ended. The time seems ripe for a new birth of religious and spiritual life, which may remould society, as no less potent force would have the strength to do."[15]

There is an interesting episode in the life of Aurangzeb, the Mughal emperor. Once a scholar who had taught him in his early years approached him for some favour. Aurangzeb did not oblige him and said, "If you had taught me that philosophy which adapts the mind to reason, if you had made me acquainted with nature of man, accustomed me to always refer to principles – first and given me adequate concept of the universe I would have been more indebted to you than Alexander was to his teacher Aristotle." He further added that "it was necessary for a ruler to know the distinguishing feature of every nation of the world; its resources and strength; its mode of warfare; its manners, religion, form of government;

and also have a regular course of history and knowledge of the events or errors which led to great changes in the world order and revolutions." What Aurangzeb thought necessary in his times for a ruler to know is now necessary for all responsible citizens, for it is they who have to elect their rulers or administrators.

## REFERENCES

1. Quoted from Christine I. Bennett's, *Comprehensive Multicultural Education*, pp. 281–82.
2. Vadim Zagladin, to Restructure and Humanize Inter-national Relations, pp. 61-62.
3. Dr. Karan Singh, *Essays on Hinduism*. pp. 91–92.
4. द्यौः शान्तिरन्तरिक्षं शान्तिः पृथिवी
   शान्तिरापः शान्तिरोषधयः शान्तिः
   वनस्पतयः शान्तिर्विश्वे देवा शान्ति–
   र्ब्रह्म शान्तिः सर्वं शान्तिः शान्ति–
   रेव शान्तिः सा मा शान्तिरेधि।।

   – *Yajurved* 36.17
5. Quoted in Will Durant's The Story of Philosophy, p. 284.
6. Dr. S. Radharkrishnan, *Our Heritage*, p. 49.
7. Annals of American Academy of Political and Social Sciences, May, 1963.
8. *Maj. General S.Mohindra, Terrorist Games Nations Play, p. 16*
9. Interpole General Secretariate.
10. Narcotic Control Board.
11. United Nations Drug Control Programme.
12. Human Values in the Changing World, p. 187.
13. J.N. Nanda, *Conflicts and Co-existence India*, p. 151.
14. Dr. S. Radhakrishnan, *Religion and Society*, p. 12.
15. Five Essays by Dean Inge Edited by E.A., Woodhouse, p. 137.

# APPENDICES

## *APPENDIX - I*

## BIOGRAPHICAL NOTES

*A Passage to India :* It is a famous novel by E.M. Foster, in which the author explores not only the path to greater understanding of India, but also man's quest for ultimate truth. Just as Walt Whitman's poem "Passage to India" from which the title of the novel has been derived. This poem stressed the need to combine the success of western civilization with a new exploration of spiritual experience.

*Aurobindo* : Shri Aurobindo (1872–1950) was a famous spiritual leader of Modern India. He is one of the most predominant features in the History of the Indian Renaissance and Indian nationalism. Romain Rolland regarded him as the highest synthesis of the genius of the East and the West and the 'prince among the Indian thinkers'. R.N. Tagore, a Nobel Laureate, was impressed by his genius to such an extent as he prophesied that through him India should express her message to the world, he described him as the 'messiah of Indian culture.

He was a great poet, a profound thinker, notable metaphysician, a great seer and ardent patriot. Among his works these are noteworthy–a defence of Indian Culture, Savitri (epic), The Future Poetry, The Human Cycle, the Ideal of Human Unity. He was the propounder of the idea of 'the Supermind'. According to him "The Supermental change is a thing decreed and inevitable in the evolution of earth, consciousness for its upward ascent is not ended and mind is for its last summit. The Supermental being only can say :

"I shall know mystic truths, seize occult powers,
I shall slay my enemies with a look or thought,
I shall see the unspoken feeling of all earth."

– *Savitri,* p. 583

*Asuras :* Demons. According to Hindu Mythology they were divine beings; but as opposed to the gods, they were generally evil. They frequently fought with the gods and troubled human beings. In Zend-Avesta, 'Ahur Mazda' means wise lord. Later on the word Ahur was changed into 'Asura', which was used in Assyria for the supreme lord. For some time Assyrians were rulers of the Persians.

**ASA – Ameican Standards Association**

*Arthasastra* : A famous treatise on statecraft written by Vishnugupta Chanakya (Kautilya) preceptor of Chandra Gupta Maurya, a founder of Mauryan empire in India. His doctrine, like that of Machiavelli, was the separation of politics and ethics. Alike Machiavelli he maintained that even wicked actions become good when they benefit the community. It is only the promotion of public welfare that justifies immoral deeds.

*Annie Beasant* : Annie Beasant (1847–1933) was the president of the Theosophical Society for the last 26 years of her life.

*Aristotle* : (384-322 B.C.), A noted Greek philosopher and disciple of Socrates. His famous treatise named 'Republic' established the supremacy of nature over the tradition.

*Ali* : Cousin and son-in-law of prophet Muhammad, who appointed Ali as his successor. On the plain of Kerbala Ali and his son Hussain were assassinated by his rivals.

*Bishop Berkeley* : Berkeley (1688–1753) was the bishop of Cloyne, in Ireland, and the famous idealistic philosopher. His main works are – Essay towards a New Theory of Vision (1709), the Treatise on the Principals of Human knowledge (1710) and Alciphron.

*Bismark* : Prince Bismark (1815–1898) was the founder of the German Empire. Held the office of Imperial Chancellor from the foundation of the empire up till March, 1890, when growing disagreements with the emperor, william II forced him to resign.

*Charles Goodyear* : Goodyear (1800-was born at New Haven (USA). For years together he was obsessed with rubber. To invent rubber which does not become sticky during summer and hard like rock during winter was the mission of his life. Ultimately he accomplished his mission. Goodyear is today a famous tyre manufacturing company. In fact, it is one of the biggest rubber-manufacturing companies in the world. The company was named in recognition of his pioneering work on rubber. After forty years of his death English Chemist Joseph Priestley found that it could rub-off pencil marks and it was re-named as 'rubber' Earlier the substance was called 'Caout Chouc' (pronounced as "Koo-Chook". One of associates of Goodyear, William Brockedon called the rubber-sulphur mixture "Vulcanization" after the Roman God of fire, Vulcan. Napolean III awarded him the Grand Medal of honour and the Cross of the Legion of Honour. His 'Pontoons' (rubber boats) came into use only in World War II.

*Charles Parson* : Parson (1854–1931) was an engineer of Britain, who invented steam turbine. A steam turbine works just like a water wheel or a windmill. A jet of high pressure steam is allowed to strike an angle blades attached to the rim of a wheel, as a result the wheel is set into circular motion. His first turbine-driven dynamo generated about 7.5 kilowatts (KW) of electricity.

His turbine became very popular. He received orders even from Germany for his turbines. He also invented turbine derived ships. Parsons firm received an order from British Navy for building a big turbine–run battleship. It was launched in 1906 creating naval history. The 38,000 ton passenger linear Mauretania build by Parson's firm won the "Blue Ribbon of the Atlantic" and remained the fastest ship for no less than 20 years.

*Chipko* : A movement of environmentalists where on-violent protection of trees is attempted by embracing them, thus foiling the wielders of the axe. Sunderlal Bahuguna was one of the prominent leaders of the movement.

*Charles Darwin*: Darwin (1809-1882) is the discoverer of the principle fo evolution through natural selection, a discovery which changed the whole current of modern scientific thought. For Darwin's many works, which cover the various kingdoms of evolving organic like the most celebrated are — Origin of Species (1859), and descent of Man (1871).

According to Darwin a man is just biological being, which was not accepted by the theistic community. If the theory of natural adoption is accepted, an idealist youth burning with generous enthusiasm cannot become a betterman when advancing years cause him to fall into the line, more and more with the dead level of the common thought of his time. Thus in the spiritualistic themes it does not fit.

*Charvak* : Ancient Indian sage of pre-vedic age, who taught unadulterated materialism with no acknowledgment of soul or God.

*Dean Inge*: A religious leader of a very high order in the Christian world, born on 6th June 1860 and became Dean of St. paul in 1911. Many rare honours were conferred to him for his scholarly works on religion, ethics and classical literature. It is said that "no writer of the day, not even Bernard Shaw, has been bolder or more resolute than Dr. Inge in the expression of unpopular views".

*Divine Theory* : Manu and other writers have confirmed the theory of King's divinity in Ancient India. Mahabharata contains a contradictory view. On the one hand it says that the king deserves all divine dignity, as it has been narrated in the "Divine Theory of Hobbes (19th century), on the other, it does not impose on citizens an absolute obligation to bow to his authority. The great epic clearly mentions that the king's divinity should be honoured only till such time as he does not deviate from the path of righteousness (Dharma)".

*Desecrates* : A French philosopher, who argued "I think, therefore, I exist".

*Decalogue* : The Ten Commandments, derived from the Greek word dekalogos.

*Dharma* : Righteousness, often translated as religion in English.

*Elias Howe* : He was born on July 9, 1819 at spencer, Massachusetts (USA), to a farmer. The idea of inventing sewing machine struck him at the age of 21. After a great struggle with the help of one of his friend, George Fisher, whom he promised to share half of the profit that the manufacturer of the machine on a large scale would entail. One day he became a millionaire, as he dreamt after he won the case against Singer Company. Before he died (1867) at Brooklyn (New York) he had received the "Grand Cross of the Legion of Honour", the highest honour bestowed on a person by the French Government.

*Eli Whitney* : Whitney (1765–1825) was a son of American farmer, who invented 'cotton gin' – an engine for separating fibres from seeds of cotton, the then American President Thomas Jefferson called him "the artist of the country" because he changed America into a rich and prosperous country. His next invention of 'parts of gun'. In those days every gun was built separately. Whitney thought of manufacturing parts of a gun separately so that by assembling the parts, guns may be prepared on a large scale. This was an attractive proposal for US Government.

*Easter* : Easter is a great day in the Greek calendar.

*Hammurabi* : Hammurabi was the greatest Baby Lonian ruler, who united the whole of what is now called Iraq into a single Kingdom by 1800 BC. He gave his people a code or a system of Laws, which covered every aspect of life. It is popularly known as "Hammurabi's Code".

*Heraclitus* : A Greek philosopher, who argued that everything is in a flux.

*Henry Ford* : henery Ford (1863-1946) of Dearborn (near Detroit-USA) invented a car. He was one of those rare inventors, who was very practical and knew the tricks of the trade. He, therefore, made his product a very saleable one within ten years of inventing the car he rose from a modest engineer to a multi-millionaire. Today Ford Motor Company is one of the leading car manufacturers in the world. He became one of the most influential persons in the USA. His company also manufactured aeroplanes. After his death it now builds satellites and space modules also.

*Hegel* : He was a great German thinker, who carried Kant's thought to its logical conclusion in idealism.

*Herber Spencer* : (1820–1903), The founder of Synthetic Philosophy, an attempt to co-ordinate the results of evolutionary in one all embracing system of thought. His writings can be divided into four Biology, Psychology, Sociology and Ethics.

*Havelock Ellis* : (b. 1859). A leading writer on sociological and psychological subject chiefly known for his elaborate studies in the psychology of sex.

*Hugo Grotius* : Hugo Grotius (1583–1645) is one of the most celebrated names in the history of Internaitonal Law, his great work on the subject remaining, for a long period, the standard authority. In it he developed a new the old Greek idea of a "national law" as the foundation of the law governing the intercourse of nations, and worked it out into a carefully formulated and detailed system of rules.

*Hague Tribunal* : An International Court of Arbitration to settle disputes between nations, set-up at the Hague in 1899 at the instance of the Czar, Nicholas II, of Russia.

*George Stephenson* : George Stephenson (1781–1848) built the first steam locomotive in 1814 and was appointed principal engineer, in 1826, of the Liverpool and Manchester Railway. He also invented 'safety lamp'. The lamp enabled coal-miners to use it without any harm to their person. He believed : "If the country made rail roads, railroads will make the country". France, Belgium, Germany etc. took his help to build their own railways.

*Johann Goltfried Herder* : Herder (1744–1803) was a German philosopher and poet. His greatest work is Id as on the achievement of Making (1784–1791) in which he goes far to anticipate modern evolutioanry theories. Herder regards Man not to merely as the culmination of all previous developments, but as the first indication of still loftier stages in the scale of existence, with which it is his duty gradually to identify himself by the cultivation of his spiritual nature. His idea of mankind, to a great extent, resembles with the idea of 'the supermind' of Shri Aurobindo, a revolutionary turned philosopher of modern India. He says, "The Supermind is a 'Real Idea', a truth Consciousness' it's a imperishable and immutable substance.

*Joseph Glanvill* - Glanvill (1636–1680) is regarded as an early apostle of free thought. He was the author of the vanity of Dogmatizing (1661) and of a couple of books on witch craft and apparitions. Readers of mathew Arnold's poetry will remember that the story of the 'scholar Gipsy' is taken from Glanvill:

> "And near me on the grass lies Glanvill's book.
> Come let me read the oft-read tale again."
>
> – Scholar Gipsy, line 31

*Industrial Revolution :* The term "Industrial revolution" was first used by Arnold Toynbee. Later on it was assigned to the epoch-making changes which were brought about in the industrial world by the mechanical inventions of the latter part of the eighteenth century in England.

*Indian Opinon:* "Indian Opinion" was a Journal launched by Mahatma

Gandhi in 1904 when he was in South Africa. Like *Young India*, *Navajvan* and *Harijan* and *Indian Opinon* was also a mirror of his life.

*ISRO* : Indian Space Research Organisation (ISRO) indicates the position of India in the field of space-research. Recently US imposed sanctions for contracting to buy cryogenic rocket engines and technology from Russia. The development of Agni and the next logical step in going on to build intercontinental ballistic Missiles, will lead to greater democratization of the international decision-making process since there could then be no arms control negotiations without India's participation.

As per one of the estimates "in all likelihood, India's missile systems will be available for export to selected countries by the year 2000".

*Imam* : A spiritual Leader in Islam. The term is derived from Imam Hussain a descendant of Ali.

*Jalianwala Bagh Massacre* : On April 13, 1919 about twenty thousand people had gathered for a public meeting in a small square surrounded by houses in the midst of Amritsar City, with a narrow passage as entrance to the square. General Dyre entered the square with some troops and ordered firing in which 400 persons died and about 2000 were wounded. This incident and Rowaltt Act (1919) created nation-wide stir leading to more intense struggle for freedom in India.

*Jean Jacques Rousseau* : (1712–1778) A noted political philosopher influenced in his ideas by Plato and Locke. He propounded the theory of "social contract" which contains the key to the understanding of the political philosophy of Rousseau, who said, "Man is born free, and every where he is in chains".

*John Gogie Baird* : Baird (1888-1946) invented the television. The television that is seen today is an electronic modification of the devise. Sending pictures by wireless that he invented. Later on it was modified by others using cathode Ray Tube and thus replacing the mechanical system he had invented.

*Johannes Gutenberg* : Johannes Gutenberg (1397–1468) was the inventor of Printing Press. He was born at Mainz (Germany). Like a rubber stamp, Gutanberg made stamps of hard metal of each and every letter in reverse) of latin, the popular language of the time. His invention for mass production of books revolutionised the book world. Bible was the first book he printed in 1282 pages, which became popular as 'Gutenberg's Bible'. Another book he brought out was 'Catholicon', a 13th century compilation of theological thoughts. After Germany, Italy was the country to start its own printing press.

*James Watt :* James Watt (1736–1819) was the first person to turn steam to practical account and was the inventor of the separate condenser, the air pump and the steam jacket for cylinders.

*Kant* : Kant was the eighteenth century German philosopher who brought a revolution in modern philosophy.

*Karma* : Deeds that bear fruit in this or the next life.

*Konstantin E. Tsiolkovsky* : Russian inventor Tsiolkovsky (1857–1935) is called a father of Rocket. It was he who first thought that travel to stars was possible. Man can be whirled into space and reach stars. He devoted his entire life to make this reality and made a rocket 'fly' into space. His prophetic words "Mankind will not remain bound to earth" are carved on his obelisk where has was laid to rest.

His real breakthrough in the field of rocketry came in 1903 when his paper "Exploration of space by Rocket Devices" appeared in a prestigious journal "scientific Review" after it was held up for publication for five years. It gave a complete outline (50 pages) of the principles of the rocket that would take man into space. It was the result of 20 years of obsession with space lights. He was awarded "Red Banner of Labour". In 1957, due to his researches, Russia could launch the first satellite sputinik-1 into space. In his honour Tsiolkovsky Gold Medal is awarded every year to one space-scientist in the world.

*Kinesies* : Kine means a recordable movement of the body. Kinesics is a new science dealing with the interpretaiton of body-movements, popularly known as body language. It is based on the assumption that all movement of the body have meaning.

*Khalsa* : It is a Sikh panth created by Guru Govind Singh, the last Guru of Sikh Lineage. He declared that after him there will be no one in human form shall be Guru; only Adi-granth shall succeed him. Khalsa shall be the Guru and the Guru the Khalsa. He said:

> "Khalsa is my tangible soul,
> Khalsa is the life of the life.

*Max Muller* : Max Muller was a great German Philosopher, who settled in England. He was deeply interested in Indian philosophy and literature. He popularised Vedic Literature and Indian philosophy in Europe. His acute intelligence and his scientific approach have made his studies impartial. His monumental work is *Sacred Book of the East* in 40 volumes.

*Martin Luther King, Jr.* : Martin Luter (1929) was a great champion who fought for the plight of Negros in order to procure justice, equality, and freedom to them. In one of the public meeting (1958) he said : "America must begin the struggle for democracy at home. . . To Negro Americans it is ironic to be governed, to be taxed, to be given orders, but to have no representation in a nation that could that would defent the right to vote abroad. On his visit to Indian in 1959, Dr. King said : "To other countries I may go as a tourist, but to India I come as a pilgrim. This is because India means to be Mahatma Gandhi, a truly great man of our age. He fought through out his life for the Negro. He was awarded Nobel Prize for peace in 1964. He is also the recipient of award for International understanding posthumously. On his gravestone is inscribed a line from an old Negro song "Free at last, free at last, thank God almighty, I'm free at last."

*Monochronic culture* : A culture in which events occur according to time schedule.

*Mazzini* : Guiseppe Mazzini (1805-1872) was the fiery Italian patriot and champion of Liberty, whose eloquent pen and unceasing activities played so great a part in the unification of Italy and in freeing her from the papel, Austrian and Bourbon Yokes.

*Mother Terresa* : Mother Terresa's original name was Agnes Gouxha Bojaxha, who had an intense desire to serve the poor. In the beginning she was a teacher at St. Mary's High School in Calcutta and later became its Principal, she was also incharge of the Daughters of St. Anne', a religious order attached to the Loreto Sisters.

*LTTE* : A group of terrorists of Shri Lanka known as 'Liberation Tighers of Tamil Eelam'. Presently Prabhakarna is the leader of the group.

*Mahabharata*: The great epic of Ancient India containing about one lac verses. Basic plot is based on the family feud of cousins-Kauravas and Pandvas. It is an epic of growth wherein there had been many interpolations and manipulations from time to time and this process continued upto Gupta period, i.e., 5th Century A.D. It is divided in 18 books (parvans). Many notable works like Bhagvadgeeta, Vidurniti, Anugeeta, Harivanspurana etc. form the part of this great epic. It is called Mbh. on account of its greatness, enormity in size and weightiness. In fact, it is eight times bigger than Homer's Illiad and Odyssi taken together.

There are variety of disciplines incorporated in it–Religion, Politics, Philosophy, Education, Economic, foreign trade and Commerce and what not. Olderberg calles it the heritage of arts, literature, culture, religion and social phenomena since the dawn of civilization.

Dr. V.S. Sukathanker opines that "This mighty work is primarily concerned with finding a solution to the problem of evil in life, nay, to the problem of existence itself".

*Machiavelli* : Niccolo dei Machiavelli (1469-1527) was an author of 'Prince' and several other historical and political works as well as a treatise on the 'Art of War'. He is universally known for his classical work "The Prince", which was designed as a manual of instruction in statecraft. "The Prince" can be easily compared with the "Arthashastra" of Kautilya (Vishnugupta Chanakya), who was the mentor of Chandragupta Maurya, founder of Mauryan empire. He maintained the difference between politics and ethics saying that "Politics deals with the rules of conduct of State, and Ethics deals with the rules of conduct of individual.

*NASA* : National Aeronautics and Space Administration (NASA) is worldfame American organisation where scores of Indian scientists are at work. The doors to a new era of space exploration was opened when (14th April 1981) NASA'S Space Shuttle Columbia made a perfect landing like a glider on the Dryden's dry lake, California, after climbing up into space like a rocket from Kennedy Space Centre. Vital addition to the shuttle is the space–lab, a multidisciplined laboratory, which is assembled by European Space Agency.

Nasa's target is to have 60 shuttle launch into space every year. Besides NASA's shuttle, efforts are underway in Russia and Japan to build their own Shuttles. Thus, shuttle era has begun. India has also come to the front a the progressive Indian Space Research orgnaisation (ISRO) reveals.

*Navajo* : Navajo is a member of an American Indian people native to

New Mexico and Arizona.

*Nelson Mandela* : Dr. Nelson Mandela, a strong Negro leader was imprisoned for 26 yrs. He fought for the Liberation of South Africa and ultimately he succeeded in his noble mission. After the historical release he became a main figure of the African National Congress (ANC). His further mission is to establish non-racial democracy in South Africa in particular and to help solving the problems of Negros, in general. He is the recipient of Jawahar Lal Nehru Award for International understanding.

*Nihilism* : Nihilism is the theory that denies the reality of everything and accepts the reality of the void.

*Nietzse* : Friedrick Wilhelm Nietzshe (1844-1900) was a famous German philosopher. His philosophy denounces all religion and regards the ordinary laws of morality as a Christian superstition invented for self-protection of the weak against the strong.

*N.A.M.* : Non-Aligned Movement of nations who do not join the military pacts in opposition to each other.

*Nanak* : Guru Nanak (1469-1538) was the founder of Sikhism. In Sikhism from Nanak to Guru Govind Singh there had been, in all, ten Gurus– Nanak, Agad, Amerdas, Ramdas, Arjundev, Hargovind, Har Ram, Harkrishana Rai, Teg Bahadur and Guru Govind Singh. Last Guru, Govind Singh declared *Adi-Granth* of Nanak as Guru. Henceforth it came to be known as Guru Granth Sahib.

*Old Testament* : The scripture of the Christians is in two parts – Old Testament and New Testament. The former contains several books and is related to the period prior to Jesus Christ. It begins with the book of Genesis. New Testament contains the books after the time of Jesus Christ. The first four books of the new Testament are called the Gospels and contain the story and teachings of jesus.

*Organic Nature of State* : According to Mahabharata their are seven parts of a state : King, minister, territory, fort, treasure, military, and allies (friendly states). Many, Kautilya and Shukracharya also refer to this concept. Comparing these to parts of human body Shukraniti maintains that king is like head, ministers like eye, friends are like ears treasury is like mouth, military power is like mind, fort is like hand and territory is like legs.

*Panchayati Raj* : Village self-government through elected village councils known as Panchayats in existence in India from hoary past, now being used as an instrument of de-centralization in an Indian version of Perestroika.

*Percy Brown* : Percy Brown is very notable art critic and historian. He made a systematic and sympathetic study of Indian painting. Unlike many art-critics, he expresses accurately what he had observed. He translates painting into literature.

*Polychromatic Culture* : A culture where many things are accomplished at a time.

*Paralanguage* : It is a type of non-verbal communication, which includes all production of sounds, like laughing etc. and also sound like *shhh* etc.

*Polus* : A sophist and rhetorician of 5th Century B.C., and advocate of the "might is right" doctrine.

*Plotinus* : Plotinus (204-270 AD) has been described as greatest of the philosophers of the Neoplatonic school.

*Plato* : Plato was a worthy discipline of secretes. He has immortalised his great 'master' by depositing him as a central character in almost all his dialogues. The whole of Plato's philosophical structure is based on the following three doctrines of socrates :

1. Socrates' dictum that virtue is knowledge.
2. His theory of reality.
3. His theory of knowledge.

Plato's dialogues remain one of the priceless treasures of the world and the best of them, *the Republic* is a complete treatise in itself, "Plato is philosophy, and philosophy Plato", says Emerson.

*Perestroika* : The policy of openness adopted by Mekhail Gorbachov in USSR, also known as the policy of glossnot. Grobachov had to go out of corridor of power, since it was thought as main factor for degeneration and lapse of USSR.

*Roger Bacon* : Roger Bacon (1214–1294) was a monk of the Franciscan order. Traditionally he is celebrated as the inventor of gun-powder and the magnifying glass. He was the author of several philosophical and scientific treatises, of which the most celebrated is his opus majus (Greater Work), written in 1265.

*Ramayana* : Ramayana composed by Balmiki, is the premier epic of India, which is appropriately called "Adi Kavya" in sanskrit literature. Mahabharata is "epic of growth" which was developed through the eyes by various scholars, whereas *Ramayana* is an "epic of art". Rhetrorically the latter is considered better than *Mahabharata*. The critics attach greater artistic value to *Ramayana*. In it Rama is a symbol of righteousness whereas Ravana is a symbol of evil forces.

According to R.C. Dutta "No work in Europe, not Homer in Greece or Virgil in Italy, not Shakespeare and Milton in English–speaking lands is the national poetry of the same extent as the epics of India are to the Hindus. No single work except the Bible, has such influence in affording moral instructions in Christian lands as the Mahabharata and Ramayana in India. . . ."

*Rowlatt Act* : In India the Britishers passed this act in 1919 to provide special powers to the then British Government to suppress movements aimed against the state. It authorised arrest and detention, without trial of persons suspected of anti–government activities.

*Social Contract Theory* : In Ancient India this theory was propounded by Bhishma, in Mahabharata. It was subsequently followed by other. Modern philosophers like Rousseau and Locke. According to this theory for a proper sharing of the people in state affairs the contract between king and subject was considered essential.

*Spinoza* : A Jewish philosopher, who believed that 'Reality' has the two properties of thought and extension.

*Samuel Crompton* : Samuel Crompton (1753–1827) invented the spinning mill and was the earliest of the spinners of fine unbroken yarn.

*SAARC* : The South Asian Association for Regional cooperation groups India, Bangladesh, Bhutan, Maldives, Nepal, Pakistan and Shri Lanka. It was organised in 1985 with the aim to unite these six countries for better economic ties and interaction. Presently it is gripped by a serious political crisis threatening its existence after a decade.

*Sankya* : One of the six systems of Indian Philosophy founded by the sage Kapila. It presents the nature of the universe in terms of twenty five categories.

*SWAPO* : South West Africa People's Organisation.

*Shelley, P.B.* : A famous romantic poet of Elizabethan age. He was a great poet of nature.

*Schiller* : Johann Christoph Freidrich Schiller (1759–1805) was a poet and dramatist; after his friend and contemporary Goethe, a leading name in German literature it was he, who said, "War always swallows up the best."

*Sociotypes* : Sociotypes are accurate generalisations about social groups. The term is just opposite to stereotypes.

*Stereotypes* : Stereotypes are erroneous beliefs based on generalization or overgeneralization about social groups.

*Shias* : Factionist Muslims are called Shias. Most Persians are Shias.

*Sunnis* : Traditionalist Muslims are called sunnis, who constitute the vast majority of Muslims of India and Trukey.

*Sybarite* : One who loved in the old Greek colony of Sybaris in Italy. It was famous for its life of luxurious pleasures.

*Sermon on the Mount* : It is teachings delivered by Jesus on a mountain side. It is incorporated in the New Testament (Mathew Chapters V to VII).

*Swamy Vivekanand* : He was one of the great thinkers and reformers of Indian Revitalising Indian religion and outlook, he sought to elevate the masses spiritually, socially and culturally lecturing in America and Europe he revealed the greatness of Indian thought and culture. He established Shri Ram Krishan Mission and made cultural revival, a necessary prelude to the nation.

*Sagala* : Sagala (or Sakala) is a place in India where king Milind is said to have ruled, which has been identified with Sialkot in the Rechna Doab by J.F. Fleet, who combined the evidence of the epics with that of Chinese pilgrim Husan Tsang. It was a great centre of trade, a capital of menander and Mihirkula.

*Sufism* : The cult followed by Sufis came to be called as 'Sufism' which represent liberalism of Islamic faith. H.G. Rawlinson says : "A point of contact between Hinduism and Islam destined later on to produce far-reaching results was established through the influence of Persian Sufis, a school of mystics, which included the famous poets such as Sadi, Jalal-ud-din Rumi and Hafiz, who held, under the forms of orthodoxy, views which approximated more or less closely to Hindu pantheism."

*Sir Thomas Roe* : Thomas Roe was the ambassador from Britain who visited India during the regime of Akbar, the Great.

*Sufi* : The etymology of the term "Sufi" is not certain. According to some scholars the word is connected with safi, the pure. The more general view refers it to sufi, or coarse wool, as these mystics used to wear woollen garments. In fact, the spread of purity, generosity service of neighbour or stranger were the basic ideals of pre-Islamic Arabia. Later on rigidity crept into it. Arabian mystics came to be called Sufis.

*Socrates* Socrates (470-390 B.C.) was a preceptor of noted greek philosopher, Plato. Socrates' mission in his life was to convince those people of their ignorance who claimed to be the wisest. At the age of 70 he was prosecuted in the court of Athens on the charge of "Corrupting the Yourth" and was sentenced to death. He exposed the hollowness of the sophists who claimed to be the teachers of Athenians. He undertook a crusade against sham knowledge, and became the preacher of genuine wisdom by adopting dialectic method. His doctrine of reality is really the progenitor of that all known as "idealism" in philosophy and political thought.

*Theocracy* : A theocracy is a form of government in which whole life is ordered in relation to a religious idea and in which the chief authority centres in the priesthood.

*Thomas Alva Edison* : As an inventor Edison (1847–1931) set a record of inventing 1093 new things, of these he is very famous for two electric bulb and phonograph. In his own life-time he became a legend. He was born at Milan, Ohio (USA) to a carphenter father and school teacher mother, who has agreat credit to make her son a great inventor. Poverty forced him to earn at the age of 12 by selling petty goods like newspaper. Vegetables etc. In 1862 he became telegraph operator at a railway station. Michel Farday's book "Experimental researchers in Electricity" gave him insight and inspiration.

Later on he set-up a company to invent new devices and started producing a new invention every month. Most of his inventions were products of team of experts who worked in his laboratory, and not of single hand as one often believes. He invented "phonograph" the granddaddy of gramophone. His famous phrase "genius is one per cent inspiration and ninety nine per cent perspiration" aptly holds for him. He had a great faith in machine, which he used to refer to as "Hope of Humanity".

*Thomas Robert Malthus* : Malthus (1766-1834) is the author of the "Essay on the Principle of Population", in which he endeavours to gather together and systemize the factors determining the fluctuations of population, tracing historically the conflict between the natural impulse towards the increase of life and the restraints imposed upon this by number of checks, such as war, pestilence, infanticide, celibacy, etc. together with the general relation of population to food supplies, mathus theory of population is very famous in Economics, wherein he maintains that our resources like food-supply etc. do not increase in proportion to the increase in population. This theory is now acclaimed world wide by the economists of the modern world.

*The Renaissance* : The renaissance, or revival of classical learning, is dated historically from the capture of constantinople by the turks in 1453, which scattered numbers of greek refugees of the ancient classical literature. Dean Inge includes the 13th and 14th centuries and the first half of 15th century in his "glacial age of the spirit".

*Tolstoy* : Count Leo Tolstoy (1828–1910) was the famous Russian novelist, mystic and social reformer. Although wealthy and of a noble family, from the year 1862 onward he voluntarily lived the simple life of a peasant. Mahatma Gandhi, in his autobiography, "My Experiments with Truth", refers to Tolstoy as he was greatly impressed by the life-style of the former. Mahatma Gandhi established an Ashram, popularly known as 'Tolstoy Farm' in South Africa in the year 1910.

*Tamil* : Tamil is a language of Dravidian family. Of the four i.e., Tamil, Telgue, Kannad and Malyalam, the first one is the most ancient and rich and spoken by about six crores of people today. It has the history of 2500 yrs. and more. besides South Indian it is spoken by the Tamils who live in Shri Lanka, Singapore, Fiji, mauritius, South and East Africa and in many other parts of the world.

Thirukkural was a great Tamil poet. The cilappatikaram is the first Tamil native epic. Besides Indians many foreign scholars have also recorded its greatness. Winslow in his "A comprehensive Tamil and English Dictionary he says : "Tamil is more polished and exact than the Greek, and in both dialects, with its borrowed treasures, more copious than the Latin. In its fullness and power it more resembles English and German than any other living language.

*Thomas Aquinas* : St. Thomas Aquinas (1227–1274) was a famous political thinker. The political philosophy of Aquinas is just the reconciliation between Aristotles's philosophy and Christian doctrine. He accepts Aristotalian philosophy of nature as an axiom. Thomas believed that state is also a God-established institution. He is rightly called "a Christianised Aristotle" he declared that church is superior to the state and secular rulers are subordinate to the pope.

*Thucydides* : Thucydides (471–400 B.C.) was the great athenian historian, who wrote the "history of the Peloponnesian War" (431–404 B.C.) in eight books. He has depicted the disaster of Athens in his fifth book of history and quoted the same as an example of "the pride that goeth before a fall."

*UNESCO* : United Nation Education, Scientific and Cultural Organisation (UNESCO) its aim is to promote inter-governmental co-operation in the fields of education, science and culture, in order to foster the forces of peace and security. It looks after human rights and fundamental freedom irrespective or race, sex, language or religion, Headquarter : Paris, Director General – Amodou M'Bow (Senegal).

*Universal Declaration of Human Rights* : The U.N. adopted on Dec. 10, 1948 the Universal Declaration of Human Rights. It is a statement of moral standards to be followed by all nations. It stresses the fact that every one has the right to life, liberty and security of person, equality before law, freedom of movement, etc. irrespective of race, religion, sex or language.

*U Thant* : U thant (1909-1974) assuming the office of Secretary General of UNO in June 1967, described his post as symbolising the conscience of Mankind. He had been Burma's representative in the world body since 1957. Since then he had to face many international issues of trickish nature; but because of his impartial and humanistic attitude he could reconcile with them successfully. He wrote many articles and books including *The League of Nations*.

He held that "political ideologies are also moving towards a stage of peaceful co–extistence in the same way as religious befliefs.

He added good many feathers to his cap by solving many disputes through behind–the scene negotiations, which include admission of China to the UNO, Vietnam war, Indo-Pakistani conflicts (1965) and many others.

*William H. Perkins* : Perkins (1838-1907) was a German chemist who invented dye. In June 1857, he started a dye-making factory at Greenfield near Harrow alongwith two other partners. He raised a company named "perkins & Sons". Later on it became the first modern dyestuff industry in Britain and probably in the world. He also invented a perfume "Coumarin", which was very expensive in those days. In 1906 king Edward VII knighted him for his contribution to dyestuff industry and declared him one of the greatest chemists of the time.

*WRAC* : Women's Royal Army Crops (in the U.K.).

*WRAF* : Women's Royal Air Force (in the U.K.).

*William Jones* : (1746–1794) as a champion of Indology, who said sanskrit is more copiou than Latin and more perfect than Greek. He translated Abhigyan Shakuntalam, a famous play of the great Sanskrit poet, Kalidas and compiled sanskrit dictionary also. The most important thing is that he unfolded the treasure "Sanskrit Literature to the West.

*Weltanschavung* : A theme which deeply concerns like today in socialist country like Russia. In Marxist terminology it is the theory of scientific atheism.

*Yuga Purana* : In the Gargi Samhita, a work on Astrology, is a section named the Yuga Puran, which contains some historical information, including among other matters the story of the attack on Saket (Ayodhya) and Patliputra (Patna) in which the Yavanas took part. Scholars are almost unanimous in regarding the Yuga Puran as the earliest among the extant works of Puran type, and as exhibit of an independent tradition.

*Yavan* : The Bebrew word Yavan (Javan) was also originally the designation of the Ionians, but it gradually came to be used for the whole greek race and the ethnic name denoted also a political entity. The term yavan may also well have been first applied by the Indians to the Greeks of various cities of Asia minor who were settled in the areas contiguous to north-west India. Some scholars hold that the term 'Yavana' is of Indian origin as it is referred in many ancient works including the great epic. Mahabharata.

# *APPENDIX -II*

## WORLD'S MAIN EVENTS : AT A GLANCE

About the year 1000 B.C. the Aryan peoples were establishing themselves in the peninsulas of Spain, Italy, and the Balkans, and they were established in North India, Cnossos was already destroyed and the spacious times of Egypt, of Thothmes III, Amenophis III and Rameses II, were/three or four centuries away. Weak monarchs of the twenty-first dynasty were ruling in the Nile Valley. Israel was united under her early kings; Saul or David or possibly even Solomon may have been reigning. Sargon I (2750 B.C.) of the Akkadian-Sumerian Empire was a remote memory in Babylonian history, more remote than is Constantine the Great from the world of the present day. Hammurabi had been dead a thousand years. The Assyrians were already dominating the less military Babylonians. In 1100 B.C. Tiglath Pileser I had taken Babylon. But there was no permanent conquest; Assyria and Babylonia were still separate empires. In China the new Chou dynasty was flourishing. Stonehenge in England was already some hundreds of years old.

The next two centureis saw a renascence of Egypt under the twenty-second dynasty, the splitting up of the brief little Bebrew kingdom of Solomon, the spreading of the Greeks in the Balkans, South Italy and Asia minor, and the days of Etruscan predominance in central Italy. We begin our list of Ascertainable dates with

B.C.

800 The building of Carthage.

790 The Ethiopian conquest of Egypt (founding the XXVth Dynasty).

776 First Olympiad.

753 Rome built.

745 Tiglath Pileser III conquered Babylonia and founded the New Assyrian Empire.

722 Sargon II armed the Assyrians with iron weapons.

721 He deported the Israelites.

680 Esarhaddon took Thebes in Egypt (overthrowing the Ethiopian XXVth Dynasty).

664 Psammetichus I restored the freedom of Egypt and founded the XXVIth Dynasty (to 610).

608 Necho of Egypt defeated Josiah, King of Judah, at the battle of Megiddo.
606 Capture of Nineveh by the Chaleaand and Medes. Foundation of the Chaldean Empire.
604 Necho pushed to the Euphrates and was overthrown by Nebuchadnezzar II.
(Nebuchadnezzar carried off the Jews to Babylon).
550 Cyrus the Persian succeeded Cyaxares the Mede Cyrus conquered Croesus.
550 Buddha lived about this time. So also did Confcius and Lao Tse.
539 Cyrus took Babylon and founded the Persian Empire.
521 Darius I, the son of Hystaspes, ruled from the Hellespont to the Indus.
His expedition to Scythia.
490 Battle of Marathon.
480 Battles of Thermopylaes and Salamis.
479 The battles of Platea and Mycale competed the repulse of Persia.
474 Etruscan fleet destroyed by the Sicilian Greeks.
431 Peloponnesian War began (to 404).
401 Retreat of the Ten Thousand.
359 Philip became king of Macedonia.
358 Battle of Chaeronea.
336 Macedonian troops crossed into Asia. Philip murdered.
334 Battle of the Granicus.
333 Battle of I S sus.
331 Battle of Arbela.
330 Darius III killed.
323 Death of Alexander the Great
321 Rise of Chandragupta in the Punjab.
The Romans completely beaten by the Samnites at the battle of the Caudine Forks.
281 Pyrrhus invaded Italy.
280 Battle of Heraclea.
279 Battle of Ausculum.
278 Gauls raided into Asia Minor and settled in Galatia.
275 Pyrrhus left Italy.
264 First Punic War, 'Asoka began to reign in Bihar to 227.'
260 Battle of Mylae.
256 Battle of Ecnomus.
246 Shi Hwang-ti became king of Ts'in.
220 Shi Hwang-ti became Emperor of China.

214 Great Wall of China begun.
210 Death of Shi Hwang-ti.
202 Battle of Zama.
146 Cathage destroyed.
133 Attalus bequeathed Pergamum to Rome.
102 Marius drove back Germans.
100 Triumph of Marius. (Chinese conquerring the Tarim valley).
89 All Italians became Roman citizens.
73 The revolt of the slaves under Spartacus.
71 Defeat and end of Spartacus.
66 Pompey led Roman troops to the Caspian and Euphrates He encountered the Alani.
48 Julius Caesar defeated Pompey at Pharsalus.
44 Julious Caesar assassinated.
27 Augustus Caesar Princips (until A.D. 14).
4\. True date of brith of Jesus of Nazareth.

A.D.

14\. Augustus died. Tiberius Emperor.
30\. Jesus of Nazareth crucified.
41\. Claudius (the first Emperor of the legions) made Emperior by pretorian guard after murder of Caligula.
68\. Suicide of Nero. (Galba, Otho, Vitellius, Emperors in succession.)
69\. Vaspasian.
102\. Pan Chao on the Caskian Sea.
117\. Hadrian succeeded Trajan. Roman Empire at its greatest extent.
138\. (The Indo-Scythians at this time were destroying the lasttraces of Hellenic rule in India.)
161\. Marcus Aurelius succeeded Anthoninus Pius.

164\. Great plaugue began and lasted to the death of M. Aurelius (180). This also devasted all Asia. (Nearly a Century of war and disorder began in the Roman Empire.)
220\. End of the Han Dynasty. Beginning of four hundred years of division in China.
227\. Adrashir I, First Sassanid shaha, put an end to Arsacid line in Persia.
242\. Mani began his teaching.
247\. Goths crossed Danube in a a great raid.

251. Great victory of Goths. Emperior decius killed.
260. Sapor I, the second Sassanid shah, took Antioch, captured the Emperor Valrian, and was cut up on his return from asia Minor by Odenathus of Palmyra.
277. Mani crucified in Persia.
284. Diocletian became Emperor.
303. Diocletian persecuted the Christians.
311. Galerius abandoned the persecution of the Christians.
312. Constantine the Great became Emperor.
323. Constantine presided over the Council of Nicea.
337. Constantine baptized on his death-bed.
361.3 Julian the Apostate attmepted to substitute Mithraism for Christianity.
392. Theodosius the Great Emperor of East and West.
395. Theodosius the Great died. Honourius and Areadius redivided the empire with Stilicho and Alaric as their masters and protectors.
410. The Visigoths under Alarci captured Rome.
425. Vandals settling in south of Spain. Huns in Pannonia, Goths in Dalmatia. Visigoths and Suevi in Portugal and north Spain. English invading Britain.
439. Vandals took Cart age.
451. Attila raided Gaul and was defeated by Franks, Alemanni, and Romans at Troyes.
453. Death of Attila.
455. Vandals sacked Rome.
476. Odoacer, king of medley of Teutonic tribes, informed Constantinople that there was no emperor in the West. End of the Western Empire.

A.D.

493. Theodoric, the Ostrogoth, conquered Italy and became King of Italy but was mominally subject to Constantionple. (Gothic kings in Italy. Goths settled on special confiscated lands as a garrison.)
527. Justinian Emperor.
529. Justinina closed the schools at Athens, which had flourished nearly a thousand years. Belisarius (Justinian's general) took Naples.
531. Chostroes I began to reign.
543. Great Plague in Constantinople.
553. Goths expelled from Italy by Justinian.
565. Justinian died. The Lombards conquered most of north Italy (leaving Ravenna and Rome Byzantine)

570. Muhammad born.
579. Chosroes I died.
(The Lombards dominant in Italy.)
590. Plague reigned in Rome. Chosroes II began to reign.
610. Heraclus began to reign.
619. Chosroes II held Egypt, Jerusalem, Damascus, and had armies on Hellespont. Tang dynasty began in China.
622. The Hegira.
627. Great Persian defeat at Nineveh by Heraclius. Tai-tsung became Emperor of China.
628. Kavdh II murdered and succeeded his father, Chosroes II. Muhammad wrote letters to all the rulers of the earth.
629. Muhammad returned to Mecca.
632. Muhammad died. Abu Bekr Caliph.
634. Battle of the Yarmuk. Moslems Took Syria. Omar second Caliph.
635. Tai-stung received Nestorian missionaries.
637. Battle of Kadessia
638. Jerusalem surrendered to the Caliph Omar.
642. Heraculius died.
643. Othman third Caliph.
655. Defeat of the Byzantine fleet by the Moslems.
668. The Caliph Moawkja attached Constantinople by sea
687. Pepin of Hersthal, mayor of the palance, reunited Austrasia and Neustria.
711. Moslem army invaded Spain from Africa.
715. The domains of the Caliph wallid I extended from the Pyrenees to China.
717. Suleiman, son and successor of Walid, failed to take constantinople.
732. Charles Martel defeated the Moslems, near Poitiers.
751. Pepin died.
771. Charlemagne sole King.
774. Charlemagne conquered Limbardy.
786. Haroun al Rashid Abbasid Caliph in Baghdad (to 809)
795. Leo III became Poppe (to 816)
800. Leo crowned Charlemagne Emperor of the West.
802. Egbert, formerly on English refugee at the court of Chalemagne, established himself as King of Wessex.
810. Krum of Bulgaria defeated and killed the Emperor Nicephorus.
814. Charlemagne died.
828. Egbert became first king of England.

843. Louis the Pious died and the Carlovingian Empire want to pieces. Until 962 there was no regular succession of Holy Roman Emperors, though the title appeared intermittently.
850. About this time Rurik (a northman) became ruler of Novgorod and Kiev.
852. Boris first Christian King of Bulgaria (to 854).
865. The fleet of the Russians (Northman) threatened Constantinople.
904. Russian (Northmen) fleet off Constantinople.
912. Rolf the Ganger established himself in Normandy.
919. Henry the Fowler elected King of Germany.
936. Otto I became King of Germany in succession to his father Henry the Fowler.
941. Russian fleet again threatened Constantinople.
962. Otto I, king of Germany, crowned Emperor (first Saxon Emperor) by John XII.
987. Hugh Capet became king of France. End of the Carlovingian line of French Kings.
1016. Canute became king of England, Denmark and Norway.
1043. Russian fleet threatened Constantinople.
1066. Conquest of England by William, Duke of Normandy.
1071. Revival of Islam under the Seljuk Turks. Battle of Melasgird.
1073. Hildebrand became Pope (Gregory VII) to 1085.
1084. Robert Guiscard, the Norman, sacked Rome.
1087-89 Urban II Pope.
1095. Urban II at Clermond summoned the First Crusade.
1096. Massacre of the People's Crusade.
1099. Godfrey of Bouillon captured Jerusalem.
1147. The second Crusade.

A.D.

1169. Saladin Sultan of Egypt.
1176. Frederick Barbarossa acknowledged supremacy of the Pope (Alexander III) at Venice.
1187. Saladin captured Jerusalem.
1189. The Third Crusade.
1198. Innocent III Pope (to 1216). Frederick II (aged Four), king of Sicily, became his ward.
1202. The Fourth Crusade attacked the Eastern Empire.
1204. Capture of Constantinople by the Latins.
1214. Jengis Khan took Peking.
1226. St. Francis of Assisi died. (The Franciscans.)
1227. Jengis Khan died, Khan from Caspian to the Pacific, and was

succeeded by Ogdai Khan.

1228. Frederick II embarked upon the sixth crusade, and acquired Jerusalem.

1240. Mongols destroyed Kiev. Russia tributary.to the Mongols.

1241. Mongol victory at Liegnitz in Silesia.

1250. Frederick II, the last Hohenstaufen Emperor, died. German interregnum until 1273.

1251. Manu Khan became Great Khan. Kublai Khan governor of China.

1258. Hulagu Khan took and destroyed Bagdad.

1260. Rublai Khan became Great Kha .

1261. The Greeks recaptured constantinople from the Latins.

1273. Rudolf of Babsburg elected Emperor, The Swiss formed their Everlasting League.

1280. Kublai Khan founded the Yuan Dynasty in China.

1292. Death of Kublai Khan.

1293. Roger Bacon, the prophet of experimental science, died.

1348. The great Plague, the Black Death.

1360. In China the Mongol (Yuan) Dynasty fell, and was succeeded by the Ming Dynasty (to 1644).

1377. Pope Gregory XI returned to Rome.

1378. The Great Schism. Urban VI in Rome. Clement VII at Avignon.

1398. Huss preached Wyeliffism at Prague.

1414.18 The Council of Constance. Huss burned (1415)

1417. The Great Schism ended.

1453 Ottoman Turks under Muhammad II took Constantinople

1480. Ivan III, Grand duke of Moscow, threw off the Mongol allegiance.

1481. Death of the Sultan Muhammad II while preparing for the conquest of Italy.

A.D.

1486. Diaz rounded the cape of Good Hope.

1492. Columbus crossed the Atlantic to America.

1493. Maximilian I became Emperor.

1498. Vasco Da Gama sailed, found the Cape to India.

1499. Switzerland became an Independent republic.

1500. Charles V born.

1509. Henry VIII King of England.

1513. Leo X Pope.

1515. Francis I King of France.

1520. Suleman the Magnificent, Sultan (to 1566), who ruled from Bagdad to Hungary, Charles V Emperor.

1525. Babar won the battle of Panipat, Captured Delhi and founded the

Mogul empire.

1527. The German troops in Italy, under Constable of Burbon, took and pillaged Rome.

1529. Culeiman besieged Vienna.

1530. Charles V Crowned by the Pope. Henry VIII began his quarrel with the Papcy.

1539. The Society of Jesus founded.

1546. Martin Luther died.

1547. Ivan IV (Terrible) took the title of Tsar or Russia.

1556. Charles V abdicated. Akbar, Great Mogul (to 1605). Ignatius of Loyola died.

1558. Death of Charles V.

1566. Suleiman the Magnificent died.

1603. James I king of England and Scotland.

1620. Mayflower expedition founded New Plymouth. First Negro slaves landed at Jamestown (Va.)

1625. Charles I of England.

1626. Sir Francis Bacon (Lord Verulam) died.

1643. Louis XIV began his reign of seventy-two years.

1644. The Manchus ended the Ming dynasty.

1648. Treaty of Westphalia. Thereby Holland and Switzerland were recognized as free republics and Prussia became important. The treaty gave a complete victory neither to the Imperial crown, nor to the Princes. War of the Fronde : It ended in the complete victory of the French crown.

1649. Execution of Charles I of England.

1658. Aurangzeb Great Mogul. occupied throne Cromwell died.

1660. Charleds II of England.

A.D.

1674. Nieuw Amsterdam finally became British by treaty and was renamed New York.

1683. The last Turkish attack on Vienna defeated by John II of Poland.

1689. Peter the Great of Russia (to 1725)

1701 Prederick I first King of Prussia.

1707 Death of Aurangzeb. The empire of the Great Mogul disintegrated.

1713. Frederick the Great of Prussia born.

1715. Louis XV of France.

1755-63 Britain and Franch struggled for America and India. France in alliance with Austria and Russia against Prussia and Britain (1756–63) : The seven years' war.

1759. The British general, Wolfe, took Quebec.

A.D.

1760. Napoleon Bonaparte born.
1774. Louis XVI began his reign.
1776. Declaration of Independence by the United States of America.
1783. Treaty of Peace between Britain and the new United States of America.
1787. The Constitution Convention of Philadelphia set up the federal Government of the United States. France discovered to be bankrupt.
1788. First Federal Congress of the United States at New York.
1789. The French States-General assembled. Storming of the bastille.
1791. Flight to Varennes.
1792. France decalred war on Austria; Prussia declared war on France. Battle of Valmy. France became a republic.
1793. Louis XVI beheaded.
1784. Execution of Robespierre and end of the Jacobin republic.
1795. The Directory, Bonaparte suppressed a revolt and went to Italy's commander-in-chief.
1798. Bonaparte went to Egypt. Battle of the Nile.
1799. Bonaparte retunred to France. He became First Consul with enormous powers.
1804. Bonaparte became Emperor. Francis II took the title of Emperor of Austria in 1805, and in 1806 he dropped the title of Holy Roman Emperor. So the 'Holy Roman Empire' came to an end.
1806. Russia overthrown at Jena.
1808. Napoleon made his brother Joseph King of Spain

A.D.

1810. Spanish American became republican.
1812. Napoleon's retreat from Moscow.
1814. Abdication of Napoleon. Louis XVIII.
1824. Charles X of France.
1825. Nicholas I of Russia. First railway, Stockton to Darlington.
1827. Battle of Navarino.
1829. Greece independent.
1830. A year of disturbance. Louis Philippe ousted Charles X. Belgium broke away from Holland. Leopold of Saxe-Coburg-Gotha became king of this new country, Belgium, Russian Poland revolted ineffectually.
1835. The word 'socialism' first used.

1837. Queen Victoria.
1840. Queen Victoria married Prince Albert of Saxe-Coburg-Gotha.
1852. Napoleon III Emperor of the French.
1854-6 Crimean War.
1856. Alexander II of Russia.
1861. Victor Emmanuel first King of Italy. Abraham Lincon became President, USA The American Civil War began.
1865. Surrender of Appomatiox Court House. Japan opened to the World.
1870. Napoleon III declared war against Prussia.
1871. Paris surrendered (January). The King of Prussia became German Emperor. The Peace of Frankfort.
1878. The Treaty Berlin. The Armed Peace of Thirtysix years began in Western Europe.
1888. Frederick II (March), William II (June), German Emperors.
1912. China became a republic.
1914. The Great War in Europe began.
1917. The two Russian revolutions, Establishment of the Bolshevik regime in Russia.
1918. The Armistice.
1920. First metting of the League of Nations, from which Germany, Austria, Russia and Turkey were excluded and at which the United States was not represented.
1921. The Greeks in complete disregard of the League of nations made war upon the Turks.
1922. Great defeat of the Greeks in Asia Minor by the Turks. Fascist March on Rome.
1924. Lenin died.
A.D.
1927. The feud of Stalin and Trotsky developed and Trotsky became an exile.
1928. Beginning of the First Russian Five-Year Plan.
1930. The Hitlerite Party appeared in force in the German Reichstag.
1931. Financial crisis in Great Britain and abandonment of the Gold Standard. The League of Nations refused to permit an Austro-German customs union. Spain became a Republic.
1932. Creation of Manchukno by Japan. Franklin Roosevelt elected President of the United States of America.
1933. Fire in the Berlin Reichstag and Naxi Coup d etat Hitler became dictator of Germany. Futile world economic conference in London. Japan (April) and Germany (October) left the League of Nations.

1934. Russia entered the League of Nations. Assissi nation of Kirov.

1935. The Saar returned to Germany. Abyssinia appealed fruitlessly to the league of nations against Italy. Jews deprived of German citizenship and their marriage with 'Aryans' forbidden.

1936. Death of King Geoge V of England. Virtual conquest of Abyssinia by Italy. Franco revolt in spain. Abdication of King Edward VIII of England.

1937. Siege of Madrid and gradual exhaustion of the Spanish Government forces.

1938. Germany invaded and incorporated Austria without armed resistance.

1939. Second World War breaks out.

1940. Germany occupied Norway, Denmark, Holland, Belgium, Fall of France. Hungary., Rumania and Slovakia joined Axis. Unsuccessful invasion of Greece by the Italians. Churchill British Prime Minister. Roosevelt re-elected President of USA for Third Term, Britain leased Atlantic basis to USA. Trotsky assassinated in Mexicao.

1941. Fluctuations of the war in North Africa. The British advanced into Libya in 1941, withdraw again in the spring, advanced in November and withdrew again in the pring of 1942. Bulgaria joined axis. German occupation of Greece, Yugoslavia and Crete. Liberation of Abyssinia. British and French occupy Syria. German Invasion of Russia (June 22nd). Atlantic Charter, occupation of Iran by British and Russians. Fall of Kiev to Germans. German offensive against Moscow failed. Japan attacked USA. USA declared war on Germany.

A.D.

1942. Fall of Singapore, Japanese conquests in Pacific and Burma. Midway Island Battle. Rommel's offensive in Libya brought Germans to Egypt. Battle of Egypt. El Alamein. British and American landings in North Africa. Tunis Remainded in German hands until 1943, when North Africa was completely cleared. Assassination of Darlan in Algiers. Fall of sebastopol to Germans, who entered Caucasus but were halted before Stalingrad. 'Quit India Movement' in India.

1943. Casablanca Conference. 'Unconditional surrender' insisted upon. Anglo-American occupation of Tunis. Invasion of Sicily. Invasion of Italy, American progress in Pacific. Russians recaptured Kharkov, Smolensk, Kiev. Quebec Conference. Teheran

Conference.

1944. Allied landings in France. France, Belgium liberated. Allies fighting on borders of Germany. Greece liberated. Russians swept through Rumania and Bulgaria into Hungary, Yugoslavia, Czechoslovakia, Roosevelt re-elected for fourth Term. Americans landed on Philippines.

1945. Unconditional Surrender of Germany. Death of Roosevelt.

1945. First Radio Station set-up in China (5th September).

1945. United Nations Charter.

1945. Manchester Pan-African Conference.

1947. India got independence (15th August) Formation of Pakistan.

1947. Jawahar Lal Nehru resumed the office of PM of India and held in office till 1964.

1948. Brussels Pact.

1948. Mother Teresa became Indian Citizen.

1948. Universal Declaration of Human Rights.

1948. Independent Republic of Israel came into existance.

1948. David Ben Curion became premier of Republic of Israel (1948-1963).

1948. Death of Mahatma Gandhi.

1949. China becomes people's Republic with the establishment of communist political system.

1950. Nasser came to power in Egypt.

1950. Adoption of Indian Constitution.

1950. Agrarian Reform Law of China regime. Five year plans started in India.

1951. San Francisco Peace Treaty.

A.D.

1951. Japanese American Security Treaty.

1952. US-Japanese Mutual Security Treaty.

1952. Dr. Sarvepalli Radhakrishnan became Vice President of India (1952-1962)

1953. Vijayalaxmi Pandit was elected President of eighth. General Assembly session (first Indian as well as first woman to hold the position).

1953. Ascent of Mount Everest (29 May).

1954. Trade and Intercourse Agreement between India and China.

1954. The first constitution was adopted in China.

1955. Bandung conference.

1955. CENTO (Central Treaty Organization).

1955. South-East Asia Treaty Organization (SEATO).
1955. Warsa Pact.
1956. Nasser's Seizure of Suez Canal.
1957. Attempt to remove Nikita Khrushchev.
1957. U.S.S.R. Launched first sputnik in space.
1958. Life peerage Act passed in England.
1960 Mrs. Sirimavo Bandarnaike became Prime Minister of Shri Lanka
1960. Liberation of Congo.
1960. Nigeria became free.
1962. Algerian Independen.ce
1962. Indo-Chinese War.
1963. Collaboration Treaty of France-West Germany.
1963. Agitation by Martin King Luther for equality between the balck and the white.
1964. Death of Jawaharlal Nehru (May 27).
1964. Lal Bahadur Shastri became PM of India.
1964. Pope Paul VI Visited India (first pope to visit India).
1965. Indo-Pakistani War.
1965. Socialist Transformation of China.
1966. Mrs. Indira Gandhi resumed the office of PM (First Woman PM).
1967. Egypt – Israel War.
1967. Chou En-Lai apologizes to Sihanauk.
1968. Wilson Government (England) issued a white paper of Lords reforms.
1969. Hague Conference.
1969. Nigerian Civil War.
1969. Man-Landing on Moon (Neil Armstrong *et. al.*).

A.D.

1970. Crown Courts Act of England.
1970. Equal rights of admission to the children of Black and White in U.S.A. (Decision of Supreme Court).
1970. Death of Nasser and resuming the office of President of Egypt by Anwar Sadat.
1971. Bangla Desh came into existence after Indo-Pakistani War.
1971. Berlin Agreement.
1971. Treaty of friendship and cooperation between the Republic of India and the Union of Soviet Socialist Republics (U.S.S.R.).
1972. Paris Conference.
1973. Copenhagen Summit.
1973. War Powers Act of U.S.A.

1974. Trade Reforms Act of United States of America .
1974. Portugal recognized the independence of Guinea-Bissan.
1974. Second Constitution of China was adopted.
1975. Mozambique became independent (25 June) "Cape verde Islands became indpendent (5 July).
1977. Morarji Desai Assumed office of PM of India. at the age of 81 (oldest to become PM).
1977. Breznev constitution introduced in U.S.S.R. (first Russian Constitution introduced in 1936).
1978. New Constitution was adopted in China (After the downfall of the gang of four).
1979 Mother Teresa won Nobel Peace Prize for selfless work among slum dwellers, destitutes, leprosy settlements of Calcutta.
1979. Charan Singh became PM of India.
1980. Mrs. Indira Gandhi cameback to power.
1982. Present Constitution was adopted in China
1984. Assasination of Mrs. Indira Gandhi, Prime Minister of India.
1984. Rajeev Gandhi became PM of India, Youngest (40) to become PM.
1986. Introduction of Perestroica by Mekhael Gorbachev in U.S.S.R.
1989. Communism collapsed.
1989. Nehru Centenary Celebration.
1989. Janta Dal came into power in India and Vishvanath Pratap Singh became PM.
1990. Chandra Shekhar resumed the office of PM.
1991. Liberalization in Indian Economy started.
1991. Rajeev Gandhi was assassinated at Sriperumbudur on May 21, 1991 in Tamilnadu, Narasimaha Rao became PM of India.

A.D.

1992. The third summit of the group of 15 developing countries (G-15)
1993. US president George Bush, and the Russian President, Mr. Boris Yeltsin Signed a Landmark nuclear arms control treaty.
1993. Sino-Russian Pact–a new chapter in Sino-Russian relations.
1994. Rirst Advanced Pastoral Leadership Seminar for the bishops of Asia at Hong-Kong.
1994. General Agrement on Tariffs and Trade (Gatf) Signed by 124 Countries.
1994. Giani Zail Singh, Former President of India died (December, 25).
1994. Organization of Islamic Countries (O I C) Foreign Ministers Summit.

1994. Nelson Mandela took the oath of office to become South Africa's first black Preident (May, 10).

1994. Ethnic Voilence in Rwanda in which about 2 lakh People were killed.

1994. PLO set-up its self-rule government.

1994. Russia's armed intervention in Chechenya taking it as prestige issue to warn other feuding republics.

1994. Miss Chandrika Kumartunga became President of Shri Lanka, First Woman President .

1994. Israel and Jordan signed a peace treaty.

1994. The Israeli Prime Minister Mr. Robin, The foreign minister Mr. Shimon Peres and PLO leader Mr. Yassir Arafat received 1994 Nobel Peace Prize.

# BIBLIOGRAPHY


Abdul, L.S., *Outline of the Cultural History of Islam*. Hyderabad : Institute of Indo-Middle East Cultural Studies, 1958.

Abhai Maurya, (Ed.), *India and World Literature*, Indian Council for Cultural Relations, New Delhi, 1990.

Abraham, Heschel, *The Earth is the Lord's, Abelard*, New York, 1949.

Ahmad, Aziz, *Studies of Islamic Culture in the Indian Environment*, London : Oxford University Press, 1964.

Ahmad, Imtiaz, *Secularism and Communalism*, Econ. & Pol. Weekly, July, 1969.

Alfred Deoblin, *The Living Thoughts of Confucius*, Jaico Publishing House, Bombay 1957.

Allian, B. Cole, *Japanese Society and Politics*, Bostan, 1956.

Ameer Ali, *The Spirit of Islam*, Christophers, London, 1922.

Anderson, N., *Urbanism and Urbanization*, London : C.J. Brill Publication, 1949.

Anthony de Reuck and Julie Knight (ed.), *Conflict in Society* (A Ciba Foundation Volume). J&A Churchill Ltd. London, 1966.

Aron, Raymond, *Peace and War : A Theory of International Relations*, N.Y. Double Day, Garden City, 1954.

Arthus, Waley, *Ways of Thought in Ancient China*, paperback.

Aurobindo, *Hymns of the Mystic Fire*, Shri Aurobindo Ashram, Pondicherry, 1952.

Aziz, K.K., *Muslim in India and Britain*. London : Heinemann Publ., 1963.

Baig, M.R.A., *The Muslim Dilemma in India, Delhi* : Vikas Publishing House Ltd. 1967.

Barbara, Ward, *India and the West*, Publication Division India, 1961.

Barnett, H.G., *Innovation: the Basic of Cultural Change*. New York : Mcgraw Hill, 1953.

Basham, A.L., *The Wonder that was India*, Rupa & Co. 1967.

—–, *Cultural History of India*, OUP, Delhi, 1985.

Baverly, B. Cassara (Editor), *Adult Education in a Multicultural Society*, Routledge, London & New York, 1990.

Ben Spiecker & Roger Straughan, *Freedom and Indoctrination in Education*, Cassel Educational Lt., London, 1991.

Beijing Review, *Progress in Urban Reforms*, Beijing Review Publication, Beijing.

Bergson, Henri, *An Introduction to Metaphhsics*.

Bernard, B. Fall, *Two Vietnams*, New York, 1963.

Bhagwandas, *A study in the Theory of Avataras*, BVB, Bombay, 1962.

Biswas & Biswas, *The World's Famous Speeches*, Arya Book Depot., New Delhi, 1992.

Boulding, Kenneth E., *The meaning of 20th Century : The Great Transition*: N. York. Harper 1969.

Bose, N.K., *Cultural Anthropology*, Asia Publ. House, 1961.

Boris Ford (Editor), *The Modern Age, Penguin Books*, Reprint, 1966.

Bowser, B.D. & R.D. Hunt, (Ed.), *Impacts of Racism on White Americans*, Baverly Hills, 1981.

Bouguet, A.C., *Comparative Religion*, Pelican, 1933.

Brass, P., *Language, Religion and Politics in North India*. Delhi : Vikas Publishing House, 1975.

Brij Mohan, *India's Social Problems*, Allahabad : Indian International Publ., 1972.

Bronowski, J., *Science and Human Values*, Harper Torch books Science Library, 1950.

Brown, I.C., *Understanding other cultures : Theory and Practice*.

Buchanan, William, *How Nations see Each Other: A Study of Public Opinion*, Uni of Illiois Press Urbana, 1953.

Buddha Prakash, *Aspects of Indian History and Civilization*, Shivlal Agrawal & Co., Agra, 1965.

Camps, Mirium, *Britain & European Community (1995-1963)*, Prinecton Uni. Press, Princeton, 1964.

Carsun Chang, *The Development of New-Confucian Thought*. 2 Vols, New York, 1957, 1962.

Chamanlal, *India : Cradle of Cultures*, IBH, Delhi, 1979.

Chapekar, Nalini M., *Ancient India and Iran*, Ajanta Publications, Jawahar Nagar, Delhi-7. 1932.

Charles Wighton, *Eichmann, His Career and Crimes*, Odham, 1961.

Chattopadhyaya, S., *Traditional Values in Indian Life*, India International Centre, New Delhi 1961.

Chavan, C.R.S., *Nationalism in Asia*, New Delhi : Sterling Publishing, 1973.

Chen Shou yi, *Chinese Literature : A Historical Introduction*, New York, 1961.

Cherry, C., *On Human Communication*, New York : Science Editions, Inc:. 1961.

Christine, I. Binnett, *Comprehensive Multicultural Education* : Theory and Practice, Allyan and Bacon, London, II Edition, 1990.

Chopra, V.D. *et al.*, *India-Hungary-Cooperation in Action*, Patriot Publishers, New Delhi, 1985.

Claude Inis, *Power and International Relations*, Random House, New York, 1962.

Craemer, A.J., *A Cultural Self-awareness : Approach to Improving Intercultural Communication skill* ERIC ED. April 1973.

Dalal, M.N., *Wither Minorities*, Bombay : Taraporewala, 1940.

Dalwi, H., *Muslim Politics in India*, Bombay, Nachiketa, 1968.

Dagny, Carter, *Four Thousand Years of Chinese Art*, New York, 1948.

Damodar, Dharmanand Koshambi, *An Introduction to the Study of Indian History*, Sangam, Books Ltd., London, 1985.

Dandekar, R.N., *Some Aspects of History of Hinduism*, Poona, 1967.

Dean, V.M., *New Patterns of Democracy in India*, Cambridge:Harvard Univ. Press, 1969.

Debary, W.T., *Sources of Chinese Tradition*, New York, 1960.

Desai, A.R., *Social Background of Indian Nationalism,* Bombay:Popular Book Depot., 1968.

Devandan, P.D. *Religion and National Unity in India Religious Roots of Communalism*, Quest (21) April./June. 37-42, 1959.

Devendra Handa & Ashvini Agrawala(Ed.), *Ratna Chandrika - Panorama of Oriental Studies*, Harman Publishing House, New Delhi.

Dhalla, M.N., *Zoroastrian Theology*, New York, 1914.

Dhirendranath, *The Problem of Minorities*, University of Calcutta, Calcutta, 1990.

Diwakar, R.R., *Secularism, and Politics*, Bhawan's Journal. 11(7) Oct:95-101, 1964.

Dixit, P., *Communalism-A Struggle for Power*. Delhi:Orient Longman., 1974.

Donald, Kenne, *Living Japan*, New York, 1959.

Dube, S.C. and Basilov V.N.(Ed.), *Secularisation in Multi-Religious Societies*, Indo-Soviet Perspectives, Concept Publishing Co., New Delhi, 1983.

Dutt, V.P., *India and the World*, Sanchar Pubvlishing House, New Delhi, 1990.

Edward Conze, *Buddhism:Its Essence and Development,* Philosophical Library, New York, 1951.

Egner, Robert, E., Bertrand Russell's, *Best, Unvin Books*, London, 1975.

Eliot, Charles, *Hinduism and Buddhism:An Historical Sketch*, 3 Vols., New York, 1954.

Eliot, N.E., *Japanese Buddhism*, London, 1935.

Erich, Fromm *et al.*, *Zen Buddhism and Psychoanalysis*, George Allen and Unwin Ltd., London, 1960.

Ernest, F. Fenollosa, *Art Architecture and Aesthetics*, paperback.

Falk, Richard A., *This Endangered Planet*, New York, Random House, 1971.

Falk, Richard A. & Mendlovitz Soul H.(Ed), *Toward a Theory of War Prevention*, World Law Fund, New York, 1966.

Farrell, R. Barry(Ed), *Approaches to Comparative and International Politics*, North Western University Press, Evanston III, 1966.

Feagin, J., *Racial and Ethnic Relation*, Prentice Hall, Englewood Cliffs, 1978.

Ferguson, J., *Moral Values in the Ancient World*, Methuen and Co., Ltd., 1938.

Ferkiss, Victor C., *Technological Man*, New York, Braziller, 1969.

Fischer, Louis, *Russia's Road From Peace to War*, New York, Harper & Row, 1969.

Fung, Yu-Lan, *Chinese Thought from Confucious to Mao Tse-Tung*, paperback.

Fyoyd David, *Mao Against Khrushehev*, New York, Praeger, 1963.

Gayor, F., *A Dictionary of Mysticism*, New York, 1933.

Gauba, K.L., *Passive Voices. A Penetrating study of Muslims in India*, New Delhi : Sterling Pubishers Pvt. Ltd., 1973.

Gautam, V., "*Minorities" In India Since Indepndence* edited by Dube S.C. New Delhi : Vikas Publ. House, 1977.

George Alexander Lensen, *Europe and China : A Survey of their Relations from Earliest Time to 1800*, paperback.

George Macaulay Trevelyan, *History of England*, Longman Green and Co. London, II edition, 1945.

Gerbner, G., Mass and Human Communication Theory. In : *Human Communication Theory* : Original Essays edited by Frank, E.X. Dance. New York : Hott, Rinehar & Winston Inc., 1967.

Ghurye, G.S., *Social Tensions in India*, Bombay : Popular Prakashan, 1968.

Godnon, M.M., *Assimilation in American Life*, Oxford Uni. Press, New York, 1966.

Gordon, M.M., *Assimilation in American Life : The Role of Race, Religion, and National Origins*, New York.

Gudly W.B. Kunst and Y.Y. Kim, *Communicating with Strangers : An Approach to Intercultural Communication*, New York addition-wesley 1984.

Gunnar, Myrdal, *The Challenge of World Poverty*, New York, Pantheon, 1970.

Gunnar, Myrdal, *Asian Drama (Abridged Edition) Allen Lane*, The Penguine Press, London, 1972.

Gupta, N.L., *A Search for Human Values*, Arya Book Depot, New Delhi, 1992.

—., *Creativity and Values*, Arya Book Depot, New Delhi, 1992.

—., *Value Education : Theory and Practice*, Chetna Prakashan, Shirke Rd. New Shukrawari, Nagpur, II Edition, 1994.

—., *Education and Values in the Mahabharata*, Concept Publishing Co., New Delhi, 1995.

—., *Contribution of Western Indologists,* Mohit Publications, New Delhi-1996.

Harba, J., *American Ethricity*, F.E. Peacock, Itasca, 1975.

Hajime Nakamura, *Ways of thinking of Eastern Peoples*.

Haldar, M.K., Hindu Values : Myth and Reality, In : *Tribe, Caste and Religion*. Edited by Ramesh Thapar, Dlhi : Macmillian Pub. 1977.

Haq, M.R., *Islam in Secular India*, Simla : Indian Institute of Advanced Study, 1972.

Har Dayal, *Hints for Self-culture*, Jaico Publishing House, Bombay Reprint 1985.

Harold, M. Vinacke, *Modern Constitutional Development in China*, Princeton University Press, New Jersy, 1920.

Harold, C. Hinton, *A Short History of Chinese People*, Paperback.

Harris, Thomas A. *I am OK you are OK*, Avon Books, New York, 1977.

Hassn, S.E., *Indian Muslime, Challange and Opportunity*, Bombay : Lalvani, 1968.

Hays, Carton, J.H., *Essays on Nationalism*, New York : Macmillan Camp., 1962.

Heinrich Zimmer, *The Philosophies of India,* Pantheon Books, New York, 1951.

Henry Brandon (Ed.), *As we are, Popular Library*, New York, 1960.

Herman Khan, *The Emerging Japanese Superstate : Challenge and Response*, Englewood Cliffs, NJ, Prentice Hall, 1970.

Herschel Webb, *An Introduction to Japan*, 2nd Ed. New York, 1960.

Herry, J. Benda, *The Crescent and the Rising Sun : Indonesian Islam under the Japanese Occupation, 1942-45*, The Haugue, 1958.

Hinstey, F.H., *Power and the Pursuit of Peace*, Cambridge University Press, New York, 1963.

Hodiwala, S.K., *Indo-Iranian Religion with Parallelism in Hindu & Zoroastrian Scriptures*, Bombay, 1925.

Hoops, D.S., *Intercultural Communication Concept and the Psychology of Inter-cultural Exprience.* In M.D. Puseh (Ed.) Multicultural Education : A Cross-cultural Trg. approach, La Grange Park III Intercultural Network.

Horace Alexander, *Gandhi through Western Eye*.

Humphries, Robert, *The Imperifed Environment*, Vista (March-April) 1970.

Hunter, W.W., *History of Indian People*, Cosmo Publication, New Delhi, 1984.

Hussain, S.A., *The National Culture of India*, Bombay, Asia Publishing House, 1961.

Huston Smith, *The Religions of Man*, New American Library, First Printing, 1959.

Hu-Chang-tu *et al, China, : Its People, Its Society, Its Culture*, New York, 1960.

Hugh Borton, *Japan's Modern Century*, New York, 1955.

Indian Penal Code, 1860.

James, Legge, *The Travels of Fa-Hien, Oriental Publishers*, Delhi-6, 1972.

James, *The Chinese Classics*, 5 Vols., Hong Kong, 1960.

John, F. Cady, *Southeast Asia : Its Historical Developments*, New York, 1964

——., *A History of Modern Burma*, Ithaca, 1958.

John D. Montgomery, *The Politics of Foreign Aid : American Experience in Southeast Asia*, New York, 1962.

John, Turner, *The New Japan : Government and Politics*, 1956.

John, K. Faribank, *China's Response to the West*, Hardward University Press, 1963.

Jones, K.W. Communalism in the Punjab, the Arya Samaj Contribution In : *Journal of Asian Studies* XXVIII(1), 1968.

Jotwani, Motilal, *Sufis of Sindhi*, Publication Division, New Delhi, 1986.

Julius Fast, *Body Language*, Pocket Book, New York.

Kaplan, Morton A. (ed.), *New Approaches to International Relations*, St. Martin's, New York, 1968.

Karan Singh, *Essays on Hinduism*, Ratna Sagar, New Delhi 1993.

Kartz, D., *Psychological Barrirs to Communication*, Annal American Acad. Political Social Science. 250 : 17-25, 1947. Kapur, J.C., *India : An Uncommitted Society*, Vikas Publishing House, New Delhi 1982.

Karunakaran, K.P., *Religion and Political Awakening in India Meerut,* Meenakshi Prakashan, 1965.

Kato, M., *The Lost Ward*, New York, Alfred A Knopf, 1946.

Keay, F.E., *Kabir and His followers,* OUP, Calcutta, 193.

Kenneth, Cragg, *The Call of the Minaret*, OUP, New York, 1956.

Kluchkhohn, C., *Mirror for man : The relation of Anthropology to Modern Life*, New York, McGraw Hills, 1949.

Knapp, L., *Non-verbal Communication in Human Interaction*, New York, Holt Rinehar and Winston, 1972.

Lavine, R.A. & D. Campbell, *Ethnocentricism : Theories of Conflict, Ethnic Attitudes & Group Behaviour*, John-Wiley & Sons, New York, 1971.

La Barre, W., *Paralinguistics, Kinesics, and Cultural Anthropology in Intercultural Communication* : A Reader, edited by Larry Samouar and Richard E. Parter, Belmont, CA : Wards Worth.

Lenebitz, L., *Nonverbal Communication : A guide for Teachers Skokie III* : National Text Book, 1973.

Lester, R. Brown, *World Without Borders*, Affiliated East West Press Pvt. Ltd., New Delhi, 1972.

Lin Yutang, *The Wisdom of China and India*, New York, 1942.

Linton, R. (Ed.), *The Science of Man in World Crisis*, Columbia Uni. Press, New York, 1945.

Louis, Fischer, *Life of Mahatma Gandhi*, London 1951.

Macdonell, A.A., *Lectures on Comparative Religion*, Calcutta, 1925.

Majumdar, B., *Militant Nationalism and its Socio-religious Background*, Calcutta; Central Printers and Publication Pvt. Ltd., 1966.

Majumdar, R.C., *History of Freedom, Movement in India*, Vol. II Calcutta; Firms K.L. Mukhopadhyaya, 1963.

——., *Hindu Colonies in the Far East*, II edition, Calcutta, 1963.

Marius, B. Jansen, *The Japanese and the Chinese Revolutionary Movements 1895-1915*, New York, Columbia Uni. Press, 1970.

Mary, K. & F. Engers, *Selected Correspondence*, Moscow, 1956.

Maslow, A.H., *New Knowledge in Human Values*, New York, Harper and Row Pub. Inc., 1959.

Maulana Abdul Kalam Azad, *India Wins Freedom*, Orient Longman, 1988.

Max Beloff, *Soviet Policy in the Far East 1944-1951*, London, 1953.

Mead, Margaret, *Culture and Commitment: A study of the Generation Gap*, Natural History Press, New York Doubleday, 1970.

Menon, K.T.R., *Soldiers of Peace*, N.B.T. New Delhi, 1980.

Miller, J.B.D., *Survey of Commonwealth Affairs*, Oxford University Press, London, 1974.

Mishan, Ezra J., *The Costs of Economic Growth*, New York, Praeger, 1967.

Mirashi, V.V., *Studies in Indology,* Motilal Banarasidas, Varanasi.

Mohammad Iqbal, *The Reconstruction of Religious Thought in Islam*, OUP, London, 1934.

Mohindra, S., *Terrorist Games Nations Play*, Bancer Publisher Pvt. Ltd., New Delhi, 1993.

Monier, Monier Williams, *Indian Wisdom*, Cosmo Publications, New Delhi, 1978.

Morris, C.M., *Varieties of Human Values*, University of Chicago Press, Chicago, 1956.

Morse, H.B., *The International Relations of the Chinese Empire*, Longmans, Green & Co. Inc. New York.

Moon Penderel, *Strangers in India*, New York : Reynal and Hitchcock, 1945.

Mujeet, M., *Education and Traditional Values*, Meerut : Meenakshi Prakashan, 1965.

Mukherjee, Rekhakamal, *A History of Indian Civilization*, Hind Kitab Limited Bombay, 1956.

Mukherjee, S.N., *India-History and Thought Subarnrekha*, Calcutta, 1982.

Naidu, Ratna, *The Communal Edge to Plural Societies*, Delhi : Vikas Publ. House, 1980.

Nanavati, M.B., *Vakil G.H., Group Prejudice in India-a Symposium*, Bombay : Vora Publ., 1951.

Nanda, B.R., *Gandhi and His Critics*, OUP, Delhi, 1985.

Nanda, J.N., *Conflicts and Co-existence India*, Concept Publishing Company, New Delhi, 1991.

Narayan, A.K., *The Indo-Greeks*, Oxford University Press. Amen House London, 1962.

Needham, Joseph, *Science and Civilization in China*, Vols 1-4 to date, Cambridge, England 1954-62.

Neustadt, Richard, *Alliance Politics*, Columbia Uni. Press, New York, 1970.

Nehru, J.L. *Glimpses of World History*, OUP, Forth impression, 1987.

Niccolo Machiavelli, *The Prince*, Penguine Books, 1981.

Nore Barlow (Ed.), *The Autobiography of Charles Darwin,* London, 1958.

Norman, Angell, *The Great Illusion-Now*, Penguine Books, London, 1939.

Norman, E. Robert, *Japan's Emergence as a Modern State*, Institute of Pacific Relations, Inc. New York, 1940.

Oman, J.C., *The Mystics, Ascetics and Saints of India*, Cosmo Publ., New Delhi 1984.

Pace, Danny, F., *Concept of Vice, Narcotics and Organised Crime*, Prentice Hall Inc., 1961.

Panchbhai, S.C., Intercommunal Stereotypes in a Plural Society, *Anthropological Quarterly*. 331-44, 1966.

Pannikar, K.M., *Hindu Society at Cross Road Cant and Democracy*, Bombay Asia Publishing House, 1955.

Park, R.L. and Tinta, *Leadership and Political Institution in India*, Madras Oxford University Press.

Patrick, Pingle, *Great Discoveries in Modern Science*, George G. Harrap & Co. Ltd. Toronto, 1955.

Paul Carus, *The Gospel of the Buddha*, Open Court, Chicago.

Percival, Spear, *A History of India*, Vol. 1-2 Penguine Books, reprint 1968.

Peoples Publ., *House, Role of State Sector in Developing Countries*, New Delhi.

Pearson, Lester B., *The Crisis of Development*, New York, Praeger, 1970.

Philip Hitti, *The Arabs : A short History,* Princetion University Press, 1949.

Progress Publisher, *Philosophy in USSR* — Problems of Historical Materialism, Moscow, 1981.

Radhakrishanan, S., *Religion and Society*, George Allen and Unwin Ltd., Indian Edition, 1959.

——., *Our Heritage*, Orient Paper Back, Madras, 1976.

——, *Hindu View of life*, Macmillan, New York, 1927.

Raghavan, M.D., *India in Ceylonese History, Society and Culture*, Asia Publishing House, Bombay, 1969.

Ram Gopal, *Indian Culture During and After Muslim Rule*, M.D. Publications, Pvt. Ltd. New Delhi 1994.

Ram, P. and Murphy, C., Recent investigations of Hindu-Muslim Relations in India, *Human Organisations* II (2) : 13-22, 1952.

Rawlinson, H.G., *India–A Short Cultural Hisotry*, London : The Cresset Press, Paper-back, 1965.

——, "Early Contacts Between India and Europe", in *Cultural History of India*, by A.L. Basham, OUP, Delhi, 1985.

Revel, Jean-Francois, *Without Mary or Jesus*, New York, Double day 1971.

Rex, J. and Moore, R., *Race Community and Conflict*, London : Oxford University, Press, 1967.

Rissler, Clark, *Man and Culture*, London, 1923.

Robbert Schwantes, *Japanese and Americans : A Century of Cultural Relations*, New York Harper and Row, 1955.

Rolf, Sidney E. & Damm Walter (eds), *The Multinational Cooperation in the World Economy*, New York, Praeger, 1970.

Romain, Rolland, *The Life of Vivekanand*, Advait Ashram, Calcutta, 1993.

Romila Thapar, *Ancient Indian Social History*, Orient Longman Ltd., 1978.

Roy, C. Marcidis (Ed.), *Foreign Policy in World Politics*, 5th Edition, Prentice Hall of India, New Delhi, 1979.

Russel, Bertrand, *Why I am not Christian*, George Allen and Unwin, 1967.

Russel, H. Fifielf, *Southeast Asia and the World Today*, paperback.

Ruth, Gruber, S., *Science and the New Nations*, Pyramid Books, New York, 1965.

Sachar, A.L., *History of the Jews*, Knopf, New York 1953.

Sakharov, Andrei D., *Progress, Coexistance and Intellectual Freedom*, New York, Norton, 1969.

Sansom, G.B., *Japan : A Short Cultural History*, New York, 1931.

Saral, T.B. *Consciousness Theory and Inter-Cultural Communication, Portland Oregon* (Paper Presented and International Communication Association, Portland Oregon.

Saxena, N.K., *History and Facets in the World and India*.

Sellin Thorsten, *Annals of American Academy of Political and Social Sciences*, May 1963.

Shriniwasan, *Inside Present Day China*, Popular Book Depot Bombay, 1963.

Sharma, S.R., *The Soul of Indian History*, BVB, Bombay, 1967.

Sinha, Jadunath, *Outline of Indian Philosophy*, Sinha Publishing House, Calcutta, 1963.

Sprout, Herald and Margaret, *Towards a Politics of the Planet Earth*, New York, Van Nostrand Reinhold, 1971.

Swami Nikhilanand, *The Essence of Hinduism*, Beacon Press, Boston, 1948.

Swamy Abhedanand, *Life Beyond Death*, Vedant Math, Calcutta VI edition, 1978.

Sweder, R.A. & R.A. Le Vine (ed.), *Culture Theory : Essays on Mind, Self and Emotion*, Cambridge Uni. Press, 1986.

Tagore, R.N., *One Hundred Poems of Kabir*, Macmillian & Co. first edition, 1915.

Taraporewala, J.S., *The Divine Songs of Zarathustra*, Bombay, 1951.

Thompson, Kenneth W., *Christain Ethics and Dillemas of Foreign Policy*, Duke Uni. Press, Durham N.C., 1959.

*The Koran*, Penguine Classics Series, 1985.

Triandis, H.C., *Attitude and Attitude Change*, John Wiley & Sons, New York, 1971.

Tyler Bennett, *Americans in East Asia,* Williams College, Williamston, Massachusetts, 1922.

Vadim Jagladin, *How to Restructure and Humanize Inter-National Relations*, Novosti Press Agency, Moscow, 1989.

Victor, C. Ferkiss, *Technological Man : The Myth and the Reality*, George B. Aziller, New York, 1969.

Vincent, A. Smith, *The Oxford History of India*, OUP Oxford, 3rd impression, 1983.

Wager, W. Warren, *Building the City of Man : Outline of a World Civilization*, New York, New York Grossman, 1911.

Wallia, C.S. (ed.) *Towards Century 21*, New York, Basic Books, 1970.

Walls, H.G., *A Short History of the World,* Penguine Books, 1960.

Walter, C. Langsam Otis C. Mitchell, *The World Since 1919*, p. 681, Surjeet Publications, Delhi-7. Eighth Edition, 1971.

Walter, Hutchinson, (Ed.), *Customs of the World*, Vols. I-II, Concept, New Delhi, Second Indian reprint, 1985.

Waltz, Kenneth, *Foreign Policy and Democratic Politics little Brown*, Boston, 1967.

Whetaker, Ben, *The Forth World, Schodress Brothers*, New York, 1972.

Whitney, A. Grisworld, *The Far Eastern Policy of the United States*, Harcourt. Brace and World Inc. New York, 1938.

Wilkins, W.J., *Hindu Mythology*, Vedic and Puranic Rupa & Co. New Delhi.

Williard Throp (Ed.,), *The United States and the Far East*, 2nd ed., Englewood Cliffs, N.J., 1962.

Will Durant, *The Story of Philosophy*, Pocket Books, New York, *Pleasures of Philosophy*, New York, 1952.

William Irwin, *The Old Testament : Schuman*, New York, 1952.

William Sergant, *Battle for the Mind*, Pan Books Ltd. London, 1959.

Woodhouse, E.A., (Ed.) *Five Essays by Dean Enge.*

Wolfe, Thomas W., *Soviet Strategy at the Crossroads*, Cambridge, Harward University Press. 1964.

Yang, C.K., *Religion in Chinese Society*, Barkelay, 1962.

# INDEX